Exploring the Southern Sierra:
West Side

Traveling in the mountains entails unavoidable risks of which you need to be aware. The fact that a route appears in this book does not guarantee that it will be safe for you. Trails and roads vary greatly in difficulty, as do the degree of conditioning, agility and skill you need to enjoy them safely. Routes may have changed or conditions may have deteriorated since the descriptions were written. Also, conditions can change even from hour to hour owing to weather. A trip that is safe on a dry day or for a highly conditioned, agile, properly equipped person may be completely unsafe for someone else or unsafe under adverse weather conditions. If conditions appear dangerous, and you are not prepared to deal with them safely, choose a different trip. It is better to have wasted time and effort than to be the subject of a mountain rescue.

These warnings are not intended to frighten you, as millions of people have safe and enjoyable mountain adventures every year. However, the beauty, freedom and excitement of the high country includes the presence of risks that do not confront you at home. When you travel in the mountains you assume those risks.

Exploring the Southern Sierra: West Side

J. C. Jenkins
and
Ruby Johnson Jenkins

Wilderness Press
Berkeley

Jim

He was a sincere young man with a deep love of the wilderness, admired and respected by all who crossed his path. A decade ago he dedicated himself to learning all he could about the southern Sierra Nevada, preserving its pristine high country, and writing about it. From his facile pen came four guidebooks, detailing the roads, the camps, the trails, the natural and human history of his beloved Southern Sierra. He knew this gentle wilderness as few others have known it.

As a person he was unique. There was nothing artificial or temporal in his makeup. He sought truth and meaning in life, and these qualities radiated into all who were fortunate enough to know him. Truth is reflected in his writings. His books, so painstakingly and thoroughly researched, are monuments to accuracy. He was a genial and gentle person, willing to go to almost any length to help a friend or acquaintance in need. His intellect was straight-forward and captivating, his sense of humor delightfully subtle. He will be sorely missed by many.

My most treasured memories of Jim date back to the summer of 1973, when we were working together on two guidebooks for Wilderness Press. We criss-crossed the Kern Plateau and Mineral King country that summer, checking out landmarks and trails. Jim toted a heavy pack and pushed along a mileage wheel to measure trail distances, much to the astonishment of passing hikers. He insisted on absolute accuracy, even when it meant discomfort to him. I remember one late afternoon, the sun low on the western horizon, trudging along the West Stringer Trail from Volcano Meadow toward the Kern River. We had walked twenty miles that day, and I felt we had covered enough of the trail and needn't continue the final four miles to the river. Jim was tired too, but he insisted on walking the entire distance and back. He returned to camp well after dark, totally fatigued but in good spirits. His sense of honesty and responsibility to his readers would allow him no shortcuts.

In subsequent years Jim covered every trail and feasible cross-country route from Sequoia National Park south to Tehachapi Pass. Out of all this toil, sweat and tears was born *Self-Propelled in the Southern Sierra, Volume 1,* one of the finest trail guides ever written. Fortunately Jim finished work on Volume 2 before his passing.

Jim's rich but all too short life came to a tragic end on Interstate 5, near Fort Tejon, on the afternoon of August 27th. He was returning to his duties as a summer ranger in Sequoia National Forest when he stopped on the shoulder of the highway with car trouble. Standing behind his VW camper, he was killed instantly when struck by a wayward vehicle. Fate plays cruel and unfathomable tricks on some of us. How tragic that Jim's "turn" came when he had so much life ahead of him.

John Robinson
Author/Historian
1979

James Charles (J. C.) Jenkins
"Jim"

1952–1979
(Son of co-author Ruby and her husband Bill)

The research and writing of J. C. Jenkins' *Self-Propelled in the Southern Sierra, Volume 2: The Great Western Divides,* 1979, formed the basis of this book. All of the trails and mountains described in Volume 2 were hiked and climbed, some several times for this revision. Many trails and mountain climbs were added, and car tours were included. While much has changed over the years, care was taken to retain the essence of Jim's original work.

FIRST EDITION September 1979 (entitled *Self-Propelled in the Southern Sierra, Vol. 2: The Great Western Divides*)
SECOND EDITION June 1984
Second printing September 1986
Third printing April 1990
REVISED THIRD EDITION January 1995 (entitled *Exploring the Southern Sierra: West Side*)

Cover photo by Ruby Johnson Jenkins *Trail, Flowers and Peaks* The Little Kern River headwater basin
Book design by Ruby Johnson Jenkins
Cover and page production by Michael Batelaan, Lake Design
Printed in the United States of America
A Frontier Trail Book
P.O. Box 1544
Kernville, CA 93238

International Standard Book Number 0-89997-181-4
Library of Congress Card Catalog Number 94-45200

Library of Congress Cataloging-in-Publication Data

Jenkins, J.C. (Jim C.), 1952-1979.
  Exploring the Southern Sierra, west side / J.C. Jenkins and Ruby Johnson Jenkins. — Rev. 3rd ed.
      p.   cm.
  A companion vol. to: Exploring the Southern Sierra, east side. 1992.
  Rev. ed. of: Self-propelled in the Southern Sierra. Vol. 2. 1979.
  Includes bibliographical references and index.
  ISBN 0-89997-181-4
  1. Hiking—Sierra Nevada (Calif. and Nev.)—Guidebooks.
2. Outdoor recreation—Sierra Nevada (Calif. and Nev.)—Guidebooks.
3. Sierra Nevada (Calif. and Nev.)—Guidebooks. I. Jenkins, Ruby Johnson. II. Jenkins, J.C. (Jim C.), 1952-1979. Exploring the Southern Sierra, east side. III. Jenkins, J.C. (Jim C.), 1952-1979. Self-propelled in the Southern Sierra. IV. Title.
GV199.42.S55J45 1995
796.5'09794'4—dc20   94-45200
                                                        CIP

Photo Credits

Pictures by Ruby Johnson Jenkins except for the following:

Tom Highberger, NFS: X
Richard C. Burns, NPS: XVI, 2, 216
National Park Service: 7, 176, 214
Jeffrey P. Schaffer: 13
Beverly Steveson: 15, 17, 76, 102, 215
J.C. Jenkins: 19, 30, 37, 67, 104, 132, 139, 146, 148, 150, 180, 206, 209, 232
Brian Jones: 35, 62, 78, 100
Bob Powers Collection: 38
Sierra South Mountain Sports: 42
Greg Iger, CALM: 54

Mike Mortenssen, NFS: 85
Larry L. Norris: 91, 98
Bill Jenkins: 105
Lyn Haber: 111
Claus Engelhardt: 124
Pat Clark: 131
Fred Hoeptner: 170
Lee Strand: 172, 205
Bill Jones, NPS: 182, 230
Gary Kenwood: 186
Elwyn Beach: 224
Dick Beach: 240

Acknowledgments

I had wonderful adventures while doing fieldwork in the Southern Sierra for this book. They were made even more enjoyable by friends who accompanied me on many trips: Roberta Abbe (nearly every trip!), Pat Clark, Vonnie Diggles, Ellen Halpin, husband Bill Jenkins, Bonnie Strand, Bob Tollefson and Bill Whities. I had interesting conferences with, or received informative material from, several who gave generously of their time: David Baskin, Bill Deisman, Jerry Enoff, Nolan Fritz of Sequoia National Forest; David Dulitz of Mountain Home Demonstration State Forest; William Tweed of Sequoia and Kings Canyon National Parks; and Michael Diggles of U.S. Geological Survey, Menlo Park, California. I was greatly encouraged in my effort and received editing with excellent suggestions while doing desk-work for the book from my friend, Lyn Haber. Many thanks to each one of you.

Throughout the six years it took to complete the field and desk work for the two volumes of *Exploring the Southern Sierra,* I appreciated the support I received from my family and friends. They understood my desire to continue the effort begun by Jim. Through his highly acclaimed books, *Self-Propelled in the Southern Sierra: Volumes 1&2,* the first guidebooks to the area, Jim introduced people to the gentle Southern Sierra: its flora and fauna, its geology and history, and its many paths that crisscrossed the vast land. And so this, a continuation of Jim's work, is dedicated in his memory to those who find pleasure exploring these mountains and surrounding areas, and to those of our family and friends who, like Jim, have too soon left our earthly paths.

Ruby Johnson Jenkins

Aspen trees of autumn glow in waning light along Western Divide Highway

Contents

Part 1   Introduction to the Southern Sierra: West Side

Part 2   Adventures in the Southern Sierra: West Side

Section 1   Highway 58 to Highway 178
—Piute & Breckenridge Mountains & Surrounding Area—

Section 2   Highway 178 to Parker Pass Drive (J22)
—Greenhorn Mountains & Surrounding Area—

Section 3   Parker Pass Drive (J22) to Sequoia National Park
—Western Divide Mountains & Golden Trout Wilderness—

Section 4   Sequoia and Kings Canyon National Parks
Jennie Lakes Wilderness & Surrounding Area

Part 3   Appendix

Part 1

Introduction to the Southern Sierra: West Side

Squirrel Creek's cascades and potholes above Mineral King Road

Chapter 1: Features

Come, explore the west side of California's vast Southern Sierra: unveil its pleasures, listen to its secrets.

This book describes the country in the Sierra Nevada Mountains that stretches west of a line extended along the North Fork Kern River between Highway 58 in the south and Highway 180 in the north.

As you travel the trips progressing from south to north, grouped into four sections, you visit in Section 1 the west side of the Piute Mountains, then west of them, Breckenridge Mountain; both parted from the main body of the Sierra Nevada by the canyons and valleys through which Highway 178 winds. These mountains ascend from high deserts to pine forests and between them spread pastoral valleys. This area now lightly traveled once crawled with prospectors who sought veins of gold and left behind lands rich in history.

To the north of Breckenridge abruptly rise the Greenhorn Mountains of Section 2 where in pioneer days on the western foothills, stage coach routes connected budding villages. Historic lookouts and peaks with panoramic views reach above the tree-clad slopes while to the east Isabella Lake beckons fishermen and other water sports enthusiasts.

The Greenhorn Mountains meld into the Western Divide range of Section 3; a land where awesome giant sequoia trees invite viewers to linger. Here expansive Golden Trout Wilderness offers hikers and equestrians an abundant variety of enticing trips along rivers and atop crests.

The classic country of Sequoia and Kings Canyon national parks and Jennie Lakes Wilderness of Section 4 front the serrated Great Western Divide mountains of the High Sierra. Here abound lakes and meadows and backcountry trips as well as the renown largest living things on earth, the stately giant sequoia trees.

This book and its companion, *Exploring the Southern Sierra: East Side*, which describes routes and attractions stretching east of the North Fork Kern River between Highway 58 and the north border of Golden Trout Wilderness, offer exciting experiences and adventures across the entire Southern Sierra, a land of memorable beauty.

Giant Sequoia Trees *Mammoth trees with crowns in misty heavens congregate in cathedral groves and raise their boughs as if in solemn tribute to their creator.*

Giant Sequoias, the most massive living organisms in the world, possess delicate, lacy clusters of stems entirely covered by overlapping, ¼ inch-long leaves. When mature the trees display soft, cinnamon-colored, deeply-furrowed bark wrapped around huge, straight trunks. Although this evergreen's great bulk and height significantly dwarf the viewer, it radiates an intimacy. Each one soon becomes distinct as its crown and bark show individual traits. This book describes numerous trips to sequoia groves in the national and state forests and the national parks.

The giant sequoia, *Sequoiadendron giganteum*, of the Sierra Nevada belongs to the same botanical family as the imposing coast redwood, *Sequoia sempervirens*. However, no common fossil ancestor has been found, according to the late Richard J. Hartesveldt, PhD., whose life work was devoted to the study of giant sequoias. He and other botanists suggested the sequoias were related to extensive groves of Northern Hemisphere trees that existed in the Cretaceous period, 125 million years ago.

Today there remain only 75 scattered groves of giant sequoias located exclusively on the Sierran west slopes and mostly in the Southern Sierra in a 260-mile belt, 15 miles wide, between elevations of 5000 to 7500 feet. The General Sherman tree in Sequoia National Park's Giant Forest ranks as the world's largest tree by volume, in fact, largest living organism. It may also be the world's fastest growing tree. As a sapling, about 2500 year ago, its vertical growth was probably as much as 1 to 2 feet per year. Now the vigorous old General's increased girth each year would create a tree 50 feet tall and one foot wide!

The mature sequoia produces about 2000 small, 2½ × ¾ inch, egg-shaped cones each year, which harbor an average of 200 seeds each. Of the prodigious number of seeds released, few take root and survive. But in the long life span of each sequoia, it takes only two of its seeds to survive to double the grove's size. During the first hundred years sequoias display a conical tree shape; then, as the trees begin to grow above other varieties, their crowns fill in, giving the tree tops a full, rounded shape. In time the majority of mature trees lose their crowns to lightning, or die back due to fire-damaged trunks, but the

Majestic *Sequoiadendron giganteum*

trees continue to live. Sequoias are protected from disease and ground fire by their bark that thickens to an average of 10 inches with sections reaching up to 30 inches. Strangely, this overwhelmingly large tree whose girth can reach a base diameter of 30 feet or more and height of 300 feet or more, has shallow roots, although extensive, and no tap root. Death results most often by its toppling.

The 25 largest trees by volume are identified in the groves visited by trips in this book. The information was gleaned from *To Find the Biggest Tree* by Wendell D. Flint, a man who has crisscrossed the sequoia belt in search of the biggest trees. The individual tree ranking noted was updated in 1993 and will no doubt change again as he discovers more sequoia behemoths.

Since the time of its discovery, the role of the giant sequoia in society has been controversial. Many major groves received protection from logging when Sequoia and Grant Grove, the second and third national parks to be formed in the United States, were designated in 1890. But before the current policies precluding logging of sequoias on public lands, many noble trees were felled, much to the distress of early day environmentalists.

Presently the controversy swirls around grove management. Several strategies have been tried with mixed results. For the sequoias to reproduce, their seeds need to fall on mineral soil and their seedlings need sun and moisture. Since 1916 when the National Park Service was established, all mountain fires were aggressively fought. This allowed shade tolerant trees and shrubs to proliferate around the sequoias and forest litter to accumulate. Sequoia seeds found little open soil in which to germinate and insufficient sun light in which to grow.

In the early 1970s prescription burning, a controlled, man-set fire, became the method of opening the forest canopy and reducing the understory. It was found that the fire's warmth also caused sequoia cones to release their seeds.

Sequoia National Forest, home of 38 groves, replaced controlled burning in 1982 with clear-cutting in sequoia groves. Only mature sequoias, defined as trees with a diameter of 8 feet or more, were saved. All other growth, including "young" sequoias several hundred years old, were removed. The felled trees were used for wood products, and all the ground around the few standing sequoias was exposed for seed development. This practice raised a storm of protest from the public who decried that the once beautiful groves with giant sequoias became gouged land with solitary trees. These trees, they said, were threatened by damage to their shallow root system during the logging process, by decrease of soil moisture due to lack of shade and by exposure to strong winds. The policy was rescinded and a management plan with input from many interested parties was established in 1990 by the Forest Service with assurances for protection of the trees. However, sequoia devotees want statutory protection for these national treasures that cannot be changed by political caprice. They hope for a congressionally mandated Giant Sequoia National Forest Preserve of approximately 440,000 acres, which would protect all giant sequoias in Sequoia and Sierra national forests.

Rivers *Springtime swift, dancing; autumn placid, reflective: a western river's changing rhythm responds to the seasons.*

Several major rivers, each with extensive branching, race down canyons of the Southern Sierra's west side. The North Fork Kern River, the longest and the only one in this book that received the honor of inclusion into the National Wild and Scenic Rivers System, flows south through a magnificent gorge to Isabella Lake from its headwaters above timberline at the Kings-Kern Divide; then the main stem Kern below the lake descends abruptly west to slake the thirst of Bakersfield and green the fields of San Joaquin Valley. The river was named by U.S. Army Captain John C. Fremont for his cartographer Edward M. Kern. Kern, in 1846, camped at the confluence of the river's north and south forks while on Fremont's third expedition.

The Tule, originating on the Western Divide mountains, and the Kaweah, on the Great Western Divide slopes, tumble steeply west in deep, rocky canyons to be captured in reservoirs that serve their nearby towns and valley. Tule received its name from the tule or bulrush that was so abundant at its mouth, and Kaweah honored the local Indian Tribe. Before and into the early 1900s, each of the three rivers created marshy, mosquito infested lands on the vast valley floor.

Reservoirs The Kern River's Isabella Lake, one of the largest reservoirs in California and at an elevation of 2600 feet, the highest of the three in the Southern Sierra, sits in the cup of stark 5000- to 7000-foot mountains. Tule River's Success Lake and Kaweah River's Lake Kaweah fill low land valleys surrounded by typical California oak-studded, rolling hills. All offer attractive camping facilities and a variety of water sports year round.

Fishermen along the shores or bobbing in boats, angle for large mouth bass, catfish, bluegill, crappie, redear, sunfish and trout. You can swim, sail and wind surf, jet and water ski in ideal surroundings. Wind sports are especially inviting on Isabella Lake. There, too, fishermen have derbies and other water sports have competitive races.

Whitewater Sports Since 1980, inflated rafts with ecstatic, shouting, water-drenched people have been shooting the rolling rapids of the North Fork and lower Kern River. Today, during spring and early summer snowmelt runoff, commercial rafting companies in the Kern River Valley whose expertise assures you a thrilling yet safe ride offer a gamut of excursions, from one hour rides known as Lickety Splits to multiday trips, an exultation for ages six and older. Limited rafting awaits experts on the Kaweah River below the park during high water, as well.

Whitewater kayaking and canoeing flourish on the Kern River, too. Lessons are a must before you plunge into this sport. Also, exciting competitive races involving these activities are held in Kernville each spring.

Body boarding the Kern River began in 1993. This entails challenging the crashing rapids at eye level, head first. Equipment for this living-on-the-edge sport includes a 2×4-foot, plastic-foam slab, a helmet, life vest, wet suit, shin and knee guards, swim fins and webbed gloves—all can probably be rented in the valley.

Swimming and Tubing   Each year as the temperature soars, people flock to the cool, inviting rivers and reservoirs. After snowmelt the mighty upper Kern offers some safe stretches—check for locations with the Forest Service. The attractive pools and slabs along the cascading Tule River lure large numbers of valley residents. Similar pools offer bathing in the Kaweah River near the lower campground.

The lower Kern River is closed to swimmers and waders and fishermen need to be especially careful. Every year the numbers increase on the signs counting the river deaths, mostly on the lower Kern resulting when people do not heed the warning signs. The river can appear deceptively calm.

People drift with the current along the upper Kern in large rubber tubes after the river's tumultuous roar decreases to a murmur in late summer.

Fishing   Spearing, hooking or trapping the plentiful fish in several waterways of the Southern Sierra furnished food for Indians and early settlers. Today, angling attracts an enthusiastic following to these waters, and many fishermen help keep the sport excellent by volunteering their time to habitat improvement.

The California Department of Fish and Game (CDF&G) oversees the Southern Sierra fisheries. It plants hatchery-bred fish in most lakes, rivers and viable streams on a regular basis. As a further addition to the fishing excitement, in 1994 the CDF&G selected Isabella Lake as one of five state reservoirs to participate in the agency's trophy bass program. Management under this designation will produce an ever increasing number of bass 10 pounds or over.

With the encouragement of fly fishing groups, CDF&G introduced regulations that extend to the headwaters of the Kern River in the national park, the prime wild trout fishing that now exists on the river's four mile stretch north of Johnsondale Bridge, 19.6 miles north of Kernville, and that exists on the North Fork Tule River. To promote sizable fish and at the same time increase the propagation of the Kern River rainbow trout that until recently was thought extinct in the Kern River, only barbless hooks and artificial lures may be used. A limit of two rainbow trout 10 inches or less or two brown trout of any size may be kept. By establishing a maximum size for bows, mature fish that are most likely to spawn will create natural brood stock. As the

Isabella Lake in a winter setting

numbers of large rainbow increase, the maximum size will be moved upward. These regulations will in time return all of the extensive upper Kern River above Johnsondale Bridge to a nationally known quality wild trout fishery and will increase the number of Kern River rainbows. (Kern River rainbow trout are really golden trout; they are more closely related to goldens than to other rainbow.)

Another CDF&G program began in 1977 after years of research, when the Little Kern golden trout was federally listed as a threatened species. The listing precipitated an extensive effort to save the trout in the Little Kern River basin—Section 3 of this book. Over nearly two decades every lake and stream in the Little Kern watershed was treated with rotenone, which removed all fish. Following the treatment, the streams and lakes were replanted with pure strains of golden trout genetically correct for each body of water. The basin now offers good fishing for the beautiful, lively goldens that many anglers enjoy, and it will improve each year.

CDF&G once planted fish in the waterways of Sequoia and Kings Canyon national parks. The parks' management plan now emphasizes the enhancement of natural flora and fauna within its lands and the diminution of all that is nonnative. The Kern River rainbow trout project is within this purview; fish planting in its waterways is not.

When glaciers receded from these park lands, numerous lakes and streams were left in their wake. All were barren of fish until the 1870s when travelers in the backcountry, and later the CDF&G began putting trout in them. These fish thrived and today many rainbow, brook, golden and hybrids ply the parks' waters. Although not native, there are no plans to remove them en masse.

Mountains *"Climb the mountains and get their good tidings. Nature's peace will flow into you as sunshine flows into trees. The winds will blow their own freshness into you and the storms their energy, while cares will drop off like autumn leaves."*

John Muir

The mountains' tranquillity expressed by Muir belies their turbulent growth. In an attempt to understand the mountain building process, two vastly different theories developed in the 1900s. Early on, mountains were thought to rise as the earth cooled from a molten state and shrank. The earth's skin wrinkled into mountains on the stationary continents.

A different theory of mountain building began to take shape in 1915 when Alfred Wegener noted in *The Origin of Continents and Oceans* that if the continents were placed together they would fit like pieces of a jigsaw puzzle into one continent that he called "Pangaea." Thus, he said, they must have separated and drifted. His theory was advanced when rocks, fossils and mountain ranges found on widely separated continents matched when the masses fit together to form Pangaea. But how could continents drift?

Then in the 1960s it was discovered that an upwelling of molten material from mid-ocean ridges pushed the sea floor outward, and it road as if on a conveyor belt. By 1968, both continental drift and sea-floor spread concepts were united into a theory called "plate tectonics" where plates of rigid, exterior earth crust (lithosphere), under oceans and continents alike, road on mobile molten interior material (asthenosphere), the earth's thermal engine. Within this theory scientists were able to outline plate borders and to indicate plate drift direction.

Under the plate tectonic theory, mountains appear due to the interaction of the plates. The ancient Sierra Nevada developed about 80 million years ago from volcanoes that built up on the surface of the North American plate caused by the heat derived from the diving (subduction) of the Pacific plate beneath it. Also, continental crust material on the Pacific plate (west of the San Andreas fault) collided with the continental crust of the North American plate (east of the San Andreas fault). This collision led to the major uplift of the Southern Sierra.

While some forces build mountains, other forces whittle them down. Francois E. Matthes said in numerous publications based on his research beginning in 1914, and subsequent scientists concurred, that ice was the greatest whittler and that mountains were reshaped and reduced primarily by glaciation, sighting wide, U-shaped valleys as an example of reshaping. But in the mid-1990s, Jeffrey P. Schaffer challenged that theory in "Yosemite Valley and the Sierra Nevada: relative ineffectiveness of glaciers in an ancient granitic landscape." His research suggested that intense tropical weathering and erosion for millions of years, not glaciation, led to the stripping away of the overlying rock. This stripping exposed the granitic rock, which originally solidified in the earth's crust several miles or more below the surface, and rose during mountain building. The erosion created landscapes similar to the unglaciated granitic Dome Land Wilderness with its wide floored valley, described in this book's companion volume. When the somewhat tropical climate finally changed dramatically about 34 million years ago, weathering and erosion were greatly reduced, and the mountains appeared almost as they do today.

Schaffer agrees that some mountain reduction and reshaping occurred by glaciers that were effective enough in their *upper parts* to excavate basins in locally fractured bedrock. Up high, glaciers left as evidence various lakes and ponds, polished and striated bedrock, and scattered, glacier-transported boulders (erratics) and sparse, coarse sediments. In places where the topography was favorable, glaciers left as evidence terminal and lateral moraines (masses of rock and mountain debris). Moraines can be seen by people on trips in Section 4 and on a few trips in Section 3.

These rock deposits appear to be from two distinct glaciations: the Tahoe, which may have been at its maximum about 150,000 years ago, and the Tioga, which was at its maximum about 20,000 years ago. During these periods, thick glaciers descended from the heads of the higher canyons, often converging to form trunk glaciers that then descended the major river canyons to mid-elevations. By 13,000 years ago they had essentially disappeared. Since then there

have been several times when small glaciers have formed on the shadier slopes of the highest peaks; one is seen on T99.

The process of mountain building and reducing continues, but in geological time. To visitors the mountains embrace the peace and offer the welcome they seek.

The Southern Sierra mountains are subject to two governmental policies. In general, the Bureau of Land Management governs the low elevation public land while the Forest Service sets policies for the higher, forested reaches. Both these agencies apply the congressionally mandated multi-use concepts, which means caring for the land while allowing commercial and recreational use. In contrast to both these agencies, the National Park Service's mandate is to preserve the land in its natural state. While people are to be allowed the enjoyment of that environment, no commercial use other than the care of its visitors is permitted.

Wildernesses A vast swath of 306,916 acres straddling the North Fork Kern River across Sequoia and Inyo national forests became Golden Trout Wilderness by an act of Congress in 1978. This huge wilderness was created both to protect the beauty of the land and to protect the streams for golden trout—California's state fish. The Golden Trout Wilderness west of North Fork Kern River, the area detailed in this book, ranges in elevation from 4660 feet at the river to 12,432 feet at Florence Peak on the Great Western Divide. Solitude can still be enjoyed in this hinterland of pine forests, high mountain lakes and miles of clear creeks and rivers.

Jennie Lakes became a wilderness area in 1984. Only 10,971 acres, a tiny piece by comparison, it occupies picturesque land between Sequoia National Park and Kings Canyon National Park. This montane gem of wildflowers includes two glacial-carved lakes tucked below ragged peaks. The book includes trips to both these lakes.

Magnificent wilderness stretches to Mount Whitney and the Sierra crest behind the popular area traversed by Generals Highway of Sequoia and Kings Canyon national parks. This book offers some trips in the wilderness

Cross-country (nordic) skiing in the Southern Sierra

east of the frontcountry and many trips in the scenic remote Mineral King area.

National and Historic Trails To be included in the National Recreation Trail System a trail must be open to all types of use, easily accessible, interesting and scenic. One trail qualified for that distinction on the west side: the Summit Trail. The beginning of the trail, the only part that now qualifies for this honor, is an attractive climb through a mature red fir forest over Slate Mountain. The middle section fell victim to trailside logging and repeated path slashing by logging roads. The highly scenic, lengthy end section travels through Golden Trout Wilderness and as such is open to foot and hoof travel only. The complete Summit Trail, divided among several trips, is described in this book.

The three historic trails, two of which cross the Summit Trail, are Dennison, Jordan and Hockett. These trails that followed Indian and game routes, were forged in the 1860s when a rich silver strike was discovered in the Coso Mountains east of the Sierra Nevada range. Prospectors in the busy town of Visalia, west of the range, traveled these toll routes across the Sierra to the strike.

Of the three trails the Dennison Trail was the first. The route seems to be known to historians, but not the man. They know only that he was a mountaineer who was accidentally killed by a gun he had rigged to kill a bear. The Jordan Trail, probably the best known of the three, gained notoriety because John Jordan drowned in the North Fork Kern River on his return trip to Visalia to announce the completion of his route. The Hockett Trail built by John Hockett apparently was the most traveled.

These historic trails were used very little as toll routes after the Walker Pass road opened, but over the years they remained accessible. The trails are mentioned occasionally in trips in this book when they overlap current paths. Many features in the Southern Sierra carry the names of these three trailblazers.

Other abandoned trails are sometimes old enough to be considered historic. They have particular appeal for pathfinders as well as history buffs. The text mentions them and this book's map shows them only if they appeared on the 1950s 15 minute USGS topographic maps.

Cross-Country Skiing Nordic skiing referred to as cross-country skiing ranks high among the most esthetically rewarding sports. Good snow for this type of skiing covers the Southern Sierra at around 6000 feet during most normal winters. A network of logging roads in the national forest near the mountain crests make excellent easy-to-follow routes. Those with mountaineering skills will find plateaus, hilly slopes or peaks within reach of the mountain roads.

The Piute Mountains have four unplowed access roads. You can drive up all the roads to snowline except the gated northwest entry. Piute Mountain Road off Kelso Valley Road (T17 in *Exploring the Southern Sierra: East Side*) offers the easiest approach. The route to the most snow, however, may be the southwest entry out of Walker Basin, also called Piute Mountain Road (T6 in reverse). That road reaches the highest snow at 8000 feet. You may have this winter mountain all to yourself!

Breckenridge Mountain assures you solitude, too. Its plateau area averages an elevation of 6000 feet with the lookout road to 7500 feet. The long, winding approach from Bakersfield, Breckenridge Road (T10), remains open to snowline or to its gate that crosses the road near the top. The approach from the east side is closed in winter.

In the Greenhorn Mountains, State Highway 155 (T27), which crosses the range, is plowed, but usually requires chains. Greenhorn Summit at an elevation of 6000 feet offers several roads south where invigorating alpine and nordic skiing are offered on marked routes at Shirley Meadows Ski Area, and north (T32) for extensive ski routes. Parker Pass Road, J22 (T41), over the Greenhorn Mountains is open to snowline and has good skiing on marked trails at 6500-foot Parker Meadow. This road is plowed from the east to Johnsondale R-Ranch. The county road M-109 is open to Sugarloaf Mountain Park.

Western Divide mountains can be reached on State Highway 190 (T74), plowed to Ponderosa Village at an elevation of 7100 feet, south of Quaking Aspen Campground. Excellent skiing exists on roads and some marked trails north of the campground and south of the village. Parking is limited. Stop on your way up at Tule River Ranger Station for latest information on cross-country trails.

Bear Creek (T77) and Balch Park roads to Mountain Home Demonstration State Forest are open to snowline. The elevation of the county park and state forest ranges between 6000 to 6500 feet. This area offers beautiful skiing among the sequoias.

Mineral King of Sequoia National Park offers ideal skiing on the Hockett plateau and winter accommodations at Silver City by reservations: phone (209) 734-4109. The twisty Mineral King Road (T89) is open to snowline or to its gate just prior to Atwell Mill Campground.

State Highway 198, the Generals Highway (T84) to Sequoia National Park proper is plowed to Lodgepole Campground (or Wuksachi Village) and usually to Kings Canyon National Park. Its major ski center, Wolverton—converted from alpine to nordic—offers rentals, lessons and the ultimate ski trip to Pear Lake Hut. Lodgepole Campground nearby remains open with no fee in winter.

Highway 180 (T112) to Kings Canyon National Park is plowed to Grant Grove's winter center. Privately operated Montecito-Sequoia Lodge, under Forest Service lease, lies between the two parks off the Generals Highway. Phone 1(800) 843-8677.

The park areas offer winter sports and lodging and many groomed cross-country ski routes, often among the giant sequoias. The reddish-brown trunks of sequoias amid snow-laden pines and deep glistening drifts surely rank among the most inspiring winter sights anywhere.

Native Americans The first people to dwell in the Southern Sierra lived harmoniously with one another and successfully within the bounty of the seasons.

Those referred to by the white man as Indians migrated to the North American continent from Asia where they crossed the Bering Strait over a land bridge. Eventually some settled along the foothills of the Southern Sierra. Artifacts found in the San Joaquin Valley indicate prehistoric Indians lived there at least 7600 years ago.

In historic times Indians called Yokuts dwelt in or near the valley: the Paleiyami lived in the area of Linns Valley along Poso Creek; the Yowlumne occupied the Kern River land where Bakersfield now stands; the Yaudanchi thrived in the Tule River country.

The Shoshonean Tribe had a presence in the Southern Sierra: the Tubatulabal settled in the Kern River Valley; the Kawaiisu ranged from the Tehachapi Mountains to the Kern River; a band of Monache Indians called Gaweah enjoyed the lower Kaweah River area; the Patwisha lived in the higher reaches of the Kaweah.

These Native Americans gathered in villages and established outlying camps near their food sources, which were fish, game, nuts, seeds and other vegetation. Most often their houses were round and cozy, made of willows and tules, insulated with mud. An opening in the center let the smoke escape from their fire. They needed few if any clothes in summer: a breechcloth for men, a front and back apron for women; in winter they enjoyed the warmth of animal firs.

The tribes met with one another on occasion. They exchanged food and hunting articles, played games and held religious ceremonies. They were peaceful, content and friendly.

The Indians welcomed the first Caucasians, but problems quickly arose. The white man settled on their land, treated them as inferiors, caused them to contract diseases for which they had little resistance and exchanged alcohol and guns for their beautifully crafted baskets and carefully treated firs. The Indians eventually fought for their lands and their way of life, but by the 1850s they ended, decimated, in government created Indian Reservations.

Mortars developed in rocks where Native Americans ground acorns

Chapter 2: Precautions

Outings   A well-planned trip most often results in a successful outing. Read the trip text, study the maps and gather your equipment several days before departure.

Picture yourself on your selected trip. Are you able to meet the physical demands and time constraints of the outing? Remember that increased elevation and rough terrain require extra energy and hours. Are you mentally ready to be away from the comforts of your home? Do you have someone with whom you can leave your itinerary and a phone number to call if you do not return when expected? See Chapter 3 for agencies and phone numbers.

Consider your transportation. Be sure your vehicles function well. All of the car tours and trailhead approaches in this book, including the ones over unpaved roads, can usually be made in a conventional car. Most often bicycles used on paved roads are multi-geared; on unpaved roads or trails are all-terrain (mountain bikes).

Carefully plan your clothing and gear. For the outdoors, dress in layers and prepare for all types of weather. Carry some clothing of wool or of a synthetic material that provides warmth even when wet. Protect yourself from sun, bugs and scratchy brush. Be sure to

include a first aid kit, compass, reflector, flash light, matches and extra snack food for emergencies. Take this book along or a copy of your trip. Carry a map. For backpacking, be sure it is the area topographic map. Carry a polarshield emergency blanket in your day pack; it weighs only two ounces but helps you retain 90% of your body heat. Beyond these items, pack only what you need—you will soon regret any extra weight.

For your car, have a full tank of gas upon entering the mountains, carry the usual car tools and while driving on dirt roads, include a shovel to fill in deep road ruts if needed and a saw to cut away fallen trees. Always pack in extra water and a blanket.

If touring on a bicycle, you need to take special precautions. Sinuous mountain roads and roller coaster hills hide your presence. For your safety it may be best to pull off the road when you hear cars coming from either direction. If bicycling on a trail, you may find that winding, narrow paths across steep slopes sometimes hide hikers or equestrians. For their safety and yours, control your speed to prevent colliding with them.

Dehydration is always a threat during outdoor activities, but especially on hot days and difficult or extended trips. Carry water in

Consider your transportation—

your pack. The extreme minimum amount of water an adult requires on a hot day is two quarts per 10 miles. This book tells you where you will find streams to refill your supply.

Mountain streams in the backcountry during snowmelt can be life-threatening: the current can be deceivingly swift, the depth uneven with unseen deep pockets and the water extremely cold, quickly reducing your body temperature. When crossing streams look for the widest section: those will be the shallowest. Remember that rocks and logs may be slippery and wobbly. Use a walking stick for balance and wear shoes (without socks) for stability. Never cross directly above a waterfall or a partially submerged log. Unbuckle the hip strap of your backpack for easy exit if you fall. Do not tie yourself into safety ropes. Plot your course, preferably angling downstream. Above all, use good judgment. It is better to abort the trip than risk a hazardous crossing.

Giardiasis This intestinal disease is caused by the parasite *Giardia lamblia,* which sometimes lives in untreated water. The debilitating, unpleasant symptoms are nausea, diarrhea, abdominal pain and physical weakness. The incubation period ranges from six to fifteen days. If untreated the disease recurs.

The cysts can be killed by boiling your water three to five minutes or by filtering it with a commercial water filter with a pore size of 0.5 micron or less. Use treated water for drinking, tooth brushing and dish washing.

Hypothermia Now and then you hear of someone known to be logical and intelligent using poor judgment on an outing and dying because of it. The most likely cause is hypothermia, a subnormal body temperature that causes the reduction of blood flow. This can happen in temperatures between 30° to 50° when you are wet or exhausted or exposed to wind. Continuous shivering is an early sign; slurred speech, clumsiness and impaired thinking follow.

At the first sign of uncontrollable shivering, make camp, get into dry clothes and a sleeping bag, rest but do not sleep.

Drink warm fluids. Return your body to its normal temperature before you sleep or progress. If you wait until serious symptoms like confused thinking occur, you may not be able to save yourself.

Lightning Summer showers in the Southern Sierra are infrequent, but when they occur they are usually accompanied by lightning. The moist air of the storm and the sun-heated ground of the high country are major ingredients for lightning, which can be cloud to ground or ground to cloud. Lightning usually seeks the highest point in its strike area.

During these storms, avoid peaks, lakes, open areas, lone trees or shallow caves. Seek forested areas away from the tallest trees. If caught in the open, sit on insulating material (foam pad) atop a small rock, with your feet also on the insulation.

Altitude Sickness Camp near the trailhead the night before, if you can, and ascend slowly the first day until you adjust to the altitude. Mild symptoms of illness like headache or nausea can be treated with rest, but if you are wheezing, are vomiting, have a severe headache, have shortness of breath, return immediately to lower elevations and get help.

Wild Animals Probably very few animals will be visible to you on your trips. Mule deer, black bears, mountain lions and most of the little critters will flee long before you arrive. They are suspicious of you the intruder in their domain.

Should a lion cross your path, do not run as that triggers the chase instinct in him. Talk calmly but firmly to him, make eye contact, make yourself look as big and bold as possible but nonthreatening. Do not stoop except to quickly pick up little children, slowly back off facing him and fight if attacked. However, few people ever see this majestic animal in the wilds.

Should you encounter a bear, especially a sow with cubs, retreat quietly. If one comes near your sleeping quarters, make lots of noise. Be calm, the bear is seeking your food, not you.

Most bears in the Southern Sierra are shy and do not associate food with people. To maintain this, keep your camp clean and at night hang anything with an odor: food, garbage, toothpaste, etc. Directions for counterbalance bearbagging can be obtained with your fire or wilderness permit. If bruin gets your food, he has become your guest—do not interfere.

In Sequoia and Kings Canyon national parks, bears do associate food with people, and bears have become a serious problem. They will seek food they see or smell on tables, in ice chests, in tents or in cars and are not threatened by people.

The parks spent a great deal of money and much time educating the public in a successful effort to reduce this problem. They have supplied heavy metal, bear-proof food lockers at most popular camping areas. Use them, share them, and help keep them clean. As an alternative, when you pick up your wilderness permit you can rent or purchase an ingenious bear-proof canister that weighs under three pounds and fits nicely in a backpack.

Some animals are visible and friendly such as marmots and ground squirrels. Do not feed them, they fare better on their own food; do not pet them, they may carry diseases.

Rattlesnakes   The Southern and Northern Pacific rattlesnakes, a subspecies of the Western Rattlesnake, frequent the areas described in this book. The snakes range from 16 to 64 inches and have broad diamondlike markings that become rings near the rattles at the end of their tails. A new rattle is added each time they shed their skin, three or four times a year, but sometimes the rattles fall off. These members of the Pit Viper family have broad heads on thin necks and retractable hollow fangs in their upper jaws, which they use to pierce the skin of their prey and to inject venom. The venom contains digestive enzymes that act on the prey. The snakes cannot hear or see well, but they sense heat and feel vibrations. Their forked tongue aids in their sense of smell.

Although their preferred homes are rock outcrops, you will find snakes in grassland, blue oak savannah, digger pine/live oak chaparral and riparian areas up to 11,000 feet elevation. They sun in the cool of day and seek shade during the heat. Snakes feed on small creatures and help the environment by keeping the rodent population in check.

This rattlesnake shows more aggressive behavior than some species, usually after emerging from hibernation; however, all rattlesnakes prefer to be left alone and to leave you alone. They defend themselves by striking, but only when provoked or stepped on. They usually warn you by rattling. They can strike one third to one half of their length and can bite even after they have been killed. A bite is not fatal for most people; small children are at greater risk. Envenomation does not occur with each bite. Numbness and tingling around your mouth indicate that venom has been injected. Do not cut the fang marks or apply a tourniquet; in fact, do nothing to the bite, but do try to stay calm, rest the affected area if possible, and get to the hospital. Suction devices now on the market may help to reduce venom from the wound.

Bugs   *Ticks* rank as the most sinister and sneaky of the four nuisance bugs encountered in the Southern Sierra. Ticks can cause serious diseases that, fortunately, are uncommon in this area: most notably Lyme disease and Rocky Mountain Spotted Fever. Lyme disease usually presents a ringlike red rash around the bite; spotted fever causes reddish-black spots. Both diseases involve flu-like symptoms. Specific antibiotics offer a cure and should be given early in the illness.

Ticks seem most prevalent in late winter and spring. They neither jump nor fly, but transfer from grass or brush to animals or you. You hardly see them and often do not feel their bite. This eight-legged creature can be as tiny as a dot of an i (larvae), to ¼ inch (adult). Remove them with tweezers by gently pulling up. Try not to crush them as that releases their fluid into the bite. Inspect your clothes frequently while in brushy, grassy areas.

Yellow Jackets can be pesky; they sting if molested. Unless you react to their juice, the sting will be painful but cause no further problems. Bright colors and perfume attract these black- and yellow-banded wasps. They land on meat and sweets, which they feed to their young, and buzz around water. Yellow Jackets retreat at dusk.

Mosquitoes, the ubiquitous bug everyone knows and universally dislikes, apparently were put on earth as food for fish, birds and other insects. Mosquitoes leave their watery nursery during spring and early summer, then usually remain around damp areas. They become inactive during cold nights and crispy days, and disappear when the area dries. Many people prefer late summer and early fall for their mountain adventures to avoid these irritating bugs and their itchy bites.

Black Flies, which also develop in water, may be the most exasperating of all as you hike. One or two of these tiny pests hovering around your face can be bothersome, but swarms of them become unbearable. At the first opportunity, they dive for your eyes. As with mosquitoes, the female is the biter, but the bites cause less annoyance than the swarming.

Poison Oak This, the most wide spread shrub in California, occurs from sea level to 5000 feet. Poison oak is deciduous. It has three ovate leaves on a stem with the terminal leaf the largest. Each leaf cluster alternates on the branchlet. The margins can be toothed or lobed. This attractive plant, frocked with spring green leaves that turn a brilliant red, has no thorns. It displays panicles of tiny white flowers and later produces small berries.

The oil of poison oak causes an irritating dermatitis. You can become affected by touching the leaves or the leafless stems, by touching clothing that has brushed against it, even by walking through smoke of burning poison oak bushes. To remove the oil, wash yourself and your clothing thoroughly with strong soap as soon as possible. If you do get a poison oak rash, ask your pharmacist which over-the-counter lotions effectively reduce the irritation. Best to avoid touching any three-leafed bush or vine until you are certain it is not poison oak.

Poison oak: widespread in California

Chapter 3: Resources & Regulations

Agencies

(Summer hours vary depending on budget constraints; therefore, they are not listed here.)

Kern County Parks & Recreation Department
1110 Golden State Avenue
Bakersfield, CA 93301
(805) 861-2345
Hours 8:00–5:00 weekdays

Greenhorn Mountain Park
(619) 376-6780

U.S. Department of the Interior Bureau of Land Management Bakersfield District
Hours 7:30–4:15 weekdays
Information, BLM maps, fire permits

Headquarters
3801 Pegasus Drive
Bakersfield, CA 93308-6837
(805) 391-6000

Caliente Resource Area—For Piute Mtns,
Breckenridge Mtn,
S.W. Isabella Lake, Sierra foothills
Address same as Headquarters

U.S. Department of Agriculture Forest Service Sequoia National Forest
Hours 8:00–4:30 weekdays
Information, books, F.S. maps, fire permits,
Golden Trout Wilderness permits

Headquarters
900 West Grand Ave.
Porterville, CA 93257-2035
(209) 784-1500
Camping Reservations 1 (800) 280-2267

Greenhorn Ranger District—For
Breckenridge Mtn,
Piute Mtns, Greenhorn Mtns.
15701 Highway 178
P.O. Box 6129
Bakersfield, CA 93386-6129
(805) 871-2223

Lake Isabella Visitor Center
4875 Ponderosa Dr.
P.O. Box 3810
Lake Isabella, CA 93240
(619) 379-5646

Cannell Meadow Ranger District—For
Isabella Lake, North Fork Kern River
105 Whitney Rd.
P.O. Box 6
Kernville, CA 93238
(619) 376-3781

Hot Springs Ranger District—For
Greenhorn Mtns, Western Divide Mtns.
43474 Parker Pass Dr.
Route 4, Box 548
California Hot Springs, CA 93207
(805) 548-6503

Tule River Ranger District—For
Western Divide Mtns,
Golden Trout Wilderness
32588 Highway 190
Springville, CA 93265
(209) 539-2607

Hume Lake Ranger District—For
Jennie Lakes Wilderness
35860 E. Kings Canyon Rd.
Dunlap, CA 93621
(209) 338-2251

U.S. Army Corps of Engineers

Success Lake
P.O. Box 1072
Porterville, CA 93258
(209) 784-0215

Lake Kaweah
P.O. Box 346
Lemoncove, CA 93244
(209) 597-2301

California Department of Forestry
Mountain Home Demonstration State
Forest
Hours 8:00–4:30 weekdays
Information, maps
P.O. Box 517
Springville, CA 93265
(209) 539-2855 (Winter)
(209) 539-2321 (Summer)

Tulare County General Services
Balch Park
County Civic Center, Room 7E
Visalia, CA 93277
(209) 733-6612

U.S. Department of Interior
National Park Service
Sequoia and Kings Canyon
National Parks
Hours 8:00–4:30 daily
Information, maps, books, fire &
wilderness permits
Three Rivers, CA 93271
(209) 565-3134
Camping reservations 1 (800) 365-2267

Mineral King
(209) 565-3768

Lodgepole Visitor Center
(209) 565-3782

Grant Grove Visitor Center
(209) 335-2856

A pack train carries supplies

Community

Kern County Museum
3801 Chester Ave.
Bakersfield, CA 93301
(805) 861-2132
Hours 8:00–5:00 weekdays
10:00–5:00 weekends
(Ticket office closes at 3:00)

California Living Museum (CALM)
14000 Alfred Harrell Highway
Bakersfield, CA 93306
(805) 872-2256
Hours   Please call
Admission fee charged

Packers

Golden Trout Wilderness Pack Trains
P.O. Box 756
Springville, CA 93265
(209) 539-2744 (Winter)
(209) 542-2816 (Summer)

Balch Park Pack Station
P.O. Box 852
Springville, CA 93265
(209) 539-2227 (Winter)
(209) 539-3908 (Summer)

Bedell Pack Trains, Mineral King
P.O. Box 61
Three Rivers, CA 93271
(209) 561-4142 (Winter)
(209) 561-3404 (Summer)

Horse Corral Pack Station, Wolverton
P.O. Box 641
Woodlake, CA 93286
(209) 564-2709 (Winter)
(209) 565-3404 (Summer)

Campgrounds, Campsites and Fire Safe Areas

Campgrounds Amenities offered at most campgrounds include the following: individual sites, tables, fire rings, grills, faucet water (off in winter) and toilets—often of the outhouse variety—a vanishing American institution. See the chart for campground listings and detailed information on the enclosed map.

Campsites Any suitable place on public land in the mountains can serve as a campsite. See the map for camp etiquette. However, you are required to camp only in campgrounds while in Mountain Home Demonstration State Forest and in Sequoia and Kings Canyon national parks' frontcountry.

Fire Safe Areas Numerous selected areas scattered throughout Sequoia National Forest considered at minimum fire risk are indicated by signs as "Fire Safe." In these areas you may have camp and cooking fires at any time.

Permits

Campfire A fire permit for campfires and camp stove use outside developed campgrounds is required on all public land. One permit from any of the land governing agencies suffices; it remains in effect for one calendar year. A wilderness permit also serves as a campfire permit.

In addition to wildfire prevention suggestions mentioned in the etiquette column on the map, during extreme hazardous conditions further regulations become necessary. When a Fire Restriction is in effect, you can not have a campfire outside campgrounds or Fire Safe Areas; you may use only stoves with gas, jellied petroleum or pressurized liquid fuel. Smoking is prohibited outside enclosed vehicles, campgrounds or Fire Safe Areas. OHVs are restricted to roads only. For information on the few exempted areas, check with the governing agencies.

Wilderness Golden Trout Wilderness campers need to obtain a wilderness permit for each trip; day hikers need no permit. Permits may be obtained at any Forest Service district office. They are free of charge as of 1994. Permits are not required for Jennie Lakes Wilderness.

At Sequoia and Kings Canyon national parks all over night backcountry trail use requires a permit. Permits are limited under a quota system. A portion of the quota for each trailhead remains on a first-come, first-served basis for those who do not have reservations. Reservations can be made by mail or FAX only, postmarked no earlier than March 1st or requested at least 15 days in advance of your trip. To reserve a permit, state entry and exit dates, trailhead, method of travel, group size and approximate camping sites in a letter addressed as follows:

Wilderness Permit Reservations
Sequoia and Kings Canyon National Parks
Three Rivers, CA 93271
Telephone:(209) 565-3708
FAX (209) 565-3797

Pets under leash may accompany you in national forest wildernesses; no pets are permitted in national park wildernesses or on any park trails. Mechanized equipment including motorcycles, bicycles and chainsaws are not allowed. In the national forest, although unnatural to the wilderness ethic, cattle grazing, hunting and fishing are allowed. In the national parks only fishing is permitted. Weapons are prohibited.

River Use Commercial and private rafters, kayakers and canoeists need to obtain a permit at the Greenhorn or Cannell ranger stations or Lake Isabella Visitor Center before floating on the Kern River.

Fishing A fishing license is needed for all people 16 years of age or older. Since a mix of regulations exist in the Southern Sierra, and may change every two years, obtain information on your area of interest when you buy your fishing license.

Chapter 4: Trip Format

This guidebook could be called a written map. Its information guides you to the trailhead, then helps keep you on route even though the trail may be vague, unsigned, covered with snow or crossed by a myriad of logging roads, animal trails or motorcycle paths. This written map guides you on country car and bicycle tours as well as foot trails. Although the book helps you plan your trip at home, it is also meant to be carried along as you travel by car, bicycle, horse or foot. To lighten your load you may wish to take only copies of the needed pages. The same format is used for each trip description.

Car Tours These tours offer sightseers guidance and information about the mountains and foothills. They may also offer directions to trailheads, thus doubling as resource material for those heading to hiking trips described in this book. The text mentions road names when appropriate and also their code numbers if the numbers are shown on maps or roadside paddles.

Most car tours described connect with other tours from Highway 58 (Tehachapi Pass) to Highway 180 (Kings Canyon National Park). You may need to link several tours to get to your destination. Occasionally the mileage reading will be the most obvious clue that you have reached the destination you seek.

Each car tour includes brackets with two or three figures (6030/0.5/6.3): elevation, mileage from point to point and cumulative mileage. You find elevations at the beginning and end of trips, at low and high points of grades, and at departure points for other car tours. Cumulative mileages appear in one direction only starting at the tourheads. Note that all tours on major roads progress from south to north and from west to east. When traveling in the opposite direction, simply subtract your point of interest from the total mileage.

Bicycle Tours Many car tours serve well as bicycle tours and are indicated as such in the title. Several day hikes and backpack routes accommodate all-terrain bike trips as well

and are listed in the Tripfinder Table found in the appendix. For simplicity, the trip descriptions refer to drivers or hikers rather than bicyclists.

Day Hikes With few exceptions, day hikes carry you less than 10 miles over well-defined trails.

Peak Climbs Most peak ascents follow cross-country routes. If the peak is apparent, you climb up its slopes picking the best way to approach as you go. If not apparent, you consult your map and compass. Sometimes the easiest route is marked by a series of small rock piles called "ducks." Often a dim path called a "use" trail develops by repeated climbs up the same route. If an engineered trail ascends the peak it is listed in this book under day hikes.

Backpacks Overnight trips in the backcountry are called "Backpacks." (Of course pack animals can carry your supplies instead of you.)

Excursions When an optional day hike, peak climb or car tour appear within a trip, it is referred to as an "Excursion."

Equestrians Hikes that accommodate equestrians are listed in the Tripfinder Table in Part 3 of this book. As with bicycle tours, to simplify description, these trips refer to one user group, hikers, and are not intended to ignore another, equestrians.

Side Trips Trips that venture outside the Southern Sierra, but relate to the mountains historically or biologically are called "Side Trips."

Bicycling: a family sport

Trail blaze carved on tree trunk

Format Headings By scanning the headings you can quickly tell whether the trip promises the kind of outing you desire. To determine the difficulty of a trip for you, consider the distance, steep ascents, elevation gain and skills involved, then factor in your capability and your time limitation. To approximate the duration of a trip, decide on the average number of miles you can comfortably hike on a fairly level trail in one day. Add one mile for every 1000 feet of elevation gain to the trip's mileage. Now divide the trip's total mileage by your daily mileage estimate. The accepted generalization of hikers' speed is 1.0 mile per hour on uphill trails; 2.0 miles per hour on level paths; 3.0 miles per hour on downhill treks if the grade is not extreme. Allow extra time for cross-country hiking; for rough trails; for carrying a backpack or heavy day pack; for snack breaks; for observing the flowers; for listening to bird songs; for exploring whatever wonders present themselves along the way.

Distance This indicates the total distance of the trip. Field surveys with a measuring wheel yielded most of the readings; distances on terrain impassable for a wheel were taken from topographic maps. A *round trip* means that you follow the same route to your destination and back. A *loop trip* means that you return on a new route, but it may include a maximum of 2.0 miles of your outgoing trail; a *semiloop trip* combines a loop and a significant round trip portion. As with a loop and round trip, you always return to your starting point. In a *shuttle trip,* you begin and

end your journey at different locations. This means you will need to arrange transportation at both ends. You have several options: you can leave a vehicle at each trailhead; be dropped off and/or met; hitchhike; split your group, hike in opposite directions and trade cars. The mileage given is for one way. A *one-way trip* appears on car and bicycle tours only.

Steep Ascents Here you have an approximate figure that indicates the sum total of grades around 21%—that is 21 feet elevation gain in 100 feet.

Elevation Gain This is approximately the trip's total gain excluding minor trail undulations. Most elevations were taken from the U.S. Geological Survey provisional topographic maps.

Skills: Day Hikes To assist novices, day hikes are rated. An *easy* rating promises a hike of several miles on fairly level terrain; *moderate* means a longer duration and includes some elevation gain; *moderate-to-strenuous* includes significant gain, perhaps some rough terrain, and may require some pathfinding skill; *strenuous* day hikes do not appear in this book. The ratio of miles to elevation gain is a factor in determining the rate, also.

Skills: Route Finding *Easy route finding* means well-defined trails or roads. Cross-country routes, if any, are short or obvious.

Intermediate route finding includes cross-country routes where the destination cannot be seen at departure, or trails with obscure sections (when scouted). When the trail becomes obscure, look for these clues to guide you: blazes on trees either in the form of a vertical rectangle with a square above carved in the tree trunk or a metal diamond nailed to the trunk; orange plastic ribbons tied to protruding objects; low stacks of rocks known as ducks. Usually there is a series of like clues. Look also for the subtle clues: remains of downslope retaining walls; sections of an unnatural linear depression along the contour of the ground; smooth cuts on branches of trees and shrubs made during trail construction or maintenance; a line of dark grass through a meadow.

Advanced route finding trips are not included in this book.

Skills: Climbing This book describes Class 1 to 4 climbing routes and identifies a number of interesting, more difficult route possibilities. *Class 1* terrain requires no particular expertise, and ordinary, comfortable walking shoes are adequate. *Class 2* requires good balance and shoes or boots that afford good traction on boulders. Rock climbing falls into this category when the degree of difficulty assures a challenge, but good hand and foot holds assist your ascent, and there are no precipitous drops. *Class 3* may have sheer cliffs, exposure, arêtes, narrow hand and footholds and precipitous drops. You may wish to use a rope for belay. *Class 4* refers to steep, exposed rock with narrow holds; you will need to use a rope as well as your best climbing skills. *Class 5* routes refer to technical climbs.

Seasons This heading indicates the time of year for the trip's most temperate climate.

Maps In the 1980s, the U.S. Geological Survey published photographic revisions and new provisional editions of topographic maps of the Southern Sierra in the large, easy-to-read 7.5-minute series. These maps, listed in order of use, appear next to the heading in each trip as additions to the map included with this book. You can buy the 7.5-minute maps at your mountain supply store, your map store or order them as follows:

USGS Map Sales
Box 25286
Denver, CO 80225

In 1993 the cost was $2.50 per map. Prepayment is required; include $1.00 handling charge if order is under $10.00; list maps within a state alphabetically; allow four weeks.

The offices of the Bureau of Land Management sell maps of areas within their jurisdiction. The maps include points of interest and some have road and trail numbers, as well. Offices of Sequoia National Forest have maps for a nominal price that include road and trail numbers in their area. The Tourist Center in Lone Pine offers at little cost an Inyo National Forest, USGS 15-minute topographic map that includes all of Golden Trout and South Sierra wildernesses. Their map differentiates between main and secondary trails on the forest. Sequoia and Kings Canyon National Parks' contour maps cover their entire area and are reasonably priced.

Wilderness Press sells a wide variety of maps including a 15-minute, plastic coated topographic map of Mineral King. It cost $4.50 in 1994. The Map Center specializes in quick delivery.

Map Center: Wilderness Press
2440 Bancroft Way
Berkeley, CA 94704
(510) 841-6277

Trailheads and Tourheads To avoid repetition and to increase interest while driving, *trailhead* directions are included in the car tour descriptions. If a trailhead serves only one trip, its concluding spur road directions, if any, appear in the trip's format. Otherwise that information appears within brackets in the car tour. Check the odometer while driving to trailheads—mileage often becomes the best guide. All parking areas accommodate at least five cars. *Tourheads* serve car and bicycle tours.

Description A detailed account of each trip is given so that a traveler, unfamiliar and inexperienced, can journey safely and confidently. The account includes information

"Duck": a low stack of rocks

about campsites, water sources, viewpoints and elevations for specific locations en route with mileages between locations (6720/2.3). To enhance the adventure, cameos of natural and human history, geology and geography, flora and fauna appear as part of the text. To aid in quick identification, salient features of a few birds and numerous flowers are described and are listed in the index. Those identified in the *East Side* book are not repeated in this, the *West Side* book.

Trail signs occur at trailheads and junctions and dependably remain in place inside the national parks. Outside the parks they are inexplicably destroyed by people, toppled by cattle and sometimes chewed by bears. To assure a successful trip in those areas, do not depend on signs, but follow the maps and book descriptions and note the landmarks as you hike. Sequoia National Forest uses codes

and names for trails and roads along with destinations: CLEAR CREEK TRAIL 33E45, BROWN MEADOW 10 MILES; sometimes only code numbers appear on the sign: 33E45. These numbers are mentioned in the text. In contrast, the parks use signs indicating destinations and mileages only: HOCKETT LAKES, 8.9 MILES.

Some trails described in this book provide passage for motorcycles. Cyclists tend to drive on the weekends, but they are prohibited from all trail travel during fire restrictions. "M'cyclepaths" identify the trails open to motorcyclists.

Trip logs appear in the description where two or more trips overlap while heading in the same direction. The point-to-point elevations and mileages given in the logs help you identify corresponding text and locate your position in the field.

Blowdowns cut during trail maintenance often outline a trail

Part 2

Adventures in the Southern Sierra: West Side

Section 1

Highway 58 to Highway 178 —Piute & Breckenridge Mountains & Surrounding Area—

Pinus sabiniana (Digger Pine): lacy pine of Southern Sierra foothills

T1   Tehachapi Railroad Loop Side Trip

One of the wonders of the railroad world, this section of track gains 77 feet and makes such a tight loop that you can watch a freight train's engine circle over its caboose. The Tehachapi Loop is among the most photographed railroad sites on this continent.

Distance   None
Steep Ascents   None
Elevation Gain   None
Skills   Easy access; paved road
Seasons   All year
Map   Kern County road map
Trailhead   1. From Highway 58 (0.0/0.0), take the Keene offramp, then turn right on ***Woodford-Tehachapi Road*** (KC Road 481) and drive east. The offramp is 29.7 miles east of Highway 99 in Bakersfield and 29.3 miles west of Highway 14 in Mojave. Drive under the freeway, pass Keene, zigzag then level out where you pass an unpaved road branching to the left (2.6/2.6). The loop's tunnel No. 9 is 0.1 mile to the right of that road. Continue on the paved road to climb to the marker viewpoint (0.8/3.4), **TH1**.
Description   Rising from the floor of the San Joaquin Valley on a 2.2% grade, the

Southern Pacific Railroad curls up Tehachapi Pass canyon through 17 tunnels and around this famous loop before reaching its 4032-foot summit. The train route surrounding the loop looks like a wriggly doodle on maps: the tracks curve and broadly zigzag. The loop below is fully visible from the viewpoint where a monument sits at the left side of the road overlooking the Walong siding. This siding on the loop was added in 1909 and named Walong in honor of District Roadmaster W. A. Long.

Sometimes several trains arrive in a short period; other times not many. Bring chairs to use at the edge of the road, or a ground cover for use on the slopes, or plan to visit the loop in spring when viewing the wildflowers will absorb your waiting time. After you see a few trains curve around the loop, descend to No. 9 tunnel, which you passed 0.8 mile back, to

One end of a train circles over its other end

see one end of a train in the tunnel and the other end riding on top of it—if the train is more than 4000 feet long.

The Southern Pacific Railroad Company (SP) incorporated in 1865. A year later an act of an expansionist Congress authorized SP to build a line from San Francisco to the Colorado River where it would connect with tracks arriving from the east.

Construction of the railroad south commenced in 1869 and reached the Kern River five years later. From there it pushed southeast up Tehachapi Pass canyon, arriving at Caliente in 1875. From Caliente to Mojave became an engineering feat that made its surveyer, William Hood, famous in railroad annals. "It was just a common sense plan," said Chief Engineer Hood who declined having the loop named for him. As many as 3000 laborers, mostly Chinese, laid the tracks and blasted the 22-foot-high, 16½-foot-wide tunnels. Accidental explosions killed many.

Ownership and control of SP at that time belonged to Mark Hopkins, Leland Stanford, Collis P. Huntington and Charles Crocker who were known as the "Big Four." David D. Colton became an associate. These names remain familiar to Californians today; for example, the Mark Hopkins Hotel in San Francisco, the Stanford University in Palo Alto and the Huntington Library in Pasadena.

T2   Caliente-Bodfish Historic Car & Bicycle Tour
(With Directions to Trailheads 2–5)

This trip unfolds on a nineteenth century stagecoach route called the "Old Lions Trail." It passes intriguing places steeped in the history of that period. Along the way the route journeys over rounded hills and mountain slopes that display seasonal flows of youthful wildflowers and aged leaves.

Distance   35.0 miles, one way
Steep Ascents   None (Long hard grades for bicyclists)
Elevation Gain   4095 feet
Skills   Easy route finding; paved road
Seasons   All year (Bicyclists avoid summer)
Map   Kern County road map
Tourhead   2. The junction of Highway 58 and Bealville Road is **TH2**. It is 24.7 miles east of Highway 99 in Bakersfield and 34.3 miles west of Highway 14 in Mojave.
Description   From the freeway (2062/0.0/0.0) descend north on winding **Bealville Road** as it crosses over and under railroad tracks then merges with **Caliente-Bodfish Road** (KC Road 483) (2.0/2.0). After bridging the wide wash of Caliente Creek, you arrive at the general store and post office of Caliente (0.1/2.1).

The sleepy hamlet of Allen's Camp became Caliente when in 1875 the Southern Pacific Railroad established a railhead here. For one year it served as home base for 2000 to 3000 laborers, mostly Chinese, who laid the rails. The town further burgeoned with gamblers, thieves and thugs who frequented the nearly two dozen saloons that lined the north side of its main street. When the railroad pushed farther east to Tehachapi, the workers and many businesses moved with it. For a time the town remained an important terminus for stagecoaches, handling their freight and serving their passengers to and from Los Angeles, Havilah and the Kern River Valley. Now a skeleton of its former self, it serves as a railroad siding.

Your route travels near Caliente Creek, a stream lucky to have a trickle of water most years, but occasionally it swells with massive runoff from the western slopes of the Piute Mountains and roars down the wide wash playing havoc with anything intruding upon its path. It has caused six major floods since 1932. Swollen waters inundated several communities in 1983 causing $40 million damage.

The road soon arrives at a forked junction

(1545/3.1/5.2) with Caliente Creek Road at **TH3** for T3, a loop car tour that later rejoins this tour. Here proud citizens of the area erected a WELCOME TO SCENIC WESTERN COUNTRY sign.

Now ascending a moderate grade on the left fork, still the Caliente-Bodfish Road, the route enters Oiler Canyon, named for John F. Oyler, a saloon keeper and road overseer. The old trail climbed this canyon before the stagecoach road opened in 1865. It was so steep early settlers from the north traveling to Los Angeles or Visalia for provisions had to lower their wagons by ropes or cables. On their return they unloaded their wagons to hoist them up, then horses carried the contents up the trail. Residents refer to this route as the "Old Lions Trail."

The road switchbacks deeply then again to a lesser degree. It offers few shoulders on the narrow steep slopes; therefore, bicyclists need to be extra alert for cars even though they cannot be driven very fast. Then the grade eases as the pavement traverses along the ridgecrest. In late winter, early spring a wildflower mosaic borders the way, and blue oaks on gently rounded hills unfurl their leaves. While on a nearly level grade, the road passes the unpaved, private, westward-bound Baker Grade Road (3900/8.3/13.5). Enterprising Colonel Thomas Baker, founder of Bakersfield, established this as a toll road in 1867. It became one of the first to be forged from San Joaquin Valley to the gold strikes north of Walker Basin.

Still on the paved road, you quickly descend past broad views of Walker Basin and past the entrances of Rankin Ranch and Walker Basin Road (1.3/14.8). Rankin Ranch has been in the Rankin family as a continuously working cattle ranch since established in 1863. It also served as a stagecoach stop at one time, and from 1965 it has operated as a guest ranch as well. The charming white building facing Walker Basin Road, the home of the owner, was built in the 1870s from plans in "Godey's Ladies Book." A plaque at the road junction placed by the Kern Valley Indian Community honors Little Lucy, a Native American, and the family of Lavenia Lightner Rankin. The family raised Little Lucy after she nearly died of starvation during the U.S. Cavalry enforced march of Owens Valley Indians through Walker Basin to the Tejon Reservation.

The road, hedged by fences and rabbit-brush, passes Julia Lake, a tiny reservoir on Walker Basin Creek, and continues straight along Walker Basin's west hem, the line of the Breckenridge fault. In prehistoric times this was the scene of grinding quakes as Breckenridge Mountain rose and Walker Basin sank. Some seismologists link this fault with the Kern Canyon fault to the north and the White Wolf fault to the south as one continuous fault. They align directly and together make this an awesome rupture line. The most movement along this extended fault in recent times occurred on the White Wolf segment in 1952. That quake measured 7.7 on the Richter Scale and caused extensive damage in the Bakersfield and Tehachapi areas.

At the north of the basin the road turns abruptly right then left at a junction (3380/2.7/17.5) with Walser Road where T3 returns to join this tour. Moving ahead, your road leaves Walker Basin, enters the sparsely populated hilly habitat of live and blue oaks and penetrates a zone of metamorphic rocks laced with limestone. An unmarked road to the right leads to the Tungsten Chief Mine. Discovered in 1918, this mine's greatest yield occurred between 1940 and 1950 when about 4000 tons of ore were removed averaging around 1.0% tungsten. One use for this

The 1870 Rankin house

Replica of first court house

mineral found along junctions of granitic and calcareous rock is the filament in light bulbs.

Beyond the mine's road, Piute Meadows Trading Post (4277/3.2/20.7)—groceries, drinks, snacks—straddles the pass. Views from here include Isabella Lake with Split Mountain to its left and upper Kern Canyon extending far to the north. Kern Canyon fault joins Breckenridge fault beneath as you descend into Havilah Canyon past a scattering of houses, apple orchards and paved Breckenridge Road (3510/2.1/22.8) to the left. This junction is the terminus of car tour T10 that takes hikers to **TH10** of T11 in the Breckenridge Mountains. In 1.8 miles on your route you pass public phones at the Forest Service's Havilah Work Center, then arrive at Havilah and the Havilah Museum (2.3/25.1).

Today's quiet village bears little resemblance to the 1860s when thousands of people roamed its streets following the discovery of gold in the Clear Creek diggings. Prospector Asbury Harpending laid out the town and called it more profitably than reverently after the biblical Havilah: ". . . where there is gold . . ." Genesis 2:11. Harpending retired to San Francisco on the $800,000 he made while mining the miners. The town with its 150 buildings became the hub of much activity. It was named the first seat of Kern County in 1866 and remained so until 1874 when Bakersfield gained the title.

Old tombstones, a few adobe walls and some foundations were about all that remained visible from the town's rambunctious past until a few citizens instigated an effort to reconstruct some buildings and preserve its history. Now there stands replicas of the schoolhouse and county courthouse—the town's museum. The museum, open on weekends, houses a rich display of pictures, maps and artifacts. Between the buildings the proud people of Havilah constructed cement tables for your picnic pleasure.

Still in Havilah Canyon, your route touches **TH4** of Ts4&5 (3030/0.6/25.7) to the right for hikes along Clear Creek. Also to your right along this stretch, granite Bald Eagle Peak of T7 dominates the northwest edge of the Piute Mountains. Ahead your road climbs to the V-shaped pass between Hooper Hill, west, and Ball Mountain, east. At the pass (3779/3.6/29.3) a dirt road drops west to Lathum Tunnel, dug in a futile attempt to find a gold vein. Unpaved SNF Road 27S02 (a.k.a. Piute Mountain Road, Ball Mountain Road, Saddle Spring Road), **TH5** for car tour T6, leads east to **THs6–8**, Ts7–9 on the plateau lands of the Piute Mountains.

Ahead on your descent beyond the pass, you view spacious scenes of the Greenhorn, Kern Plateau and Piute mountains, all of which rise dramatically to confine the Kern River Valley in a virtual showcase. The royal blue of Isabella Lake appears foreshortened and snug in the most distant part of the valley.

Four switchbacks ease you down to Hot

Frontier buildings at Ghost Town

Spring Valley and the town of Bodfish, named for George Bodfish who established a wayside station here on the stagecoach route. Then your route passes a T junction (2674/2.9/32.2) with Kern Canyon Road of car tour T13, and your road becomes *Lake Isabella Boulevard*. Quickly the boulevard crosses under the flume of Borel Canal and passes privately owned Silver City Ghost Town (0.6/32.8). This interesting outdoor museum, open to the public for a fee, features a cluster of frontier buildings collected from surrounding historic towns.

As you drive through the town of Lake Isabella, you may notice to the right, tucked back from the road, a skeletal structure and puffs of steam (1.8/34.6). Closer inspection of the structure reveals an upright pipe gushing 130° water from within, and behind that, the concrete remains of a swimming pool. This is the site of Scovern Hot Springs House. Here a hotel, hot spring baths and a plunge attracted many people from 1866 until interest waned, and the complex fell into disrepair. The crumbling buildings remained unused until they were consumed by flames in 1971.

Your lengthy country tour of historical sites and rolling hills ends at the junction of State Highway 155 (2504/0.4/35.0). This junction is **TH17** for lake circling car tour T21 and also marks the end of Kern Canyon car tour T12.

T3   Caliente Creek-Walker Basin Car & Bicycle Tour

Paved roads on which few cars travel enhance the attractiveness of this region where once man came in search of wealth. Narrow canyon, quiet stream, broad valley, spring wildflowers, rolling hills and old mines provide scenic diversity on this leisurely trip in the country.

Distance   28.0 miles, one way
Steep Ascents   None
Elevation Gain   2735 feet
Skills   Easy route finding; paved roads
Seasons   All year (Bicyclists avoid summer)
Map   Kern County road map
Tourhead   3. The junction of Caliente-Bodfish Road and Caliente Creek Road is **TH3**. This is 5.2 miles north of Bealville exit on Highway 58. It departs from car tour T2.
Description   From the tourhead junction (1545/0.0/0.0), *Caliente Creek Road* (KC Road 487) curves east into nooks and around fingers of Caliente Creek's narrow scenic canyon, crossing the creek 12 times. During rain storms this placid little stream expands dramatically and periodically floods the road, carrying off chunks of asphalt. Some of the houses you pass show signs of undercutting by high water. The stone fortified terrace and house visible on the south bank that was once owned by renowned author of western fiction, the late Louis L'Amour, shows flood water damage—and extensive

vandalism.

In time you pass the hamlet of Loraine (10.8/10.8), tucked next to the confluence of Indian and Caliente creeks. Frenchmen who worked the local mines within a triangle of rich deposits between Harper, Eagle and Stevenson peaks, settled here in 1890—about the center of the triangle. They found productive veins that appeared where rhyolite dikes intruded granitic and metamorphic rock.

Amalie mine and mill

Former schoolhouse: circa 1934

Rhyolite, a volcanic equivalent of granite, flows sluggishly when erupted due to its highly viscous magma form. Between 60 and 25 million years ago molten rhyolite welled up here filling widespread fissures that developed deep in this southernmost granite of the Sierra Nevada. Local bluffs of white to buff, yellow, or reddish-purple exemplify the rocks of this intrusion and help you recognize it. But it takes a trained eye to locate the metals it may harbor.

Next, the Amalie Mine and Mill (0.6/11.4) sprawl to your left. Gold, silver and other metals extracted here totaled about $600,000 by 1912. While inspecting the mine, notice the embossed metal that covers the interior walls of the building closest to the road.

Gaping Sand Canyon appears to the left, then you see grayish limestone ridges and outcrops as you continue. Such remnants as these, widespread in this part of the range, predate both the rhyolite and granite. In minutes the little red schoolhouse occurs to the right, circa 1934, which now houses Twin Oaks General Store where food is also served. The school's blackboards remain on the walls. Next you pass Back Canyon Road (2.7/14.1): a private, gated road to the right that connects with other roads to meet Highway 14.

As you leave the zone of volcanic rock, heading north among the rounded hills, you pass the road (2.0/16.1) to Piute Mountain School. Built in 1984, this attractive school employs energy conservation ideas from the past: it abuts an excavated side of a hill and has a sod roof. The energy saved by that construction allows it to have glass across the entire front of the school, giving the kindergarten- to eighth-grade students a wide-angle view of the mountains and valleys.

Soon your road passes the spring-fed reservoir and housing development of Piute Springs Ranches; then, curving west, it ascends to a saddle and a junction (4258/3.3/19.4) with Piute Mountain Road. This highest elevation point on your journey marks the terminus of car tour T6 on one of four access roads to the Piute Mountains. Now your road becomes **Walker Basin Road** (KC Road 475), and passes the Kern County Fire Station built in the 1980s.

You next arrive at the entrance (3.6/23.0) to privately owned Cowboy Memorial and Library open to the public for a fee. A large collection of branding irons and work-worn saddles are among the artifacts on display. Long range plans call for an Indian village as well. Two plaques stand at the entrance: one refers to the memorial, and the other presents the enigma of the origin of the valley's name.

On the final leg of your country journey, now in Walker Basin, your route passes several roads to houses; one reaches the Joe Walker Gold Mine, closed to the public. Discovered in 1865, ore was taken from a quartz vein and milled in a 20-stamp mill on the site for 10 years before water forced the mine's closure. It was again worked profitably for a short time in the 1950s. Since then the bore has furnished local irrigators with a wealth of water.

A sea of baby blue eyes

While oak-dotted slopes of Harper Peak rise to the left, you head west, then zigzag on *Johns*, *Williams*, *Daily*, and finally *Walser* roads to the junction (3380/5.0/28.0) with Caliente-Bodfish Road and the end of this tour. Finish your trip on the route of car tour T2.

T4   Clear Creek Day Hike

Wildflower enthusiasts who visit the foothills of the Piute Mountains in springtime will find these slopes dabbed with the pastel blue of baby blue eyes. This native wildflower, abundant here, has been cultivated and treasured in English country gardens for centuries. In the canyon beyond the flowered slopes, the hidden creek flows lazily where you arrive; its tree-shaded banks invite you to pause and picnic.

Distance   4.6 miles, round trip
Steep Ascents   None
Elevation Gain   830 feet
Skills   Easy route finding; easy-to-moderate hiking
Seasons   Fall, winter, spring
Maps   USGS 7.5-min. *Miracle Hot Sps, Lake Isabella So*
Trailhead   4. See car tour T2.
Description   The first two miles of this trail cross private property; the owners ask that you do not hunt, cut wood, camp or linger on their land.

This walk begins on *Clear Creek M'cyclepath 33E45* at a stock-fence gate (3030/0.0) next to the Caliente-Bodfish Road, north of Havilah. It heads generally southeast, first among rabbitbrush, then buck brush, blue and live oak and digger pine. The path soon follows a ravine, and then crosses a saddle. In good years, baby blue eyes cover these slopes with a sea of powder blue, but most any spring you will find puddles of these delightful blooms. The clear blue flowers have five petals and white centers. The flowers are bowl-shaped, about ½ to 1 inch in size and average around 12 inches high. Their pinnately divided, oblong leaves grow opposite on the stem.

The trail ascends in the Clear Creek watershed where rocky Bald Eagle Peak of T7 perches dominantly on the north divide. The path takes you along corrugated slopes over many gullies, passes through another gate into Sequoia National Forest, and then arrives at Clear Creek (3810/2.3).

Here in late fall before winter rains, the year-round creek barely pools enough water to satisfy the watercress that floats on the stream's surface. Alders and willows crowd the banks. Scattered boulders offer seats for a lunch stop before your return trip or further exploration of the creek environs.

T5   Clear Creek Backpack

The hills respond to the call of spring with pastel wildflowers, and the canyon to autumn with bronze, gold and crimson leaves. In any season the rusted artifacts of gold mines recall the time the canyon of Clear Creek bristled with prospectors after gold was discovered there in 1864.

Distance   20.2 miles, round trip
Steep Ascents   0.2 mile
Elevation Gain   3700 feet
Skills   Easy route finding
Seasons   Fall, winter, spring
Maps   USGS 7.5-min *Miracle Hot Sprs, Lake Isabella So, Piute Pk* (trail not does appear on this provisional edition)
Trailhead   4. See car tour T2.
Description   The beginning of this trip is described in T4.

Southeastbound Trail 33E45 Log

T4	Trailhead	3030	0.0
	1st Clear Cr Xing	3810	2.3

An easy step or boulder-hop deposits you on the opposite bank of Clear Creek, the first of 29 fords of the creek on this trip. After the ford, *Clear Creek M'cyclepath 33E45* immediately crosses it again along with a tributary. Then the path ascends a moderate grade where you perhaps disturb a family of California Quails. They can be seen walking with peanut-sized fledglings lined up behind. Often the male stands guard while his family pecks about for food. Their distinct call of "where-are-you," the second note higher and accented, resounds through the canyon. One way this gray and brown bird differs from his cousin the Mountain Quail of the yellow pine and lodgepole pine belts, is by the head plume that curves forward. A Mountain Quail's slender head feather reaches high and flows back.

The canyon grows deeper beside you; numerous spindly yuccas pin the far slopes. The exposed trail advances among sagebrush and mountain mahogany along with a few oaks and pinyon pines and one huge old juniper. It passes through another gate and hugs steep slopes where it sloughs off somewhat at times. The path travels over metamorphic chunks, curves alongside the creek, then crosses it among alders and stinging nettles, the third Clear Creek crossing (4880/2.7).

A campsite appears on a ledge under golden oaks after the fifth crossing. The trail passes under a leaning, dead tree that has an unusual thorny trunk after the seventh. A seeping spring appears after the eleventh ford. A terrace with black and golden oaks, a spring, room for camping, heavy mining artifacts and a rusted pipe that parallels the trail on the creek's north bank mark the thirteenth. Here a barely visible path (5435/1.4) ascends a side canyon north to Valley Vista Mine.

You ford the creek again; then you reach a large flat suitable for many tents. Ahead the grade steepens and Clear Creek chortles down through a set of cascades, its white water bold against round mossy boulders. Now you careen across the creek several more times, zigzag steeply up, then drop to another ford.

The path, now on the south side of the creek, ascends by curves and switchbacks above the canyon floor. Chinquapin, white pine and Jeffrey pine accompany the route. After a third triangle blaze, some people head across the creek to inspect Burton Mill site (6700/2.2). The mill is gone, but the cabin, hidden from view, has been restored and NO

One of Clear Creek's many little falls

TRESPASSING signs have been tacked about.

Continuing to Brown Meadow, the trail crosses the creek above the mill site area, curves next to a barbed wire fence and fords the stream five more times. The narrow canyon supports creek dogwoods whose leaves turn crimson in autumn and willows whose leaves turn golden: an additional touch of beauty to the snug little canyon.

After following close to Clear Creek for 7.8 miles, you cross it for the twenty-ninth time—this time on logs—and arrive at a Fire Safe Area of campsites bordering spacious

Brown Meadow (7280/1.5). The meadow lies cupped in a semicircle of peaks and ridges, 500 vertical feet below Saddle Spring Road to the east. Spring water captured in a tank by the meadow often overflows, making it easy to refill your water. An ideal place to linger or camp.

Rumor has it that Charlie Brown had a substantial house where the campsites are, and that he cultivated the meadow. But one day while plowing the field his tractor turned over on him. He did not recover. The meadow and a peak to the west carry his name.

T6   West Piute Mountains Car & All-Terrain Bicycle Tour
With Excursion A: Piute Mountains Lookout Site (With Directions to Trailheads 6–8)

From above Isabella Lake to Walker Basin, this dramatic road winds along the west side of the Piute Mountains, clings to its steep slopes, and presents broad vistas of Kern River and Havilah valleys. It bisects a botanical area of rare trees as it travels through successional flora zones and reaches the high country of the Piute Mountains.

Distance   25.0 miles, one way
Steep Ascents   None (Long, hard grades for bicyclists)
Elevation Gain   4245 feet
Skills   Easy route finding; unpaved roads
Seasons   Spring, summer, fall
Map   Kern County road map
Tourhead   5. The forked junction of Caliente-Bodfish Road and SNF Road 27S02 on the pass between Harper Hill and Ball Mountain is **TH5**. This is 4.2 miles north of Havilah and 2.9 miles south of Bodfish. This trip departs from car tour T2.
Description   For safety, bicyclists may opt to drive up the narrow, ascending road with its numerous blind curves, then mount their bikes at the Bald Eagle Peak trailhead.

Your tour on bladed, maintained *SNF Road 27S02* begins at the pass (3779/0.0/ 0.0). This road is most often referred to as Saddle Spring Road, but appears on some maps as Piute Mountain Road. Ascending southeast past a road gate (closed in winter), the road curves around Ball Mountain, then

hangs onto steep slopes offering grand views of Isabella Lake and the surrounding area, but offering little room to pass oncoming cars. In just over 3.0 miles and after crossing into Sequoia National Forest, your tour enters the Bodfish Piute Cypress Botanical Area where you can find a place to pull off for a closer examination of these rare cypress trees.

Piute cypress trees, *Cupressus nevadensis,* according to the late botanist Ernest C. Twisselmann, once covered the region occupied by the Mojave Desert. Now only six known groves exist, of which this is the largest. This cypress grows in any soil, but does not compete well with shrubs. The cones seem to need the heat of fire to release their seeds; thus you usually find even aged trees in a grove. Cypress trees are often confused with juniper trees as both have minute, fragrant, overlapping, scalelike leaves. But you can identify a cypress by its cones that have seams like those on a soccer ball and a point between each seam. The cones of junipers have frosty looking coats and are uniformly round and bumpy.

Back on the narrow road you negotiate a series of switchbacks; then, no doubt with some relief, reach a wider roadbed and a pullout on a minor saddle (5.5/5.5) at **TH6**. Climbers of T7, the prominent Bald Eagle Peak protruding northwest, debark here alongside thriving fremontia bushes and yuccas.

Continuing on SNF Road 27SO2, the southeastern ascent carries you near the ridgetop into a mixed forest of pine, fir, and oak and through a community of summer cabins. The road next reaches the Fire Safe Area of shady Saddle Spring Camp (4.8/10.3). Most of the amenities of the former campground have been removed, but the grills remain, and an upright pipe delivers a trickle of water. Still a nice place to camp.

Climbing up the ravine beyond the camp, you quickly arrive at a saddle with a two-pronged entrance of a road (1.1/11.4) to the right. This is **TH7** for climbers of Liebel Peak, T8. The descending road leads to Burton Mill of T5, the Clear Creek Backpack.

Ahead you ascend below Liebel Peak along the western slopes of a watershed divide to pass a T junction (3.6/15.0) with SNF Road 28S18. (That road curves above Brown Meadow of T5 and continues to Solomons Ridge with Brown Peak—nice country for extra exploring.) You soon reach a gate, then a junction (7970/1.4/16.4) with the end of SNF Road 28S01. A not-to-miss tour to Piute Mountains Lookout site begins here.

Excursion A: Piute Mountains Lookout Site

At the site you are treated to a comprehensive view of the nearby peaks and the distant, misty silhouettes of the outlying ranges. In your near view, chartreuse lichen form designs on metamorphic shards.

Distance   6.6 miles, round trip
Steep Ascents   None
Elevation Gain   360 feet

Skills   Easy route finding; unpaved roads
Description   From the junction with SNF Road 28S01 (7970/0.0/0.0), you turn left, still on *SNF Road 27S02*. You descend north and quickly arrive at a swale and a T junction (0.4/0.4) with *SNF Road 28S17*, the lookout road on which you turn left again. (SNF Road 27S02 continues eastward beyond the lookout site road to cross the Piute plateau and then descend to Kelso Valley Road. It connects with tours on the Piute Mountains described in *Exploring the Southern Sierra: East Side*, this book's companion edition.)

Drive north on the easy undulating ascent of maintained 28S17 along the backbone of the Piute Mountains through forest, some logged, some replanted, past spur roads to a junction (2.6/3.0) with a fork to the left where you park next to a large campsite.

Now you continue on foot along the road, which steepens and becomes rough, to the former lookout parking area (0.2/3.2) where a cabin-sized cement slab remains. Here you find the path to the right, hidden among chinquapin, and climb up the rock steps to the site (8326/0.1/3.3) where a lookout once crowned the peak. Single logs of the former building supported on concrete piles afford an ideal place to sit, inhale the clean mountain air and enjoy the panoramic view.

*   *   *   *   *

On this tour you turn right at the junction onto *SNF Road 28S01*, also called Piute Mountain Road on maps, to curve below 8000-foot peaks, the highest on the Piute Mountains. You reach **TH8** of T9, a climb of the peaks, at the apex (1.0/17.4) of the road's U curve, a mile from the junction. Here, to the right, you can usually obtain water by walking a bit down-canyon, where you will find a tank filled with an underground flow from Piute Spring. A campsite rests in the canyon below the tank.

Now you begin your long descent south out of the mountains. Bicyclists may want to return the way they came at this point. The road is steep at times and winding, but has few blind curves and precipitous side slopes. In a little over a mile, you pass a ramshackle group of structures and the ruins of Buxton Sawmill, the last of three mills in the Piutes, closed in the early 1960s.

You soon leave Sequoia National Forest, enter the chaparrel zone, view distant Walker Basin and note the road code change to **KC Road 501** on the paddles. Private roads to mobilehomes and structures depart yours. You cross Rancheria Creek. Then, after endless driving on unpaved roads, suddenly find yourself on pavement just prior to meeting Walker Basin Road (4258/7.6/25.0), the end of your journey on the Piutes. Car tour T3 describes this road.

T7   Bald Eagle Peak Climb

Bald Eagle Peak, perched on a protruding northwestern ridge of the Piute Mountains, looms with a commanding presence over its domain, the Havilah Valley.

Distance   1.2 miles, round trip
Steep Ascents   0.1 mile
Elevation Gain   585 feet
Skills   Easy-to-Intermediate route finding; Class 2 climbing
Seasons   Spring, summer, fall
Map   USGS 7.5-min. *Lake Isabella So*
Trailhead   6. See car tour T6.
Description   The access to this peak looks inaccessible due to the thick blanket of buck brush and associated xerophytic bushes—an arduous bushwhack at best. And it would be, without the valiant efforts of the members of the Hundred Peaks Section, Angeles Chapter, Sierra Club who keep the brush trimmed along a use path.

Upon leaving SNF Road 27S02 (6060/ 0.0), the route follows a **use path** northwest while weaving through an aisle of head-high brush. It stays close to the crest, reaches a metamorphic rock outcrop, then drops to the southwest side and descends to a saddle.

Sometimes openings in the brush lead to a false route; cut stubs of branches indicate the correct way.

From the saddle you ascend along the ridgeline, climb two tiers of granite rock—the second being the most difficult—and pass by a few Piute cypress trees in the southern extension of their grove. A scramble up another tier, and you attain the summit (6181/0.6). Spectacular views beyond the remarkable adjacent cliffs present the Kern River and Havilah valleys.

It is not likely that you will see bald eagles from this peak, although they are returning to winter by the lake and rivers of the Kern River Valley in increasing numbers. The cragginess of this peak would suggest an aerie for this federal and state listed endangered bird of prey, our national symbol, but bald eagles usually nest in trees within a short distance of their favorite food: fish.

Piute Mountains' Bald Eagle Peak

T8   Liebel Peak Climb

This peak climb in the Piute Mountains is usually done in tandem with Bald Eagle Peak. Whereas the Eagle climb stretches out, this stretches straight up. The combination of the dissimilar peaks makes an interesting and invigorating day's outing.

Distance   1.0 miles, round trip
Steep Ascents   0.5 mile
Elevation Gain   855 feet
Skills   Easy route finding; Class 2 climbing
Seasons   Spring, summer, fall
Map   USGS 7.5-min. *Lake Isabella So*
Trailhead   7. See car tour T6.
Description   Across SNF Road 27S02 (7180/0.0) from an unsigned triangle junction, you ascend steeply east on a *cross-country* route. The lower part of this mountain has been heavily logged and sparingly replanted. You climb up the disturbed terrain, crossing the switchbacking loggers' road five times. It might be easier to hike up the road from its beginning just right of your cross-country route, and leave the road at its fourth switchback. At this point you ascend straight east, just left of a ravine, out of the cut area into the shade of pines and firs to reach the boulders at the summit (8035/0.5). Scramble up the surrounding rocks for views of the Piute Mountains, Isabella Lake and beyond. As you may have guessed, Liebel was a pioneer rancher.

T9   Piute Peaks Climb

Most peakbaggers climb these easily accessible peaks because they reach the highest elevations in these mountains and at the same time offer satisfying views.

Distance   0.8 miles, round trip
Steep Ascents   0.1 mile
Elevation Gain   400 feet
Skills   Easy route finding; Class 2 climbing
Seasons   Spring, summer, fall
Map   USGS 7.5-min. *Piute Pk*
Trailhead   8. See car tour T6.
Description   Uncertainty exists as to which of the two northern points under the map's "Piute Peak" carries the official name. The peak with the USGS mark usually receives the name, which is the one described here. Upon exploration, you may decide otherwise.

At the wide hairpin curve of SNF Road 28S01 (8020/0.0), above the canyon where a leaky tank captures Piute Spring water, you ascend north on a moderately steep *cross-country* route to the saddle. The south face of the peak you are climbing was cleared of timber, and the footing may be uneven over the scarred slope. As you pick your way carefully, or follow what remains of the logging road, you may notice diminutive "belly plants" that go by several common names: blue lips, maiden blue-eyed Mary or just blue-eyed Mary. (This is why botanists frown upon using common names.) Blue lips seems the most descriptive, however. The ¼-inch-wide flowers have an upper lip of two white lobes bent up and a lower lip of two blue lobes projecting forward. The narrow leaves of this plant grow opposite near the base.

While enjoying this flower distraction, you soon reach the saddle (8300/0.3). Here you turn left to climb the summit rocks of VABM Pah Ute by circling north to a west approach (8417/0.1). Wires, stakes, a USGS Geological Survey marker and a register tablet rest here.

Inspect the other two nearby points; then, to complete your tour of the Piute Peaks, return to the saddle and climb steeply southeast to the unnamed highest of the peaks (8450'), then to the most eastern point, VABM Piute (8435').

T10   Cook Peak Day Hike

Cook Peak in the Piute Mountains reaches 2600 feet above the south shores of Isabella Lake. From the peak's former lookout site, views unfold of Kern River Valley, its surrounding mountains and the distant ghostly pinnacles of the High Sierra.

Distance   10.4 miles, round trip
Steep Ascents   None
Elevation Gain   1965 feet
Skills   Easy route finding; moderate hiking
Seasons   Fall, winter, spring
Map   USGS 7.5-min. *Lake Isabella So*
Trailhead   22. See car tour T21. From Highway 178, drive south on *McCray Road* (0.0/0.0). Turn right on *Cook Peak Road* (1.0/1.0). Drive southwest, ascend beyond the pavement to park after a U turn on a flat at a forked road junction (1.4/2.4), **TH22**. You can drive the unpaved, maintained road in conventional cars to the first saddle on the crest, but once committed it is difficult to turn back. The last 0.8 mile beyond the saddle to the peak and radio facility becomes steeper and rougher.

Description   Your hike begins on the left fork (3441/0.0) continuation of unpaved *Cook Peak Road*, which you follow to the top on a gentle incline averaging a 7% grade. (The right fork at this junction leads to abandoned prospects.)

A California Gray Squirrel may bound by while you prepare to hike. This muscular 1½- to 2-pound rodent climbs on overhead branches and leaps from tree to tree using his bushy 9½- to 11-inch tail as a counter-balance and rudder. He attaches his stick nest high in conifer trees. This cuddly-looking squirrel often sits in a crotch of a digger pine where he showers pine cone scales on the unexpected below while hunting for the cone's seeds.

Hiking on a road, as opposed to a path, allows you freedom to scan the views while you walk. Here they include the Lynch Canyon hamlets of Squirrel Mountain Valley and Mountain Mesa below and the angular landform of Owens Peak on the distant Sierra Crest to the east; also Isabella Lake with Split Mountain and Cannell Point flanking the

valley to the north. Junipers, digger pines, blue and interior live oaks block this open view on occasion, but offer you little shade.

Here you find sagebrush—the common tridentate leaf variety that grows profusely in the Southern Sierra. It prefers light soils where moisture escapes quickly. This 3- to 6-foot, hardy plant dominates other shrubs on open slopes and invades meadows that dry out because of over grazing. A variety of wild life depend on it for food and shelter. Cattle and sheep browse it. Sagebrush's identifying pungent aroma intensifies when you crush its gray, wedge-shaped leaves.

Fractured meta-sedimentary rocks, some standing on end, easily flake to the touch in this Cook Peak fault zone. Below, the band of exposed, grayish limestone rock on Lynch Canyon's east slopes extends across Isabella Lake.

After advancing on twin long-legged switchbacks, you traverse south on steep slopes, then abruptly turn northwest. Next

California Gray Squirrel

you negotiate a series of four short switchbacks, and pass east of jumbled Peak 5170 to cross the crest (4940/4.5) with its breathtaking lateral views. This saddle allows a wide place to park for those in cars.

The road steepens as you pass two lesser peaks of granitic rock rich in potasium feldspar, then levels when you reach the saddle next to the peak (5280/0.7). (The road continues 0.1 mile to the radio tower.) Here you look to the right for the old lookout path ascending from the road, not the more prominent path curving east around the peak that leads to mining prospects.

Your route twists among sagebrush that occasionally grows on it to the concrete steps and foundation of the former lookout atop the summit (5405/0.1). From the site you gaze down upon the towns of Hot Spring Valley and the head of lower Kern Canyon to the west, the intense blue of Isabella Lake and the canyon of the North Fork Kern River to the north and the wide valley of the South Fork Kern River far to the east.

T11 Breckenridge Mountain Car & Bicycle Tour
With Excursion B: Breckenridge Lookout
(With Directions to Trailheads 9&10)

The history of this mountain spans from subsistence hunting and nut gathering to gold and uranium exploration; from cattle grazing and timber cutting to vacation cabins; from a fire lookout to TV transformers and radio towers. The old Breckenridge Road has served many of these activities over the years. A ride along its tortuous route reveals snippets of the past, but mostly it envelops you in the tranquility of rolling hills and highland woods.

Distance   39.7 miles, one way
Steep Ascents   None (Long, steady grades for bicyclists)
Elevation Gain   6170 feet
Skills   Easy route finding; paved road
Seasons   Spring, summer, fall
Map   Kern County road map
Tourhead   9. The junction of Highway 184 (Morning Drive), in east Bakersfield, and Breckenridge Road is **TH9**.
Description   Because of the many blind, sharp curves in the road ahead, bicyclists need to be aware of cars from either direction and take protective precautions. Also bicyclists will find water en route only during early season.

The first few miles east of State Highway 184 (450/0.0/0.0) on **Breckenridge Road** (KC Road 218) through residential country, citrus groves and vineyards, comprise the only stretch of straight road for the entire trip. The road begins to curve through the low hills prior to intersecting Comanche Drive (4.2/4.2). Along the way giant buglike rigs dip their heads methodically, sucking up oil from Miocene sands in the Racetrack Oilfield, while along the gulches, tamarisk bushes spread their roots profusely, sucking up waste water from the oilfields. Suddenly to the right, a stunning mansion tops a hill: perhaps a harbinger of future development in this foothill country. Soon the road crosses the usually dry bed of Cottonwood Creek, which receives its flow from streams that descend the south and west of Breckenridge Mountain.

Close to 3.0 miles from Cottonwood Creek, geologists identify silt in the road cuts that bears pebble conglomerate interbeds and thick oyster shells, which, they say, characterize brackish-marine conditions. Here ancient swampy shorelines evolved to the present spring profusion of wildflowers on rolling green hills. Turning to inspect a portion of the contemporary phenomena, a predominant carpet of lavender, you find it composed of common phacelias. To identify the plant look for the many purple blooms with projecting stamens on tight coils at the ends of finely-haired 8- to 32-inch stems. The

1- to 4-inch leaves are pinnately divided—like bracken fern.

After much twisting and turning, the road passes the site of Rock Spring Station to the right, where watering troughs and pipes remain at the spring, then passes the paved approach (11.6/15.8) to Mt. Adelaide, the prominent mountain to the left. Near the 3430-foot peak soar the transmitting towers of station KGET. Cow Flat Road (SNF Road 28S09) (1.5/17.3) also branches off to the left. This section of Breckenridge Road, along with Cow Flat Road, was used in 1902 to supply machinery by wagon train to the first Kern River electric plant. For the next 22 years this was the only access road to the upper power plant system near the river. It was also used by visitors to the hot springs resort: a frazzling two-day journey with an overnight at Rock Springs Station. Narrow Cow Flat Road is accessible to 4WDs today; it exits 0.3 mile above the Democrat Hot Springs entrance on Highway 178 in lower Kern Canyon.

Your paved road narrows at times, winds past live oak and buckeye trees, ascends into a digger pine and blue oak woodland, and into Forest Service governed land where it acquires a new code: *SNF Road 28S06* (5.9/23.2). Soon it passes a ranch at Pine Flat (1.7/24.9) and travels among stately black oaks, white firs and sugar, Jeffrey and ponderosa pines. At seasonal Lucas Creek (2.2/27.1) a sign lauds all the wonderful things that happen when these trees are logged! Thickets of willows sheltering Lucas Creek, however, stir no interest in loggers. This plant's proximity to water, its catkins and slender, pointed leaves that turn yellow in autumn help identify it. Twenty-four species of willows occur in the Sierra of the 350 species worldwide. Sometimes what looks like willows may be *Baccaris viminea* of the sunflower family. This riparian shrub has flowers—disk and ray—while the willow's flowers are its catkins.

Beyond the creek, roads peel off to the right and left toward summer cabins. This area was a popular retreat for Bakersfield people before air conditioning in their homes tempered the valley heat. A road gate stops winter driving beyond the cabin exits. At a U bend in the road, you cross seasonal Mill Creek, then pass the Mill Creek Trail directional sign to arrive at Squirrel Meadow and a junction (6620/3.7/30.8) with the road to Breckenridge Campground and the lookout tower. The following excursion takes you to these facilities.

Excursion B: Breckenridge Lookout

Views from the catwalk circling Breckenridge Lookout include distant mountain silhouettes of the Great Western Divide, Death Valley, Sierra crest, San Gabriel and Los Padres, while spacious Walker Basin seems a stone's throw below.

Distance 8.0 mile, round trip
Steep Ascents None
Elevation Gain 930 feet
Skills Easy route finding; unpaved road
Description From the road junction (6620/0.0/0.0) turn right and drive on

Total frustration

unpaved **SNF Road 28S07**, the campground/tower road, and ascend to the Breckenridge Campground entrance (0.6/0.6). The inviting, widely-spaced campsites are spread out among white fir, black oak and Jeffrey pine at the headwaters of Mill Creek. Do not count on water after snowmelt.

Your road next winds past logging spurs, access roads to transmitting towers for Bakersfield's KERO, KBAK, and a radio facility, and ends at the foot of the lookout (7548/3.4/4.0).

If the trapdoor is open, you are welcome to climb onto the catwalk and perhaps enter the station. The person on duty can spin many interesting stories of life as a lookout and can point out the various points of interest. His job is to collect information on temperature, humidity, rain and snow amounts, and fuel moisture as well as to spot fires and assist with rescues. The functions of lookout towers and their personnel will probably be replaced by satellites and computers when money becomes available.

This tower was built in 1931. Before then, the lookout climbed a pine tree that had a wooden "tree house" balanced precariously on top.

Unlike most features in the Southern Sierra that took on the names of ranchers who grazed their animals there, Breckenridge Mountain was named during the Civil War era by local supporters of the Confederate cause. Its misspelled name honors John C. Breckinridge, Confederate general, U.S. Vice President, 1857–1861, and candidate of the Southern Democrats for president in 1860, opposing Abraham Lincoln.

*　　*　　*　　*　　*

The next leg of your journey uses a portion of the Breckenridge Road (SNF Road 28S06) that was rerouted and paved during the 1980s to facilitate logging. From the campground/lookout road, head east then northeast as your road traverses the slopes on a gentle descent furnishing views of Walker Basin, Havilah Valley, Bald Eagle Peak and Isabella Lake to the east through openings in the forest. You soon pass the unmarked exit of the old road, followed immediately by a

road gate, and arrive at Lightners Flat (2.7/33.5) where your road abruptly bends right. (The dirt road straight ahead at the bend takes hikers to **TH 10** of T12, a climb of Lightner Peak.)

The next stretch of road, also paved and improved in the 1980s, quickly descends east from a mature black oak forest to chaparrel. The twisting, switchbacking grade scarcely eases until the road reaches the Caliente-Bodfish Road (3500/6.2/39.7) of car tour T2, in Havilah Valley and the end of this tour. (Bicyclists can create a loop trip by traveling south on this road and west on Edison Highway.)

The first Breckenridge Lookout

T12   Lightner Peak Climb

The hike to Lightner Peak alternates between sunny slopes and shady woods. It offers views of Southern Sierra landmarks en route, and from the summit, snatches of Isabella Lake and the distant High Sierra.

Distance   5.2 miles, round trip
Steep Ascents   0.1 mile
Elevation Gain   1210 feet
Skills   Intermediate route finding; Class 1 climbing
Seasons   Spring, summer, fall
Map   USGS 7.5-min. *Miracle Hot Sps*
Trailhead   10. See car tour T11. From the junction (0.0/0.0) at the descending bend of Breckenridge Road on Lightners Flat, drive north on unmaintained *SNF Road 28S19* to the road fork cul-de-sac (0.6/0.6). This is **TH10**. With care 4WDs can go 0.9 mile farther to a swale.

Description   Leave the cul-de-sac (6020/0.0) where views west usually include brownish smog or Tule Fog smothering the San Joaquin Valley, and hike north past the 4×4 ONLY sign along increasingly rutted *SNF Road 28S19*. Upon curving east, descend to a wide swale (5950/0.9) where high clearance cars park.

The faint trail starts here, but at this writing its obscurity makes it easier to continue to descend along the road, which passes beyond a fence and quickly becomes steep and rough. The road winds down among black oaks, breaks into the open, levels, then arcs to the left. (Another jeep road (5620/0.3) departs for a short stint to the right.) Your road now crosses a willow-lined gulch just above O'Brien Spring. The willows apparently deplete what little water the spring furnishes during normal rainfall years, as none surfaces. Pipes and a catch basin down-canyon suggest a sometimes flow. Your road meanders back into the woods and ascends continuing northwest. Old blazes on trees appear near the road, but hardly a path; stay on the steepening road until the point where it suddenly descends, curving left then right (5800/0.3). Here to the right the outline of a path can be detected although overgrown, which you take. A duck may mark the trail's entrance.

Now you are hiking on *Remington Ridge M'cyclepath 32E15:* watch for the reassuring old blazes on oak trees. The path becomes easier to follow as you skirt Hobo Ridge's Peak 6302. Next you switchback to climb along the right side of a gulch and curve north through oak brush. To the northeast pointed Owens Peak appears, an easily distinguishable landmark of the Southern Sierra crest. The Spanish Needle group of peaks rise to the north of Owens; rounded Mount Jenkins to the south. Climbs of these peaks are described in this book's companion edition.

You climb over a ridge and drop toward the west where you look for a lightly carved L blaze on a sugar pine above the path in a wide ravine. At the L you leave the path (6160/0.8) for a *cross-country* 60-foot climb southwest up the ravine to a saddle. At the saddle turn right where you pick up a *use trail*, climb northwest, curve right to round a lower knob and ascend to the top of Lightner Peak (6430/0.3). The peak and flat commemorate Abia Lightner, a local pioneer of the 19th century.

The summit offers an ideal place to dry camp. You will find the register can to the north of the clearing, atop a granite boulder hugging a tall "finger" rock pointing northwest.

Lightner Peak's finger rock

T13   Lower Kern Canyon Car Tour:
Bakersfield to Isabella Lake
(With Directions to Trailheads 13–17)

The magnificent Kern River flows forcefully through the granite-walled lower Kern Canyon near the end of its wild journey. It began as droplets of snowmelt on the slopes of the High Sierra in the craggy country north of Mount Whitney. This river and its lower canyon offer the highway traveler scenic diversity and a wealth of geological and man-made history.

Distance   33.2 miles, one way
Steep Ascents   None
Elevation Gain   1780 feet
Skills   Easy route finding; paved road
Seasons   All year
Map   Kern County road map
Tourhead   13. The junction of Highway 184 and Highway 178 is **TH13**. This is 9.4 miles east of Highway 99 in Bakersfield.
Description   *State Highway 178* leads northeast from the tourhead junction (740/0.0/0.0) to enter a residential area, then meets Alfred Harrell Highway (1.3/1.3) where people heading for **TH14**, the fascinating California Living Museum of T19, turn left. Next the straight-ahead highway skirts the Rio Bravo Country Club with its upscale houses before suddenly descending into orchard country where you may want to pause at the Father Garces Historical Monument (1.6/2.9) to the left. Father Garces named the river "Rio de San Felipe" long before it was known as the Kern River. (The Mexicans later called it "Rio Bravo"—the brave river.)

In 0.1 mile you drive past Rancheria Road, which loses its pavement on its way to Greenhorn Summit. In 1994 Sequoia National Forest began renting its retired Oak Flat lookout tower as a unique mountain retreat 15 miles north on Rancheria Road. If successful, other unused, historical, fire observation towers currently scheduled for demolition will be offered for rent instead.

After bridging Cottonwood Creek, your route passes the office (1.1/4.0) of Sequoia National Forest's Greenhorn Ranger District, located to the right in a niche among orange trees. For services see Chapter 3.

Next your road passes the unattractive concrete conduit of the Rio Bravo hydroelectric power plant built in the late 1980s, and then, in the grove to the left, the rambling two story home that used to belong to country/western singer Merle Haggard. One of Haggard's popular songs laments the loss of a friend who drowned in the Kern River.

The dramatic Kern River drops 1800 feet in 32 miles in this canyon. In places it presents a calm surface, but strong currents that lurk below pull people under and trap them against submerged rocks and brush. Although signs warn of the danger, people still enter to swim or wade causing a horrifying 177 deaths between 1968 and 1993 in the Kern County section of the river, excluding Isabella Lake. Most drownings occur at the Richbar, Democrat and Miracle areas of the river. Well-trained, well-equipped kayakers and commercial whitewater rafters ply the water safely, but inexperienced private rafters and kayakers tempt death.

Several points of interest can be observed at the mouth (1.6/5.6) of the canyon. The scarp of the Kern Gorge fault reveals itself to the trained eye. Contact between the bedrock of the Sierra and soils of the San Joaquin can be seen here. Also, here you see the Pacific Gas and Electric (PG&E) power plant, built in 1912 with a capacity of six megawatts per hour. One megawatt of power supplies enough energy to light 1000 homes. The plant's 2.0-mile aqueduct tunnels through the mountain on the north side of the river. The running ledge high above the river supported the aqueduct prior to the tunnel system.

Once in the canyon you immediately pass

at road level to the right a tunnel that was cut along a quartz vein in search of gold. Across the river as you progress, aqueduct tailings and remnants of ancient landslides appear. Should a major earthquake occur in this vicinity, new landslides could easily dam the river, and, of course, block the road. This scenic road of many curves was built in bits and pieces and finally completed in 1926. It has been improved in like manner ever since. In the early 1970s a freeway to replace the canyon section was begun at the east end, but decreased state money provided only a fragment of freeway.

If you arrive in the lower Kern Canyon in early spring, the slopes will be a weave of white popcorn flowers, gold fiddlenecks and California poppies, blue lupines and baby blue eyes. In late spring this multicolor tapestry is replaced with a pale, pinkish-purple blanket of farewell-to-spring flowers. This cuplike flower has four ½- to 1-inch petals with large purple splotches in the center end. Its stems grow 1- to 3-feet tall with linear leaves. The genus name, *Clarkia*, honors Captain William Clark of the Lewis and Clark expeditions.

Upon entering Sequoia National Forest, the highway reaches the Edison hydro-electric plant, Kern River Number One (1.8/7.4), built in 1902, 10 years earlier than the PG&E plant, and with a capacity of 27.5 megawatts produces three times more energy. Its 19-tunnel, 8.7-mile aqueduct bores through the mountain at the right above the road to the dam near Democrat Hot Springs. During the building of the aqueduct system, a Mr. L. B. Hicks was trapped for 16 days under an ore car in a construction tunnel cave-in. His ordeal and sensational rescue made headlines throughout United States.

Materials for the plant system were hauled by mule along trails visible as you continue on. Farther ahead, the vague, high canyon trail on the right side is used occasionally by Edison aqueduct inspectors. Below the road next to the river, a few terraces appear that were natural valley floor before the river cut deeper.

Several miles after passing usually dry Pechacho Creek, you reach the first (3.8/11.2) of three delightful riverside picnic

The Kern River appears calm along stretches of lower Kern Canyon

areas within the next mile: Live Oak, Lower and Upper Richbar. Each is tree-shaded and offers picnic tables and restroooms with faucet water at the Richbars. A summertime use fee is charged. In 0.3 mile beyond the first picnic site a stream from an aqueduct leak bounces down a canyon crease. In 0.2 mile after the second, next to Stark Creek, a road leads to the aqueduct trail. Beyond the third, hydraulic mining occurred before that procedure was outlawed in the late 1800s to protect the fisheries.

As you drive on you see green-tipped road paddles stenciled with "Sal." These signs alert road crews to the presence of the state listed threatened Kern Canyon Slender Salamander, only found here. This 2- to 5-inch, lungless creature appears wormlike, with delicate legs and feet. It absorbs oxygen through its skin, and it curls up like a spring when disturbed.

Well after you pass Dougherty Creek—which also carries water from an aqueduct leak—and pass Lucas and Cow Flat creeks, you can see the Edison intake dam far below. You pass its approach road, then notice a left road (7.4/18.6) to Democrat Hot Springs and Raft Takeout. This dirt road leads to an attractive day use only area by the water. The Kern River rates high among the most popular rivers for white water rafting and kayaking in the country, and the lower Kern attracts the heaviest use. A private, gated, side road part way down takes the owners and their guests to Democrat Hot Springs, named as might be guessed, for the political party. A 15-room hotel and several cottages were built in 1908 to accommodate up to 100 people. The resort with its hot baths was immensely popular, but currently (1994) the facility is closed to the public.

Just 0.1 mile ahead on your highway and to the right, a large boulder on the side of the ravine covers a gold miner's tunnel to a quartz vein. Following that, again to the right, Cow Flat Road (SNF Road 28S09) (0.3/18.9) angles in. This twisting, unpaved 4WD road winds its way to Breckenridge Road just as it did when it was built in 1902 by the Edison Company to transport material

for its power plant system. The road makes a great cool weather day hike or bicycle run. Next, to the left, the road to China Garden (0.4/19.3) transports today's gold seeker to a placer gold mining claim and campers to a Fire Safe Area for camping by the river. Then your route meets the first major junction (2280/0.9/20.2) in the canyon at **TH15**. Shortly beyond here, Highway 178 flares into a four-lane freeway on which you continue, while here the old road becomes Kern Canyon Road (KC Road 214) of car tour T14 and **THs18&19**.

Relieved of the tight curves, you zoom along to your road's first crossing of the river. Immediately before the bridge on the right side (1.9/22.1) is **TH16** for T20, the wildflower day hike. Around the curve and next to the river, below the EMERGENCY PARKING ONLY sign (0.5/22.6) is privately owned

White-water sports on Kern River

Delonegha Hot Springs, not open to the public. Once a resort thrived at this beautiful location. There remains two sets of crudely built, three-tiered hot pools overlooking the Kern River. Many bathed here without apparent harm despite exposure to radioactive uranium and radon dissolved in the water.

Ahead, notice the diagonal banding in the road cuts. These bands are known to geologists as pegmatites. When the granodiorite cooled and hardened it cracked. Into the cracks poured elements that had not crystalized earlier. This pegmatitic liquid then hardened into large crystals.

The next point of note is Greenhorn Cave just off the route (2.3/24.9) to the left. The large boulders that form the cave, 0.5 mile up the ridge road or trail, rest in Greenhorn Gulch where in 1854 the first gold was found in the area, starting the Kern River Gold Rush. The cave's floor is said to have unseen holes big enough to fall in. A miner's cabin sits at the site with NO TRESPASSING signs

posted, but you can visit the cave.

Next, the highway passes through a fault zone where several productive uranium mines were worked in 1954 to 1956. Placer gold claims reach up some of the canyons to the left. Soon the road bridges the river to pass a T junction (4.6/29.5) with the paved road to Borel Powerhouse and to Bodfish. In 0.1 mile beyond the junction, unpaved SNF Road 27S08, to the left, descends to a popular Fire Safe Area for camping next to a curve of the river at Black Gulch South.

You cross over the river for the third and fourth time, then continue ahead as a road (2.2/31.7) to the town of Lake Isabella departs to the right. Also to the right on cold days, puffs of steam rise from the flow of the hot spring winding in the wetlands between the town and the highway. Presently you arrive at the turnoff to Kernville and the junction (2504/1.5/33.2) with State Highway 155, the end of this tour at **TH17**. The trip around Isabella Lake is described in car tour T21.

T14   Old Kern Canyon Road Car & Bicycle Tour
(With Directions to Trailheads 18&19)

Power plants, uranium mines, hot springs: these are three dissimilar entities that currently affect the area of this trip and historically left fascinating tales to recount. The absence of traffic on this road replaced by the freeway, makes it particularly appealing to bicyclists.

Distance   13.4 miles, one way
Steep Ascents   None
Elevation Gain   395 feet
Skills   Easy route finding; paved road
Seasons   All year (Bicyclists avoid summer)
Map   Kern County road map
Tourhead   15. The junction of Highway 178 and Kern Canyon Road (KC Road 214) is **TH15**. This is 20.2 miles east of Highway 184 via Highway 178 and 16.2 miles west of Lake Isabella. It departs from car tour T13.
Description   From the tourhead junction (2280/0.0/0.0), the old road journeys east, to the right, where it immediately passes a

Forest Service fire station. Crews from this station quickly reach the canyon fires that frequently flare; careless motorists, careless campers, lightning, dry brush and canyon winds spell trouble hereabouts. But as if to quickly cover the fire scars, the burned hillsides blaze with prodigious numbers of wildflowers in the spring following a fire.

Beyond the station the road traverses slopes spottily clothed with interior live oak, blue oak, buckeye and digger pine, then dips to cross year-round Mill Creek in its densely foliaged recess. The Mill Creek Trail hikes, Ts15&16 at **TH18** (1.5/1.5), follow shortly after the crossing.

A controversial proposal that springs up periodically, involves the addition of a power plant on the Kern River at the mouth of Mill Creek. (The lower Kern already supports four plants.) The plan calls for one dam 200 feet high at Mill Creek—that is 15 feet higher than Isabella Dam—and a second dam 27 feet high 10 miles upriver. Water would be diverted into pipes and troughs from the last remaining free-flowing section of the lower river. Environmentalists, fishermen and rafters oppose the proposal. Meanwhile, the Forest Service has found that the 13.2 mile free-flowing section of the Kern River, which includes the project's area, is eligible for inclusion into the National Wild and Scenic Rivers System. This would protect it from development.

Moving ahead on the tour, you pass a parade of gated, dirt roads that mostly access idle uranium mines and prospects. Over the years Kern County nourished dreams of wealth with the discovery of placer and hard rock gold, and in the 1950s, of rare uranium deposits. Encouraged by the support of the Atomic Energy Commission that needed the mineral for its bombs, an epidemic of would-be miners with Geiger counters in hand swarmed over the slopes of Kern Canyon. Kergon, Little Sparkler and Miracle mines situated in this area on a north-south fault zone of crushed altered quartsdiorite became the producing uranium mines. By 1956 the boom went bust.

Continuing on, you arrive at **TH19** (6.5/8.0), the end of Remington Ridge Trail, T16. Backpackers on this trip park their shuttle cars on the lot just ahead. If a bath in an open air tub flowing with hot spring water, overlooking the Kern, appeals to you, descend on the use path at the end of the lot. However, it, like the rest of the hot springs in this fault area, registers high amounts of radioactive uranium and radon. Tiny amounts of these carcinogens can be absorbed through the skin and inhaled from the steam. The cumulative effect of the small amount entering the body is unknown.

Your road soon arrives at the Hobo complex (1.6/9.6). An unused, deteriorating Forest Service Station remains upright on the land next to Clear Creek, and some campground sites spread away from the dirt road above the forlorn station. The paved road below reaches the main riverside Hobo Campground, a long favored year-round retreat for generations of families. This campground and Sandy Flats Campground ahead serve nicely for picnicking and lazing by the river as well as camping. A road branching to the left off the campground road arrives at a day use area for rafters' river access. On this site once stood the Miracle Hot Springs Resort.

From the 1870s on, this serene hot springs area next to the placid-appearing river offered solace to miners and power plant workers, and no doubt long before that to Native Americans. The Hobo Hot Springs sturdy three-story hotel that opened in 1928, served an ever-growing clientele. A garage, store and post office were on the premises. There was also a mill with a cyanide plant for the recovery of gold and silver from ores.

The resort was renamed Miracle Hot Springs in 1947 for the soothing powers of the mineral waters. Twenty years later an RV park was added, but drastic events lurked ahead. In 1975 fire completely destroyed the hotel and although the RV park survived and flourished it later received a fatal blow when the "miracle" baths were closed by the health department because of the presence of benzene. For a more detailed history on this and the lower Kern Canyon read *Kern River Country* by Bob Powers, sold in the Kern River area.

Your tour quickly passes spacious Sandy Flats Campground (0.9/10.5), constructed in 1993. An 0.5 mile riverside trail conveniently connects the two campgrounds and is a delight to fishermen. The road next passes the penstocks and canal that send water to the 10.6 megawatt Borel plant situated on bedrock granodiorite below. This plant once sent electricity to Los Angeles to power its famous red cars: a long-gone transit system that reached all of far-flung LA. Your route travels beyond the paved connector road (0.8/11.3) to Highway 178.

On the concluding miles of this trip you pass a cluster of homes, the Bodfish Post Office and a curious Historical Landmark that sits 7.0 miles from the site of Havilah that it commemorates. Your tour ends at the junction (2674/2.1/13.4) of Caliente-Bodfish Road described in car tour T2.

T15   Mill Creek Day Hike

Easy access and vivid settings attract hikers to this trip. In this canyon intimate woods-sheltered streams and hideaways harbor a colorful salamander, the Sierra Newt, while open grassy slopes showcase dazzling displays of seasonal wildflowers.

Distance   5.4 miles, round trip
Steep Ascents   None
Elevation Gain   970 feet
Skills   Easy route finding; easy-to-moderate hiking
Seasons   Fall, winter, spring
Map   USGS 7.5-min. *Miracle Hot Sprs*
Trailhead   18. See car tour T14.
Description   From Kern Canyon Road, *Mill Creek M'cyclepath 31E78* (2370/0.0) switchbacks south across slopes above the road. These lower slopes always bear a sparse growth of oaks, often nurture grass bitten short by cattle and sometimes display a flamboyant array of lustrous wildflowers. Prairie star, a plant usually found in northern states, appears among the flowers. Five white petals of the ½- to 1-inch bloom are deeply cleft into three slender lobes, resembling a snow flake more than a star. Raceme flowers on thin, reddish stems reaching a foot or more and basal leaves further identify this delicate wildflower.

Quite soon the path rounds a ridgelet, enters the canyon of Mill Creek, then undulates gently up-canyon, crossing a cattle guard en route. The polka-dotted bark of an aged digger pine to the right of the trail has little remaining space for more woodpecker holes; the bark of buckeye trees along the route seem untouched. Clusters of poison oak appear next to the path and in the woods, as well as in the colonnade of alders and sycamores at the first boulder-hop of Mill Creek (2515/0.9).

Next, the path crosses a saddle, recrosses Mill Creek, passes a large campsite, and then on the flat of a ridge, splits off from a wide path that leads north to a mining prospect. On the right fork, your route continues southeast to ford the creek twice, and then climbs six switchbacks to a broad swale with a corral. Here you branch off to the left on a rem-

Observing salamanders in Mill Creek

nant of the former *Farmer Riggs Trail* (3260/1.7) while backpackers on T16 continue up the Mill Creek Trail. You descend slightly to the creek's branch (3255/0.1) where a large, flat-topped granite boulder overlooks a quiet pool; an ideal lunch spot before returning the way you came. (For buffs of abandoned trails, the unmaintained Farmer Riggs Trail to Lightners Flat, long deleted from the Forest Service trail system, presents difficult but possible pathfinding along the creek then up the canyon.)

This pool seems to be a favorite habitat for the salamander, Sierra Newt, a subspecies of the California Newt, although they are all along the creek in spring. This salamander, reddish-brown above, deep orange below, can be seen attached to the banks, burrowed under the brown sycamore leaves that cover the pool's bottom, and walking along the submerged sides of the granite rocks.

The newts emerge in March or April from underground shelters to enter the water for mating. The female lays her eggs in a gelatinous mass that she attaches to vegetation in the water. These amphibians survive better when not handled; their special coating protects them from infection.

T16   Breckenridge Mountain Backpack

The ascent and descent involved in this backpack between the confines of lower Kern Canyon and the highlands of Breckenridge Mountain present a test of physical fitness and stamina. Hikers prepared for this challenge appreciate its varied views, its often cool, wooded heights and its rare Piute cypress trees. This hardy adventure is best enjoyed in early spring when hills of wildflowers surround Mill Creek, or in late fall when shades of gold fleck the forests.

Distance   18.6 miles, shuttle trip
Steep Ascents   0.9 mile
Elevation Gain   4330 feet
Skills   Easy-to-intermediate route finding
Seasons   Spring, fall
Maps   USGS 7.5-min. *Miracle Hot Sprs, Breckenridge Mtn*
Trailheads   18&19. This trip begins at **TH18**. See car tour T14. It ends at **TH19**. There are 6.5 miles between trailheads.
Description   The beginning of this trip is described in T15.

Southeastbound Trail 31E78 Log

T15	Kern Cyn Rd	2370	0.0
	1st cr xing	2515	0.9
	Farmer Riggs Tr	3260	1.7

Plan, if possible, to hike in the late afternoon to this point in the journey where you can camp near the Mill Creek tributary. This will assure a fresh start for the most challenging part of the Mill Creek Trail: 4.1 miles of exposed moderate-to-steep ascent, gaining 3440 vertical feet. Also fill your water bottles and hydrate yourself well here; the next seasonal water is at Breckenridge Campground, 5.1 miles ahead. Fall travelers will have to obtain water here for the rest of the trip.

From the Farmer Riggs Trail junction next to the corral, you head south on *Mill Creek M'cyclepath 31E78*. You immediately pass a large campsite near the creek to the left, then ascend a moderate grade amid live oak and buckeye trees along a shallow ravine with a harvest of miner's lettuce. The round, edible, succulent leaves of this plant supplied miners and Indians with greens. The stem has a raceme of tiny white flowers and appears to grow through the center of the leaves.

A pair of switchbacks leads you around the ravine, and then four more take you to a north-trending ridge offering possible dry camping. The trail, now mostly sliced through brush, steepens considerably up the ridge between the canyons of Mill Creek and its tributary, but allows brief reprieves along ridge tops where you can camp or rest and view the watershed and surrounding peaks. Switchbacks constructed in 1993 help ease the climb. The route at length rises into the welcome shade of occasional digger pine and black oak, and soon after of Jeffrey, ponderosa and sugar pine and white fir. It eventually rounds a ravine west where a TRAIL sign indicates direction, and where occasional trickles muddy the soil. The path turns southeast again, zigzags and climbs another ridge, then a ravine, and ends at a saddle with a trailhead sign, a large campsite

and a transverse dirt road (6700/4.1) that you ignore.

Here the wide path takes you straight ahead to another more prominent unpaved road at the north end of Squirrel Meadow (6670/0.1). This road, the former Breckenridge Road, now blocked to vehicles east of Squirrel Meadow, eventually winds north to

Mill Creek Trail among twisted oaks and flowered slopes

meet the present paved Breckenridge Road. If you are a late season hiker, turn left here and subtract 1.3 miles from your total mileage. But early season hikers' concern is to obtain water for the rest of the trip. A seasonal stream, the headwaters of Mill Creek, provides water at Breckenridge Campground. To reach the campground, turn right on the *old road*, which soon bends south and merges with the paved *Breckenridge Road* (SNF Road 28S06) (6600/0.3). A sign here states fenced Squirrel Meadow is used for administrative pasture. On the paved road you quickly meet unpaved *SNF Road 28S07*, the campground and lookout road (6585/0.1) onto which you turn right.

Now walk southwest soon crossing Mill Creek and its line of willows. Here the forest parts around a bilobed, grassy meadow, then rises southward to the crest of Breckenridge Mountain. Beyond the creek you reach the campground (6630/0.5). With ample water for the remaining trip, you return to paved *SNF Road 28S06* (6585/0.5) and turn right. This road north was aligned and paved in the 1980s and does not appear on the 1972 topo map.

Probably your idea of hiking in the mountains does not include a trek along asphalt, but this gives you a break between the demanding ascent and descent of Breckenridge Mountain. You lose elevation slowly on this lightly traveled road, shaded by a mixed forest that parts on occasion to reveal Havilah Canyon and the Piute Mountains. You soon meet the old road (6300/1.1) blocked by a downed tree. Here late season hikers rejoin the route. You then pass a road gate, round Point 6235 and arrive at Lightners Flat (5837/1.6) just minutes beyond the unmarked, faint head of Farmer Riggs Trail.

At Lightners Flat the Breckenridge Road turns right and descends while you continue straight ahead, north on unpaved *SNF Road 28S19* signed O'BRIEN SPRING 2. After the road splits to a left cul-de-sac (6020/0.6), your route as far as Lightner Peak's climb is described in T12.

Northbound SNF Road 28S19 Log

T12 cul-de-sac	6020	0.0
4X4 pkg area	5950	0.9
O'Brien Spr	5620	0.3
Remington Rdge Tr 32E51	5800	0.3

Northwestbound Trail 32E51 Log

SNF Rd 28S19	5800	0.0
X-country rt	6160	0.8

From the junction of the cross-country route, you continue on the *Remington Ridge Trail 32E51*. In 0.2 mile, as you begin a gentle descent north, you pass the return use trail from Lightner Peak. Soon after, you drop into open chaparral, getting a heady northward view that includes the near Kern River Valley and the far High Sierra.

At length you outflank Hill 5582, then bend northeast along the ridge and enter BLM land through a stock fence with a grate instead of a gate. Here you find the rare Piute cypress trees. (For information on this tree see T6.) This grove reestablished itself after a devastating 1966 wildfire. You touch a deeply rutted road (4973/2.0), then reach cypresses that shade the only good resting place (or small campsite) for miles around.

Beyond the trees you turn abruptly northwest. The surface ahead becomes jarringly hard where you pound down the trip's steepest grade, losing 1860 vertical feet in 1.4 miles. Midway down the grade, you reenter national forest at a stock fence with a grate, and soon after find a cool nook with a refreshing seep spring. The descent ends temporarily in a swale, then you rise slightly, passing a fence, and head generally northeast, encountering many cow paths that can be misleading.

As you continue your descent, you may notice occasional excavations that were made by prospectors who swarmed this area looking for uranium during the early 1950s. Soon switchbacks and zigzags curve among seasonal colonies of impressive arrowleaf balsam root. This plant of the sunflower family produces a single 4- to 5-inch yellow, daisylike flower on a leafless stalk 8 to 32 inches high. Its arrow-shaped leaves, up to a foot long, stretch from a stem of equal length. After these diversions, you reach paved Kern Canyon Road (2480/2.8) and the end of your trip.

Section 2

Highway 178 to Parker Pass Drive (J22)
—Greenhorn Mountains
& Surrounding Area—

Pines, sycamores and oaks accompany hikers along lower Kern Canyon trail

T17   Kern County Museum Side Trip

The Kern County Museum abounds with enrichment for Southern Sierra visitors. The displays in the main building reach back to the early Indian days while the outdoor village depicts rural life in the mountains and foothills as well as the valley dating back to the middle nineteenth century. The Smithsonian Guide to Historic America *(1989) praises this museum as "One of the Nation's best efforts to preserve an area's heritage by moving historic buildings to a single site."*

Distance   The museum occupies 14 aces of land.

Steep Ascents   None

Elevation Gain   None

Skills   Easy walking; paved paths (wheelchair accessible)

Seasons   All year

Map   Museum guide

Trailhead   11. From Highway 178 (0.0/0.0) in Bakersfield, drive north on ***Chester Avenue*** past Garces Circle to the museum parking lot (1.0/1.0), **TH11**.

Description   Allow a full day for your visit, much of which will be outdoors. Wear comfortable walking shoes and remember that although usually temperate, Bakersfield becomes exceedingly hot in the pitch of summer and penetratingly cold in the Tule Fog of winter. Consider touring the exhibits in the main building first, then rest or picnic at one of the several tables available throughout the grounds. Take your own food. Once refreshed, plan to walk around the village shaded by graceful trees that appear as old as the buildings, then visit the gift shop before you leave. There you will find a nice selection of books, souvenirs and handcrafted items. Arrange another day for your youngsters to visit the Lori Brock Children's Museum next door. It provides playacting experiences in "Kid's City." Consult Chapter 3 for the museum's schedule.

At the entry of the museum, you will see the Moorish-style Beale Memorial Clock Tower that complements the Spanish Mission architecture of the main building. The tower, a Bakersfield landmark on Chester and 17th Street since 1904, was reconstructed after the 1952 earthquake on the museum grounds where it again serves as an important landmark.

The first acquisition for the outdoor museum was Barns Log Cabin in 1946. Now the grounds host over 50 structures dating from 1860s to 1930s: originals, restorations and replicas, most with interior glass panels for easy viewing, and all with collections of antique, relevant accouterments.

A number of events are staged here. At the village each year, hobgoblins and things that go bump in the night entertain children of all ages on Halloween. Elves and their helpers festoon the buildings with period decorations, then welcome visitors to December's candlelight tours. The chapel, gazebo and

Beal Memorial Tower

bandstand accommodate those desiring an old-fashioned wedding at any time of the year.

Several attractions in the village relate to trips in the Sierra. Barnes Log Cabin was constructed of logs washed down Kern River in the flood of 1868; an event discussed in T57. Quinn Sheepherder's Cabin, one of several Harry Quinn built, recalls another larger, sturdier cabin of his seen on T63. The

locomotive resting here pulled boxcars around the Tehachapi Loop as described in T1. Bena Railroad Depot is the same circa (late 1800s) as the depot that was in Caliente, visited in T2. Havilah, represented here by the *Havilah Courier Newspaper,* which later became *The Bakersfield Californian,* and the Havilah Courthouse/Jail replica, is visited on T2. Woody General Store stood among the other buildings seen on T27.

T18   Sierran Foothills Car & Bicycle Tour: North of Highway 178 to Highway 190

Ideal for bicyclists, a must for history buffs, a scenic country outing for every-one: this Sierran foothills tour travels on old stagecoach routes among oilfields, rolling hills, oak woodlands and historic towns.

Distance   68.2 miles, one way
Steep Ascents   None
Elevation Gain   3700 feet
Skills   Easy route finding; paved road
Seasons   All year (Bicyclists avoid summer)
Maps   Kern & Tulare county road maps
Tourhead   12. The junction of James Road and Bakersfield-Glennville Road in Oildale is **TH 12**. It is 2.4 miles southeast of Highway 65 on James Road and 5.7 miles north of Highway 178 and Union Avenue.
Description   To begin this trip of gentle grades and sparse traffic from the tourhead junction (600/0.0/0.0), turn north onto **Bakersfield-Glennville Road** (KC Road 363), which here lies over the Kern Front fault. You progress over land abundant with nodding oil well pumps. Oil, along with agriculture, comprises Kern County's prevailing commercial interest. Not far to the southeast, 0.7 mile north of China Grade Loop on Round Mountain Road, rests a monument at the Discovery Well site of Kern River Oil Field. The well was hand dug in 1899 to the depth of 40 feet and gushed 42 gallons of oil a day. Its oil was used to produce energy for the first drilled well in this field.

The dry, hilly country through which this route now travels barely supports enough forage for grazing cattle. Trees survive only near washes and creekbeds. Immediately

after crossing Poso Creek, usually dry here, on the northeast corner of the junction (7.3/7.3) with Round Mountain Road, a forlorn monument, sans plaque, marks the site of the Poso Station, a stop on the Butterfield Overland Stage Route. Between 1858 and 1861, John Butterfield's stages plied the Los Angeles-Stockton Road, an old emigrant path. He was paid handsomely by the U.S. government to deliver mail twice weekly. Passenger fares and freight also proved profitable. The outbreak of the Civil War ended the service here.

Traveling north through country crosshatched with oilfield pipes, now atop Poso fault, you soon pass Famosa Road to take a right turn on **Granite Road** (KC Road 421) (6.1/13.4). After ascending mildly among lichen-decorated boulders, you arrive at Granite Station (5.3/18.7). The small forsaken structure is all that survived in a 1993 fire that consumed the 30 × 100-foot, old wooden main building.

In the early 1870s, the first owner, John Elden, offered food and supplies here at what was then called "Five Dogs," a wayside station on the Bakersfield-Glenville stage route. The place saw several owners and at one time was just a rowdy bar but "ain't no one got kilt!" After additional structures, the station became a place to sheer sheep for herders traveling with their flocks to and from the

Mojave Desert. The main building had been refurbished with valuable antiques and memorabilia of the era—all lost in the conflagration.

Beyond the station your route ascends gently on Granite Road through a junction (1.0/19.7) with Woody-Granite Road, and minutes later, with Poso Flat Road, both inviting side trips. In a serene blue oak woodland, your road descends to cross willow-sheathed Poso Creek, crosses it again, and then reaches a T junction (3015/12.0/31.7), where you turn right on **State Highway 155** of car tour T27. Briefly heading northeast on the highway, your route again bridges the sinuous creek and turns left to Linns Valley on **Jack Ranch Road** (KC Road 421) (3035/0.7/32.4).

Pastoral Linns Valley lies to the left. Numerous ditches spread the water of Poso Creek as it meanders through the valley. During wet years a scattering of vernal pools appear. As the pools shrink, a riot of aquatic and terrestrial plants bloom in succeeding concentric circles around each pond, and the pond animals adapt to the change. Majestic California white oaks (valley oaks) spread generous boughs along the fringe of the valley. Their slender acorns once provided food for grizzly bears and Native Americans; Acorn Woodpeckers are among the present day feeders. This medium sized, black-tailed, black-winged bird has a red crown, yellow bib and white belly. He stores his acorns in tight-fitting tree holes and shares them, as well as all duties, with his extended family. Marauding squirrels cannot extract the acorns.

William P. Lynn settled here in 1854. He is best known for building the Bull Road to the Kern River Valley gold fields in 1856. David Lavers constructed a hotel next to the road in Linns Valley, which became a trading center known as Lavers Crossing. A few descendants of the first settlers here still live along Jack Ranch Road. Beyond the junction of White River Road, you pass Oak Grove Cemetery containing the names of many of those pioneers.

On Jack Ranch Road, you cross Poso

Granite Station gutted by 1993 fire

Creek for the fifth and last time in this tranquil country before the road ends at the T junction with **Old Stage Road** (TC Road M-109), (3254/5.4/37.8) the highest point on your route, on which you turn left. This former Indian path was followed in succession by Spanish explorers, fur traders, gold seekers and stage drivers, all of whom preferred it to possible routes through the San Joaquin Valley's mosquito-infested marsh lands. It became Tulare County's first public road.

Heading west, eventually above the valley of incipient Arrastra Creek, where the road narrows on steep slopes, you arrive at a one-lane bridge (9.4/47.2) over sycamore-shaded White River, more a creek than a river. At this site over a century ago, after gold was discovered in the vicinity, a mining town was erected called "Tailholt." The name was characteristic of gold-rush miners' humor for its source was a piece of cow tail with which a miner pulled open his front door. Refinement overcame coarseness, and it became known as White River. The mines that kept the town alive petered out by 1909, and so did the town.

After the bridge, gated and locked Grapevine Road branches off your route twining its way to Parker Pass Drive. Your road zigzags to cross a divide, then descends along grassy hills sparingly studded with blue oaks, boulders and assorted structures, in time passing the nicely landscaped buildings of California Department of Forestry's Fountain Springs Fire Station. It then arrives at Fountain Springs (790/7.8/55.0) and its wood-framed saloon. Here it intersects Parker Pass Drive (TC Highway J22) of car tour T41.

Straight ahead, again on the old Los Angeles-Stockton Road and Butterfield Overland Stage Route, your tour northwest undulates mildly through treeless hills, then threads between orange groves, crosses Deer Creek and finally curves onto **Plano Road** (TC Road 252), on which it continues north to end this country journey in Porterville at busy State Highway 190 (460/13.2/68.2), the subject of car tour T74. The Sierra foothill adventure continues north from here on T75.

T19   California Living Museum Side Trip

A visit to this special outdoor museum introduces you to the fauna, flora and natural history native to California. Here you view mountain animals that are usually unseen on your Southern Sierra adventures; you identify plants from a range of habitats; you distinguish among rocks and remnants from various geological ages. A trip to the mountains or a journey among the rolling hills of California will be greatly enhanced if preceded by time spent at this evolving, living museum.

Distance   The museum grounds cover 13 acres

Steep Ascents   None

Elevation Gain   None

Skills   Easy walking; concrete and dirt walks (wheelchair accessible)

Seasons   All year

Map   None

"Whiskers" at CALM

Trailhead   14. See car tour T13. From Highway 178 in east Bakersfield (0.0/0.0) drive north on **Alfred Harrell Highway**. This road's name honors the memory of the editor and publisher of *The Bakersfield Californian*, 1897–1946. The road curves west to the museum's parking area (3.1/3.1). (Ahead is Hart Memorial Park honoring former County Supervisor John O. Hart who in 1921 spearheaded the project.)

Description   Your amble through the museum occurs mostly in the unshaded and unprotected outdoors, so dress accordingly, and remember to wear your most comfortable shoes. Allow plenty of time. A pavilion and occasional picnic tables throughout the grounds provide places to rest or lunch. Take your own food. (See Chapter 3 for further information.)

As you wander from exhibit to exhibit in the museum, known by its acronym CALM, keep in mind that the animals you see were injured, orphaned or imprinted on humans when they arrived at CALM for care. Those that could be returned to the wild were released; the others receive the best life possible.

Of particular interest to Southern Sierra travelers may be the raptors. Here you see eagles and hawks up close that soar high above you in the country. Also visit the mountain lions. It may be chilling to know these large animals came from the Southern Sierra where you tread, but mountain lions are so illusive you probably will not see one in the wild. By the time you visit, an expanded natural-setting lion enclosure may be in place. The snake house is an important stop for you. There you will see the reptiles that frequent the Southern Sierra. Scattered about the acreage you will find plant communities with named species. Several endangered plants and animals, such as the Bakersfield cactus and the San Joaquin kit fox receive special care at CALM.

The number of animals and plants here varies from time to time, but around 300 animals representing 100 species and a collection of perhaps 1100 plants with 115 species thrive on the grounds. A total of 88 acres obtained on a 99-year lease in 1980 from the Kern County Board of Supervisors await full development. The DiGiorgio

house, donated to CALM by the Kern County pioneer family of that name, serves as the staff office, gift shop and education, resource and training center. It showcases interesting displays as well as traveling exhibits. In 1993 CALM received a fossilized baleen whale skull unearthed from nearby Hart Park, which added a large dimension to its fossil display.

The museum, a non-profit facility founded by Mike Hopkins in 1983, is patterned after the well-known Arizona Sonora Desert Museum near Tucson. CALM depends on contributions for its existence. It is run by a few paid employees and a large number of volunteers who serve as docents, educators, grounds keepers, animal caretakers and builders. It hosts educational programs such as the CALM Curriculum for students from grades K to 8 and a student summer program series. Each year, this very exciting museum grows and changes. With each visit, you will find more to learn and to enjoy.

T20   Lower Kern Canyon Day Hike

Wildflower devotees favor this trail in spring when the hills display a montage of colorful blossoms. Others find this hike a peaceful retreat in fall or winter when the spacious canyon's multicolors dissolve to amber, and the raucous Kern River far below speaks only in whispers.

Distance   6.6 miles, round trip
Steep Ascents   None
Elevation Gain   700 feet
Skills   Easy route finding; easy-to-moderate hiking
Seasons   Fall, winter, spring
Maps   USGS 7.5-min. *Miracle Hot Sprs, Democrat Hot Sprs* (trail does not appear on provisional editions)
Trailhead   16. See car tour T13.
Description   Because the freeway starts here and it is illegal to park along it, the trailhead is south of the bridge. Cross over the bridge, alert to the traffic, scramble down the bank, then under the bridge and beyond where you find **Kern River East M'cyclepath 32E49** (2070/0.0). The trail is sometimes referred to as the "Old Kern River Mule Trail." On it you immediately meet a

fork with a path that ascends a ravine. (It connects with dirt roads and eventually reaches the Greenhorn Caves or Black Gulch North, up river.) You travel down river high above as it rushes through its bouldery canyon to serve the people of Bakersfield and the agribusiness of the southern San Joaquin Valley. Across the river the steady stream of cars seems a world away.

In spring the wildflowers immediately greet you; the variety sends naturalists reaching for their field guides. Among the flora present are the California poppies, the state flower. The seeds of this plant germinate abundantly if the sun's warmth and the soil's moisture are just right. Under those optimum conditions whole slopes along the canyon flame orange, the color of this plant's bloom. The four wide petals of the 1- to 2-inch flower

California poppies: the state flower

Along the trail you dip and climb among occasional blue oaks and digger pines, well above the euphonious river. After curving around usually dry Tucker Creek, you step over a cow fence on a stile (2320/1.7): the fence divides permittees' cattle allotments. Next you hike on an extended curve that corresponds to the outstretched slope slashed with roads of China Garden across the river. You soon arrive at a junction (2220/1.6) of old trails on a saddle of a ridge, reaching the end of the day hike. Here you can relax on the slopes, picnic and enjoy the open views.

(If you wish to explore further, you have several choices: a cross-country route with tree blazes that used to be the extension of your trail, takes you west along the river opposite Democrat Hot Springs; an old jeep trail from the junction takes you north to meet Badger Gap Trail 31E76, then on it west to Rancheria Road. You can also descend south to view from the ridge the gracefully curving Kern River, the popular camping area of China Gardens across the river and the private property below, which includes a river spanning bridge.)

unfold in sunlight and close at dusk. This plant, 8 to 24 inches tall, has fernlike leaves that add a softness to its radiant beauty.

T21   Isabella Lake Loop Car & Bicycle Tour
With Excursions C-E:
Keyesville, Indian Massacre & Old Kernville Sites
(With Directions to Trailheads 20–22)

This scenic tour circles the lake touching campgrounds, villages, historic sites and natural wild areas. It offers pullouts where you can view the semiarid setting of the lake and its surrounding mountains bathed in hues of blue and brown dotted with muted greens. You may see boats and windsurfers displaying colorful sails, jet skiers and water skiers creating sparkling plumes or, in a quiet shoal, a boat drifting on calm water with fishermen casting shiny lines.

Distance   35.4 miles, loop trip
Steep Ascents   None
Elevation Gain   1350 feet
Skills   Easy route finding; paved roads
Seasons   All year (Bicyclists avoid summer)
Map   Kern County road map
Tourhead   17. The junction of Highway 178 and Highway 155 at the southwest end of Isabella Lake is **TH17**. It departs from car

tour T13.
Description   Bicycling is not recommended along the west side of the lake because of traffic on the winding two-lane highway and lack of road shoulders.

Ahead of the junction you will notice two earthen dams. They were built by the U.S. Army Corps of Engineers, authorized by the Flood Control Act of 1944. Their construction caused the Kern River Valley to buzz with activity over a five year period. By 1953 the 185-foot-high, 1725-foot-long Main Dam and the 100-foot-high, 3257-foot-long Auxiliary Dam were ready to impound water from the rivers. These two riprap dams were built to provide flood control for Bakersfield and San Joaquin Valley farmers and to supply their water needs. Recreation was also a consideration. The dams are maintained by the Corps employees who inspect them regularly and after each Southern California earthquake—the dams sit within the Kern Canyon fault zone. The employees also provide daily lake and weather information. In addition, the main dam had a privately owned 12-megawatt hydroelectric plant retrofit that became operational in 1992.

The dams spawned Isabella Lake, one of the largest reservoirs in Southern California. This vast lake rests in the hollow of the Kern River Valley surrounded by mountains and clusters of small towns. The reservoir covers the confluence and the valley beds of the north and south forks of the Kern River: their former courses are marked by the lines of snags that usually pierce the lake's surface. Along the banks of the rivers and inland were ancient Indian villages, historic towns, ranches and farms—all now submerged.

The lake, at a capacity elevation of 2606 feet, boasts a 38-mile shoreline containing 570,000-acre feet of water. Capacity, however, has only happened three times since the lake's birth: 1969, 1980 and 1983. But even at the drought level of 30,000 acre feet, the lowest allowed, it has more water than most other Southern California reservoirs and ample room for all water sports.

The lake gave rise to campgrounds. Sports enthusiasts and family groups enjoy the eight conveniently located, comfortable Forest Service campgrounds of which six flank the highway along the west side of the lake. Beside the amenities listed on the enclosed map's chart, you will find flush toilets at all campgrounds and a tot's playground at most. Hungry Gulch, Boulder Gulch and Tillie Creek offer wheelchair accessible sites. Tillie Creek has an amphitheater where talks and slide shows featuring local attractions are given during the summer. Along with the camping areas around the lake, there are three marinas: two on the west side, one on the south.

Traveling north on *State Highway 155* from the overpass (2520/0.0/0.0) of State Highway 178 to circle the lake, you could see perspiring runners practicing for the brutal, annual ultra-marathon Dam Tough Run, which also circles the lake. You may want to stop at the visitor center (0.5/0.5) where you can view the lake and obtain information and permits. Next you bridge an area of the Kern River referred to as the "sluicebox"; here below the dam, the regulated flow of the Kern races down a narrow polished-granite gorge. Then you arrive at the T junction (2500/0.5/1.0) of Keyesville Road where the following excursion is of special historic interest.

Excursion C: Keyesville Site

Keyesville was the first town in the valley during the Kern Gold Excitement of the middle 1850s. An historical landmark at the site describes how frenzied people of the colorful town protected it from an anticipated Indian attack that turned out to be just rumor.

Distance   4.0 miles, round trip
Steep Ascents   None
Elevation Gain   320 feet
Skills   Easy route finding; paved road
Description   From the junction (2500/0.0/0.0) with State Highway 155, turn left and drive southwest on *Keyesville Road* (KC Road 485) into the rolling hills. Many people are drawn here to compete in a grueling mountain bicycle race, the Keyesville Classic. Other people arrive here to attend a ceremony that honors the servicemen who died December 7, 1941 at Pearl Harbor. (To reach the commemorative site, turn left on unpaved Pearl Harbor Drive (1.0/1.0). In 0.8 mile you reach the peaceful fenced enclosure where trees were planted as a living memorial. Flag poles march along the gated dirt road within the fenced area; trees amid

wood chips grace the entrance. This memorial was developed and is maintained by the Pearl Harbor Survivors Association.)

Continuing on Keyesville Road, you reach the end of the paved road where you turn right at the fork to park at the historical landmark (2820/1.0/2.0) on Fort Hill. In the mid-1800s Dickie Keyes, a Cherokee Indian, struck gold in a rich quartz vein that became the Keyes Mine, located a few hundred yards northwest up Hogeye Gulch. The Mammoth Mine to the south was found shortly after. These discoveries gave rise to Keyesville, a typical, shabby mining town that took on a measure of respectability when the mines prospered. It had the first post office and stores in the Kern River Valley. The stores often obtained meat from the hunter, Grizzly Adams, who stood out among the milling miners because he had two pet grizzly bears. The story of Grizzly Adams was featured in a TV series in the 1980s.

One structure remains from the Keyesville era: the wooden house with the native stone chimney seen to the south. This private dwelling has been enlarged over the years and has had a number of occupants, the locally notorious Shootin' Walkers among them.

The son of one of the Walkers was Ardis M. Walker, born in the old house in 1901. In contrast to his rough beginnings, Ardis became a naturalist and a poet. He and his wife Gayle worked many years toward the preservation of the Southern Sierra, a land that was the subject of many of his poems. The result of their leadership was the establishment of the Golden Trout Wilderness. Ardis returned often to old Keyesville where until his death in 1991 he conducted tours of the site and the house of his birth.

(If you wish to travel farther on the Keyesville Road, it continues unpaved from Keyesville through oak- and pine-dotted rolling hills. The road was constructed in the mid-1930s by the Civilian Conservation Corps. In 2.4 miles SNF Road 27S30 branches left to descend to Black Gulch North where the old Kern River East Trail 32E49 was reworked in 1993. Mountain bikers will find this trail especially inviting.)

Legitimate mining continues in the country served by the Keyesville Road, but many squatters with no intention of mining file claims under the antiquated mining law of 1872 and live free on the land. However, the managing agency, the Bureau of Land Management, has an increasing regulatory presence in the area.

*   *   *   *   *

Ahead on Highway 155, you pass Main Dam and Pioneer campgrounds and a marina and arrive at French Gulch Recreation Area (1.5/2.5) where after 1995 you can visit the Lake Isabella Native American Interpretive Center. It will feature Native American history, culture, and values associated with this area and present artifacts returned home to this land of their inception. It will have displays from other Californian tribes as well. The center will enrich all who tarry among the exhibits and provide a place where native traditions can be taught to all interested Indians who may be out of touch with their tribal ways.

Continuing on, you pass Hungry Gulch and Boulder Gulch campgrounds and a marina, then Live Oak and Tillie Creek campgrounds and arrive at an intersection (2680/4.0/6.5) where Highway 155 turns abruptly left to climb over the Greenhorn Mountains. Car tour T27 joins your route here. At this point you can continue straight ahead or turn right on Evans Road to the infamous site of an Indian massacre, described next.

Excursion D: Indian Massacre Site

Every book relating the history of Kern County includes a section on the Indian Massacre. The unmarked site was a village located near the foot of Tillie Creek in the valley of the Kern; today the same site rests on a peninsula near the wind ruffled waters of Isabella Lake.

Distance   1.6 miles, round trip
Steep Ascents   None
Elevation Gain   100 feet
Skills   Easy route finding

Description Drive east on *Evans Road* (2680/0.0/0.0) past Wofford Heights Park. Park off the road near the El Segundo Rod & Gun Club (0.7/0.7). Here you climb south, up the hill to your right that supports a lake beacon, then turn east (2660/0.1/0.8).

In the spring of 1863, Indians from surrounding tribes, mostly from Owens Valley, gathered in the local Tubatulabal Tribe's village to discuss their increased resentment over the acts of the white man, particularly the killing of their leader and the confiscation of their land. Although the local tribesmen desired to remain at peace, the others wished retaliation beyond the small skirmishes and the plundering of the white man's cattle in which they had at times engaged.

After hearing of the gathering and of a miner's death by an Indian, Capt. Moses McLaughlin and his company, fearing an uprising, swooped down upon the village at first light, removed the women, children and old men and killed the rest of the defenseless

men—to make examples of them, as he later reported—and galloped off.

The captain and his men had killed the peaceful Tubatulabals; those suggesting revenge had already left.

The Hill of Three Crosses stands silhouetted against the sky above the massacre site. Here each Easter since 1950, worshipers who gather at sunrise stand among the bedrock mortars where nuts were ground by the peaceful villagers before that tragic day.

* * * * *

Now driving north on *Burlando Road* you pass through the community of Wofford Heights (W-off-ord) located on the old Wofford cattle ranch. Here bicyclists can mount their bikes and ride safely along the bike paths that flank the road. The paths continue to the airport; beyond that is open country where bicyclists can easily be seen by motorists. North of Wofford Heights you arrive at the unsigned road (2700/1.5/8.0) to the old cemetery and to historic old Kernville.

Indian massacre site and the Hill of Three Crosses

Excursion E: Old Kernville

When Isabella Lake was created by the dam, the government offered to either move the structures to higher land or compensate the owners for their lost buildings. Several were moved to new Kernville. When not under water, you can visit the remaining foundations of old Kernville and picture in situ life as it was before the 1950s.

Distance   0.4 mile, round trip
Steep Ascents   None
Elevation Gain   120 feet
Skills   Easy route finding; unpaved road
Description   Turn right on the ***old cemetery road*** (2700/0.0/0.0), drive right at the fork to descend to the flat (2580/0.2/0.2), where you park your car.

The Kern Valley Museum in Kernville offers a free map showing the street and building locations of Old Kernville. Members of the Kern River Valley Historical Society lead guided tours here and to the Big Blue Mine each year during the Whiskey Flat Days Celebration over the Presidents Holidays.

Old Kernville's history intertwines with that of the Big Blue Mine located on private property (open to tours only) above Burlando Road. One day in 1860, Lovely Rogers, a Cherokee Indian from Arkansas, scuffed along the hot, brushy country looking for his wandering mule. Annoyed, he picked up a rock to throw at the wayward animal—the rock was veined with gold! He worked his claim for several years, then sold it to Joseph Sumner, who added a small stamp mill. Around that time Adam Hamilton decided the miners needed a convenient place to spend their money. He set up two barrels on the flat here by the Kern River a mile from the mine, placed a plank across the barrels and called his "bar" Whiskey Flat. A village began and grew as the mine prospered. Refinement inched in and in 1864 Whiskey Flat changed its name to Kernville.

Several mines developed along Lovely's rich vein in the Kern Canyon fault zone, collectively known as the Big Blue Mine,

named for the presence of blue quartz. Eventually an 80-stamp mill replaced the original mill. The Big Blue changed ownership several times. In 1883 the owners met with adversity in other investments and pulled out, leaving unpaid workers who angrily torched the mine. It was repaired and reworked several times until 1942.

By the time the mine burned, old Kernville had a solid economy, thanks mainly to the commerce created by the A. Brown Company. Old Kernville typified many prosperous mining towns; it had schools, churches and hotels as well as saloons, and in time it had movie street—false fronts erected for Hollywood filming. Roy Rogers, William Boyd, Humphrey Bogart, Gary Cooper, John Wayne and many other actors portrayed their characters before the cameras on Movie Street.

To locate some of these sites, first look up-canyon from the parking area where you see the concrete square of the water tower in the hills marking the northern border of Old Kernville. Walk along the ***dirt road*** south where you pass concrete steps that remain of

Old Kernville site

a former residence nearly hidden among the willows. Farther on, the foundations of the school house appear prominently, then of the Methodist Church. Most of the buildings in Old Kernville, however, did not have foundations. Movie Street stretched between the church and the square reservoir to the right of it.

*   *   *   *   *

Burlando Road next passes the cemetery; the old section from 1860 lies below to the right. Ahead you can make out sections of reinforced path where a tramway transported ore from the Big Blue Mine to the mill. Just beyond, your route descends past a chimney downslope to the right, the remains of a Big Blue Mill guest house in the vanished town of Millville. Then the narrowing rocky canyon holds in a startling contrast to itself, the plush green nine-hole golf course, open to the public. Picturesque Riverside Park stretches just beyond the golf course. Play areas, picnic tables and huge cottonwood trees that line the sinuous river make this the most popular park in Kern County.

Now in Kernville, you arrive at a forked junction (2.8/10.8) just beyond the park. You curve right on **Kernville Road**. Those seeking the U.S. Forest Service Cannell Meadow District office or **TH20** continue north, left at the fork.

Ahead on **Burlando Road** (0.0/0.0) you quickly reach the log building facing Whitney Drive (0.2/0.2) that houses the Forest Service. Here you obtain your permits and other services listed in Chapter 3. Continue north to the cul-de-sac end (1.8/2.0) for **TH20**, Whiskey Flat Trail, Ts22–24. Camping is discouraged here.

The charming town of Kernville keeps its frontier roots with its stores displaying western-style fronts. The stores, several arrayed around the village green, Circle Park, cater to the traveler's needs and interests. The town has numerous motels, restaurants, antique shops, sports outfitters and a fine museum.

Two notable buildings among the many

moved into the new Kernville reflect the old west's genteel side: the Country Gourmet restaurant and the Neill House Bed and Breakfast. The cedar-barked Country Gourmet at the west side of Circle Park retains its original late 1880s exterior—the interior was refurbished in the early 1990s in motifs reflecting the buildings age. The 100-year-old Neill House was split into four sections so that it could be transported from its original location on the lake's flood planes in Weldon. This Bed and Breakfast was completely restored and furnished in Victorian style.

Across the bridge on the east side of town, you turn right on **Sierra Way** (2706/0.5/ 11.3). Those seeking **TH21** turn left. All of Sierra Way and the trips to the east of the road are detailed in *Exploring the Southern Sierra: East Side*.

To reach **TH21** for Ts24–26 drive north on **Sierra Way** (0.0/0.0) which later becomes **TC Road M-99**. Between Camp Owens, a low security facility for young men, and the river lies Kern River Fish Hatchery, currently (1994) breeding Little Kern golden trout and serving as a holding tank for other trout. Visitors are welcome. Drive beyond the hamlet of Riverkern and many Forest Service campgrounds to arrive at the parking lot (15.1/15.1), **TH21**, between McNalley's Restaurant and Fairview Campground.

Your route south on Sierra Way passes the airport (2.5/13.8), then Camp 9 (2.1/15.9), a shadeless camp offering serenity except on the Fourth of July when crowds flock to its premises to watch the Wofford Heights Improvement Association's fireworks explode in the evening sky above the lake. The road next ascends to the saddle east of Rocky Point. With several turnouts for viewing, it drops and climbs among coves and points on the north side of Isabella Lake. It passes the Model Aircraft Flying Field (4.6/20.5) where people send their small crafts soaring over Hanning Flat.

You next arrive at the South Fork Wildlife Area (1.9/22.4). This area straddling the South Fork Kern River is a wooded place

Great Blue Heron

with Fremont cottonwood and red willow trees; a wild place with occasional black bears, mountain lions and mule deer; a gentle place with nesting sites for numerous birds.

Great Blue Herons nest in the wildlife area, one of the heronries in the valley. These large 42- to 52-inch-long and 48-inch-tall birds, well adapted for fishing with their long legs, necks and beaks, usually build their stick nests in the crowns of trees, but sometimes on the ground or in bushes. They return each spring to refurbish their nests for the next brood. Sometimes a colony of herons nests in the same sturdy tree; sometimes herons share the tree with other water fowl, owls or hawks: a condominium of un-segregated feathered friends.

Your route subsequently crosses the South Fork Kern River. Flanking the highway here along the river, the international nonprofit Nature Conservancy manages 1127 acres of riparian land, one of the finest cotton-wood/willow stands left in California. The conservancy selected this particular area to protect the remaining forest and enlarge it

primarily for the benefit of two endangered birds: the Yellow-billed Cuckoo and the Southwestern Willow Flycatcher. Both nest here.

The 5- to 7-inch, olive-brown flycatcher is being eradicated by Brown-headed Cow-birds. Parasitic cowbirds lay their eggs in the nests of the flycatcher and other birds that build open-cup nests. The host birds then raise the aggressive young cowbirds often at the expense of their own young. You are very likely to see cowbirds if you take a minute to observe grazing cattle. The 6- to 8-inch grayish-brown female and greenish-black male with a brown head dine on seeds and flock around cattle, eating the bugs that are flushed out. This bird's population exploded here when cattle grazing and alfalfa growing increased open space in the valley.

A long-term study of the flycatcher was conducted by the Kern River Research Center, the conservancy's neighbor. The center, a non-profit agency, specializes in conservation biology here and throughout the country. The study revealed the dangerous impact of the Brown-headed Cowbird on the Southwestern Willow Flycatcher and several other birds. The conservancy and the research center have numerous study projects ranging over the wealth of flora and fauna present in the Kern River Valley. The location is a remarkably rich study area because of the proximity of mountains, desert, rivers and valleys.

Curving south, your road ends at *Highway 178* (2630/2.0/24.4) where you again turn right. (If you turned left you would find within 2.0 miles the entrance to the preserve and Fay Ranch Road, which takes you to the research center.) This book's companion edition has many trips east branching off High-way 178.

Heading west now on Highway 178, you will see a KOA Campground, then unpaved Patterson Lane (1.9/26.3), which once crossed the valley, but currently gives access to the south side of the wildlife area. Now on the south side of the lake at the foot of the Piute Mountains, you drive by the community of South Lake, cross over the Lime

Point peninsula where road cuts reveal marble rock and travel next to the residential town of Mountain Mesa. Those heading for **TH22**, Cook Peak of T10, turn left onto McCray Road (3.5/29.8). (A turn here also takes you in 0.4 mile to the Kern Valley Hospital and its emergency center.)

Your road next approaches the Forest Service's Paradise Cove Campground (1.8/31.6). To the east of the cove formations of metasedimentary rock are visible while the roadcut to the west reveals slate and shist of metavolcanic rock. Your route passes South Fork boat ramp and meets a T junction (2.5/34.1) with paved Isabella Boulevard. This is the main street of the relocated Lake Isabella town in Hot Spring Valley, the most commercial of the towns around the lake, named for Columbus' patron queen. Old Isabella Road leads to a boat ramp, but

formally it led to the old Lake Isabella town, now submerged. The historical landmark at the junction refers to Edward M. Kern, for whom the river was named, the cartographer during U.S. Army Captain John C. Fremont's third expedition.

Ahead, you see the auxiliary dam, camping area, boat ramp, marina and Engineer's Point, favorite places for water skiers and wind surfers. You pass the Kern County Courts, Administration and Library Complex completed in 1990. The Borel Canal which you bridge transports water to the power plant in the canyon. You then take the on ramp to Highway 155 (2520/1.3/35.4) where you began this circumnavigation of the lake. The canyon trip from Bakersfield to here is described in car tour T13, and from Tehachapi Pass in car tour T2.

T22   Bull Run Smelter Site Day Hike

This smelter operated from the late 1890s to the early 1900s, serving the many gold mines in the area.

Distance   2.8 miles, round trip
Steep Ascents   None
Elevation Gain   405 feet
Skills   Easy route finding; easy hiking
Seasons   Fall, winter, spring
Map   USGS 7.5-min. *Kernville*
Trailhead   20. See car tour T21.
Description   From the cul-de-sac at the end of Burlando Road in Kernville (2755/0.0), pass through the gate onto *Whiskey Flat Trail 32E35*. Leave the trail immediately where a brief *path* to the left takes you to a wide *road*. Ascend in a westerly direction on the road up a gentle grade through land spotted with brush, interior live oaks and digger pines.

Here patches of early blooming popcorn flowers, filarees and goldfields announce the coming of spring. You can recognize all three. Popcorn flowers have several white, round, small five-petaled flowers with a central yellow circle that pop from a tight coil at the end of a branched stem. Their hairy, lance-shaped leaves grow mostly in basal rosettes,

and when crushed, leave a red stain. Filaree flowers are also small with five petals, but they are purple. The blossoms and fernlike leaves grow close to the ground. The long, slender storkbill pods enclosing their seeds twist into the ground when mature or hook into your socks. Goldfield flowers are yellow. They have ten petals; they resemble miniature daisies with golden centers and petals. These three plants often bloom en masse, creating a mosaic of color on open hillsides.

To the left of the trail just after a discontinuous barbed wire fence, about 0.3 mile into the trip, a scattering of brick chips lie hidden among the brush. "Perhaps the bricks for the smelter were made here," muses Bill Burlando, a long time Kernville resident. The trench you can see in places to the right he thinks may have brought water to the site. Soon a path (2920/0.7) to the left leads in 0.6 mile of bushwhacking to one of the mines in the area. The tale varies, but it is said that between $80,000 to $150,000 worth of gold was recovered from one rich-veined Bull Run mine hereabouts.

Very soon your stony road arrives at a three-way split (3100/0.6): the right fork goes to a boulder hedge of unknown origin and use; the center fork, over the trunk of a downed digger pine, leads past rock-wall remains of a hut, then to the "Matterhorn," a big boulder next to a small fortified campsite. Beyond that the path reaches another campsite, creek cascades and an inviting pool. You, however, take the **left fork** at the split, climb among nonnative ivy, curve south and quickly arrive at the smelter ruins (3160/0.1). Unmortared, parallel stone walls and foundations stand as the most prominent remains; most of the bricks from the smelter have been carried away.

Burlando suggests that the area below the ruins encircled by boulders may have been a tailings pond. The cook house, he recalls, sat north of the smelter near a rock-lined arch dug into the top of the creek's bank, which may have been used for storage. "Trash was of no concern then; it was merely dumped over the bank." You may find remains of buildings and artifacts if you poke around the site—

With open views of Harley Mountain beyond the Edison penstocks, the unshaded ruins make a good place to picnic on a crisp winter day; on a sizzling summer day, the slabs, cascading water and bathing hole beyond the "Matterhorn" make a better place to linger.

T23   Whiskey Flat Trail Day Hike

This hike along the west side of upper Kern Canyon offers open views of the mountains that line the wide valley of the North Fork Kern National Wild and Scenic River. The tumbling river, especially when backed by peaks touched with snow, etches a visual treasure.

Distance   6.0 miles, round trip
Steep Ascents   None
Elevation Gain   200 feet
Skills   Easy route finding; easy hiking
Seasons   Fall, winter, spring
Map   USGS 7.5-min. *Kernville*
Trailhead   20. See car tour T21.
Description   The faded sign at the end of Burlando Road next to the trailhead proclaims in large letters NO TRESPASSING! The warning applies only to the private property surrounding the trailhead. Sparse shade and the canyon's penchant for retaining the sun's warmth suggest moderate-to-cool days as the most enjoyable time to travel on this trail. Creek crossings during snowmelt or after a torrential rain call for caution: you may take a deep wade through swift-flowing water or even have to abort the trip.

Begin your hike at the gate (2755/0.0) and stroll north along wide **Whiskey Flat Trail 32E35**, formerly the bed of an unpaved road. Several roads peel off your trail, but yours is the most conspicuous. You briefly parallel a

residential road. Then, a bit later, the sound of rushing water reaches you as you near year-round Bull Run Creek. Most of the time you can step from boulder to boulder to cross the creek (2740/0.5). This is the most difficult creek crossing on the day hike.

Beyond the ford and below to the east of the river, the hamlet of Riverkern nestles near the foot of Cannell Creek. An exposed pipe of Southern California Edison Company's mountain tunneling aqueduct carries river water across the creek's canyon. The canyon also marks the divide between Kern and Tulare counties, here approximately delineated by a fence.

Several cattle fences cross the length of this trail. Most of the gates become a tangle of downed barbed wire, but if possible, please close them after you. To the right of the trail an aged corral appears, while unnatural ground depressions give evidence of bygone water trenches.

A TRAIL sign indicates a path split from the road. You ascend the path, pass a fence and arrive at a gently sloping terrace that was cleared for a safety zone during the massive Stormy Complex Fire of 1990. The fire flared in the mountains to the west, consuming 24,200 acres.

You may see Red-tailed Hawks soaring and gliding on the day's thermals. In flight this large bird has a wing span of up to 4½ feet. The hawk holds its wings virtually motionless and, broad tail fanned, exerts little energy while performing aerial displays for his mate or while searching for ground mammals. Light tan with dark trim below, rich brown above, this hawk shows a glimmer of the red in his tail when he banks to change directions.

You may see milkweed flowers alongside the trail. The 1- to 3-foot plant blooms with a burst of creamy starlike flowers: five lobes bent backward, five hoods circle the center. The stem and its long, opposite growing leaves carry a thick, milky juice. Milkweeds host the egg and larva stages of the stain-glass appearing, orange-and-black Monarch Butterfly. Most of the 2000 species of this plant are poisonous: a property shared with the butterfly.

After rounding the wide ridge that divides the watersheds of Bull Run Creek and Chico Canyon's creek, and passing beyond the third cattle fence on the trip, you briefly dip through another usually dry creek bed and

arrive at a vague dirt road (2870/1.3) widely cleared of brush. This 4WD road leads to a mine prospect claimed in 1982, unlike most digs along the river that occurred in the late 1800s.

From a small terrace just beyond, the view across the canyon reveals the north end of Headquarters Campground and an undeveloped campground on a flat. Behind them looms a massive kaleidoscope of colorful rocks and shadow patterns known locally as Yellow Jacket Peak, T42 in this book's companion edition. In 0.3 mile the path fords another seasonal stream, which carries the combined flows of Chico and Dark canyons. On a terrace again, the route heads directly toward distant Baker Point of T39, which dominates your northern views.

Along the way you sometimes hear voices wafting across the canyon from Camp 3 Campground; you usually hear the roar of the cascading river; and lastly you see the river. Here at this picturesque moment along the trail, the day hike ends (2920/1.2). You may wish to pause, have lunch, get out your binoculars and search for rock climbers scaling Class 4&5 routes on the Kern Slabs: the smooth, exposed granite on the river side of Yellow Jacket above Camp 3. Or you may wish to hike farther on the trail as described in T24.

Yellow Jacket Peak east of Whiskey Flat Trail

T24   Upper Kern Canyon Backpack North of Kernville

Colorful outcrops of metamorphosed sediments abut granite along the Kern Canyon fault zone, evident at several points in the deep canyon of this off-season backpack. Cameos of scenic North Fork Kern River and the opportunity to camp on an isolated beach add to the pleasure of this trip.

Distance   13.9 miles, shuttle trip
Steep Ascents   0.4 mile
Elevation Gain   2540 feet
Skills   Easy route finding
Seasons   Fall, winter, spring
Maps   USGS 7.5-min. *Kernville, Fairview*
Trailheads   20&21. This trip begins at **TH20**. See car tour T21. It ends at **TH21**. There are 17.7 miles between trailheads.
Description   The beginning of this trip is described in T23.

Northbound Trail 32E35 Log

T23	prkg area	2755	0.0
	Bull Run Cr	2740	0.5
	4WD Rd	2870	1.3
	viewpoint	2920	1.2

Easy walking continues as you follow **Whiskey Flat Trail 32E35**, which quickly drops to cross Stormy Canyon's year-round creek (2910/0.4). This aptly named canyon seems to funnel storms to the Kern Plateau, while nearby Kernville gets nary a drop. You next hike inland from the North Fork Kern River: it curves around a protrusion of Yellow Jacket Peak, located on the opposite shore, with Hospital Flat Campground visible at the foot of the mountain's north-facing slope.

Now with an open view of the river, the trail drops to a sandy flat. Equestrians will want to dismount and lead their animals on the next segment of trail: it briefly swings up a steep, narrow path across the face of a metamorphic rock bluff, and then plummets to reach a sandy beach next to the river with good camping possibilities. Across the water you can see Corral Creek and Corral Creek Picnic Area.

The path next cuts across a broad terrace where the river makes a wide arc to the east. A lookout atop Baker Point (T39), attracts attention to the west. Soon your trail approaches the river near the sprawl of Gold Ledge Campground on the east bank. To the right of your path (3340/5.2), a steep, unmaintained lateral marked by a duck leads to a sandy, grassy beach by the river—a good middle-of-the-journey place to camp. Turning west shortly after the junction, the path, 32E35, heads up a moderate grade, tops a hill with car-sized boulders, and drops via zig-zags to a boulder-hop ford of Ant Canyon's alder-shaded, year-round creek (3460/0.5).

Ahead a moderate-to-strenuous grade leads northwestward up a canyon to a spur-ridge saddle in the longest ascent of this trip, a 640-foot gain on a deeply gouged path. The Whiskey Flat Trail, developed years ago as a horse trail, does not offer the luxury of contemporary paths graded to avoid such water-caused rutting. Your thoughts may be diverted by the dulcet song of a Canyon Wren—a descending series of clear notes that seem to tumble down the scale. This 5-inch, finely-mottled brown bird with white throat and rust tail hops about on large boulders.

On the long descent to the river after crossing the saddle, look east for Salmon Falls dropping from the rim of the Kern Plateau. Its upper and most noticeable falls spills over sheer rock oriented northwestward, while its lower falls faces west. To the north you see the Monopoly-sized houses of Fairview and beyond them, a grayish, diagonal band of limestone slashed across the mountains. Around the bend from the houses and below the limestone is the end of this trip.

Many layers of sediment—the oldest of which became limestone—were deposited on an ocean floor roughly 320 million years ago, then buried deeply, heated, pressured, chemically altered, faulted, folded, stood on end, broken up and isolated amid engulfing molten granite—a process that lasted until close to 100 million years ago. Since then, erosion has exposed these metamorphic rocks to view.

Chamise, a densely-branched bush that can reach 12 feet and is often found in impenetrable thickets, is prominent here. Its evergreen bundles of short, linear leaves and its panicles of tiny white flowers give the bush a soft, somewhat lacy look.

With snippets of the river in view, the trail rounds a Greenhorn Mountain ridge, then crosses year-round Tobias Creek (3500/3.8), a deep wade during snowmelt. Then the path ascends and curves to the right. Rocks lining the curve close a replaced section of trail that led to the Tobias/Flynn trail junction. Your path ahead overlays a ditch dug by Matt Burlando in the early 1900s to divert water from Tobias Creek to his property. The ditch traversed along the steep slopes, then dropped 50 feet where Burlando installed a Pelton waterwheel to power his generator. For more history of the upper Kern Canyon, read *North Fork Country* by Bob Powers. You pass the concrete remains where the ditch turned, then meet a junction (3620/0.5) with the Tobias Creek Trail 32E34. Next your trail zigzags down to sandy turf, passes a path to the river, then continues between a fence and the river.

Turn right at a junction (3520/0.4) with the private Fairview Mine Trail and onto the

Distant Salmon Creek Falls

suspension bridge crossing the tumultuous river. The torrent captures your attention when snowmelt runoff peaks in this river. Turn left at the end of the bridge. Next walk along the dirt road of the trailer park to the parking lot (3550/0.1), **TH21**.

T25   Tobias Creek Day Hike

Creekside seclusion awaits the hiker of this short, vigorous trip. An ambitious turn-of-the-century irrigation project spices the journey with history.

Distance   5.2 miles, round trip
Steep Ascents   0.2 mile
Elevation Gain   920 feet
Skills   Easy route finding; easy-to-moderate hiking
Seasons   Fall, winter
Maps   USGS 7.5-min. *Fairview, Johnsondale*
Trailhead   21. See Car tour T21.
Description   The latter months of the year are recommended for visits to Tobias and Flynn canyons for then the sun's warmth is welcomed and the brush harbors very few if

any ticks.

From the parking lot (3550/0.0) north of McNalley's Fairview Resort, descend on the **dirt road** through a small colony of house trailers to **Whiskey Flat Trail 32E35** at the east end of the suspension bridge spanning the North Fork Kern River. The bridge sometimes sways lightly, which, coupled with the swirling water below, can make you feel somewhat insecure. The river, a masterful stroke of beauty, especially during peak snowmelt, nevertheless compels you to linger as you cross.

At the bridge's west abutment, you turn left through a junction (3520/0.1) with the private Fairview Mine path. Southwest along the sandy trail between fenced private property and the river, you pass a flat layer of tufa: sedimentary rock of calcium carbonate created of limestone with the help of springs, some of which bubble from the river bed. Shortly you climb up zigzags to a junction (3620/0.4) with *Tobias Creek Trail 32E34*. Here you leave the Whiskey Flat Trail, which lies atop a trench that once transported water from Tobias Creek to the flats below, and take the upper path. Continue on a moderate-to-steep grade to a junction (3740/0.2) with Flynn Canyon Trail atop the bluff where people heading for Flynn Canyon of T26 take the right fork, while you take the left.

Your path, still Tobias Creek Trail 32E34, gently descends south through a thick cloak of buck brush, fremontia and mountain mahogany pierced occasionally by digger pines: all of them accompanying vegetation on much of this trip. The obscure irrigation ditch crosses your trail about 200 feet before you reach the wide, bouldered, usually dry bed of Flynn Canyon's creek (3600/0.3). A short side trip up this creek bed reveals a pipe unseen from your route. Now rusted and broken, it was used by the trench builders to bridge the creek.

Your trail also turns up the dry bed for a few steps, leaves it and proceeds to ascend southwest into Tobias Creek's canyon, high above the year-round flow. Your path, now on red-brown metamorphic soil, again crosses the nearly unseen trench just before the ditch finally converges with the water below. Your trail passes tufa here as well as farther ahead and descends to a flat (3760/0.6) by the creek. Shaded by oaks, alders and willows near the whispering cascade and quiet pools, this beach makes an attractive place to pause or camp.

After climbing higher in the canyon, which follows a bend in the stream far below, you again descend to Tobias Creek (4190/1.0), the goal of this trip. Incense cedars and ponderosa pines provide a shady retreat among creekside boulders and level spaces: an inviting retreat to picnic or camp, dip in the creek or fish.

Boulders assure a dry creek crossing if you wish to venture farther; one rock with a non-Indian petroglyph indicates H. Mars crossed here in 1904. (The unmaintained trail beyond the creek climbs steeply up a ridge to circuitous, paved SNF Road 23S16 on the upper reaches of the Greenhorn Mountains.)

T26   Flynn Canyon Day Hike

Peaks of limestone show strikingly above the secluded retreats along Flynn Canyon's stream. This leisurely hike takes you to creekside slabs dappled with shade from mature oaks, pines and incense cedars and suggests, for the more energetic, a climb to a ridgeline view of the surrounding country.

Distance   6.8 miles, round trip
Steep Ascents   None
Elevation Gain   1250 feet
Skills   Easy route finding; easy-to-moderate hiking
Seasons   Fall, winter
Maps   USGS 7.5-min. *Fairview, Johnson-dale*
Trailhead   21. See car tour T21.
Description   The beginning of this trip is described in T25.

Southbound Trail 32E35 Log

T25	parking lot	3550	0.0
	Fairview Mine Tr	3520	0.1
	Tobias Cr Tr	3620	0.4

Westbound Trail 32E34 Log

Whiskey Flat Tr	3620	0.0
Flynn Cyn Tr	3740	0.2

After the junction with Tobias Creek Trail 32E34, your trail, **Flynn Canyon 32E33**, heads west, rounding a finger of dominant Speas Ridge: a feature of metamorphic rock interlarded with limestone. Fremontia, mountain mahogany, buck brush and manzanita bushes line the route. Also among these grow the silk tassel bushes, named for their elegant, tassel-like catkins strung with tiny saffron-yellow flowers. The catkins hang like tinsel on a Christmas tree. Silk tassel's thick, elliptical, yellow-green leaves grow opposite each other on erect yellowish branches. The bush can reach 10 feet in height.

The path dips to cross the creek (3990/1.3). Below the crossing a succession of slabs and tumbling water invite you to pause awhile. A bit after the ford a grayish limestone peak appears to the north, and numerous thorny stems of blackberry bushes drape over the trail. Continuing above the creek channel, the path heads northwest under a forest canopy of mature incense cedars and golden and black oaks. The route passes a campsite among the boulders under a huge golden oak, good for picnicking, and then crosses the creek again, the second of several crossings.

Two more step-across creek fords, then the path, covered inches deep with leaves, passes a few downed logs. In winter these logs and surrounding leaf litter are used by hibernating ladybugs, crowded together for warmth. This phenomenon occurs in selected locations of middle elevation in the Sierra and illustrates a need for downed wood to be left in place.

After more creek crossings, at a fork in the canyon, a rusted but still intact bed with springs sits forlornly on a flat: another spot for picnicking or camping and a good place to end the day hike (4640/1.4). You may wonder if Matt Flynn, for whom this canyon is named, used this place to rest while herding sheep over 100 years ago. Surely the bed postdates Flynn.

(The trail continues up a usually dry north branch of the creek, narrows as the slope sloughs onto the canyon floor, and in half a mile, turns sharply left to cross the creek bed. Here the unmaintained trail leaves the canyon and climbs steeply up a ridge, with the help of switchbacks, to Speas Ridge Trail 32E32, which eventually takes you to Johnsondale R-Ranch. Some day, the Forest Service plans to make this a good riding trail.)

Catkins hang like tinsel on silk tassel bushes

T27   Highway 155 Car Tour:
Delano to Isabella Lake
(With Directions to Trailheads 23–26)

The rolling countryside unfolds as you climb and curve among its hills to gain the summit of the Greenhorn Mountains and then descend to Isabella Lake. The country's history of pathfinders, early settlers, gold seekers, land developers and stagecoach stations adds a fascinating dimension to this sweeping setting of foothills, mountain crest and lake.

Distance   45.7 miles, one way
Steep Ascents   None
Elevation Gain   5515 feet
Skills   Easy route finding; paved road
Seasons   All year (Snow removed)
Map   Kern County road map
Tourhead   23. The intersection of north-south Highway 65 (Porterville Highway) and east-west Highway 155 is **TH23**. This is 11.1 miles east of Highway 99 in Delano.

Description   From the tourhead intersection (590/0.0/0.0), drive east on *State Highway 155* as it cuts through low, barren hills: some cultivated, all fenced on each side of the road to contain the cattle. In about 10 minutes there appears to the left of the road the first of three historical monuments (7.6/7.6) along the route. This marker honors the first recorded Christian baptism in the San Joaquin Valley. It took place on May 3, 1776 in Grizzly Gulch three miles north of the monument. The baptism was performed by Father Francisco Garces, who is recorded in history books as a humble, kindly priest from

Church moved to Woody in 1909

Spain. A solitary pathfinder, he succeeded in crossing the often hostile desert, leaving his mission in Arizona to travel to California: he was the first Caucasian known to cross the land into the San Joaquin Valley. He was warmly welcomed by most of the Native Americans as he traveled, but was murdered at the age of 43 by a rioting mob of Indians outraged at the broken promises of the Spanish Government. Father Garces is well-remembered in Kern County today: an imposing statue in the traffic circle on Chester Avenue in Bakersfield; a school and the west extension of this highway bear his name; several roadside historical monuments recount his deeds and travels.

The baptism site, Grizzly Gulch, was no doubt named for some grizzly bear incident, as these animals were numerous around the mountain foothills. Hunted to extinction in the Sierra, the last grizzly sighting occurred in the early 1920s.

Many miles ahead blue oaks begin to appear on the rolling grassland; then you see a tiny white church tucked among the hills to the left on the western outskirts of Woody. The Elberon Christian Church, which was moved piece by piece from Glennville in 1909, celebrated its centennial in 1990.

To the right in the hamlet of Woody, a historical landmark (7.8/15.4) next to an aged frame building informs travelers that Dr. Sparrell Woody established a ranch here after his property, in what became Bakersfield, was inundated by the Kern River flood of 1861–62. His remains rest in the Blue Mountain Cemetery nearby. Among the cemetery tombstones sits a unique 6-foot-tall memorial with names of people who lived in

Woody but died and were buried elsewhere. Woody Road next to the historical landmark is one of the many paved, lightly traveled network of roads in the foothills ideal for bicycling.

Beyond Woody, the road passes the old cemetery, climbs alongside a ravine with oaks, cottonwoods and willows, then passes Blue Mountain Road (1.9/17.3) leading north to a radio tower. Blue Mountain yielded some gold around 1884. During that period miners worked gulches hereabouts with vivid names such as Rag Gulch, Five Dogs Gulch and Howling Gulch. Granite Road of car tour T18 (3015/6.2/23.5), the route on which Julius Chester ran a stage from Bakersfield in 1873, comes in from the south. After your road crosses Poso Creek, Jack Ranch Road (3035/0.7/24.2), also of T18, leaves to the north.

Quickly you arrive at the historic town of Glennville. Cumberland Presbyterian Church established in 1867, is one of Kern County's first churches. You will find another historical landmark at a reconstructed adobe house next to the fire station (1.4/25.6). The adobe, built before the Civil War as a trading post, stood at the junction of a pair of Indian trails. After 1864 it served the McFarlane Toll Road, which climbed over the Greenhorn Mountains to the mining fields in Kernville somewhat along the lines of Highway 155. The old east-end toll house still stands in the Kern River Valley, now on private property.

Glennville, named for James M. Glenn, who had a home and blacksmith shop in the area, was a thriving community by 1871. Today it offers a country atmosphere in a peaceful setting. However, once a year, during the annual Spring Rodeo, the tiny town burgeons with 10,000 people and their horses. The event began in 1948.

Climbing east of Glennville, the road passes ranch houses and Sequoia National Forest's Fulton Work Center. Zigzagging, it ascends among numerous buckeye trees, digger pines, live oaks and ceanothus bushes. The lovely California buckeye trees, adjusting to available water, appear impatient and

defiant. They are among the first to leaf out in the spring with five leaflets (palmate) on a long stalk, which grows opposite other stalks on a branch. They quickly adorn themselves with lengthy, fragrant clusters of white flowers that curve up at the ends of the branchlets. They then become the first trees to withdraw their leaves' chlorophyll, and by late spring already appear cloaked in brown. In a parting gesture, while going dormant, they dangle large pods with seeds that are poisonous to most animals.

Soon the road curves around the Jameson Ranch, a camp offering a variety of outdoor activities for young people. It then quickly arrives at Sandy Creek Fire Road (SNF Road 24S07) (4860/6.8/32.4) to the north, the return route of T34, and SNF Road 25S04 to the south, Alder Creek Campground for the shuttle car of T28: both roads are gated in winter.

Traveling on, you skirt the savannah hills around Bohna Peak and arrive at sylvan Cedar Creek Campground (2.5/34.9), **TH24** for Ts 28&29. Beyond the campground you pass to your left a pipe hanging over a staircase of moss-covered rocks where cold water flows from Spout Spring. In the mile to the summit you also pass to your left a graceful dogwood tree whose white spring blossoms appear to float unattached. You then quickly top out at Greenhorn Summit (6102/3.2/38.1), **TH25**, the hub of several trips. To the left car tour T32 takes you north to **THs27–30;** to the right the following

1867 church in Glennville

description takes you south to **TH26** and Shirley Meadows Ski Area.

For T31 and the ski area, turn right on paved ***Rancheria Road*** (SNF Road 25S15; KC Road 465) (0.0/0.0). You quickly pass the self-guided nature trail of T30 to your right which parallels this road, then pass the entrance to county Camp Kaweah and several logging roads, to arrive at the parking area (2.3/2.3) for skiers and **TH26**. The former Shirley Meadows Campground now houses maintenance equipment shaded in part by sequoias. Only because these trees were planted do they fail to qualify as the Sierra's southernmost grove. Two cross-country ski routes begin just north of the parking lot on unplowed logging roads. To the left in 0.1 mile, the 3.0 mile, one way, Windy Gap route on SNF Road 25S17 leads along the west slopes to join Rancheria Road. To the right in 0.7 mile, the 5.7 miles Shirley Loop route of T31, on SNF Road 25S21 circles east around Shirley and Cooks peaks to the parking lot.

At about half the price charged by larger complexes, Shirley Meadows Ski Resort, at 6800 feet, offers two chair lifts with runs for beginners to advanced. It also rents equipment.

(Rancheria Road, sans pavement, continues south to Highway 178. The former Rhymes Campground, now a Fire Safe Area with no amenities, is located 2.0 miles down the road. Evans Flat Campground, 2.5 miles farther, with sites interspersed among pines and firs at the headwaters of Greenhorn Creek and the lower edge of Evans Flat Meadow, offers the usual amenities plus equestrian accommodations.)

Around you, as you begin your descent from the summit on Highway 155, appear the Forest Service maintenance station, houses and cabins of forested Alta Sierra, and the inviting Greenhorn Mountain County Park and campground. For a nominal nightly fee you can camp for 21 days at this spacious, cool park shaded by incense cedar and white fir trees. Camp Yenis Hante, formerly a logging camp, and the smaller Camp Kaweah, situated within the park, offer cabins, showers, recreation and dining halls to organizations at a reasonable rate.

A highway sign advises you to use low gears as the grade varies from 11% to 13%— advice you definitely should heed. Before leaving the cool, mixed woodlands, you may notice trees in the forest about you that are yellowing and dying, mostly because of the bark beetle. Almost every conifer has its community of beetles, which are kept in check by healthy trees. During stressful times, such as periods of extended drought or smog, the beetles conquer the trees. When beetles overcome a tree, usually the top dies first.

Isabella Lake appears below and far east of it appear the bluish Sierra crest with prominent Mount Jenkins. While descending the north side of the brushy deep canyon, you pass the ranches, houses and mobile homes of Wofford Heights. At the end of the often steep descent you reach the junction (2680/7.6/45.7) of Burlando Road in the commercial section of Wofford Heights situated above the lake. Highway 155 turns right here. The trip around the lake is described in car tour T21.

T28   Cedar Creek Day Hike

On this cross-country stroll you are not constrained by a trail, but governed by fleeting whims: hop across the shadow-dappled creek at any desirable moment; lunch by its banks at any pleasurable locale; wander about to investigate any curious object. The tranquil setting along Cedar Creek, shaded by numerous cedars, oaks and pines, beckons the wanderlust in all free spirits.

Distance   6.0 miles, round trip
Steep Ascents   0.1 mile
Elevation Gain   900 feet
Skills   Easy route finding; easy-to-moderate hiking
Seasons   All year
Map   USGS 7.5-min. *Alta Sierra* (Trail does not appear on provisional editions)
Trailhead   24. See car tour T27. (This hike can be shortened to a one-way shuttle trip ending at Alder Creek Campground, 3.0 miles south on SNF Road 25SO4 (Closed in winter). This is 5.5 miles from **TH24**.)
Description   Because trees shade much of the way, you can take this hike in summer, but spring is the most desirable time for this whimsical adventure.

Begin your hike across Highway 155 (4800/0.0) south along SNF Road 25S14 into lower Cedar Creek Campground. Leave the road (4740/0.1) before it crosses the creek to find the unsigned *Cedar Creek Trail 31E69*, south of Campsite 8 above the creek. Although this trail belongs to the Forest Service network of trails and can be found here, it has all but disappeared elsewhere. If you miss it, it is easier to make your own way along the creek than to hunt for it. You descend to the creek in the shade of black oaks and incense cedars. After a short amble creekside you approach an idyllic site hosting a stone cabin. Its corrugated roof covers an ample room with a large fireplace. This building is one of several vacation homes that lined Cedar Creek in the early 1900s. A large campsite sprawls nearby.

Shortly a fence (4500/0.7) confronts you, separating private property from public domain. Here you turn right to follow this fence west while climbing *cross-country* out of the ravine of Cedar Creek, a steep but short bushwhack. At the top you cross the power-line road at a yellow section marker on a nearby tree. Descend along the fence and under the powerlines. Around 0.1 mile beyond the lines, cut back to the creek again, thus climbing around the private property.

Once more you are free to saunter along the creek as you see fit. Soon Slick Rock Creek from the northeast joins Cedar Creek,

and just below the confluence you skirt around another cabin that appears abandoned. Next as you descend along the creek, a north-trending canyon delivers water from branches of Cedar Creek. These canyons and the rolling hills all about, sprinkled in spring with various flowers, display the fiddleneck among them. This narrow-leafed, 1- to 3-foot plant, one of the easiest to identify, has coils of small golden blooms at the ends of hairy stems that resemble the end curve of a violin. These abundant flowers sometimes appear in pure stands covering whole hillsides.

In 0.8 mile you join a dirt road that leads in a few steps to Alder Creek Campground (3900/2.2) at the confluence of Cedar and Alder creeks. Both Cedar and Alder camp-grounds offer desirable campsites and are well-used.

When returning, be alert for a few places that may cause route confusion as you ascend along Cedar Creek. In about 0.8 mile, Cedar Creek turns right (east) where it receives a creek branch from the north; in another 0.7 mile, Cedar Creek keeps left at its con-fluence with Slick Rock Creek; again climb out of the canyon steeply when you approach the private cabin.

A Cedar Creek falls

T29 Bohna Peak Climb

Bohna Peak stands prominently above the rolling grass and oak lands of the western Sierra slopes. It ascends west of the slides and cascading falls of Cedar Creek's narrow, wooded canyon where this trip begins. Like other outlying peaks in the Southern Sierra, this peak invites climbers when other mountains become inaccessible.

Distance 3.8 miles, round trip
Steep Ascents 0.5 mile
Elevation Gain 1975 feet
Skills Intermediate route finding; Class 1 climbing
Seasons Fall, winter, spring
Maps USGS 7.5-min.*Alta Sierra* (briefly), *Tobias Pk*
Trailhead 24. See car tour T27.
Description From State Highway 155 (4820/0.0) at Cedar Creek Campground, walk upstream on a wide *path* that meanders under a coalescence of incense cedars, alders and live oaks. You crisscross Cedar Creek several times. While on the left bank you hike below mine shafts chiseled out of metamorphic rock. On the right bank you climb above a pair of falls to an enticing pool about 25 feet wide with two water slides above. Climb up their side, watching your footing on the slick rocks. The pool and the slides cue you to look to your left for a *use trail* (5060/0.5) ascending back among the miner's lettuce that flourishes abundantly in this slender canyon. The following route helps you avoid some bushwhacking. (Should you miss the path, leave the creek before you reach a broad northwest trending canyon, climb up the east-facing slopes, then head toward the defined southeast-trending ridgecrest.)

The vague use trail zigzags steeply southwest, finding clearings between trees and brush. Then it traverses west along the south slopes of the ridge to a small scooped-out area. Here the route takes you northnorthwest up the scooped slope, then between bushes to a grassy, open, sloping ridgecrest and a cairn (5700/0.5).

Along the way you may notice the low growing spring flower called five spot. This attractive plant, closely related to baby blue eyes, has white, bowl-shaped flowers with large blue-violet spots on the tips of each of its five petals. It has slender, divided leaves.

Now climbing west up the open slope, you soon reach a level area with a camper's fire ring. Continue up the ridge through a forest of incense cedar, black oak, ponderosa and sugar pines, enjoy another brief plateau, then make the final steep climb to the top of Bohna Peak (6795/0.9). Sunday Peak to the northnortheast seems a hop away while Split and Black mountains appear to the east a tad farther. Christian Bohna, whom this peak honors, built the first house in what was later to become Bakersfield. He moved away after the flood of 1861–62, established a ranch at Rag and Gordon gulches near Woody, and grazed his animals hereabouts. Colonel Baker acquired his old house and founded Bakersfield.

T30 Unal Nature Trail Day Hike

This short trip, particularly inviting to parents with young children, loops along the cool, quiet crest of the Greenhorn Mountains. The pamphlet for this self-guided tour suggests how this land would be viewed by a Tubatulabal Native American lad who lived in the Kern River Valley area before Caucasians arrived and contrasts that with information about the surrounding land as you see it. Children, who usually enjoy pretending, can imagine themselves as the young Indian lad walking the Unal Trail—"unal" to the boy would mean "bear."

Distance   3.2 miles, loop trip
Steep Ascents   None
Elevation Gain   730 feet
Skills   Easy route finding; easy-to-moderate hiking
Seasons   Spring, summer, fall
Map   USGS 7.5-min. *Alta Sierra* (Trail does not appear on provisional edition.)
Trailhead   25. See car tour T27.
Description   Obtain your brochure at the trailhead. Also copies usually are available at the Greenhorn Ranger Station on Highway 178, the Lake Isabella Visitor Center on Highway 155 and the maintenance station on Greenhorn Summit.

The **Unal Trail** (U-nall) (6110/0.0) begins at the junction of paved Rancheria Road and unpaved SNF Road 25S17, immediately south of the Forest Service's Greenhorn Summit Maintenance Station. The "Bear Trail" ascends parallel to the paved road, switchbacking twice to gain elevation. Twenty-five numbered posts situated at points of interest appear; they correspond to the numbers in your pamphlet giving you past and present information. Your path soon arrives at the junction (6280/0.3) of the return trail; you continue ahead.

The trail overlaps a retired logging road lined with incense cedar seedlings and saplings. In time the road will narrow to path width and the built-up water bars will diminish. You may see notices here of a sugar pine blister rust evaluation that began in 1990 nailed to a couple of nearby trees. Through this study sugar pines resistant to blister rust are identified and their seeds are gathered for planting.

Soon the path reaches the creek mentioned in your brochure. Shortly after the path curves back (6560/1.0) to climb higher, still on east-facing slopes. The tall, spindly looking trees, lonely in the clear-cut area, were stripped of branches by cut trees falling past them. After recrossing the slender stream, the path zigzags up to the crest (6838/0.6), showcasing views of near and far.

After enjoying the trail summit dubbed "Unal Peak," you curve around the ridge, zigzag down through a forest of bracken fern, then gently descend along the crest. At Stop 25, a Tubatulabal house and a few artifacts illustrate the lives and activities of the Native Americans who lived in this area about 100 years ago. (They are imitations and have no value as collector items.) You next cross the crest and drop via four switchbacks to the end of the loop (6280/1.0). Now you retrace your incoming steps (6110/0.3).

T31   Shirley Meadows Loop Day Hike

This trip in the Greenhorn Mountains appeals to people who enjoy walking where the air flows pure and sometimes crisp; where numerous trees grace the way, but allow portals of dramatic vistas and where the route remains gentle.

Distance   6.4 miles, loop trip
Steep Ascents   None
Elevation Gain   600 feet
Skills   Easy route finding; easy hiking
Seasons   Spring, summer, fall
Map   USGS 7.5-min. *Alta Sierra*
Trailhead   26. See car tour T27.
Description   Like only one other hike in this book, this loop around the Shirley and Cooks peaks massif uses seldom or lightly traveled roads exclusively. Although described for walkers, this route provides equal pleasure for joggers, equestrians, car travelers, family all-terrain bicyclists, and cross-country skiers.

Begin by walking north-northeast down paved **Rancheria Road** (SNF Road 25S15), leaving the Shirley Meadows Ski Area (6790/0.0) on the most traveled section of the tour. (Peakbaggers can detour on the first unpaved road to the right, which leads 1.2 miles southeast to a saddle between Shirley Peak and Cooks Peak. From the saddle a 0.2-mile climb east reaches Cooks Peak's summit, its register tablet in a can and tree-framed views of Shirley Peak and Black

Mountain. Or they can climb the steeper east-facing slopes later in the trip.)

Continuing on this trip, Rancheria Road passes other unpaved roads while curving around a slight ridge, then meets *SNF Road 25S21* (6480/0.7). Here your route turns obliquely right. This road once sported a thin coat of asphalt but now is entirely dirt surfaced. It descends gently, embraced on either side predominantly by incense cedar trees, immediately passes an old road (6440/0.1) connecting the summer home tract of Shirley Meadows and the village of Alta Sierra, then crosses over the culverts of several spring-fed branches of Shirley Creek. Soon the trees part, first displaying steep canyons, then showcasing vistas of Isabella Lake and the Kern River Valley with Split and Black mountains to the northeast.

The road rounds the divide where black oaks have become liberally mixed with conifers, then heads southwest and west, offering glimpses of Breckenridge Mountain. It ascends easily over a saddle at the crest of the Greenhorn Mountains to again meet *Rancheria Road* (SNF Road 25S15) (6420/4.2), unpaved here, onto which you turn right. SNF Road 26S07 departs west at this junction.

Now ascending north, on the broader road, you cross the crest twice, then view Cedar Creek canyon below, Linns Valley midway and San Joaquin Valley in the far west. After leaving the slopes of Shirley Peak, where a road to the right leads to its towers, you pass a road gate (the road is cleared of snow north of this gate) and arrive at the paved parking lot (6790/1.4) of the ski resort and your car.

A family outing

T32   Greenhorn Mountains East Side Car Tour
(With Directions to Trailheads 27–30)

This mountain traverse from Greenhorn Summit to Parker Pass Drive lets you explore the extent of regrowth since the devastating 1990 fire, then leads you to dense forests and beside airy meadows.

Distance   27.6 miles, one way
Steep Ascents   None
Elevation Gain   2225 feet
Skills   Easy route finding; unpaved and paved roads
Seasons   Spring, summer, fall

Maps   Kern & Tulare county maps
Tourhead   25. The junction of Highway 155 and SNF Road 24S15 at Greenhorn Summit is **TH25**. This is 38.1 miles east of Highway 65 and 7.5 miles west of Burlando Road in Wofford Heights. This trip departs

from car tour T27.

Description From the tourhead junction turn north onto unpaved **SNF Road 24S15** (Portuguese Pass Road; Forest Highway 90) (6102/0.0/0.0), gated in winter. At first you are driving within the northern extension of spacious Greenhorn County Park, shaded by incense cedar, ponderosa pine and black oak trees. As you leave the unmarked park boundary you descend gradually to meet SNF Road 25S16 (Black Saddle Road) (1.2/1.2) on the crest of the Greenhorn Mountains. Climbers seeking **TH27** of Ts35&36, Black and Split mountains, turn right while others continue ahead.

To reach **TH27**, drive east along **SNF Road 25S16** (0.0/0.0), pass roads departing left and arrive at Black Saddle (1.6/1.6), **TH27**, a clearing to the right of your road at the head of a north-facing canyon. (Beyond the clearing Black Saddle Road heads north and descends.) From the trailhead, old SNF Road 25S20 descends south and SNF Road 25S27 ascends west.

As you gradually rise north from the T junction to curve around Peak 6852, you drive along the upper slopes of Bull Run Basin where you may still see blackened devastation below with slow regeneration from the Stormy Complex Fire. Charred trees border the road to your right while unburned trees extend upslope to your left. Firefighters on line could not explain why the fire's progress halted, with few exceptions, at the road, since it was a wind-whipped crown fire.

The lightning-caused conflagration started on August 5, 1990, as two separate fires. Four days later the two united sending a mushroom cloud billowing 20,000 feet above the upper Kern Canyon. A voluntary evacuation notice had been issued to residents of Wofford Heights and Alta Sierra; the communities of Kernville, Sugarloaf and Panorama Heights were threatened. At the height of the fire 2500 personnel were involved; air tankers and fire helicopters dropped retardants continuously during daylight hours; bull dozers worked to clear an extensive fire

break west of Wofford Heights and Kernville. By August 31 the 24,200-acre, 12 million dollar fire was controlled. No residences were burned; no lives were lost. Coincidentally, an intense lightning-caused fire had burned the same extensive area in 1924.

You soon arrive at the former Tiger Flat Campground (3.1/4.3), now a Fire Safe Area for camping with a free-flowing spring. As indicated, it was safe during the fire; however, "Fire Safe Area" refers to a place where open fires are allowed even while forbidden elsewhere during periods of extremely dry conditions.

While skirting slopes and negotiating hairpin curves around Sunday and Portuguese peaks, you enter Tulare County, then minutes later arrive at SNF Road 24S28 (2.3/6.6) departing southwest to Camp Mountain Meadows, a Girl Scout Camp, where girls from grades 2 to 12 enjoy high adventure in this mountain setting. To the right of this road at the junction is **TH28**, a parking area for the popular Sunday Peak Trail 31E66 of T37.

Continue on to the next important junction, paved SNF Road 23S16 (7370/0.7/7.3), Portuguese Pass, where people on T34 turn left while you turn right.

Resuming northward, now on **SNF Road 23S16** (Sugarloaf Highway; Forest Highway 50), the road curves around Point 7782, while passing Panorama Campground (0.7/8.0) spread on a ridge to the right. The interesting view from the point of the ridge gives the campground its name. With the Kern Plateau visible to the east, the road slices into steep slopes near the Greenhorn Mountains' crest and arrives at a forked junction (7340/1.4/9.4) with SNF Road 24S50 to Frog Meadow. Here those on T33 take the left fork while you continue ahead.

The rest of your route on this narrow paved road assumes an overall descent of nearly 1900 feet. Here it passes above a massive clear-cut. The replanted trees on the bare slope escaped the Stormy Complex Fire. After a winding descent with shocking views of total fire destruction, you arrive at a sign announcing Tyler Meadow (2.1/11.5).

The vivid emerald green of the meadow dissolves into a tawny yellow after a fall frost, but the black silhouettes that line the grassy expanse no longer respond to seasonal changes: they are dead. The fire created unpredictable winds as it marched across Bull Run Basin below, causing it to suddenly blow up on both sides of Tyler Meadow, trapping around 50 firefighters at the meadow's base camp. The noise and heat were intense. Miraculously, during that frightening period only a few vehicles and a 1920 cabin were destroyed. No lives were lost.

About 71.5 million board feet of timber were logged from the fire area. After logging the commercially useful burned trees, a new method of removing slash (branches, etc.) was tried. Usually after logging an area the slash is collected into a pile and burned on site. Here a giant grinder was brought in to reduce the remaining branches to chips. These were hauled out and burned to produce energy for the sawmill in Terra Bella. This method is less polluting, less wasteful and a less costly source of fuel.

To the north of upper Tyler Meadow, you pass SNF Road 24S35 (0.7/12.2) forking southeast to **TH29**, of interest to those seeking T38, a hike into the burned acres of Bull Run Basin. Shortly beyond, at a saddle junction (0.9/13.1) with SNF Road 24S02, you continue ahead where people wishing to climb Baker Point and Peak at **TH30** turn right.

If you are heading for **TH30**, turn east on *SNF Road 24S02* (0.0/0.0), a well-graded but winding, unpaved road. After advancing from complete burn to pockets of burn and passing spur roads, you arrive at the end of the road (3.2/3.2), **TH30**, on the ridgecrest.

Beyond the burned area, linear, lush Dunlap Meadow, named for an 1850s Linns Valley rancher whose cattle grazed it, stretches to the left of the road. Next your route crosses the headwater streams of Tobias Creek, sheathed in willows, and once again hugs steep slopes where glimpses of The Needles to the north appear. A climb around densely wooded Burnt Ridge promises that in time the burn devastation you just experienced will once again become a forest. After constant curves and several road junctions, your road curves sharply left where a winding unpaved road exits to Johnsondale.

Seekers of the rumored humongous "Lost" giant sequoia of the Packsaddle

Mushroom cloud over Kernville: 1990 Stormy Complex Fire

Grove will find SNF Road 23S64 to Packsaddle Meadow at a junction (13.4/ 26.5) 1.3 miles beyond the Johnsondale cutoff. (That road twists and climbs southeast gaining 1000 vertical feet to the meadow, which is above the steep canyon containing the grove. Stories of the "Ghost Tree," perhaps the largest tree in the world, have circulated since 1885: the L.A. Times carried articles about it in 1934 and again in 1961. Wendell D. Flint, considered an expert on tree sizes, located the tree and found it impressive, but because of its broken top, it ranks only 48 by volume, and it has a 63-foot

perimeter at breast height, not the rumored 120 feet. Big, but not among the biggest; General Grant has the greatest perimeter at breast height at 90.9 feet. Two other trees in this grove also rank in his top fifty by volume.)

Finishing this trip, you pass Thompson Camp (site)—camping, but no facilities—followed by a road gate, and after crossing South Creek—it really flows east—you arrive at the end of this tour. Here you meet Parker Pass Drive (TC Road M-50) (5430/1.1/27.6) of car tour T41.

T33   Greenhorn Summit Car & All-Terrain Bicycle Tour
With Excursion F: Tobias Peak Lookout

Variety, opportunity and recent events commingle in this exploration along the crest of the Greenhorn Mountains. Light travel on graded roads makes this trip just right for bicyclists. Interesting side trips and a secluded campground alongside a velvety meadow add to the pleasure for all.

Distance   14.0 miles, one way
Steep Ascents   None
Elevation Gain   1650 feet
Skills   Easy route finding; unpaved roads
Seasons   Spring, summer, fall
Maps   Kern & Tulare county road maps
Tourhead   25. See car tour T32.
Description   The mild road undulations make this an ideal winter route for cross-country skiers. The beginning of this trip is described in T32.

Northbound SNF Road 24S15 Log

T32 Hwy 155 jct	6102	0.0
Blk Saddle Rd jct		1.2
Tiger Flat		3.1
Sunday Pk Tr jct		2.3
SNF Rd 23S16 jct	7370	0.7
Northbound SNF Road 23S16		
SNF Rd 24S15	7370	0.0
Panorama Cmpgd		0.7
SNF Rd 24S50	7340	1.4

After leaving SNF Road 23S16 (Portuguese Pass Road; Forest Highway 90), you ascend on the left fork, ***SNF Road 24S50***, a

narrow, unpaved road, and initially parallel the paved road you left, then skirt Bull Run Peak to reach Bull Run Pass (1.1/10.5). (Peakbaggers can hardly be this close to a named and quickly obtainable peak without climbing it. The easiest ascent of Bull Run Peak begins south from this pass and stays east of the crest to avoid brush. It turns sharply west when you are below the peak boulders and climbs to the 8024-foot summit where its register in a can lies under rocks. The gain is 485 feet.)

Your tour leaves Bull Run Pass, crosses the crest and meanders north along slopes heavy with brush punctured with a few firs and pines. It curves above Poison Meadow, then crosses the slopes of Tobias Peak, once shorn of trees, now replanted, but still offering open views west of the White River drainage and Sierra foothills. The road soon reaches Tobias Pass (7550/1.5/12.0) and the brief road tour to Tobias Peak Lookout described below.

Excursion F: Tobias Peak Lookout

If you enjoy vistas and lookouts, make time for this brief tour to a lookout built in 1937. Its views extend to distant horizons in all directions.

Distance   4.0 miles, round trip
Steep Ascents   None
Elevation Gain   735 feet
Skills   Easy route finding; unpaved roads
Description   From Tobias Pass (7550/0.0/0.0), turn right on *SNF Road 24S24* to ascend generally northeast. Soon you see the clearing of Tobias Meadow to the north through artificially thinned forest. In fact, much of the predominately fir forest all around has been selectively logged or clearcut. The cleared areas have been replanted with seedlings of a single species: ponderosa pine—a practice no longer employed by the Forest Service. Studies show that a forest resists disease better if it has a mix of species. Now other commercially-valued trees are planted with the favorite rapid-growing ponderosa.

At the ensuing forked junction (0.7/0.7), the route turns right on *SNF Road 24S08* and ascends south on a rather steep and bumpy road past the open gate to the parking area (1.2/1.9). A painted white line on rock steps leads you up the chinquapin-hedged entrance where a solar panel and radio facilities accompany the lookout (8284/0.1/2.0).

Who was Tobias? What did he do to be remembered with so many place names?

Historian Francis P. Farquhar wrote in 1924 that Tobias Minter homesteaded a meadow at the base of Tobias Peak—that is all. After his death in 1884, his sons named the peak for him, and much later geographers extended the name to a creek, meadow and pass because these features happened to be near the peak. This is the way most Southern Sierra features were named before the United States Board on Geographic Names adopted a comprehensive procedure by which place names are limited to honoring people who had made a positive contribution to the area; or, with major features, to the nation.

*   *   *   *   *

Your road, SNF Road 24S50, progresses north with Berry Meadow and corn lily-lined outliers of Tobias Meadow to its east. At the next junction (1.6/13.6) your route bears right onto *SNF Road 24S86* to Frog Meadow. (If you plan to backpack on T42, note this important junction. You will leave your route to reach this point on gated SNF Road 24S82 if you intend a side visit to Frog Meadow.)

Now you descend gently, passing a Forest Service guard station, and arrive at remote Frog Meadow Campground (7560/0.4/14.0). It sits in the woods at the north end of lush, spring green Frog Meadow, which hides secretive tiny white violets and showcases an aged cabin. This is an ideal place to picnic or camp if you wish for peace and seclusion before returning the way you came. You may not find water here, however, if you visit late in the season.

Frog Meadow and sagging log cabin

T34 Greenhorn Mountains Car & All-Terrain Bicycle Loop Tour

This tour, designed primarily for bicyclists who enjoy a variety of experiences on their trips, presents gently undulating, unpaved roads and a descending forest-shaded trail. It is ideally suited to car travelers who wish to experience seldom-visited pockets in the cool, wooded highlands of the Greenhorn Mountains.

Distance   Car 36.3 miles; bicycle 29.3 miles; loop trip

Steep Ascents   None

Elevation Gain   3915 feet

Skills   Easy route finding; unpaved and paved roads

Seasons   Spring, summer, fall

Maps   Kern & Tulare county road maps

Tourhead   25. See car tour T32.

Description   The beginning of this trip is described in T32.

Northbound SNF Road 24S15 Log

T32 Hwy 155 jct	6102	0.0
Blk Saddle Rd jct		1.2
Tiger Flat		3.1
Sunday Pk Tr jct		2.3
SNF Rd 23S16 jct	7370	0.7

Cars and bicyclists turn left at Portuguese Pass heading southwest on paved *SNF Road 23S16* (Sugarloaf Road; Forest Highway 50), but bicyclists be alert for Marshall Trail 31E60 (0.4/7.7) to the left immediately after the hairpin curve: you leave the road and descend abruptly on that trail. Car travelers drive on and skip to the car route description.

Bicycle Route

You promptly gear down to descend moderately to steeply on *Marshall M'cyclepath 31E60* along the right side of a nacent Spear Creek branch. You may want to stop to examine three items of interest near the beginning of the trail. First, a colony of spring-blooming, white violets reaching less than 4 inches high. The lower petals of the five-petaled flower have purple veins and a slender spur extending back. This flower barely peeks above its round leaves to bow on a slender, arched stem, giving it a "shy" or "shrinking" look. In contrast, a black and yellow sign on a section bearing tree yells ATTENTION! and threatens six months in jail or $250.00 if you disturb the section sign! Yet

another sign indicates a wildlife area.

On your bike you quickly descend to cross the creek, ride along its left bank, then down a ridge to meet a logging road (1.0/8.7). Peel Peak stands in view directly ahead. (At this point if the peak beckons, dismount and climb 0.3 mile cross-country, northwest, curving west, stay left of the lesser peak, then attain the ring of boulders that crown the 6788-foot peak. A register in a can rests at the summit.)

After the climbers' ascent, turn left onto the logging road, which takes you to Marshall Meadow, and left onto SNF Road 24S93 (0.5/9.2). On this offset trail junction, you pass spur SNF Road 24S93B and a campsite on a ridgelet to find on the south side of that minor ridge the continuation of your trail, 31E60 (0.1/9.3). Descend on it below and parallel to the road, then turn west to ride below the crest of Peel Ridge. Tree blazes mark the way.

Shortly you turn northwest, descend a lesser ridge, sometimes steeply, always in shade, to a crossing of two branches of Von Hellum Creek near their confluence. Here you also meet a road (1.7/11.0) to cabins and abodes of Panorama Heights. Find the trail as it descends gently along the creek's right bank; on it you soon meet unpaved Sandy Creek Fire Road (4700/0.4/11.4).

Car Route

You continue ahead on narrow, serpentine *SNF Road 23S16* describing a wiggly curve around the Poso Creek headwaters bowl: here its branch is Spear Creek. Near the beginning of the curve, a pipe above the road issues refreshing water from Cold Spring. Incidentally, Poso in Spanish means "quiet, repose, sediment"; all descriptive of Poso Creek during the dry season.

As you descend past spur roads leading to

clusters of cabins and drive through two hairpin curves, Sugarloaf Peak appears to your left. You cross through a gateway impeding further traffic east in winter and arrive at Sugarloaf Lodge. Here two rope tows repeatedly transported skiers up a cleared slope of Sugarloaf Peak from 1947 until 1968. Currently (1992) the lodge is run by a nonprofit corporation for the benefit of learning-impaired children.

A heavily-forested village spreads around the lodge. Soon you pass an unpaved road (5.7/13.4) departing north to White River Campground, 3.7 miles. Leaving Sequoia National Forest, your road code changes to **TC Road M-9** and you quickly arrive at a T junction (3.4/16.8) with paved **Camp Road** on which you turn left. Next turn right on paved **Poso Peak Drive** (0.9/17.7), cross Spear Creek, then at a five road junction (0.3/18.0) proceed ahead, southeast on **Sandy Creek Fire Road**. On this road at the crossing of seasonal Von Hellum Creek (4700/0.5/18.5) you meet the end of Marshall Trail 31E60, the route of the bicyclists.

—   —   —   —   —

Cars and bicycles here touring together head south on maintained **Sandy Creek Fire Road** (SNF Road 24S07), now in a lower elevation zone of black and live oaks, but still intermingled with incense cedars, white firs and ponderosa pines. A viewpoint ridge offers views of Linns and San Joaquin valleys, then you turn into the recesses of

Peel Mill Creek (2.6/car 21.1/bike 14.0). Scattered campsites sit by the banks in its shaded nook—and so do cows. Some distance from this ford, the sawmill that gave the creek its name was in service from 1886 until the depression that followed the Spanish-American War.

Your road initially ascends, sometimes steeply, into the creases of the Greenhorn Mountains and around its ridges. The grade eases. In time your road reaches Sandy Creek tumbling amid mossy boulders in its recess. Later forest portals frame views of the mountains to the west and south, and the road passes a spur to the site of Munn Camp. Soon after, it crosses the branches of McFarland Creek and enters into an oak savannah. If you look carefully, you may see a rock duck atop a boulder to the left. It indicates a cross-country route to Bohna Peak, an alternate to the one described in this book. In quick time the road reaches the pavement of **Highway 155** (4860/9.5/car 30.6/bike 23.5) where your route turns left.

Two idyllic campgrounds spread within easy access: Alder Creek Campground at the end of a 3.0 mile descent on the unpaved road south; and after you ascend east on the highway, Cedar Creek Campground (2.5/car 33.1/bike 26.0). Beyond Cedar Creek you spy a cranny where Spout Spring issues forth and in the next cranny, a graceful dogwood tree stands. Quite soon you return to Greenhorn Summit (6102/3.2/car 36.3/bike 29.2), the end of the loop tour.

T35   Black Mountain Climb

Black Mountain's panoramic views rival most views of the Kern River Valley in this book's coverage. The mountain can be easily identified from the valley, and its trailhead can be quickly reached from Greenhorn Summit, adding to the attractiveness of this climb.

Distance   3.2 miles, round trip
Steep Ascents   0.5 mile
Elevation Gain   1204 feet
Skills   Intermediate route finding; Class 2 climbing
Seasons   Spring, summer, fall
Map   USGS 7.5-min. *Alta Sierra*

Trailhead   27. See car tour T32.
Description   **Cane Spring M'cyclepath 32E46**, on which this trip should begin, has been removed from the Forest Service trail grid, and the unmaintained path was heavily damaged by activity during and after the Stormy Complex Fire of 1990. The path may

be redefined and again placed in the system of trails by the time you make this trip. If not, ascend east from Black Saddle (6230/0.0) up the steep slopes on the retired logging road to top Hill 6608. Now drop briefly to a clearing (6600/0.5). Here a rather obscure blaze indicates your trail; you do not climb ahead; rather, you turn left and traverse northeast where the trail becomes more defined. You then climb briefly but steeply east and resume a northeast direction to a wide saddle (6860/0.4). Black Mountain rises to the south.

You leave the trail at the saddle; a duck perched on a stump to the right marks the beginning of your *cross-country* climb. (More lasting clues inform you that you have passed your turnoff: next to the trail in the minor ravine ahead, an incense cedar tree displays a huge blaze; beyond the blaze the trail levels then abruptly descends into a flat above a major ravine.)

Any way up the slopes will get you to the peak. The ducked route may be the easiest, although some of these markers tend to disappear. The route slants east to the ravine above the blazed cedar. It climbs alongside the ravine then on an ascending traverse, among spotty burn sites. It curves around the east side of the first peak on the mountain. The route then drops to a saddle, which opens to great views of Split Mountain.

Cross the saddle to the west side and climb past the second peak of boulders. After dropping to the second saddle on the mountain, climb to the highest point, first on its right side as you face it, then cross over to its left and circle around the final pile of rocks to approach the easy climb up to the summit (7438/0.7). While on the summit, play the game of identifying the peaks on the High Sierra north, Sierra crest east, Piute and Breckenridge mountains south and Greenhorn Mountains west.

Louis Quirarte, in his research of peak-name origins, found that Black Mountain was named by USGS surveyor A. P. Hanson in 1883. Why Hanson named it "Black" is unknown—certainly not for geological reasons, as the mountain's composition consists of Mesozoic granitic rocks.

T36   Split Mountain Climb

The split appearance of this prominent peak attracts the attention of visitors in the Kern River Valley and invites the adventuresome peakbagger. The long, trying approach to its summit tests the determination of the climbers and guarantees that the register book there names only the most resolute.

Distance   8.2 miles, round trip
Steep Ascents   1.2 miles
Elevation Gain   3300 feet
Skills   Intermediate route finding; Class 2 climbing (Class 3–5 pitches optional)
Seasons   Spring, fall
Maps   USGS 7.5-min. *Alta Sierra, Tobias Pk, Kernville*
Trailhead   27. See car tour T32.
Description   The beginning of this trip is described in T35.

Eastbound Trail 32E46 Log

T35	Blk Saddle	6234	0.0
	clearing	6600	0.5
	Blk Mtn exit	6860	0.4

After the Black Mountain cross-country

exit on the saddle, *Cane Spring M'cycle-path 32E46* dips into a minor ravine, levels briefly, then descends through a manzanita aisle and levels again. Here a canyon drops north, to your left. You continue ahead for a short distance, then turn sharply left where another canyon drops east. Your route heads north, then curves east to descend moderately along the ridge to the left of this second canyon. Ducks and a few tree blazes mark the way on the churned terrain.

You soon reach the first of many saddles (6220/0.8) on this long ridge that extends to Split Mountain. At this first saddle, you may wish to visit Cane Spring less than 0.1 mile down-canyon to the north. A trickle from the spring waters a lush colony of bracken ferns presenting a sharp contrast to the black standing trees burned in the 1990 fire that surround it. Rejuvenation of flora appears all about as you progress on this trip. Here and there clumps of wild iris bloom in late spring. The flower of this species blooms white to pale lavender with deep purple veins. Its stem and long, slender leaves grow from bulbs.

Now you proceed *cross-country* generally east near the crest of the extended ridge. The brush that previously demanded difficult bushwhacking from hikers completely burned in the conflagration, but shows regrowth. Stump sprouting black oaks predominate, with kit-kit-dizze the most prolific ground cover. The pairs of pine seedlings you see were laboriously planted throughout the area by Forest Service personnel—it takes special care to keep from stepping on them as you tramp along. You may join a use trail of sorts that developed from the extension of Black Saddle Road as the planters walked among the seedlings.

The undulating route rises over numerous crestline hills, the highest point being Peak 6366, and drops into intervening saddles. The final and steepest drop to a saddle (5740/1.8) precedes the taxing climb following occasional ducks up the peak of Split Mountain (6835/0.6).

The cleavage that divides two separate peaks, but nevertheless inspired the mountain's name, opens dizzyingly to the east, a tempting return trip for climbers of Class 5 rock who want to exercise their skills. The stalwart hiker is rewarded with a stunning view of Isabella Lake and the upper Kern Canyon.

T37   Sunday Peak Day Hike

Atop Sunday Peak you gain views of the Southern Sierra unsurpassed by those from any other peak this far south in the Greenhorn Mountains. Energetic children with parents in tow and out-of-town guests find this hike a special treat.

Distance   3.2 miles, round trip
Steep Ascents   None
Elevation Gain   1105 feet
Skills   Easy route finding; moderate hiking
Seasons   Spring, summer, fall
Map   USGS 7.5-min. *Tobias Pk*
Trailhead   28. See car tour T32.
Description   From the parking circle next to Portuguese Pass Road, *Sunday Peak Trail 31E66* (7190/0.0) climbs a moderate grade northwest, then quickly turns southwest among chinquapin and snow brush under a canopy of fir, pine and incense cedar boughs. The grade soon moderates, and in a short time the trail reaches a saddle (7700/0.7).

(If you are a dedicated peakbagger and exploring Portuguese Peak piques your curiosity; if you are tolerant of bushwhacking, then turn right here to climb north less than 0.3 mile. After dodging trees and pushing through clumps of chinquapin that become 6 feet tall around the summit

boulders, you reach the highest rock and achieve another peak. You can find a can on one of the boulders with a register tablet—it may not be the highest point.

If you enjoy finding springs and Water Gap Spring draws your attention, it issues forth just over 0.1 mile west below the saddle—look for tall willow bushes. A sloping meadow spreads farther downslope. Both dry up during drought years.)

Continuing to Sunday Peak, trace the path south from the saddle, negotiate the switchbacks, turn a corner and note the fir forest on Sunday Peak's north slopes: the late botanist Ernest Twisselmann identified these woods as the southernmost limits of Shasta red fir. Continuing on west-facing slopes above a vale, you turn abruptly left at a junction (7980/0.5) on Telephone Ridge with defunct Telephone Trail 31E67. (Bohna Peak can be reached from here by descending west on the unmaintained trail along the ridge to Point 7473, then south on a use trail along another

Sunday Peak Lookout destroyed by the Forest Service in 1954

ridge.)

Your path, 31E66, leads east, then south to a swale, then north to exit the forest. Now it swings southeast and climbs the granite talus of Sunday Peak (8295/0.4). A lookout built here in the early years of this century housed an attendant who reported to Fulton Ranger Station near Glennville using a phone line that descended Telephone Ridge. Tobias peak blocked the view to the north, so a new lookout was built on that peak in 1937. The structure here was abandoned, and in 1954,

burned by the Forest Service. The roof of the outhouse can still be seen in the brush to the south.

A pivot atop Sunday Peak reveals distant valleys, Sierra peaks, Kern Plateau and southern mountains. In the foreground to the east appears a sweeping view of the Stormy Complex Fire area whose perimeter extends north from Split and Black mountains to Baker Point. The grooves etched on the slopes occurred during the commercially profitable logging of burned trees.

T38   Bull Run Basin Day Hike

This basin, once featured in Sunset magazine as a desirable place to camp and fish, was ravaged when the Stormy Complex Fire of 1990 roared through it. Its recovery is fascinating to see: the sequence of regrowth; the return of fish and other wildlife.

Distance   2.4 miles, round trip
Steep Ascents   0.5 mile
Elevation Gain   1080 feet
Skills   Easy route finding; moderate-to-strenuous hiking

Seasons   Spring, summer, fall
Map   USGS 7.5-min. *Tobias Pk*
Trailhead   29. See car tour T32. Drive south on **SNF Road 24S35**, skirt east of Tyler Meadow and cross a branch of Bull Run

Creek (0.7/0.7). Continue through burned and logged terrain on east-facing slopes, then in quick succession, pass a cattleguard, a left spur road and park on the wide shoulder at **TH29** (1.9/2.6)—look for the descending path near the crest of a ridge.

Description *Bull Run M'cyclepath 32E39* (6140/0.0) first makes a brief traverse, then leads steeply southeast down the ridgecrest. Manzanita and yerba santa appear among the regrowth, and kit-kit-dizze has returned as ground cover. The most vigorous growth is the stump sprouting of black oak and brewers oak. The ponderosa and sugar pines, incense cedars and white firs remain as black skeletons or have been removed for their salvageable timber. Plots of ground along the path have been replanted by volunteers under Forest Service direction. Highly commercial ponderosa trees dominate the plots, but, surprisingly, some giant sequoia seedlings appear among them. Surprising, because sequoias prefer moist, north-facing slopes; these are dry, east-facing

slopes in the rain shadow of the Greenhorn crest.

The grade finally eases at a ford of Schultz Creek prior to its confluence with Bull Run Creek. Here the trail leads across the braided cascading creek on metamorphic rocks in a refreshing glen of large-leafed thimbleberries.

Beyond the ford the path rises briefly, then descends to the floor of Bull Run Basin where it passes one of several campsites scattered across this basin. Then the trail arrives at Bull Run Creek (5060/1.2), usually an easy boulder ford. This pleasant place to pause before returning offers welcome shade and color from the fast growing alder trees among the blackened trunks.

(If you wish to explore further, the trail continues across the basin, following Bull Run, then Deep and Cow creeks. Where it nears a cluster of mines and a private road along Cow Creek, you may find a path that reaches the ridgecrest and zigzags up to a spur road. The road eventually reaches the Portuguese Pass Road south of Tiger Flat.)

T39   Baker Point Lookout Day Hike

Seen from the heights of Baker Point, Kernville resembles a tiny alpine village—a picture-postcard setting nestled in a canyon between craggy peaks. Views of the upper Kern Canyon are just as spectacular.

Distance   2.4 miles, round trip
Steep Ascents   None
Elevation Gain   350 feet
Skills   Easy route finding; easy-to-moderate hiking; not recommended for equestrians
Seasons   Spring, summer, fall
Map   USGS 7.5-min. *Tobias Pk*
Trailhead   30. See car tour T32.
Description   Uncertainty shrouds the fate of this lookout. The Forest Service stopped manning it by 1992. Whether it will be removed, or left standing as a historical building or for some other use, remains uncertain.

Baker Lookout Trail 32E37 begins east of the parking area (7420/0.0) on the crest of a slim ridge that culminates at Baker Point. In its first few hundred yards, the wide, level trail crosses a forested north-facing slope

parallel to an older path visible just down the slope. The path you tred was built during the 1960s so tractors could ferry supplies to the lookout, but construction was halted when funds ran out. Later helicopters transported supplies ending any further work on the new trail. You can see how much more blasting on this section would have been needed to accommodate tractors.

The trail soon reaches a linkage with the old path—the left fork—which you take. (The right fork suddenly stops at a cliffy protrusion.) A forest of white fir, Jeffrey, ponderosa and sugar pine offers shade and view-framing vignettes of the upper Kern Canyon to the High Sierra with prominent views of Dome Rock and The Needles in the foreground. Your path gently descends across talus to avoid the cliff face, climbs a short, steep grade, then undulates, zigzags and rounds a north-trending ridge. It ends at rocky Baker Point (7754/1.2), which was spared from the Stormy Complex Fire.

Here the venerable white-washed lookout hovers over an equally old cabin. Not far removed squats the wall-papered outhouse fully equipped with a lightning rod.

T40   Baker Peak Climb

This peak, the highest point on the extensive north-south Baker Ridge, beckons confirmed peakbaggers and would-be climbers to include it in tandem with the Baker Point hike.

Distance   1.8 miles, round trip
Steep Ascents   0.1 mile
Elevation Gain   510 feet
Skills   Intermediate route finding; Class 2 climbing
Seasons   Spring, summer, fall
Map   USGS 7.5-min. *Tobias Pk*
Trailhead   30. See car tour T32.
Description   From the Baker Point trailhead (7420/0.0), with its superb views of Kernville and Isabella Lake far below, turn west to climb *cross-country* among burn debris over an insignificant hill. Next curve

north near an even-aged plantation of planted saplings that escaped the Stormy Complex Fire. From that point on, climb north, usually just below the crest outcrops, to the farthest and highest cluster of granite, sometimes barely visible among the trees as you approach. Scramble up the brief chute on the west side to the top of the highest boulder (7926/0.9). You will find a register there.

The views, pleasant but undramatic, include to the north the canyons of Tobias and Flynn, and to the east the peaks of the Kern Plateau.

Baker Point and Ridge from North Fork Kern River

T41   Parker Pass Car & Bicycle Tour: Ducor to Kern River
(With Directions to Trailheads 31–37)

This tour broadens your knowledge of past events while surrounding you in the beauty of the forested Greenhorn Mountains. You journey through pastoral small towns steeped in nature's abundance and rooted in California's history. For a trans-Sierra route, combine this tour with a similarly stimulating journey over the Kern Plateau described in Exploring the Southern Sierra: East Side.

Distance   51.0 miles, one way
Steep Ascents   None (Long, hard grades for bicyclists)
Elevation Gain   5900 feet
Skills   Easy route finding; paved road
Seasons   Spring, summer, fall
Map   Tulare County road map
Tourhead   31. The intersection of north-south Highway 65 and east-west Highway J22, east of Earlimart in Ducor is **TH31**.
Description   The route changes code numbers several times, but remains direct and easy to follow. Although not a major thoroughfare, bicyclists need to be extra cautious because of blind dips and curves.

This tour begins east on *TC Highway J22* (Avenue 56; Parker Pass Drive) at the tourhead intersection (545/0.0/0.0). Your road immediately enters the small town of Ducor where German homesteaders settled in 1885. They called it Dutch Corners (not German Corners?). The name was shortened to Ducor when the Southern Pacific Railroad Company built their east side line through it in

Resort rebuilt in 1985

1888.

The straight ahead, roller coaster road travels by orange groves, hay fields and pastures to an intersection (790/7.6/7.6) with Old Stage Drive of car tour T18 at Fountain Springs, a hamlet consisting of a fire station, a saloon and a few far flung ranches. A landmark plaque west of the saloon informs passersby that Fountain Springs first developed 1½ miles northwest next to the springs. The springs were at the intersection of the Los Angeles-Stockton Road and a road to the Kern River mines. Between 1858–61 it served as a station on the Butterfield Overland Stage Route.

Your route continues east, now coded *TC Road M-56*. It travels over blue oak- then buckeye-dotted grassy hills that quickly turn golden by mid-spring. It passes TC Road M-15 (11.9/19.5), now a gated private road, ascends above the valley of Speas Creek, with its ponds and ranch houses, and tops a summit where views unfold of a picturesque valley extending along Deer Creek. The road descends to that quaint vale where a church is called "Lily of the Valley." Your route crosses Deer Creek and shortly arrives at Sequoia National Forest's Leavis Flat Campground (6.0/25.5) just inside the forest's border, a pleasant year-round, live oak- and sycamore-shaded campground on the banks of gently flowing Deer Creek.

Just up the road, the village of California Hot Springs seems dwarfed by sparkling white California Hot Springs Resort. Founded in 1882, it was built as a health resort. Visitors bathed in the 125° F water that spewed forth at 350,000 gallons a day, bubbling up out of the Deer Creek fault. By

1968 fires had gutted the last of the buildings. The recreation hall, with its spacious oak dance floor, was restored in 1985 along with the hot springs pool; an RV Park was added. It attracts numerous visitors today, as it did in the 1800s.

Beyond the village you come to a T junction (2.3/27.8) where you turn left on M-50. However, those heading for **THs32&33** and for White River Campground, continue on M-56, which curves right and is described within the following brackets.

Turn south on *TC Road M-56* (0.0/0.0) where you quickly reach a forked junction (0.2/0.2). Here those looking for **TH32** of T42, the Greenhorn crest hike, and others wishing to visit Deer Creek Grove, which has the distinction of being the southernmost sequoia grove, take the left fork, TC Road M-51. The grove is 3.0 miles in.

If you seek **TH33** and the campground, continue past the fork on M-56 through the village of Pine Flat (0.4/0.6). A restaurant, store, gas station, phone and laundromat serve the cozy community and others in need. Cross Capinero Creek and continue through the T junction (1.3/1.9) with Manter Meadow Drive, even though the sign says ROAD ENDS 500 FEET. The pavement and county road indeed end, but unpaved *SNF Road 23S05* abuts and on it you pass Bony Witt Fire Road, climb over Capinero Saddle, descend past Betty Waller Meadow and, just prior to the river, reach **TH33** (2.8/4.7) of T43, a trip to Ames Hole.

Campsites can be found here and at Upper White River Campground across the bridge off SNF Road 24S05. Pine- and cedar-shaded Lower White River Campground (0.4/5.1) has for a fee all the needed facilities.

Left from the T junction, traveling north, now on *TC Road M-50*, referred to as Parker Pass Drive, you immediately meet a driveway (0.1/27.9) to a phone kiosk and the inviting buildings with extensive, deep-green, manicured lawns of the Hot Springs Ranger Station. This station was previously named "Uhl," pronounced "you'll," the same pronunciation used by the contemporaries of the namesake homesteader, a vegetable truck farmer.

Your road passes the station entrance and dips to cross Tyler Creek, where overarching alders and laurels shade a campsite nook next to water riffling over boulders. Ahead your route curves right of SNF Closed Road 22S31. Merry Camp Trail 31E46 originates here; it will reopen after its realignment to avoid private property. Beyond, the road negotiates a series of U turns, passing first Dead Mule and then Cold Springs saddles en route.

Cold Springs Saddle (8.6/36.5) presents four interesting diversions: the parking area to the right is **TH34** for T44, Cold Springs Peak climb. Ahead, SNF Road 23S66 (0.1/36.6) branches left, northwest, to **TH35** for T45, a climb of Hatchet Peak. Between the two, to the right, SNF Road 23S29 descends east to reach the canyon of Starvation Creek below, where giant sequoia buffs will find the small Starvation Creek sequoia grove.

In this same canyon, the last California Condor to hatch in the wild was taken from his nest and placed under the auspices of the condor breeding program. Condors are listed as state and federally endangered birds, which provides protection for them and money to promote their numbers.

In 1980 the last 30 California Condors rode the thermals in Southern California in

Johnsondale's R-Ranch in the Sequoias

Gas pump at Lower Durrwood Lodge

search of carrion, and that number decreased. Alarmed, biologists captured the remaining condors, the last taken in 1987, and took them to the Los Angeles and San Diego zoos for care and breeding. The million dollar a year breeding program succeeded. In 1988 the first egg was laid in captivity; by 1994 there were 87 birds and the release of young condors into their natural habitat began.

These black vultures with featherless heads have a wingspread of up to 9½ feet. Their size and the white under-wing feathers help you identify them in flight. It is possible that someday they will return to soar over this canyon and perhaps other Southern Sierra sites.

Ascending again, the road skirts a ridge high above the canyon of Starvation Creek to cross the crest of the Greenhorn Mountains at Parker Pass (6443/1.9/38.5). Parker Pass separates the Greenhorn Mountains to the south from the Western Divide mountains to the north. Here the Parker Meadow Cross-Country Ski Trail offers an interesting marked route for skiers.

Next you enter a curvilinear corridor through needle-and broad-leafed forest. You may notice spring blooming dogwood lacing the high mountain countryside; you will notice a signed Penny Pines project. The

Forest Service plants trees of commercial value in areas where trees were logged or burned using funds from contributions to its Penny Pines reforestation program. Beyond the sign, you arrive at **TH36**, a T junction (6376/1.1/39.6) with northbound Western Divide Highway (TC Road M-107) of car tour T46 to **THs38–48**.

You proceed on Parker Pass Drive with Double Bunk Meadow to your right, then Double Bunk Creek, a branch of South Creek. An unnamed dome looms ahead. You soon pass to your right, winding SNF Road 23S16 (Sugarloaf Road; Forest Highway 50) (5430/3.3/42.9) the north end of car tour T32. Shortly after, as you swing north, two unpaved turnouts offer spacious views of Johnsondale's R-Ranch with Capitol Rock hovering to its northeast. To your northeast, pointed Sentinel Peak (T65) seems to be in immediate contact with the farther pinnacles of The Needles (T51). Minutes later you meet to your left a T Junction (4828/3.2/46.1) with paved SNF Road 22S82 (Lloyd Meadows Road) **TH37** of car tour T64 to **THs49–54**.

On your road, now coded *TC Road M-99*, you arrive at Johnsondale's R-Ranch in the Sequoias (0.7/46.8), an active community reflecting the growing change from commodity dominance to recreation opportunities in the Southern Sierra.

In 1935 Mount Whitney Lumber Company started operating a mill here at 750-acre Johnsondale using ponderosa, sugar and Jeffrey pine, red and white fir and incense cedar trees felled from the surrounding mountains. The company-owned town of cabins, school, post office, store, meeting hall and hospital housed between four to six hundred people during its most productive period. It closed operations in 1979.

In 1990 Johnsondale reopened as "R-Ranch in the Sequoias." The rustic cabins and other buildings had been brought up to code. A camping area, pool, lake, tennis courts and RV Park were added. Once again Johnsondale flourishes, now as a vacation resort. Snow plows keep the road east of here clear for their winter activity.

East of Johnsondale you wind high above the near canyon. Ahead, across the river canyon you see that a band of whitish granite slashes the slopes of the Kern Plateau mountains—not unusual. Beneath it you see a grayish band of limestone—much less common. Limestone is found on the east slopes of the Greenhorn Mountains and the west slopes of the plateau, reaching to Isabella Lake. If you drive south along the Kern River you may notice holes in that band that pock the very steep slopes above Limestone Campground—possible caves. Farther on you will pass the path to Packsaddle Cave of T45 in *Exploring the Southern Sierra: East Side*.

Your route leaves the trees and descends amid brush until it nears South Creek where secluded Lower Durrwood Lodge (3.4/50.2) nestles. The lodge was located here on higher ground after the original camp, ½ mile north of Road's End, washed away in a 1937 Kern River flood. The buildings of the rebuilt camp sit invitingly tucked among the huge ash, ponderosa, willow and redbud trees next to the chortling creek.

In minutes you arrive at a viewpoint for the falls of South Creek. Here the thunderous sound of the 100-foot falls resounds during snowmelt. A spectacular falls at that time, but breathtaking any time of year when seen from the narrow viewing ledge next to the road. Caution signs mean what they say. After a short descent from the viewpoint, you arrive at the magnificent Kern River where it follows the graceful curves of its colorful canyon.

The original Johnsondale bridge, now a foot bridge, was built for the lumber project at Johnsondale. The parking lot (3820/0.8/51.0) at the bridge serves whitewater rafters, kayakers, canoers, fishermen and the trailhead for the river hike described in T99 of this book's companion edition. Detailed in that book, too, are the two roads immediately across the bridge: Sherman Pass Road (T52) that climbs across the Kern Plateau to Highway 395; TC Road M-99 (T37) that travels to Kernville and Isabella Lake.

South Creek's spectacular falls

T42   Greenhorn Crest-Lion Ridge Backpack

Hikers brimming with energy, eager for a challenging trip or a conditioning hike, will find this rousing loop outing to their liking. A secluded campground at verdant Frog Meadow atop the Greenhorn crest and spacious views of San Joaquin Valley from the trail add to the appeal of this journey.

Distance   14.6 miles, loop trip
Steep Ascents   0.3 mile
Elevation Gain   3500 feet
Skills   Intermediate route finding
Seasons   Spring, summer, fall
Maps   USGS 7.5-min. *Johnsondale, Tobias Pk, Calif Hot Sprs*
Trailhead   32. See car tour T41. From the junction of TC Road M-56 east of California Hot Springs, turn left on **TC Road M-51** (SNF Road 23S04) (0.0/0.0). The road becomes unpaved. Pass the second cattle guard (1.2/1.2) where your return path climbs up from the canyon. Drive on to a right-hand clearing (0.8/2.0) above the road at **TH32**.
Description   If you take this trip in the fall, you may not find water at Frog Meadow, the only water source until Deer Creek, near the end of the trip; therefore, you will need to tote your entire supply.

From the trailhead parking lot (4460/0.0) **Deer Creek M'cyclepath 31E54** ascends east, then south, nicely shaded by incense cedars and black oaks; later white firs and sugar pines join their ranks. The object of all the halved 1935 license plates you see supplementing blazes along this trail is to guide the snow surveyors who use the trail to reach Dead Horse Meadow for measurements of the snow's depth and moisture content.

The moderate-to-steep path climbs up north-facing slopes, eases, then angles across a logging road. A spur path forges ahead, but your path turns right immediately after the crossing, then parallels the road for a short stint. The ascent becomes gentler and flats for possible dry camping appear. The route crosses the road again and just beyond meets a T junction (5840/2.0) where Deer Creek Trail ends. Your route turns left onto **Frog Meadow M'cyclepath 31E56** and heads northeast.

For the third time you angle across the same logging road, then pass an unmarked junction with Sequoia Grove Trail 31E55 (5960/0.2), which is a steep, disappointing path through scars where loggers removed pine and fir amid local sequoias in the 1920s. Of the 130+ sequoias scattered across about 180 acres in the Deer Creek Grove, 31E55 visits only one.

On your dusty path, so typical of heavily used motorcycle paths, you switchback up the Deer Creek/Capinero Creek divide. After the grade eases, you loop around two meadows and head east to join paved **SNF Road 24S82** (7670/2.2). On this road, still heading east, you arrive at a triangle junction (7680/0.1) with SNF Road 24S50. To reach restful Frog Meadow Campground, turn right at this junction for 0.1 mile. Next turn left on SNF Road 24S86 for 0.4 mile past a seldom-used Forest Service guard station to the campground located on the north edge among the conifer trees that ring emerald-green Frog Meadow. Once a hydrant gushing spring water served the camp, but now you obtain water as best you can. Across the long grass with hidden springtime white violets, a forgotten, silvery wood cabin reflects bygone years.

Continuing ahead on the route at the triangle junction, you pass the next corner of the triangle, now on **SNF Road 24S50** traveling north. Ascend slightly on the road to mount a ridge and pass a spur road that leaves to the right. Now you have a "B" added to you road code. Evidence of heavy logging remains; seedlings have been planted in clear-cut areas. The hulking Kern Plateau appears to the right while you trudge along to arrive at Sand Flat (7750/1.0) with its campsite. It seems such an inconsequential place to be named. Here you leave your road, which curves to descend east.

You march ahead still north, on another *logging road* past a gate. Watch carefully to the right upon reaching the crest of the road lest you pass the sometimes unsigned, rock-lined entrance (7800/0.1) to **Packsaddle M'cyclepath 31E53** (also called Pup Meadow Trail) ascending in a replanted clear-cut. On the trail you hike east of a pair of hills, then cross a saddle where you see below the end of the road you recently left. You now leave the Greenhorn crest for a long west-slope traverse on a gentle downgrade. Clearings en route offer westward views of the San Joaquin Valley, especially comprehensive during windy days.

A mile beyond the saddle, the trail bends around a squared-off spur ridge and runs past sloping meadows to which willows and corn lilies cling. Then the tread leads straight ahead past Speas Meadow Trail 32E31 (7600/1.7) that takes off into the forest northeast. Your path continues to twist along the headwall of the Deer Creek watershed, and brush continues to hang heavily over the path. West-trending Lion Ridge and the logging road cutting across it appear ahead. Your trail curves west, ascends onto Lion Ridge and drops below to that road you saw (7360/0.9), leaving Packsaddle Trail.

Massive clear-cutting in the late 1980s slashed the steep slopes on both sides of Lion Ridge and mauled its crest. Until Lion Ridge Trail 31E52 (your next trail) has been clearly reestablished, you turn left to hike south on the logging road, *SNF Road 23S23*, through a deep cut of metamorphic rock, then southwest, first on the left, then the right of the ridge. You stay on the road until it turns south to round the ridge at a saddle (6740/1.1), where you leave it. (The road then turns back, east, and descends into the canyon of Deer Creek.)

Look for a *path* at the saddle heading up the south side of a low hill among planted trees. On it you curve around the hill to meet **Lion Ridge M'cyclepath 31E52** (6840/0.3), which you join to course west, down the ridge under welcome boughs of uncut white fir, black oak, incense cedar and sugar pine. A

few flats offer camping possibilities on the narrow crest. Along the way broad views of bald ridges around California Hot Springs sporadically appear. Descend a stairway of switchbacks, often eroded by short-cutting motorcyclists. Ascend a small hill and walk along the ridge; then more zigzags take you onto grassy slopes. Be alert now for the next major junction which for years had been marked only by a post to the left of the path.

Turn left at the post on **Deer Creek M'cyclepath 31E54** (4980/3.0) to cross the canyon southward, here on a grassy expanse where you find another post, then more that mark the route. On the path descending a minor ridge between ravines, you drop sometimes steeply into the canyon of Deer Creek favored in spring with myriad wildflowers of five-spot, baby blue eyes, buttercups and miner's lettuce. In time you arrive at the banks of Deer Creek, the first fully-flowing, all-season stream on this journey. Its dulcet music, cool water and sylvan setting will certainly refresh any wilting spirits. Cross on boulders and depart by scrambling steeply up the path to your ingress dirt road, *SNF Road 23S04* (4240/1.2). You exit by the cattle guard.

Now on the final leg of this challenging and varied journey, you turn left to head up the road to your starting point (4460/0.8).

Forlorn cabin at Frog Meadow

T43   Ames Hole Day Hike

Along this trip, cedars, pines and oaks unfurl their awnings over the trail, which seldom leaves the White River canyon. At Ames Hole the river drops in a 30-foot, alder-framed fall before coursing over a bed of sand in the grassy glen.

Distance   4.6 miles, round trip
Steep Ascents   0.1 mile
Elevation Gain   1060 feet
Skills   Easy-to-intermediate route finding; moderate hiking
Seasons   Spring, fall
Map   USGS 7.5-min. *Posey*
Trailhead   33. See car tour T41.
Description   *White River Trail 31E58* (4180/0.0) starts across the river from Upper White River Campground and descends west, first on road then on trail where it crosses a seasonal tributary from Betty Waller Meadow. The path remains in earshot of wind chimes disguised as riffles on White River: White River, a creek disguised as a river. The trail, pungent with a catalog of fallen leaves, passes north of the White River Campground and leads through a cow fence. The path crosses flats reeking with fly-infested cow pies and passes cow paths that can cause momentary route confusion.

As you progress farther west, canyon slopes close in on the river like a vise, and your path nears the melodious water. Then the river slides away from your trail through a sequence of cascades. You continue descending, but now across slopes high in the White River canyon. Soon you enter a zone of live oak, manzanita and mountain mahogany where the trail is no longer sheltered. Then your gentle descent becomes steep momentarily as it dips down into a ravine.

Here the trail maintenance stops; brush and branches close in on the path. The gentle downgrade resumes for ¼ mile passing huge boulders. The path zigzags, sometimes steeply down a ridge between the river and a neighboring canyon, then arrives at Ames Hole (3120/2.3).

In spring, snowmelt swells the falls descent to a whirling, thundering cloud of spray and foam; by autumn its drop fades into a gentle whisper of placid water.

T44   Cold Springs Peak Climb

An easy ascent for beginning peakbaggers, this peak is often linked with Hatchet Peak for an unhurried day of climbing. Particularly good views of the valleys and hills to the south reward this effort.

Distance   0.6 mile, round trip
Steep Ascents   0.1 mile
Elevation Gain   375 feet
Skills   Easy route finding; Class 1 climbing (Class 3 pitches optional)
Seasons   Spring, summer, fall
Map   USGS 7.5-min. *Calif Hot Sprs*
Trailhead   34. See car tour T41.
Description   From the Cold Springs Saddle parking area (5780/0.0) southeast of TC Road M-50, head directly south to climb *cross-country* first gently, then moderately,

up the uneven terrain of the mountain, selectively logged to the summit. White fir, black oak and sugar and Jeffrey pine remain to shade the way and to surround the topside boulders (6153/0.3) where the register can rests.

For the nice southern views descend farther south to an outcrop. Climb around its prominence east to south to the jumble of rocks at its base. There you can sit and snack and enjoy the scenery. The outcrop itself offers fine Class 3 climbs.

Section 3

Parker Pass Drive (J22) to Sequoia National Park
—Western Divide Mountains
& Golden Trout Wilderness—

Peppermint Creek falls and cascades 200 feet over massive slabs

T45 Hatchet Peak Climb

Perched on the west slopes of the Greenhorn Mountains, this well-defined peak offers a commanding view of the California Hot Springs area and the extensive San Joaquin Valley.

Distance 0.8 mile, round trip
Steep Ascents 0.2 mile
Elevation Gain 520 feet
Skills Easy route finding; Class 2 climbing
Seasons Spring, summer, fall
Map USGS 7.5-min. *Calif Hot Sprs*
Trailhead 35. See car tour T41. From the junction (0.0/0.0) with TC Road M-50, (Parker Pass Drive) drive northwest on *SNF Road 22S66* past a cattleguard to a broad, cleared saddle cul-de-sac (0.6/0.6).
Description From the cul-de-sac (5900/

0.0), walk west southwest along a *road*, then on a *use path*, occasionally identified by ribbons, climb the steep slopes west up Hatchet Peak. A selectively logged mixed forest provides shade. Boulders interspersed with kit-kit-dizze suggest you are near your goal. Once there, you can enjoy the expansive views from the base of the summit rock, or make use of slim hand and footholds to wriggle up to the top of the boulder where you find a register can (6416/0.4).

T46 Western Divide Highway Car & Bicycle Tour
(With Directions to Trailheads 38–48)

This tour presents an array of visual diversities: distant views of rugged horizons jagged downward by canyons, upward by domes, set in green basins; and near views of meadows and streams sheltered by mixed forests laced with quivering aspen and crowned by giant sequoias.

Distance 25.1 miles, one way
Steep Ascents None
Elevation Gain 4060 feet
Skills Easy route finding; paved & unpaved roads
Seasons Spring, summer, fall
Map Tulare County road map
Tourhead 36. The junction of TC Road M-50 (Parker Pass Drive; J22) and TC Road M-107 (Western Divide Highway) is **TH36**. It is 39.6 miles east of Highway 65 in Ducor and 11.4 miles west of the Kern River at Johnsondale Bridge. This trip departs from car tour T41.
Description The highway's lack of blind curves makes this tour particularly attractive to bicyclists.

To begin, turn north from the tourhead junction (6376/0.0/0.0) onto the *Western Divide Highway*. You quickly pass an access road (0.4/0.4) to Holey Meadow Campground, the first of five campgrounds along

this trip. If you want a nonfee campsite, you will find a wide selection along the numerous logging roads.

After bridging Parker Meadow Creek, you pass through a corridor of dense forest where sequoias begin to appear. From the parking area (2.0/2.4) for the Trail of 100 Giants, outstanding sequoias of the Long Meadow Grove, **TH38** of T47, walkers and wheelchair occupants can take advantage of the self-guided tour of the big trees. This 0.6 mile loop walk winds among many sizable sequoias, and the frequent plaques along the trail supply interesting facts about the trees and grove. This stately grove is the easiest to reach of the many groves in the Western Divide mountains. Immediately beyond, Redwood Meadow Campground (0.1/2.5) offers comfortable camping for tree viewers and another access to the walk among the giants.

Now on a prolonged ascent, you journey

Ponderosa Lodge off Western Divide Highway

past SNF Road 22S08 (0.7/3.2) to Long Meadow Campground, one of two nonfee campgrounds just off this route. You next contour through the willow- and alder-graced canyon of Bone Creek, and then reach northwestbound SNF Road 22S03 (1.5/4.7) to Mule Peak Lookout and the Summit Trail, **THs39&40**. Those not seeking these features continue ahead and skip the following description.

To reach **THs39&40**, turn left onto unpaved **SNF Road 22S03** (0.0/0.0), ascend generally west on the oft-bumpy, sometimes steep, narrow surface following on the right side of Bone Creek, which lies below and out of view. Pass spur roads and the T junction (2.5/2.5) with SNF Road 22S04. Continue on 22S03, now heading north, pass Crane Meadow to a forked junction (2.0/4.5). Ascend the left fork, **SNF Road 22S03J** to **TH39** (0.1/4.6) for Mule Peak Lookout of T48.

For the Summit Trail continue on SNF Road 22S03, pass a right-hand spur to campsites in the woods near Crane Meadow, climb over a saddle, and descend through one switchback. Drive beyond the brush-hidden trail of T49 (1.4/6.0) that you seek, which angles in from the left, to park your car at the next switchback, **TH40**.

Beyond the lookout turnoff, you pass an unpaved connector road (0.9/5.6) that descends to Lloyd Meadows Road, which parallels this highway at a lower elevation, then pass Crawford Road. (This extensive road climbs the handsome Nobe Creek basin to Windy Gap, eventually reaches a corner of the Tule River Indian Reservation, passes Coy Flat Campground and ends at Camp Nelson, around 21.0 miles away: an interesting exploratory adventure for mountain bikers and drivers.)

Your wide, paved highway crosses the headwater branches of Alder Creek while rounding the southeast slopes of Slate Mountain. It soon curves in the bend of Horse Canyon and Dry Meadow Creek where contact between iron-stained quartzite and once-molten invading granodiorite has created a noticeable contrast in colors. Ahead, Dome Rock fronting The Needles occurs in northeastward captivating views. Beyond the depths of Kern Canyon, sweeping vistas of the Kern Plateau entice admiring glances. In the immediate springtime roadside scenery, the scarlet leaf buds of black oaks embellish the evergreens of pines and cedars.

Your road next crosses Dome Creek and arrives at SNF Road 21S69 (6.0/11.6) to the right, tucked in the far side of a low hill, easily missed from your direction. If time allows, a 0.6 mile drive to **TH41**, and a brief, easy walk to top Dome Rock of T50 reward you with breathtaking views. Hidden climbers may be inching up the face of this dome, so please avoid dislodging loose rocks.

Nearly opposite the road to Dome Rock exits the paved road to a Forest Service heliport and fire-crew barracks. Soon SNF Road 21S07 (0.8/12.4) leads east 0.8 mile to Upper Peppermint Campground (nonfee) next to Peppermint Creek. Shortly beyond the camp turnoff and creek, you arrive at rustic, friendly Ponderosa Resort (1.1/13.5). Here a year-round store, gas pumps, coffee shop, phone booth, winter rentals and real estate office meet the needs of both visitors and residents. The highway is cleared of snow north of here. Your trip to this point makes an inviting cross-country ski or snowmobile route, departing from the resort.

Slender, light-barked quaking aspen trees now line your route. Their roundish leaves, vivid green in spring, bright gold in fall, respond to the slightest breeze. This trembling or quivering led to the tree's name.

Soon you encounter the entrance to Quaker Meadow, the location of a church camp, then arrive at SNF Road 21S05 (1.0/14.5) to the right. After your visit to the 100 Giants and Dome Rock, the next side trip could be to the stunning Needles Lookout from **TH42** at the end of this road. (See T51.)

At the following intersection of importance (7046/0.8/15.3), unpaved SNF Road 21S99 peels off to the right heading for the Freeman Creek Sequoia Grove, **TH44** of T55. One of the 50 largest sequoias in the world grows near the path in this halcyon setting of big trees, sparkling creek and slender canyon. To the left a Forest Service Guard Station sits on the perimeter of sprawling Quaking Aspen Campground, **TH43**. This popular campground, built in 1957 among the red firs, not aspens, often offers evening slide shows and talks. Here sightseers and bicyclists may wish to end their journey north. The tour continues, however, for those seeking **THs45–48**.

Beyond the campground, the highway curves around a meadowy headwater of the South Fork Middle Fork Tule River, then it melds into State Highway 190 of car tour T74. At this point paved *SNF Road 21S50* (North Road) (6970/0.2/15.5) branches off to the right, which you take. Now your route heads north among red fir trees while skirting a willow, aspen and yarrow meadow. In minutes a triangle junction (0.4/15.9) with SNF Road 21S99 appears to the right, another approach to the Freeman Creek Sequoia Grove.

Your road straight ahead, as well as most roads in the Southern Sierra, was built for logging, and evidence of heavy cutting appears along its entire length. The route curves and twists, passes a Boulder Creek branch, then proceeds past a western segment of Lewis Camp Trail 33E01 near a Fire Safe Area campsite. At the next fork of note (3.7/19.6), your route, the left fork, loses good pavement while to the right, briefly paved SNF Road 20S79 summons those seeking **TH45** for Ts56–58 and the Golden Trout Pack Station.

To reach **TH45** from the junction (0.0/0.0), take the right fork, *SNF Road 20S79*. After an initial wiggly switchback, you travel along a rolling course, pass Deer Trail 32E17, then stay right onto *SNF Road 20S53* (2.2/2.2) when the road you were on swings north to Loggy Meadows. Shortly a WELCOME TO GOLDEN TROUT WILDERNESS PACK TRAIN sign greets you and informs you that the kitchen is open at the pack station, a cluster of several buildings (0.3/2.5). The western segment of Lewis Camp Trail 33E01 joins the road. You then arrive at a spacious parking area, **TH45** (0.7/3.2), and a few campsites with tables and an outhouse.

Those destined for **THs46–48** remain on SNF Road 21S50, now mostly dirt with patches of thin pavement. It soon passes through a junction with SNF Road 20S81 to the left. Moments later your route arrives at Clicks Creek Trailhead, **TH46** for Ts59&60 (1.5/21.1), offering plenty of parking space and a few campsites.

Continuing ahead, you quickly pass

Clicks Creek, then a Summit Trail crossing— the first of four crossings—and climb to another fork (1.3/22.4) where you stay right. The left fork, SNF Road 20S71, carries you west to Jordan Peak Lookout of T61 at

TH47. Continuing to the last trailhead, you ascend to a saddle, and then descend to a road split (2.4/24.8) where you climb on the left fork to a clearing at Summit Trailhead, **TH48** (8280/0.3/25.1) of Ts62&63.

T47   Trail of a Hundred Giants Day Hike

This cathedral of impressive sequoias overwhelms the senses and embues the viewer with a feeling of reverence. Giant Sequoia, Sequoiadendron giganteum, is a species of tree considered the largest living organism in the world by volume. A nearly level path constructed for wheelchair use provides access to these magnificent trees for people of all ages and abilities.

Distance   0.6 miles, loop trip
Steep Ascents   None
Elevation Gain   100 feet
Skills   Easy route finding; easy hiking
Seasons   Spring, summer, fall
Map   USGS 7.5-min. *Johnsondale* (trail does not appear on provisional edition)
Trailhead   38. See car tour T46.
Description   A path north of the highway gives you access from the trailhead parking lot to the loop trail. The lot provides wheelchair access restrooms. If camping at Redwood Meadow Campground, a shorter path opposite the camp entrance leads you from the highway to the loop trail.

This easily accessible *Trail of a Hundred Giants* (6140/0.0) plunges you immediately into the grove of lofty, cinnamon-colored trees. The loop trail's wide, smooth path never exceeds a 6% grade. The 13 interpretive stations along the way provide information about the sequoias and the companion trees and animals that inhabit the area. A few benches serve the viewer's desire to linger with these mammoth sentinels of the forest. Although a short walk, a full measure of time should be allowed to appreciate the wonder of these trees in the silence of the towering grove before returning to your car or camp (6140/0.6). Future plans include an additional quarter mile loop trail to a sequoia that fell around 200 years ago. Many of these trees show little signs of decay centuries after they fall. Some scientists attribute this to the heartwood's high tannin, which discourages insects and fungi. However, the logs do lose

their moisture and eventually they are consumed by forest fires.

This grove includes 125 sequoias over 10 feet in diameter—nearly double most adult Americans' heights. The estimated ages of the trees here range from 500 to 1500 years old. The largest giant in this 355-acre grove— not on this loop—measures 20 feet in diameter at breast height and 220 feet in height. It reigns among the 50 largest by volume of all measured sequoias known.

Volunteers from the Kern River Valley worked with the Forest Service on the construction of the loop path. Their labor, as indicated on a plaque, was dedicated to the late Carol Heffner, who gave much of her time to the betterment of the valley community and surrounding area, and also worked on this project.

Giant sequoias interest all ages

T48   Mule Peak Lookout Hike

An opportunity to attain an inspiring panorama and to observe a nerve center of fire-fighting operations makes this lookout-topped peak a favorite of people of all ages. Serious climbers will also be attracted here by the exclusive cliffs and pinnacles on the southwest face of the peak.

Distance   1.2 miles, round trip
Steep Ascents   None
Elevation Gain   545 feet
Skills   Easy route finding; easy-to-moderate hiking (Class 4&5 climbing optional)
Seasons   Spring, summer, fall
Map   USGS 7.5-min. *Sentinel Pk*
Trailhead   39. See car tour T46.
Description   The excursion begins from the lot (7600/0.0) a few miles west of Western Divide Highway. *Mule Peak M'cyclepath 31E43* leads west up a moderate grade across a large patch of stumps with a few standing red firs and ponderosa pines. Replanted ponderosa trees share the open space with currants and other bushes. The

palmate-leafed currant differs from the similar-appearing gooseberry in that its stems lack thorns. Both currant and gooseberry bushes have red and white flowers with thin tubes; however, on a currant bush the flower cluster, while on a gooseberry bush each flower tends to hang singularly. Both produce berries favored by brown bears.

In just over 0.2 mile the path attains the crest of the Western Divide, then switchbacks 11 times before it meanders north across the flat top of Mule Peak to the summit lookout (8142/0.6). The lookout seems squat, but it offers lavish panoramic views. Class 4&5 rock 250 yards southwest of the structure may interest climbers.

T49   Slate Mountain Crest Backpack

The contrast between the acres of trees at both ends of this journey that have fallen victim to the loggers saw and the high country in between that abounds with old growth red fir, intensifies the hiker's enjoyment of nature where man ventures only as a visitor. Scenes from a ridge viewpoint include former clear-cuts and a distant mill site, recalling the logging history of the Western Divide. The trip unfolds on the only trail in this book included in the National Recreation Trails System.

Distance   11.0 miles, shuttle trip
Steep Ascents   0.3 mile
Elevation Gain   2230 feet
Skills   Easy route finding
Seasons   Spring, summer, fall
Map   USGS 7.5-min. *Sentinel Pk*
Trailheads   40 & 43. This trip begins at **TH40**. See car tour T46. It ends at **TH43**, Quaking Aspen Campground. There are 20.0 miles between trailheads.
Description   If hiking in late summer or fall, it may be wise to pack in your total water supply, as sources along the way could be dry.

Between two switchbacks on the Mule Peak road west of the Western Divide Highway, you find north angling *Summit*

M'cyclepath 31E14 (7640/0.0). It appears tucked amid currant, manzanita and snow bush hiding the stumps of logged trees in an even-aged growth of planted ponderosa pines. The scratchy brush infringes on the trail, but does not obscure it. Half way up a moderate, sometimes steep climb, you intersect a creek destined for Mule Meadow, then negotiate a switchback and top an east-trending ridge where pussypaws parade in the trailside underbrush.

At Onion Meadow the indistinct trail first proceeds alongside the ephemeral creek, then crosses both creek and meadow. It becomes obvious again where old tree blazes mark its course. The gentle ascent past the meadow quickly becomes a moderate descent along southeast-facing slopes. Windows in the forest picture the Nobe Young bowl and the south flanks of Slate Mountain. Bitter cherry joins the trailside understory. The path then makes a sharp right turn where a downed pole once carried a destination sign. The tread becomes vague at times while descending to the right of a fence to meet Crawford Road (SNF Road 21S94 west; 21S93 east) (7540/2.0) at Windy Gap.

Turn left here and walk north on the paved road over a cattleguard to the offset junction (7510/0.1) where Summit National Recreation Trail 31E14 resumes. On the trail you curve around a moist crease, then travel north to ford a bouncing snowmelt brook. The next source of seasonal water is at Freezeout Meadow, 2.5 miles on trail, 0.1 mile down-canyon. The gully cradling the brook offers the first exposed metamorphic rock, which abounds in Slate Mountain.

The trail next bisects a tree-sheltered medium campsite, passes overreaching brush, then turns east to gain a grueling 855 feet in 1.0 mile—switchbacks assist the ascent. A cairn sits amid the forest atop Slate Mountain's ridgecrest (8560/1.7), where the trail finally arrives and turns a sharp left.

(Here you may choose to take a half-mile side trip to a viewpoint. If so, turn right on a cross-country hike southeast to gain the rocky 8769-foot summit on the crest. While admiring the view, you may be able to detect a series of large clear-cuts that are now filled in with shrubs or replanted trees, extending from this point's intermediate slopes south to a bowl where a lake marks the former lumber mill town of Johnsondale—now a vacation community called R-Ranch in the Sequoias.

Logging was rampant here. Why? According to an article in the May 27, 1940, *Bakersfield Californian*, a Michigan lumberman owned a scattering of parcels in the vicinity, including many sequoia groves. Former Forest Supervisor Joe Elliott, presumably

Snow ghosts of the Southern Sierra

spurred by the devastation wreaked by loggers on sequoias to the northwest, secured these parcels in 1935, giving protection to the sequoia groves in exchange for the right to cut local commercial timber intensely. That right extended to the Kern Plateau and Piute and Greenhorn mountains. The local commercial timber was cut and fed to the Johnsondale mill until it closed in 1979.)

Back on the Summit Trail you ascend north on the mildly undulating crest of Slate Mountain through a handsome uncut forest of red fir. (If your itinerary includes Freezeout Meadow, descend to the right in 0.3 mile after passing left of small Hill 8679; a total of 0.8 mile from the junction with the cross-country route. This lush spot of velvet green, not visible from the trail, lies in the canyon to the east. It is bordered to the north by a ridge culminating in an impressive point, but not the highest point on Slate Mountain. Several trailside ducks at intervals along the path mark departure points where hikers have descended cross-country 0.1 to 0.2 mile to the meadow.

Historian Francis P. Farquhar speculated that "freeze out," a gold-rush miners' card game in which a player drops out when bankrupt, might have lent its name to this meadow. The meadowside campsite's appeal diminishes in late summer when the brook alongside it dries up.)

You continue to trace the lengthy crestline stretch, ascending moderately to steeply over a rise, then slanting across the steep headwaters slopes of the South Fork Tule River watershed on the west side of Slate Mountain Peak. The San Joaquin Valley smog or fog laps over distant ridges, marring those views. Now western white pine join the red fir forest. In time you arrive atop a ridge at a junction (9000/2.4) with Bear Creek

M'cyclepath 31E31. Its path and yours are outlined with rocks at the junction. (For directions to a climb of Slate Mountain Peak from this point, and for information on the defunct Slate Mountain alpine ski proposal, see T52.)

Your trail at the junction stays right and descends moderately northeast around a deep north-facing canyon, then increases in steepness after a switchback. Next it moderates around a hill to cross a saddle (8540/1.1) where a climbers' cross-country route leaves the trail to seek a tooth of volcanic schist, known as Yokut Spire. The Summit Trail descends on a long traverse with a seep above the path midway, to the following saddle (8150/0.9) where it threads to the left of a granite knob.

Descending the east-facing slopes of Slate Mountain on a fall of switchbacks, you are afforded rewarding views of the High Sierra and the Kern Plateau and are gifted with a tranquil moistened pocket of thimbleberry bushes and bracken ferns. Ponderosa pines replace western white pines, and at the mountain's foot, plantations of pines grow in logged plots. Eventually, as the trail turns north, you cross an extension of Quaker Meadow and its creek, pass above the Quaker Meadow private camp, and descend to meet SNF Road 21S78 (7180/2.0) just below its gate.

Your route turns right to briefly overlap the road. It then forks left (7155/0.2) to continue, first as a retired logging road and then as path. Soon your path skirts to the left of Quaking Aspen Meadow and leaves the trail on a *spur path* (6980/0.4) that quickly ends at the campground road between campsites 23 and 24 (7005/0.1), where your journey ends.

T50   Dome Rock Day Hike

This great bulge of granite overlooking a broad basin crinkled with multiple canyons has been the setting for weddings and other special occasions. While its easy access and extensive views invite celebrations, its technical routes elicit acclaim from numerous rock climbers who scale its vertical slopes.

Distance   0.4 mile, round trip
Steep Ascents   None
Elevation Gain   100 feet
Skills   Easy route finding; easy hiking; Class 3–5 pitches optional
Seasons   Spring, summer, fall
Map   USGS 7.5-min. *Sentinel Pk*
Trailhead   41. See car tour T46. Turn east off the Western Divide Highway onto *SNF Road 21S69* (0.0/0.0), pass a right side road to reach the spacious parking area (0.6/0.6) at **TH41**.
Description   Your *use trail* starts southeast from the end of the road (7120/0.0), amid red firs; however, serious rock climbers will start east or west instead. While they descend, curving around the dome to its base,

you ascend the path's short, easy-to-moderate grade and arc onto the clearing atop the dome (7221/0.2).

On this massive dome with its dramatic views of The Needles and the Kern Plateau, everyday concerns peel away like the thin layers of exfoliating granite characteristic of this rock. Still, the loose stones and pebbles suggest careful footing for the safety of the out-of-sight climber and for you. Although the slope around Dome Rock's summit is gradual, its sides quickly curve down toward cracks and ledges where climbers have forged routes, partly with their hardware and rock-gripping boots, but mostly with their strength and nerve.

Panoramic view from Dome Rock includes The Needles

T51   The Needles Lookout Day Hike

The Needles Lookout may look precarious and spindly, but it has staunchly withstood pummeling winds, lightning strikes and rock-splitting freezes and thaws for over 50 years. Visitors who can exult in the clatter of its airy catwalks and the sheerness of the granodiorite that plunges from its heights will discover views of both spectacular beauty and a rock-climbers' paradise.

Distance 4.0 miles, round trip
Steep Ascents 0.1 mile
Elevation Gain 1165 feet
Skills Easy route finding; moderate hiking;
Class 5+ pitches optional
Seasons Spring, summer, fall
Maps USGS 7.5-min. *Sentinel Pk, Durr-wood Cr*
Trailhead 42. See car tour T46. Turn right
on **SNF Road 21S05** (0.0/0.0) off the
Western Divide Highway. Head generally
northeast then east on a winding dirt road
passing several spur roads en route. Shortly
beyond campsites to the left, you arrive at the
wide parking area (2.8/2.8), **TH42**.
Description Your approach to the lookout
begins at the east end of the parking area
(7770/0.0) where **Needles Trail 32E22**
departs. A colony of aromatic western
pennyroyals appears along the trail. The ⅝-
inch purple flowers cluster in round heads at
tops of stems that bear narrow, gray-green
leaves growing opposite each other. These
leaves make a fragrant mint tea.

The trail ascends slightly while rounding a
pair of hills. The predominant red fir trees
part to allow broad views to the north of
Hermit (T56) and Castle rocks (T72) in the
middle ground beyond the Freeman Creek
drainage; the Kaweah peaks and Mount
Whitney group in the far north; and the Kern
Plateau peaks of Kern and Olancha in the
northeast: rewarding vistas for those who end
their trip short of the lookout. Soon you spot
the lookout unbelievably perched atop the
most western needle. After the hills, the path
switchbacks down to a saddle (7820/1.7) and
a large campsite, passing a climbers' trail
branching off to the right.

With the easy hiking behind you, you now
climb up a ladder of nine switchbacks to a
small rocky cove. Rock climbers often leave
here to traverse north-facing slopes toward
the eastern needles. The Needles ranks as one
of the premier climbing rocks in the Southern
Sierra, and climbers from all over the world
come here to experience its challenges.
Weather conditions, sunrise and sunset are
posted for the benefit of climbers; important
considerations for them before they commit

to a climb.

A ladder of steps leads you up from the
cove to a pinnacle, and from there a board-
walk bears you over a knife-edged ridge. A
ladder of rungs then takes you up the highest
rock of The Needles and deposits you on the
catwalk of the lookout (8254/0.3). Built in
1938 by the Civilian Conservation Corps, the
lookout is constantly manned during fire
season. The lookout employee will readily
answer questions. He can demonstrate how
the energy from lightning strikes spreads over
the tower and down its sides, and he can show
you the stool with glass insulators onto which
he hops during lightning storms.

While taking in the grand views, look
southeast to see Wizard Needle: it resembles
a huge gorilla when the shadows are right,
with Warlock Needle looking like a bunch of
the gorilla's bananas!

The Needles Lookout atop pinnacle

T52   Slate Mountain Day Hike
With Excursion G: Slate Mountain Peak

This vigorous trip offers brief, impressive views of the distant High Sierra and nearby Needles. It takes you through open forests and patches of wildflowers; alongside fern nooks and occasional rock outcrops. At the far end, it gives you the opportunity to climb to the peak's summit or to end your journey where a chalet was envisioned in the Peppermint Recreation Area proposal for a winter resort on Slate Mountain.

Distance   9.4 miles, round trip
Steep Ascents   0.2 mile
Elevation Gain   2045 feet
Skills   Easy route finding; moderate-to-strenuous hiking
Seasons   Spring, summer, fall
Map   USGS 7.5-min. *Sentinel Pk*
Trailhead   43. See car tour T46.
Description   Your hike begins at the south side of Quaking Aspen Campground between campsites 23 & 24, west of the meadow, on a *spur path* (7005/0.0) to *Summit M'cyclepath 31E14* (6980/0.1), a National Recreation Trail. Heading south on the path that widens into a logging road, you ascend a broad ridge through tree-replanted areas to unpaved SNF Road 21S78 (7155/0.4), on which you turn right. After a short southwest stint up the road, you find the offset continuation of your trail (7180/0.2) to the left which you take. It is just prior to the road's gate.

The trail rises south to skirt the tree-shielded buildings of private Quaker Meadow Campground, then levels to cross the creek bisecting a finger of Quaker Meadow. The route passes a large red gate, incongruously with no fence, and again threads through chainsaw-cleared, replanted land before it slants southwest to begin an earnest ascent. In a pause on the ascent between sets of switchbacks, abundant seasonal flowers line the path and perfume the air. The successive north ascending sections of path offer captivating views of The Needles nearby, of Olancha and other Kern Plateau peaks across Kern Canyon, as well as of the Mount Whitney group of peaks far away northeast. Soon an unexpected nook shelters a trickling seep nourishing thimbleberry bushes and bracken ferns; then, after gaining a total of 1170 feet, the path slides over a saddle (8150/2.0) with a medium-sized campsite.

A granite outcrop, Point 8269, stands to the east: a use path ascends its flank. Farther east a granitic knob offers puzzling pitches to climbers testing techniques and tools. This saddle midway into your trip makes a good turn-around point if you are ready to start back.

Moving on beyond the switchbacks, you find the path bordered alternately with pinemat manzanita and chinquapin. Another seep oozes in a crease above the path, creating an unexpected swatch of bright green. After an extensive traverse on south-facing slopes, you arrive at another saddle (8540/0.9). (Here rocks placed in the shape of an arrow indicate the direction to Yokut Spire north of Peak 8776. Rock climbers who seek the spire, trace the peak's ridge nearly ½ mile northeast to where they can engage the spectacular tooth of volcanic schist overlooking the Tule River fork's canyon, by forging their way up the technical face.)

Beyond the saddle, you resume your ascent. Now you are walking on soils derived from the quartzite and schist that make up the bulk of Slate Mountain. Soon you tackle a steeper grade. The gradient eases and in time you arrive on a ridge separating the South Fork and Middle Fork Tule rivers' watershed at a junction with Bear Creek M'cyclepath 31E31 (9000/1.1). Slate's peak rises directly southeast. At this point you may choose to climb the peak or relax and reflect upon the ski proposal.

As indicated on a maximum capacity map outlining possible facilities for the Peppermint Recreation Area, the planners envisioned a gondola reaching this point above some of the Summit Trail you hiked, and a chalet built at this junction. They visualized a chair lift swinging over the ridge on which Bear Creek Trail descends; another over the ridge south of it. They placed most of the rest of the lifts on the east slopes of Slate: 14 in all, and a crosshatch of ski trails over the east and north slopes of the mountain. The environmentalists claimed the plan was unfeasible; the Forest Service pursued the project. However, a developer was not found and in 1989 the plan was shelved.

Excursion G: Slate Mountain Peak

The view from this peak rivals any of the lookout-capped summits in the Southern Sierra. The basin of the Tule River, the ridge of the Great Western Divide, the pinnacles of Mount Whitney, the curve of Mount Langley, the supine image of "Miss" Olancha, the wide pyramid of Kern Peak, and, nearby, the Southern Sierra's pinnacles of The Needles—all appear vividly in your sweeping overview of the horizons.

Distance   0.8 mile, round trip
Steep Ascents   0.1 mile
Elevation Gain   305 feet
Skills   Easy route finding; Class 2 climbing
Description   The ascent of Slate Mountain's peak from the ridge point on the Summit Trail at its junction (9000/0.0) with the Bear Creek Trail can be accomplished in two ways. You can angle up the slope here, then climb over the flow of large granitic boulders; or you can descend south along the trail for just less than 0.2 mile, leave it, turn left and climb steeply east along the hem between the boulders and the mass of chinquapin bushes. Both ways avoid bushwhacking.

Once on top, you will find the USGS mark on a mid-crest jumble of rocks (9302/0.4), composed of flat, colorful early Cretaceous metasedimentary material. However, one of the next two rock piles southeast appears to be the highest point on the mountain. The view is best from the rock pile topped with chinquapin bushes, but try all three.

T53   Wheel Meadow Sequoia Grove Day Hike

The oldest trees in this and surrounding sequoia groves were taking root around 1500 years ago, shortly after the mighty Roman Empire reached its zenith. These giants have outlived many institutions of man and survived the vagaries of nature, including repeated fires, which resulted in this grove's "walk-through" tree.

Distance   4.3 miles, shuttle trip
Steep Ascents   None
Elevation Gain   Negligible
Skills   Easy route finding; easy hiking
Seasons   Spring, summer, fall
Maps   USGS 7.5-min. *Sentinel Pk, Camp Nelson*
Trailheads   43 & 58. This trip begins at **TH43**, Quaking Aspen Campground. See car tour T74. It ends at **TH58**. To reach **TH58**, drive east from Highway 190 on *Nelson Drive* (0.0/0.0), the middle paved road of three, 0.6 mile east of Pierpoint Springs. Pass the county fire station, Belknap Campground (1.6/1.6) and scattered cabins to the parking area by Camp Nelson Trail 31E30

(0.5/2.1). There are 18.1 miles between trailheads.

Description   This trip, especially enjoyed by families, begins between campsites 23&24 (7005/0.0) at Quaking Aspen Campground where you take a brief **spur path** through a colony of currant bushes to **Summit M'cyclepath 31E14** (6980/0.1) and turn right on it. (Watch for it, it may not be signed.) Hiking west parallel to the campground, then north parallel to a brook emanating from Quaking Aspen Meadow, you quickly reach a mini wooden bridge minus railing, which aids your meadowy headwaters crossing of the South Fork Middle Fork Tule River. Next you meander

"Walk-through" giant sequoia

onto the shoulder of **Highway 190** (6880/ 0.4) where you turn left for a stroll west to **Camp Nelson Trail 31E30** (6780/0.4).

On the trail you abruptly descend 600 feet to the valley floor via zigzags and switchbacks. Overreaching boughs of conifers shade the way, and mats of kit kit dizze interspersed with manzanita and chinquapin border the path. Captured in your range of vision to the south stands the volcanic rock of Yokut Spire on the slopes of Slate Mountain.

At the bottom of the descent you ford the nascent river and find yourself surrounded by the venerable, stately giant sequoias of the Wheel Meadow Grove. After boulder-hops of tributaries draining Quaker Meadow and the north flanks of Slate Mountain, you rise to

traverse northeast facing slopes, then again drop to the floor among the ancient sentinels of the forest.

The graceful ferns you see scattered about the valley are abundant on earth and have been since the Paleozoic era, 345 million years ago. The vegetable matter of plants like these formed the vast deposits of coal found throughout the world. You can identify the common bracken ferns by the frond's great length and triangular shape and by the fingers (2-pinnate) of the frond. You will also find the springy humus spiny with jointed, sticklike common horsetail, sometimes called scouring rush because the plant was used to polish metal. This, too, dates to prehistoric times. Bushes of California hazelnut and Labrador tea and knots of yellow violets demurely hidden among the vegetation, perhaps not of ancient origin, also thrive on the canyon floor.

In time you walk through the wishbone opening of a great sequoia tree, living despite the forked cleavage caused by fire. Soon after you turn left on an intersecting road (5375/2.3) to find your trail continuing northwest at an offset junction. (If you mistakenly turn right, you end up in the village of Cedar Slope.)

Your trail descends easily, leaving the Wheel Meadow Grove to touch the fringes of the McIntyre Grove. High on the west ridge of this grove stands the Patriarch Tree, one of the 50 largest sequoias known. You cannot see this tree from here, but you can find it after about 3.0 miles up Bear Creek Trail 31E31 off Coy Flat Road.

Boulders ease a ford of the Tule River as you near the end of your trip. Then the path descends to cross a tributary, then McIntyre Creek and arrives at the end of your sequoia grove trip. (5120/1.1).

T54   A Stroll in the Woods Day Hike

Red fir forests and flower bedecked meadows, lyrical bird songs and muffled wind whispers highlight this pleasant hike along the Western Divide crest on the Summit National Recreation Trail.

Distance 5.2 miles, shuttle trip
Steep Ascents None
Elevation Gain 1035 feet
Skills Easy route finding; easy-to-moderate hiking
Seasons Spring, summer, fall
Maps USGS 7.5-min. *Sentinel Pk, Camp Nelson*
Trailheads 43 & 46. This trip begins at **TH43**, Quaking Aspen Campground. See car tour T46. It ends at **TH46**, Clicks Creek trailhead. There are 5.8 miles between the trailheads.
Description You begin your hike between campsites 23&24 at Quaking Aspen Campground where a brief *spur path* (7005/0.0) leads south to a right turn almost immediately onto *Summit M'cyclepath 31E14* (6980/0.1). (The Summit Trail south climbs Slate Mountain, the subject of Ts49&52.) You, however, hike west, then north, flanked by the campground and the brook from Quaking Aspen Meadow. You bridge the meadow headwaters of the South Fork Middle Fork Tule River and reach Highway 190 (6880/0.4), which you cross.

Boulders prevent 4WDs from using the retired logging road that here serves as your path. You quickly turn right off the old road (6900/0.1) onto a path and proceed on a mild ascent in cooling shade of red firs interspersed with ponderosa pines and incense cedars. Assisted by a triple set of switchbacks, you soon attain a broad saddle. A stock fence astride the north edge of the saddle offers a gate for your passage. Again you stroll along a loggers' road that was placed over the old trail. Numerous logging roads bisect and even usurp the trails on this hike, but this well-signed route is easy to follow. Next, you pass an unnamed meadow, the first in a chain of vivid greens or pale ambers, depending on the season, along this crest of the Western Divide mountains. Then at a junction (7315/1.4) the road peels off to the right; you continue ahead on the path.

The Summit Trail reaches and cuts across the northeast end of Coffee Mill Meadow, ascends moderately to cross SNF Road 20S44, then takes you parallel to the paved road (SNF Road 21S50) on which you will return at the end of this trip. The trail descends along a canyon and again meets a dirt road onto which you turn left at an offset junction (7360/0.6). (The Forest Service hopes to eliminate these set-apart, dangling trail ends.)

After walking just under 0.2 mile on the road, find the path to the right and climb up to a traverse along wooded slopes on a replaced section of trail. Across the canyon a swath of clear-cut land attracts attention. Nearby, on occasion, a snow plant's fleshy red top polking through receding snow catches your eye. If a Steller's Jay is around, you are sure to see it and hear it. Steller's Jays are about 12 inches long. They have black heads and crests, and dark, phosphorescent blue bodies. They squawk loudly at hikers; it is not one of the lyrical birds you may hear. You next meet a forked junction (7370/0.7) with Lewis Camp Trail 33E01, here a cattle driveway. You take the left fork.

To your right, linear Deep Meadow stretches north: a culvert directs its creek, Boulder Creek, under your nicely laid rock-reinforced path. A campsite rests nearby. Your path rises above the road you previously crossed, and as the path curves, it exposes hulking Slate Mountain to the south. Again your route turns onto a logging road, right, at a forked junction (7480/0.8), briefly uses the road, then leaves it on the path to the left to curl east of Smith and Failing Meadow, identified at both ends by weathered signs. The trail ascends along the meadow's creek, curves away from it, and again becomes a dirt road (7840/0.8) on which you hike north.

On the logging road, your route levels through another plantation, then crosses a well-graded road (7940/0.2) that takes climbers to a path below Jordan Peak where they can practice their skills on McIntyre Rock's face (T61: Ex-M). Your path descends to Log Cabin Meadow where it takes the right fork, *Clicks Creek Trail 32E11*, at a junction (7840/0.2). It quickly meets *SNF Road 21S50* (North Road) (7860/0.2), paved here. A large sign across the road announces CLICKS CREEK TRAIL.

You turn left, saunter north on the road to the parking lot of Clicks Creek Trailhead (7860/0.1), the end of this stroll through the woods.

(For those who wish to hike farther, the Summit Trail continues ahead for nearly 19.5 miles from the junction with the Clicks Creek Trail. It crosses North Road north of the trailhead, at fledgling Clicks Creek. Description of the trail from the creek north to the Summit trailhead appears at the end of T63. The rest of the Summit Trail is described in the beginning of T63.)

Fleshy red spears of snow plant

T55   Freeman Creek Sequoia Grove Day Hike

A sense of affection and hushed awe prevails on this stroll through the eastern-most sequoia grove in the Sierra. Along the way you visit one of the largest trees in the grove, search for a hidden picnic area and view a magnificent giant tree named the George Bush Tree.

Distance   6.4 miles, round trip
Steep Ascents   0.2 mile
Elevation Gain   1370 feet
Skills   Easy route finding; moderate hiking
Seasons   Spring, summer, fall
Map   USGS 7.5-min. *Camp Nelson*
Trailhead   44. See car tour T46. Turn onto unpaved *SNF Road 21S99* (0.0/0.0) opposite the entrance to Quaking Aspen Campground. Drive north past a short spur from SNF Road 21S50 (0.6/0.6) to the wide parking area short of the fence (0.2/0.8), **TH44**.
Description   To begin this trip of quiet beauty, you pass through the wide gateway on *Freeman Creek Trail 32E20* (7110/0.0), which starts as road but soon reduces to trail width. Then you descend on a mild slope past red firs. Shortly after crossing a minor, meadow-threading tributary, you stroll along the main trail. Stay left at a junction with a closed section of trail. Hiking along the wooded path above the elongated meadow flanking Freeman Creek, you soon ford a headwaters fork where creek dogwood, Cali-

fornia hazelnut and bracken fern, in descending order of height, deck the creek banks.

The tall rounded crowns and huge, shaggy trunks of giant sequoias begin to appear among the forest trees to the right in the 1700-acre Freeman Creek Grove. About 0.1 mile beyond the creek crossing and just before the path descends via a switchback, look to the right for the obscure end (6960/1.1) of the closed section of trail you passed earlier; slim logs line the entrance. Turn right and bushwhack along the overgrown path 0.1 mile to a large tree. Somewhere in this grove stands one of the 50 largest trees known; this may well be it. Farther down the slope near the creek, a wreath of sequoias encircles a campsite with a table, benches and a fire ring: a place to picnic and perhaps to reflect. From here you find your way back to the main trail. This makes a good end point if you prefer a shorter hike.

The trail ahead loses elevation quickly. It switchbacks, drops along a ridge, rounds it and descends north of the creek. A series of widely spaced, impressive sequoias dot the landscape; campsites appear tucked here and there among the forest trees. The well-maintained trail continues to descend north of Freeman Creek, then crosses a glassy, sand-floored tributary (5740/2.1). Here to the north and inland of the creek crossing stands a handsome, symmetrical giant sequoia dedicated to George Bush, the former U.S. president. On July 14, 1992 President Bush visited this grove and signed a proclamation designated to preserve the sequoias and protect their environment in perpetuity. You can find more information about sequoias and the proclamation in the first chapter of this book.

This impressive tree, standing tall and solemn in its easternmost sequoia grove, marks the conclusion of your trip. (You can also reach the Bush Tree by hiking 1.0 mile west of SNF Road 22S82 (Lloyd Meadows Road) on this trail, Freeman Creek Trail 32E20.)

Giant sequoia of Freeman Grove

T56   Hermit Rock Climb

The sheer, 700-foot south face of Hermit Rock has shed onionlike layers, leaving the face inscribed with a rainbow outline that beckons the skilled technical climber. The ascent's rewards are the initial awesome accomplishment and the views of a series of bolt-upright rocks in the summit panorama: the Great Western Divide in the north, Castle Rock in the east, The Needles in the southeast and Yokut Spire in the southwest—inspiration for further climbs.

Distance   1.8 miles, round trip
Steep Ascents   0.4 mile
Elevation Gain   765 feet
Skills   Intermediate route finding; Class 4 climbing (Class 5 pitch optional)
Seasons   Spring, summer, fall
Map   USGS 7.5-min. *Camp Nelson*
Trailhead   45. See car tour T46.
Description   The *cross-country* route to the backside of Hermit Rock begins at Lewis Camp Trailhead (7700/0.0) on a slight north-south ridge. It slants up a moderate, sometimes steep grade south from the parking lot through sparsely cut red fir and shortly veers south-southeast to trace a near-level section of ridge. The underbrush along this ½ mile

section, and the subsequent moderate ascent, is easily dodged. Western white pine joins the conifer overstory where you turn south-southwest onto the ridge crest between Fish and Freeman creeks.

(Climbers bound for the challenging Class 5+ routes on the face of the dome should leave the route here at the base of the exposed rock and gradually arc southwest, descending across southeast-facing slopes. To intercept the rock, do not lose more than 500 feet on this descent. Climber Fred Beckey made the first recorded ascent of Hermit Rock in 1969 and afterward described the rock as ". . . reminiscent of Yosemite's domes . . ." and ". . . one of the many surprises the

Sierra still yields." His route was a technical ascent up the south face.)

Your cross-country route skirts brush and outcrops along the crest. At the north base, the climb begins up granite slabs—some shat-tered, some intact—on the backside of the dome. Climber Jim Shevock reported in 1978 that the easiest route to the summit (8465/0.9) involved a short Class 4 pitch.

T57   Kern Lakes Backpack
With Excursion H: Hole in the Ground

Excellent fishing for native Kern River rainbow trout along the North Fork Kern River and Little Kern Lake draws fishermen to this trip. Fault, glacial and landslide formations attract geomorphologists. The grandeur of the Kern Trench and the handsomeness of the entire route entice wilderness enthusiasts of all interests to this adventure.

Distance   30.4 miles, round trip
Steep Ascents   None
Elevation Gain   5675 feet
Skills   Easy route finding
Seasons   Spring, summer, fall (Wilderness permit required)
Maps   USGS 7.5-min. *Camp Nelson, Hockett Pk, Kern Lake*
Trailhead   45. See car tour T46.
Description   See Chapter One for the Kern River's special fishing regulations.

From the large parking area east of the Western Divide Highway, *Lewis Camp Trail 33E01* (7700/0.0) heads north under a filigree of mixed conifers to loop around a ridge, then descend gently east. It intersects an extremely steep cattle driveway before advancing into Golden Trout Wilderness, following closely the border and the ridgeline. The path soon crosses Fish Creek Meadow Trail 32E12 (6925/1.8) where it unites with the route of T71.

Northeastbound Trail 33E01 Log

T71	Fish Cr Mdw Tr 32E12	6925	0.0
	Closed bypass Tr #1	6730	0.7
	Jug spr	6300	0.8
	Ltl Kern Brdg	5760	1.3

Across the bridge on *Lewis Camp Trail 33E01*, you turn right, head east through a canyon and stay on the lower trail where the path splits. While rounding a ridge above the Little Kern River, you meet *Willow Meadows Trail 33E14* where you turn left. On this path of decomposed basalt, you save one mile by cutting across the slopes above Trout Meadow and the Lewis Camp Trail, which you later rejoin. You quickly pass the other end of the closed section of this trail still used by packers. With views of the southern Great Western Divide ridge, you ascend northeast to top a minor hill, then climb easily to pass a junction (6620/1.5) with Lion Meadows Trail 32E02. Beyond the junction, you rise gradually to a saddle north of Point 6925, then descend aided by two widely spaced pairs of switchbacks on the steepest drops. At the foot near a packers' campsite and a refreshing spring, you turn left to travel again on *Lewis Camp Trail 33E01* (6340/1.7).

Heading north along the hem of Willow Meadows, the trail leaves the public pasture through a gate, crosses a nascent creek whose bed seldom carries water for any distance, and passes a packers' campsite at a creek crossing. It then ventures along through the woods atop the extensive Kern Canyon fault, which, at this point, separates the Great Western Divide to the left from Hockett Peak to the right.

In time the trail begins to descend gradually, often among foot-high, delicate, thin-leafed gayophytum plants. This tiny, white, four-petaled wildflower has a fringy center due to its eight extended stamens.

The path swings part way around a ridge and back to a U turn where you see your first views of the straight, lengthy, fault-caused trench containing the North Fork Kern River. About 75,000 years ago during the Pleistocene epoch, glaciers advanced along the Kern Canyon fault as far south as Hole in the Ground in the canyon below. Far to the north the granite of Tower Rock announces the entry to Sequoia National Park—some say the entry to "The Yosemite of the Kern River."

The trail continues to drop, crossing Angora Creek, which uses a few feet of the path on its way to the Kern. After 0.2 mile Hole in the Ground Trail 33E05 angles in to meet your trail (5845/3.6). Interested fishermen will want to investigate this secluded shore with the descriptive name; the rest skip the following trip.

Excursion H: Hole in the Ground

One fisherman claimed this to be a nationally known fishing hole; another extolled its virtues but said the rest of the Kern River was just as good. You will have to judge for yourself if fishing at the Hole is worth the extra effort to get there.

Distance   4.0 miles, round trip
Steep Ascents   None
Elevation Gain   225 feet
Skills   Easy route finding; easy-to-moderate hiking
Maps   USGS 7.5-min. *Kern Lake, Hackett Pk* (Briefly)
Description   Descend south in the sometimes shade of Jeffrey pines and incense cedars on *Hole in the Ground Trail 33E05* (5845/0.0). Drop to ford Angora Creek, then climb over a low, steep-sided notch. Near the bed of a snowmelt gully, a short spur path departs for a large campsite by a wide, placid river eddy. Zigzagging over another notch and declining steeply on the rutted trail as you approach the river, you find gravel mingled with dust thinly layered over slabs needs only an incautious step to send you flying.

As summer wanes and the snowpacks from the vast headwaters basin feeding the Kern disappear, the river is only knee-deep at this wider- and shallower-than-usual sec-

tion. But caution should always be taken when wading into the river to fish: the boulders can be slippery, unseen deep pools and tangles of wood debris can exist and the current can be stronger than the surface water suggests. Across the Kern, Right Stringer Trail climbs the steep slopes to the Kern Plateau in an area aptly named "Hell for Sure." The trail, no longer maintained, has disappeared from maps. Perhaps the area is best left to Sasquatch and the other wild creatures!

Your trail continues on, reaching more campsites and ends (5620/2.0) in a broad flood plain where the precipitous slopes of Hockett Peak pinch off any further travel along the water. Formerly, the trail climbed the slopes near here to a saddle north of Hockett Peak, then joined the Lewis Camp Trail.

*   *   *   *   *

Continuing along Lewis Camp Trail 33E01, you descend on the dusty path, which curves north and levels upon reaching the boulder-heaped Kern River flood plain. Jeffrey pine, incense cedar, alder, black and live oak, willow and black cottonwood thrive by the trailside and river ahead. Next, pass through a cattle gate following which you boulder-hop Leggitt Creek and hike past several packer-type campsites. Quite soon you approach Grasshopper Flat's primitive campground. Its widely spaced and usually shaded sites offer tables, fire rings and grills. This campground often serves as home base for fishermen, but, being in a wilderness, it will one day be dismantled.

Ahead, you splash through the water of Grasshopper Creek, enter a bouldery clearing, then zigzag up about 500 feet on trail greatly improved in 1993. You cross a slender stream en route to arrive at a saddle. Turn of the century geologist A. C. Lawson observed during his pioneering reconnaissance that this saddle eroded along the Kern Canyon fault, effectively isolating the buttress from the canyon slopes proper. He dubbed the saddle "Kerncol" and the buttress "Kernbut," terms now used by geologists to describe similar features everywhere.

The trail descends moderately, then bridges (6240/2.8) the dry bed of Little Kern Lake Creek. The creek, overflow water from Coyote Lakes nestled in the crest above, was diverted in 1954 into the trench next crossed that reaches Little Kern Lake as its only intake stream.

In another 0.1 mile you see below, sparkling, photogenic Little Kern Lake. Tree-shaded campsites ring this engaging body of water, tucked in a wide pocket of Kern Canyon. A spur path (6300/0.4) descends to its north banks. Lawson speculated that the lake was formed sometime in the early 1800s by a rock slide.

Sometime during your stay at Little Kern Lake you may wish to visit wide, shallow Kern Lake less than a mile north. Continue on the path over the next kerncol and descend to Kern Lake. There is a campsite next to the inlet stream to the left of the trail.

A massive landslide that occurred in 1868 formed Kern Lake—five years prior to the great Owens Valley earthquake. Debris from the slide blocked the flow of the Kern River, causing fright and flight among the Indians living downstream in Kern River Valley, who saw their river dry up. When the impounded water broke through the debris dam, thundering torrents of water rushed down the upper and lower Kern canyons, carrying thousands of trees uprooted by its great force. The tiny village of Bakersfield was flooded. When the river returned to normal, the ever-enterprising Colonel Baker, founder of Bakersfield, built a saw mill to cut the piles of logs into lumber.

What remained upriver of the slide was a lake a mile long with a river intake and outlet. During most of the 1900s Kern Lake and upriver to the park were used to rear native Kern River rainbow trout. The lake slowly silted in and the river intake was pinched off. The hatchery was abandoned in 1984.

Pleasant Little Kern Lake viewed from its north shore

T58   Coyote Lakes Backpack
With Excursions I–K:
Coyote Peak, Angora Mountain and White Mountain

The steep-walled Kern Trench, a pair of brilliant cirque-nestled lakes, an other-world scenario of projecting rock amid stark sand and twisted pines and the myriad sights, smells and sounds of a wilderness journey make this ambitious trip to the remote heights of the southern Great Western Divide an unforgettable experience.

Distance   45.2 miles, loop trip
Steep Ascents   1.6 miles
Elevation Gain   10,200 feet
Skills   Easy-to-intermediate route finding
Seasons   Spring, summer, fall (Wilderness permit required)
Maps   USGS 7.5-min. *Camp Nelson, Hockett Pk, Kern Lake*
Trailhead   45. See car tour T46.
Description   The beginning of this trip is described in Ts57 & 71.

Northeastbound Trail 33E01 Log

T57 Lewis Camp TH	7700	0.0
T71 Fish Cr Mdw Tr 32E12	6925	1.8
Closed bypass Tr #1	6730	0.7
Jug Spr	6300	0.8
T57 Ltl Kern Brdg	5760	1.3
Willow Mdws Tr 33E14	5960	0.6

Northeastbound Trail 33E14 Log

Lewis Camp Tr 33E01	5960	0.0
Lion Mdws Tr 32E02	6620	1.5
Lewis Camp Tr 33E01	6340	1.7

Northbound Trail 33E01 Log

Willow Mdws Tr 33E14	6340	0.0
Hole in the Gnd Tr 33E05	5845	3.6
Ltl Kern Lake Brdg	6240	2.8
Ltl Kern Lake spur	6300	0.4

Beyond Little Kern Lake on *Lewis Camp Trail 33E01*, heading north, another zig-zagging ascent takes you over a Kerncol (saddle) between a Kernbut and the mountain slopes. You now see large, shallow Kern Lake—shallow because it has only a small seasonal inlet stream and receives an average of only 15 inches of precipitation per year. With the build up of silt and the lack of adequate water, the lake is slowly turning into a marsh. One day it will evolve into a meadow, then a forested flat: a normal terrain change

you can see throughout the Sierra.

The trail descends on an easy grade to pass a campsite next to the unnamed inlet stream, leads north along moist slopes of the marsh beside a strand of river, passes a reedy pond and rises easily above the riverbank. A spur path (6360/2.5) peels off down the steep slope taking people over the bridge that spans the North Fork Kern River, then on to Kern Plateau adventures via the Golden Trout Trail of T114 described in *Exploring the Southern Sierra: East Side*. If you want to make camp now, this spur leads to inviting sites spread on the tree-shaded riverside ledge seen below, opposite the magestic Tower Rock, part of the massive wall rising 2000 feet above the river.

Your trail curves gradually west to a junction (6520/0.4) where it and Golden Trout Wilderness end and Sequoia National Park begins. You may wish to sign in at the park ranger station. The path to the right, which crosses Coyote Creek, takes you in 0.1 mile to the station, then continues upriver.

In 1926 Sequoia National Park expanded to include Kern Canyon north of this junction. It also purchased Lewis Camp, situated on the flat next to the station. The camp had begun welcoming guests around 1875, known then as the Runkel Place. It became a popular destination for campers who arrived by pack trains, and for parties of equestrians. Slowly the park dismantled it and by 1970 nature reclaimed the land.

At the end of Lewis Camp Trail, you continue ahead on *Coyote Pass Trail*. You leave the creek's side to begin a long trek up the canyon, gaining close to 3000 feet elevation before branching off to the lake trail for another 1200 feet vertical gain. Sounds dismaying, but the gain stretches out over several miles and switchbacks help you up steep slopes.

While climbing the first switchbacks, Coyote Creek comes into view, below, and you can see its dancing falls and cascades. Across Kern Canyon north of Tower Rock, you can see Golden Trout Creek's leaping ballet over the basaltic ledges of Volcano Falls. To preserve views like this was one reason Congress expanded the park, created the Golden Trout Wilderness and included the North Fork Kern River into the National Wild and Scenic Rivers System.

You soon pass camping possibilities on an extended ridge, then cross the cooling waters of Coyote Creek—wading or on nearby logs. You continue on the north shore of the creek on a path gracefully curved and briefly banked with ferns. Again you resume your ascent: a trailside string of enticing bathing holes offers an impossibly tempting mid-ascent diversion.

Labrador tea plants often dress the moist slopes hereabouts. This low-growing bush becomes especially elegant when covered with clusters of tiny white flowers whose many stamens reach beyond the petals like silken threads. Its smooth, dark green leaves tend to cloak the branch tips. Inspite of its inviting appeal, its tea is poisonous. Red mountain heather of the same family often accompany the tea bush. This low shrub has needlelike leaves and red blossoms that gather in a cluster and also show many extended stamens. It, too, is both charming and toxic.

By the time the grade eases, lodgepole pines have replaced the dominant Jeffrey pines and have partly screened you from glades backdropped with jagged, glacial-carved crags. Ford Coyote Creek, then cross a sometimes dry branch of the creek. Soon after, you meet a junction (9330/4.9) with *Coyote Lakes Trail*, onto which you turn left.

Heading south, the trail dips through the dry branch of Coyote Creek, climbs a low ridge, skirts a meadow, its flowing stream,

and a campsite at the meadow's head, then begins its long pull to the crest of the Great Western Divide: gentle at first, but increasingly steep as it progresses. While ascending through the boulder fields, the route may be hard to find, especially if you are the first out in the season and have no scuff marks to follow. The hardpan sometimes does not show the contour of the trail. After a half mile from the meadow, cross the slender stream and remain on the east side of it, then stay in its dry gully through the greater part of the ascent, zigzagging often. Campsites lie where the trail infrequently levels.

Eventually you leave tree cover and ascend a steep, gritty slope, spottily held in place with Brewer's lupine. You sink nearly mid-boot in the scree of the three long-legged switchbacks that lead you to Coyote Peaks Pass (10,540/2.1), where you exchange the park for Golden Trout Wilderness. You then negotiate a short traverse around the steep west slopes of the lesser of the two dominant Coyote Peaks where you reach a junction (10,400/0.2) with Willow Creek's hunters trail. Turn left to the saddle (10,550/0.1). From the saddle you zigzag east on the rough descent to the Coyote Lakes, pausing at intervals to view the lakes and distant Kern Peak. Soon you arrive on the north shore of the larger body of water. The path continues to the easternmost lake (10,070/0.5). Many superb campsites dot both lakes.

The Coyote Lakes, glistening gems circled by chiseled, rocky peaks, are the desired destination of many outdoor enthusiasts, but only the most stalwart hikers and those riding in on horseback realize their desire. Fishing and lazing are both quality pastimes here. History buffs enjoy forays to the east outlet in search of the old sheep driveway that dropped pell-mell from Coyote Lake to connect with Little Kern Lake below. Peak-baggers will certainly want to ascend the major Coyote Peak.

Excursion I: Coyote Peak

This huge pile of rocks looks too foreboding for the average climber when viewing its glacial-carved face from Coyote Lakes. Although steep, it is climbable as the many signatures in the summit register attest. Breathtaking views await at the top.

Distance   1.0 mile, round trip
Steep Ascents   0.4 mile
Elevation Gain   755 feet
Skills   Intermediate route finding; Class 2 climbing
Map   USGS 7.5-min. *Kern Lake*
Description   From the north side of the easternmost Coyote Lake (10,140/0.0), behind the moraine, find the shallow ravine that descends from a tarn in the saddle between the Coyote Peaks. Climb **cross-country** on the east side of the ravine, which takes you above the tarn, usually blue with lupines. The slopes steepen as you progress. The loose rocks demand complete concentration, and, because these rocks dislodge easily, do not follow close behind one another.

Make your way to the chute where the saddle bridge ends, then climb east up the larger, more secure boulders over to the summit rocks (10,892/0.5). The stellar views take in a circle of peaks and valleys as far as the eye can see.

*   *   *   *   *

When the time comes to leave the lakes, scramble up the trail to the saddle (10,550/0.5) where you turn left onto *Coyote Lakes*

Trail 32E05. Ascend south on the wind-buffeted, eerie moonscape where shards of resistant rock protrude from the gravelly slopes, and foxtail pines with twisted, cinnamon-colored trunks exist where no other tree survives. After hiking over a low hill on the crest, you next ascend to the highest point on the route, 10,850 feet, where you may want to detour briefly to climb Peak 10900, the highest peak by 8 feet on the rim surrounding the lakes.

(To climb the peak turn left off the trail, walk east to the easily climbable pile of rocks. The 360° view includes peaks clockwise from north: Kaweah, Langley, Cirque, Trail, Kern, Olancha, Spanish Needle, Owens, Jenkins, Bald, Piute and Greenhorn peaks, Slate, Jordan, Maggie, Vandever and Florence. With compass and map you will identify many others.)

Continuing on the trail, now on a protracted descent, you turn left to leave the crest (10,494/1.1). (Experienced mountaineers with compass and topo leave the trail here on a cross-country route along the crest nearly to Point 10242, then drop to the saddle and resume on the path. By the time you visit here, the Forest Service may have laid this trail; if so, take it unless you need water.)

If you need water, your trail descends east on a collection of switchbacks and curves near a branch of Grasshopper Creek whose

Hidden Coyote Lake nestled at the foot of Coyote Peak

flow is usually dependable. The sharp ridge of deformed Cretaceous granitic rocks piercing the sky above the creek resulted from the ancient Coyote Peaks fault. You may have observed the fault line division between the light granite and the dark mafic diorite granitic rocks to the east on the main Coyote Peak. The trail passes Kramer Horse Camp, spread west of the confluence, and other packer campsites as it curves southwest along another fork of the stream. Grasshopper headwaters is the last water supply until Deep Creek, approximately 4.0 miles away.

After a climb on rough trail to a saddle on the crest (9740/2.4), where cross-country mountaineers rejoin you, you descend generally south to cross a ridge above a minor saddle (9690/0.8). Peakbaggers will want to climb Angora Mountain, the southernmost named peak on the Great Western Divide.

Excursion J: Angora Mountain

Well worth the extra effort, Angora Mountain presents stunning views of the Little Kern Basin, the Kern Trench and the Kern Plateau as well as great peaks on the distant horizons.

Distance   2.2 miles, round trip
Steep Ascents   0.1 mile
Elevation Gain   510 feet
Skills   Intermediate route finding; Class 2 climbing
Map   USGS 7.5-min. *Kern Lake*
Description   From the high point of the path on the west trending ridge of Peak 10064 (9690/0.0), you have two choices of route: begin a *cross-country* southeast traverse around the slopes of Peak 10064 to the saddle (9780/0.7) between it and Angora Mountain; or descend along the trail until you see the saddle, then begin your cross-country climb. The second choice involves more elevation gain but less boulder climbing and chinquapin bushwhacking. An easy ascent from the saddle ensues southeast among the trees to the summit of Angora Mountain (10,198/0.4). According to Peter Browning's

book, *Place Names of the Sierra Nevada*, this mountain was named Angora Mountain in 1928 by a shepherd honoring his flock's leader, an Angora goat.

*   *   *   *   *

As you descend south, leaving the crest peaks of the Great Western Divide, you catch brief views of tree-clad Angora Mountain. At the head of a meadowy draw, a blank board nailed to a trailside red fir helps devotees of sheepherder camps locate Schulers Campsite, a large 19th Century retreat perched several hundred yards southeast on the other side of the meadow.

You descend dusty zigzags west, then a traverse displays southwest views of nearby White Mountain's rounded summit. Now and then thorns of snow bush scratch bare legs en route, or soft leaves of meadow garden plants caress them. After dropping 1400 vertical feet of zigzags and switchbacks from the Angora Mountain exit, you meet the north end of *Deep Creek Trail 32E06* (8276/1.6), onto which you turn left. (Continuing right would take you to Lion Meadows.) Dry camping is possible here. From the next broad saddle south (8220/0.3), you have the option of climbing White Mountain.

Excursion K: White Mountain

This easily attainable mountain sits above the Little Kern River watershed, where it offers tree-framed views of the entire basin and the peaks that rim it.

Distance   1.4 miles, round trip
Steep Ascents   0.3 mile
Elevation Gain   550 feet
Skills   Easy route finding; Class 1–2 climbing
Map   USGS 7.5-min. *Kern Lake*
Description   This excursion begins at the saddle (8220/0.0) dividing the drainage between Deep Creek and Table Meadow Creek. Climb *cross-country* southwest over the low hills on the saddle weaving among manzanita and chinquapin, then curve south to ascend the tree-shaded slopes to the bouldered high point on the rounded summit

(8740/0.7). White Mountain received its name from its Cretaceous white granite.

*   *   *   *   *

After leaving the saddle, descend south into Deep Creek's canyon among firs and pines, step across a usually dry headwaters segment of Deep Creek, then leave the forest momentarily to cross a grass- and lupine-field. A large campsite rests at the west edge of this open area near the creek, just north of a large blowdown. The trail becomes distinct again after it leaves the open field, and on it you pass a usually dry tributary and descend steeply, paralleling the east banks of entrenched Deep Creek. More campsites occur as the grade eases. After a long, gentle descent, you leap across the creek at a willow-lined ford. A large campsite sits on the east bank. In another 0.6 mile, you arrive at a T junction (6410/3.6) and turn right onto *Lion Meadows Trail 32E02*.

Hiking west now, descend a mild grade through alternating patches of manzanita and woods; listen for the scurry of lizards across pine-bark chips. In a bit you arrive at seldom maintained Round Meadow Trail 32E14 (6220/1.0) heading southwest for Grey Meadow. You continue straight ahead. Although a somewhat longer route to Grey Meadow, your better defined trail leads to the widest, shallowest ford of all Little Kern

River route crossings.

Moments after the junction, you surmount granite slabs, then cut downslope into an oft-mushy meadow with a spring-fed, sporadically present rivulet. Next you stroll through a Jeffrey pine forest where cow paths diverge from your trail, then arrive at a junction (6190/1.2) with *Burnt Corral Meadows Trail 32E13*, onto which you turn left.

Your path skirts Burnt Corral Meadows on its southeast side near some of the brownish rock remnants of the Little Kern Basalt Flow. Geologists speculate that this flow originated somewhere close to this clearing. (See T71 for further information on this flow.) You soon pass a distinct use path forking off your trail. (It descends a sandy slope, heads across the meadow and connects with the trail you just left.) An easily missed MAIN TRAIL sign tacked high on a young pine at the fork identifies your trail for those doing this trip in reverse. Your path briefly crosses a broad terrace, then descends a ravine for a wade across Little Kern River (5960/0.7).

In normal years the Little Kern basin floor receives 10 to 15 inches of rain, but drains three times that from the surrounding mountains. The river can run swift and deep during snowmelt. To cross the river when it is high, the recommended procedure is to slant diagonally downstream across the current, or

Wind-buffeted shards and pines at 10,850 feet elevation

consult your map and retrace your trail west to the foot bridge. After extended droughts a profusion of willows narrow the river channel.

Next, climb the steep bank, then wind across dry, gritty slopes to Grey Meadow where a group of campsites with tables cluster under the shade of Jeffrey pines. Sparkling, piped spring water spews forth from a meadowside spring. The old Forest Service station at the head of the meadow is home to a summertime ranger, but he is often away on patrol. A rebuilt cabin of an allottee's cow camp shares the view. In the late 1800s, the Grey brothers, Harvey P. and R. P., presumably camped here while driving sheep hereabouts. Their herd came in the middle of the summertime influx of San Joaquin Valley sheep that began in the drought of 1864 and ended some 30 years later. The federal government banished sheep in the high country after Sierran meadows had been nibbled nearly bare.

Trails radiate from the station; your *Fish Creek Meadow Trail 32E12* (6152/0.7) branches south heading for Lewis Camp Trailhead. It crosses an intermittent creek, then climbs moderately through open forest over a low saddle and descends to ford Fish Creek near campsites. Here a long gone segment of trail once followed the north banks of Fish Creek to the river.

Your trail bears a deceptive name—Fish Creek Meadow washed out more than 50 years ago. U.S. Forest Service Regional botanist James R. Shevock pointed out in 1977 that the terrain here reveals layers of peat, the remnants of at least ten previous meadows buried in the gravels of earlier floods. These lands illustrate the instability of granitic soils, the naturally brief life of the beauty they nurture and the swiftness with which land can change.

After Fish Creek, ascend a trail constructed in the early 1980s that is twice as long but half as steep as the old path—now used exclusively for cattle. You cross that cattle trail occasionally. The moderate ascent on steep slopes affords broad views of the Great Western Divide from which you came. In time you meet *Lewis Camp Trail 33E01* (6925/3.6) where you turn right. Here you retrace your incoming footsteps west to Lewis Camp Trailhead (7700/1.8), completing your extensive journey.

T59   Two Rivers Backpack
With Excursion L: Jenkins Knob

The southernmost Great Western Divide, a bulking mountain range, presents a castellated rim above the forested western flanks and broadly sloping plains of the Little Kern River basin. Its sharply dissected eastern flanks abruptly drop into an amazingly straight, deep trench occupied by the North Fork Kern River. This trip circles this massive range, cuts across its bulk at lofty Coyote Pass and visits the scenic environs of its two bordering rivers.

Distance   50.4 miles, semiloop trip
Steep Ascents   0.5 mile
Elevation Gain   9110 feet
Skills   Easy route finding
Seasons   Spring, summer, fall (Wilderness permit required)
Maps   USGS 7.5-min. *Camp Nelson, Quinn Pk, Kern Lake, Hockett Pk*
Trailhead   46. See car tour T46.

Description   During heavy snowmelt, alter your trip to avoid a potentially dangerous crossing of the Little Kern River. Begin at Lewis Camp Trailhead on Lewis Camp Trail 33E01 and follow T57 to Lion Meadows Trail 32E02. Turn left on that trail to Clicks Creek Trail 32E11. Follow this trip's description from that junction. On the return trip stay on Lewis Camp Trail 33E01 after the bridge.

The total mileage is about the same.

This extensive journey heads northeast on *Clicks Creek Trail 32E11* (7850/0.0) off SNF Road 21S50 north of Quaking Aspen Campground. At first, the trail barely descends as it wanders amid red firs. To the left, where the trees have been heavily logged, seedlings and saplings vie with each other and with currant bushes for moisture, nourishment and a place in the sun. Wayside asters appear here from time to time in moist soils. Their numerous purple petals surround a yellow disc and bloom atop a 1- to 2-foot stem with alternate, linear leaves.

Soon you step across an intermittent tributary, then pace near fledgling Clicks Creek, which you quickly boulder-hop. Next, two corrals flank the trail: the corral to the right for administrative use only; the corral and cabin to the left for teenagers who work on mountain projects and attend classes under the auspices of Community Services Employment Training. You proceed near a long grassy expanse split by the creek that you again cross on boulders. After passing into Golden Trout Wilderness, you hike over a protruding low ridge where the tumbling creek curves below trembling leaves of quaking aspen trees and through a mass of brilliant wildflowers.

By zigzags and switchbacks you lose 500 feet, then level off high above campsites located next to a meadow. Midway on this gentle terrain, a snowmelt brook moistens a slope luxuriant with seasonal flowers and blooming shrubs, the thimbleberry among them. This shrub with soft, pointed 3- to 5-lobed leaves up to 7 inches long, produces a tasty, red, thimble-shaped berry edible by humans but better left for the birds and bears.

The descent then steepens and you switchback down another 600 feet, then cross Clicks Creek once more. Small campsites appear on both sides of the waterway. In just under a half mile from the ford, Clicks Creek Cutoff 32E16 (6340/4.2) branches right heading east toward Grey Meadow Guard Station. This cutoff is part of your return loop. Meanwhile, continue ahead, northeast.

Leaving the canyon of the creek, the trail,

now under boughs of Jeffrey pines with little understory brush, arrives at an intersection (6180/1.0) with Fish Creek Meadow Trail 32E12. This is the path to Mountaineer Creek northwest onto which hikers of T60 turn left. To the right the trail goes to Grey Meadow as does the next prong of the trail (6220/0.3). Your path ahead descends to the flood plain of Mountaineer Creek and the Little Kern River.

While skirting the broad flat on a rock-lined path, you pass a Fire Safe Area with a couple of large campsites. At a junction (6085/0.5) with Nelson Cabin Trail 32E08, head for the path signed RIFLE CREEK, which crosses the river channel. During years of drought, willows creep into the channel and grow on the spit between the creek and the river. In a droughty midsummer you can step across the river on rocks; otherwise, it is a fairly shallow wade except during peak snowmelt.

Beyond the ford, the trail of decomposed granite ascends a nose between the Little Kern River at a bend and Sagebrush Gulch. A short time after a climb over slabs, it meets *Lion Meadows Trail 32E02* (6281/1.0) onto which you continue north. Clicks Creek Trail ends at this junction.

Alas, the route over rolling terrain from here to near Rifle Creek stays inland from the beauty of the river. An open forest of Jeffrey

Willows narrow Little Kern River

pines along the way allows some shade for you and lots of sun for a healthy growth of thick-leafed manzanita and holly-leafed Kern ceanothus. Several creeks intersect the trail; slender Table Meadow Creek is the first. A campsite sits to the left near the creek. The trail then skirts Table Meadow, rises over a low ridge, and approaches a sturdy fence surrounding Lion Meadows R. M. Pyles Camp. This remote, 120-acre site, purchased in 1977, offers a follow-up experience for the young men who sampled Pyles camp life at Lloyd Meadows. One of their projects keeps the nearby wilderness clean; in 1991 alone, the young men removed 1400 pounds of litter.

You cross through the gate to your left, saunter over Lion Meadows and hop Lion Creek at the meadow's far edge. After the creek, the upper end of unmarked, obscure Nelson Cabin Trail 32E08 (6622/2.1) forks west to take fishermen 1.2 miles to the Little Kern River. You continue ahead at the fork through another gate and step across a muddy branch of Lion Creek. Still on Lion Meadows Trail, you pass dim Coyote Lakes Trail 32E05 (6670/0.2) peeling off to the right, one of several approaches to the mountain top Coyote Lakes snuggled in cirques on the Great Western Divide. As you progress, views improve of the jutting crest of the Divide. Next, step across Sheep and No Name creeks, then boulder-hop Willow Creek, the best source of running water since the Little Kern River. A campsite is located near the north bank. Immediately after the ford, a Hunters Trail (6985/1.2)—unmaintained but adequately ducked—also leads to the Coyote Lakes.

Your route crosses a usually dry branch of Willow Creek, and ascends to a saddle where the bald mountains surrounding Silver Lake (T99) appear in the northern landscape. Then the trail descends to a meadow of corn lilies and crosses Tamarack Creek. "Tamarack" was the name that John Muir and his contemporaries used for what is now known as lodgepole pines. Lodgepoles are usually found at higher elevations in the Southern Sierra, but a pocket of these trees shelters

campsites along the creek here and farther up the creek at a Fire Safe Area known as "Jordan Camp."

The trail eases toward the river as it climbs a ridge. Ahead, the burned trees on a hill to the north dubbed "Jenkins Knob" come into view. Now composed of decomposed granite, the path descends to cross a usually dry gully, then rounds on the colorful metamorphics of the knob to finally bring the boistrous river into view. Across the river, the canyonside is furrowed with quartzite streaked with magenta and orange and stained chartreuse with blotchy lichens.

After passing through a gate, clinking over chunks of rock and rounding a wildflower concealed seep, you walk a slight upgrade to arrive at Rifle Creek Campground and Public Corrals, a Fire Safe Area (7400/3.8). The primitive camp consists of three widely spaced sites with tables, fire rings with grills and an outhouse located just upslope from the spring, which elicits raised eyebrows from would-be drinkers.

This was home base for co-author Jim Jenkins when he was the backcountry ranger in 1979 for the Tule River District's Golden Trout Wilderness. He relayed shortwave radio messages to headquarters from his favorite hill, which he urged people to climb for a comprehensive view of the superb Little Kern River basin.

Excursion L: Jenkins Knob

Vandever Mountain, Farewell Gap, Florence Peak and the mountains around Silver Lake and Shotgun Pass brush the artist's canvas with earthy browns to the north; clockwise, forest greens of the Great Western Divide; muted pastels of the Little Kern valley; distant blues of the river's watershed mountains and foreground sorrels of Camelback ridge complete the painting as seen from atop the knob.

Distance   1.6 miles, round trip
Steep Ascents   0.2 mile
Elevation Gain   605 feet
Skills   Intermediate route finding; Class 1

climbing
Map USGS 7.5-min. *Quinn Pk*
Description Hike east above the campground (7400/0.0) where you will find a
rough, fairly-well defined and blazed *trail*, a
retired section of the Lion Meadows Trail. On
it you curve right, south-southeast up the
gulch to a saddle (7810/0.5). There you turn
right and climb *cross-country* west and south
to the top where you circle the summit
(8005/0.5) for its many views.

*   *   *   *   *

North of Rifle Creek Campground, the
trail passes left of corrals to enter a dark
woods of Jeffrey pines, then crosses the
stream boulders of frolicsome, bubbly Rifle
Creek. The long ignored and barely per-
ceptible Little Kern Trail 31E12 (7444/0.6)
angles in near the south banks of Rifle Creek.
(Removed from the forest's system but still
used by horsemen, the east extension of that
trail climbs up Rifle Creek's crease to Coyote
Pass.) Your trail ascends a gully to top a
broad saddle and continues on a gentle
upgrade where you soon hear the rumble of
Pistol Creek. The path fords it above its
exuberant cascades. Just beyond a single,
shredded-barked juniper hovers over a few
springtime nosegays of phlox and penstemon: a blend of purples on these rust-
colored metamorphic rock slopes.

While hiking along the trail here, you may
see a female Mountain Quail describe circles
before you to distract you from her nearby
nest. Otherwise, you are unlikely to see her
perfectly camouflaged gray and brown body.
Mountain Quail have white diagonal flank
markings and a distinguishing straight, black
feather stretching high atop their heads.
Usually these birds seek cover before you
realize their nearness.

The trail suddenly switchbacks before
reaching Shotgun Creek. The piece of trail
straight ahead was closed to eliminate parallel paths. Your trail ascends to meet *Farewell
Gap Trail 31E10* (8970/2.6), on which you
continue, now southeast.

On a gradual descent of brushy slopes,
you again cross Pistol Creek, 640 vertical
feet above the first crossing, then gain eleva-

tion to reach a saddle (9044/1.2) athwart
your route. Here among foxtail pines and a
few western white pines, you find a large,
waterless, boulder-sheltered campsite and
enchanting views of the northern mountains.
Hiking beyond the saddle on an easy downslope, you step across a Rifle Creek fork
hidden in dense willows; the other forks of the
creek are usually dry after early snowmelt.

Two widely spaced pairs of switchbacks
and a traverse through an avalanche area and
a hanging garden of mixed flowers take you
into the pines where a TRAIL sign precedes a
rank of nine switchbacks. After gaining 1000
feet of elevation, the switchbacks cease at a
crossing of a stark saddle (10,395/2.1), the
highest point on this trip. The trail then
descends to campsites at the headwaters of
Tamarack Creek, banked with red heather,
Labrador tea and overarched with lodgepole
pines.

Shortly beyond the creek the route
reaches Coyote Pass (10,160/0.5) where it
leaves the Little Kern watershed of Golden
Trout Wilderness and enters the watershed of
the North Fork Kern River and Sequoia National Park—pets and weapons forbidden.
Prominent on the horizon far to the east
appear Kern and Olancha peaks, the hall-
mark mountains of the Kern Plateau. Plenty
of room on the gravel for dry camping among
the boulders and foxtail pines.

Descending on the *Coyote Pass Trail*,
northward vistas of rarely visited crags and
cirques capture attention, while an incipient
branch of Coyote Creek to the right sometimes has a trickling flow. A campsite spreads
on the flat across the creek. Soon you amble
past a metal sign indicating the junction
(9330/1.1) with the Coyote Lakes Trail of
T58. You shortly cross the slender creek
branch, stroll alongside a lush meadow and
splash through Coyote Creek below the fork
with its branch.

Your descent steepens as you hike near the
north bank of the now cascading, fizzing
Coyote Creek; you then ford on boulders a
burbling tributary arriving from lakes tucked
in cirques high to the north. Soon you wind
along a fern-edged entrance to Coyote Creek:

wade across or find a log. Possible camping exists on the low ridge immediately beyond the ford. Now the creek curves away to bounce raucously down its canyon, while your trail clings, sometimes precariously, to steep slopes. On your moderate-to-steep descent, wide views appear across the canyon of towering granitic walls and of two-tiered Volcano Falls dropping amid ancient basalt. Below the trail Coyote Creek falls also compel a pause.

In time you notice the green patch of grass far below that fronts the tree-hidden ranger cabin; then the curve of the river; then you drop below treetops and arrive at a junction (6520/4.9) with *Lewis Camp Trail 33E01*, onto which you now hike. A trail here heads north across the creek to the ranger station and beyond. (On a long trip such as this it is good policy to sign in at the ranger station.) Heading south now and again in the Golden Trout Wilderness of Sequoia National Forest, you find a spur path (6360/0.4) slanting to a riverside terrace with large, ideal campsites. (It continues to the bridge where it

meets the Golden Trout Trail that ascends the steep walls of the canyon to the Kern Plateau.)

You remain on Lewis Camp Trail 33E01, part of the historic Hockett Trail built in 1863 (See Chapter 1) to stroll above the river, which briefly passes from view as it curves around a knoll. You see the river again where it unravels into three branches creating meadow islands and walk among the outskirts of the meadow flora, sometimes on a muddy path. Soon you pass a sizable camp-site to the right near the banks of a nameless creeklet that is the only stream feeding Kern Lake ahead, a large, shallow body of water slowly silting in. Ducks find the lake and marshes to their liking and occasionally so do bald eagles that you may notice circling above the lake. Unseen by you, the Kern River flows into an adjoining embayment, away to the east.

Next, climb above the lake to pass through a saddle, then descend to tranquil Little Kern Lake, also landlocked (See T57). A scat-tering of campsites exist around its borders.

Canyon of the North Fork Kern River near Little Kern Lake

South of the lake you cross a canal diverting water from Little Kern Lake Creek to the lake, then pad over a bridge (6240/2.9) above the empty creekbed and walk through a kind of turnstile to the right of a cattle gate.

The path rises to cross behind a knoll, then drops by zigzags to the floodplain of Grasshopper Flat, crosses Grasshopper Creek, then at the flat's south end, arrives at a primitive campground with tables and grills. A short hike through the camp leads to a delightfully attractive, cottonwood-lined section of the colorful river.

After strolling past several packer campsites, you ford Leggitt Creek on boulders, pass through another cattle gate and begin a long incline out of the canyon. The river, which has followed the Kern Canyon fault for sometime, bends away to flow around Hockett Peak, but you continue along the fault line. You soon climb past Hole in the Ground Trail 33E05 (5845/2.8), a dead-end path to a popular fishing hole.

Angora Creek intersects and briefly waters the path prior to a split in the trail. The lower, newer section removes some of the steepness and at its U curve, affords lingering views to the north of the Kern River Trench. In time you level through the defile between the talus slopes of the Great Western Divide and the land form of Hockett Peak. Two trails no longer discernible but mentioned for the benefit of trail buffs, peal off to the left: the upper section of Hole in the Ground Trail departs through the pass to the east; 0.6 mile later, prior to Willow Meadows, the Hockett Meadow Trail climbs steeply up the slopes of Hockett Peak.

You next pass through a gate signed WILLOW MEADOWS PUBLIC PASTURE and hike beyond one packers' campsite to another one perched on the north slope across from the long meadow. A year-round spring with a pipe extension offers a good place to obtain water. Willow Meadows Trail 33E14 (6340/3.6), a shortcut to the Little Kern bridge by one mile, forks right from your trail.

Lewis Camp Trail 33E01 continues south on fringes of meadows and through open woods, leaving the public pasture. It passes a sign indicating TROUT MEADOWS SPRING, then meets a T junction (6180/1.6) with Doe Meadow Trail 33E10 that heads east for Kern Flat. After another stock fence gate, the route arrives at the Trout Meadows Guard Station (6170/0.2) and two large Fire Safe Area campsites with tables. Water is not always available here.

It is possible that a lodge or trading post existed at this site in the 1860s, because the three historic trails, Jordan, Hockett and Dennison converged at this point, but nothing has been found. The remains of a noticeable foundation you see here were the start of a building begun for unknown purposes sometime around World War II. By your visit the Forest Service may have a display with information and a map of the three trails.

After leaving the cabin you hike along the fence-enclosed Trout Meadows, and pass a shortcut to Doe Meadow Trail heading east across the meadow through a parallel fenced corridor (6160/0.3). Departing this bucolic scene, you ramble west over low ridges and shallow ravines inland from, but edging ever nearer to, the Little Kern River. In time you pass the south end of Willow Meadows Trail 33E14 (5960/2.1) and curve around an ephemeral brook to walk over the Little Kern suspension bridge (5760/0.6). The Little Kern River at this point invites hikers to stay awhile. Several campsites give access to swimming pools and fishing holes in this colorful basaltic and granitic canyon.

You will find that the trail divides on the south side of the bridge: your route is the right fork to Grey Meadow. Head west up the side of the ridge, then transfer to *Grey Meadow Trail 32E15* at its junction (6060/0.3), leaving Lewis Camp Trail 33E01 that you have followed since the ranger station in Sequoia National Park. On an easy traverse, you pass a connector trail (6130/0.3) to Lewis Camp Trail, then dip to boulder-hop Fish Creek. Here lies a campsite on the north bank of this creek, which lazily flows among willows and wild roses. After climbing out of the creek's canyon, you transverse the slopes on a mildly undulating path beneath a canopy of lacy pine needles, and pass a little used

Trout Meadows Guard Station

path, Round Meadow Trail 32E14 (6260/ 1.7), heading northeast. Before long you spot

Grey Meadow. You slowly begin to lose elevation, then dip across a small stream and head for the guard station (6152/0.9). Usually a summer ranger is stationed in this 1914 cabin. Cool, shady campsites spread to its north next to a refreshing spring.

To find your trail, northwest of the station, you pass the trail to Burnt Corral; then, at a three-pronged junction, take the middle path, *Clicks Creek Cutoff 32E16*. (The left is to a public pasture; the right to Mountaineer Creek.) After an easy stroll over a low ridge and across Clicks Creek—below a nice bathing hole—you arrive at *Clicks Creek Trail 32E11* (6340/1.2), the path on which you began this extended journey. Turn left onto the familiar trail and ascend west on its lengthy path, retracing your steps to the end your journey (7850/4.2).

T60   Mountaineer Creek Backpack

This trip of tumbling creeks and abundant wildflowers appeals to family groups and flower buffs. The water that spills in silvery curls and glides down smooth slabs to pool in rockbound hollows entices the young and young in spirit to linger. The wildflowers that gather in rainbow colors to hang from crannied cliffs, bank against creeks, sprinkle throughout meadows and scatter by trails beckon the novice admirer with flower guide in hand and the experienced botanist seeking a rare find.

Distance   20.0 miles, loop trip
Steep Ascents   None
Elevation Gain   4350 feet
Skills   Easy-to-intermediate route finding
Seasons   Spring, summer, fall (Wilderness permit required)
Map   USGS 7.5-min. *Camp Nelson*
Trailhead   46. See car tour T46. (This hike can be converted into a shuttle trip and shortened by 3.3 trail miles if you end at **TH48**, Summit Trailhead. There are 4.0 road miles between trailheads.)
Description   The beginning of this trip is described in T59.

Northeastbound Trail 32E11 Log

T59 Clicks Cr TH	7850	0.0
Clicks Cr Cutoff	6340	4.2
Fish Cr Mdw Tr	6180	1.0

Turning left from Clicks Creek Trail 32E11 heading northwest on *Fish Creek*

Meadow Trail 32E12, your route under dappled patterns cast by Jeffrey pines, rolls across the wrinkled, well-drained floor of the Little Kern basin, inland from the water channels. At length it drops to a boulder-heaped flood plain of Mountaineer Creek where it curves away from a path to large campsites. The route, now on rough gravels, crests an elongated bouldered hump through which the creek has found a passage. Here the water gathers, while upstream it spills through a succession of granite-bound pools. Paths from a string of campsites spread in the midst of an assemblage of shade trees access the pools. After passing gravel bars, your trail fords the creek where it debouches from the canyon (6350/1.8). The following brief, moderate-to-steep ascent zigzags, then curves by a forked junction (6500/0.2) flanking a huge blowdown; Fish Creek Meadow

Trail ends here and you continue on ***Mountaineer Trail 32E10***.

Traveling west, hike on the undulating path above the frolicsome creek, then descend to pass a campsite and stroll along a gravelly plain. A bit beyond, a large packers' campsite across the creek hides behind a downed tree—only the tops of log stools reveal its location. All along, Mountaineer Creek tumbles through a series of tempting granite-locked pools, but a short distance beyond the packers' site you reach the most inviting one of all. Before the confluence of South Mountaineer Creek, the pool fills a gorge next to a slope of gabbro bedrock where your path was carved. The long, slick slide down which Mountaineer Creek whisks into this pool, its banks bedecked with wildflowers, invite more than a passing pause (6880/2.1). If you are interested in camping nearby, you may find a remnant of the long abandoned South Mountaineer Trail north of South Mountaineer Creek. It leads west to medium campsites in 0.2 mile at the confluence of South Mountaineer and Jacobson creeks.

Venturing on, you will want to keep your flower guide handy for awhile as many varieties of wildflowers grow along the stream, in the several meadows you will skirt and along the drier trailsides. A sample would be: white—geranium, gayophytum, yampah, ranger's buttons, yarrow; yellow—Bigelow sneezeweed, groundsel, monkey flower, cinquefoil, tiger lily, buttercup; red—scarlet gilia, penstemon, paintbrush; blue/purple—shooting star, larkspur, monkshood, mountain bluebell, aster, pennyroyal and lupine. Perhaps the most abundant of all of these are lupines. Their flowers are so numerous they often bathe whole hillsides in a wash of color. The blooms range in color from purple to blue to yellow to variegated. The many species (California alone can boast of more than 60) range in size from mat ground cover to 9-foot bushes. The leaves are palmate; the flowers cluster at the ends of stalks; the seed pods are soft green and fuzzy.

The trail crosses Mountaineer Creek, hugs the flowered west bank, then fords it twice in quick succession, all easy boulder-hops. The next similar ford, reached in a moment, is not immediately apparent—it is just beyond a flat-topped rock cantilevered over the creek.

On the north bank, you hike mostly through forest for 0.6 mile, then cross the creek again. Here you loop southwest, away from the creek, while ascending a ravine with a seasonal tributary. The path on occasion becomes overgrown in meadow flora, but quickly reappears. You soon swing northwest to again cross Mountaineer Creek, then remain near its north bank. Next you hike through the fringes of flower-speckled meadows where the trail is sometimes marked with ducks; then through red fir woods where the trail is well-defined. Again cross the fledging creek, this time at the south end of Mowery Meadow, which you skirt. A large, Fire Safe Area campsite faces the meadow several paces before the crest junction (8127/2.4) of ***Summit Trail 31E14***, where you turn left.

The path, now heading south, crosses a transitory brook near a campsite and skirts a meadowy strip while crisscrossing the Western Divide crest. Then it proceeds past Jacobsen Meadow with a Fire Safe campsite to the left and Jacobsen Trail 31E21 (8360/1.3) in a red fir forest to the right. After a 250 foot switchbacking ascent, the route tops the ridge athwart the divide and offers the most expansive views of this trip.

The trail now wanders in all directions as it descends, eventually to cross South Mountaineer Creek's headwaters next to a sloping abundance of wildflowers. A medium campsite nestles nearby on a creekside ledge. Beyond the creek, the trail ascends to pass out of Golden Trout Wilderness and down to the Summit Trailhead (8280/3.7).

If you plan to hike to the Clicks Creek Trailhead, you can compare and contrast the next 3.3 miles of forest travel with the wilderness forest you just left. From here, you travel through plots of clear-cut land with replanted, even-aged trees, selectively cut forests, or as yet untouched forests.

You find the ***Summit M'cyclepath 31E14*** at the west end of the trailhead lot and hike south on it through a stump-ridden area of modest regrowth, past a former log-loading zone to descend to unpaved SNF Road 21S50 (North Road) (8160/0.4). Hike south along the road past the SUMMIT TRAIL sign and cross an open area on the east side used mostly to park vehicles with horse trailers. Descend briefly to step over the trickle of water comprising the beginning of North Fork Clicks Creek. Ascend gently on a route parallel to and below the road, then cross the road (8410/0.7) and switchback up to a saddle following the curve of the road.

For the remaining journey the trail loses elevation: it passes White Meadow; then crosses the main road again at an offset junction (8340/0.8); then descends steeply to moderately to outflank a ridge to the right and an elongated meadow bilobed by a seasonal tributary of Clicks Creek to the left.

Soon you cross a road leading to the structure and corral you saw near the beginning of Clicks Creek Trail, venture across furrowed ground and just prior to nascent Clicks Creek, exit the trail onto paved road (7780/1.1), where you stay until you reach Clicks Creek Trailhead (7850/0.3).

An inviting pool in Mountaineer Creek

T61   Jordan Peak Lookout Day Hike
With Excursion M: McIntyre Rock

The depth of the Tule River canyons contrasts with the breadth of their backgrounds—the San Joaquin Valley and the Southern Sierra—in the views from Jordan Peak: a prominence crested with spiky rock and crowned with a lookout.

Distance   1.6 miles
Steep Ascents   None
Elevation Gain   515 feet
Skills   Easy route finding; easy-to-moderate hiking
Seasons   Spring, summer, fall
Map   USGS 7.5-min. *Camp Nelson*
Trailhead   47. See car tour T46. From unpaved SNF Road 21S50 (North Road) turn left on *SNF Road 20S71* (0.0/0.0). Drive west past the gate along the rocky road still showing the remains of thin-surfaced asphalt. Pass the gated road to the tower and arrive at the cul-de-sac parking lot, **TH47** (1.2/1.2).
Description   Climb west from the parking lot (8600/0.0) on well-maintained *Jordan Lookout Trail 31E25* over slopes nearly clear-cut—a few trees were spared. Scattered brush and planted seedlings soften the mauled, rocky slopes. Ascend a series of switchbacks, zigzags and curves that begins long-legged, then decreases in length as you progress. Cross the access road and continue on the path, now among more brush and red fir trees, some western white pines. Very near the top you pass the trail to McIntyre Rock deleted from the Forest Service's system of trails. You next climb the 26-rung ladder to the lookout catwalk (9115/0.8). This 1934 Forest Service lookout operates in cooperation with the Camp Nelson Volunteer Fire Department. Camp Nelson sits out of view at the southern foot of Jordan Peak. The peak was named for the trailblazer John Jordan.

After enjoying the panorama that is as sweeping from outside the lookout as in, you may wish to sample the views from McIntyre Rock.

Excursion M: McIntyre Rock

The walk-up backside of McIntyre Rock's cracked and decomposing granite ill prepares you for the precipitous south face that suddenly drops 500 feet below you. Viewing this drop from above affords nonclimbers a taste of the zing that rock climbers often experience.

Distance   2.0 miles, loop trip
Steep Ascents   0.2 mile
Elevation Gain   500 feet
Skills   Intermediate route finding; Class 1 climbing (Class 4–5 pitches optional)
Description   The *path* (9080/0.0) descends steeply south via switchbacks and zigzags on rough terrain from the top of Jordan Peak, then the grade lessens as it curves west under cover of forest. It soon passes a trail (8560/0.6) on which you will return.

The moderate-to-steep descent, eased by switchbacks and zigzags, resumes after you hike through a meadow laced with ferns and dotted with flowers. One tall flower here that is easy to recognize is ranger's buttons. This 3- to 5-foot-tall stout plant of the carrot family has clusters of small round, white buttons composed of tiny compact flowers. Its broad, divided leaves can reach 16 inches in length.

Old blazes mark the path in the forest, and brush sometimes encroaches on the trail. In a short time you pass Hassack Trail 31E24 (8140/0.3). Before you lies an unassuming pile of boulders: McIntyre Rock. After a brief, easy walk up, you reach its plunging south face (8180/0.1). This rock, a creek and a sequoia grove were all named for Thomas McIntyre, a Tulare County pioneer and 1880s sheepman.

On your return trip, hike to the junction (8560/0.4) of the trail from the cul-de-sac, then turn right. Now easy hiking prevails as you traverse east along the path amid red firs and logging debris. The path soon melds into a retired logging road on which numerous seedlings have sprouted. On it you quickly arrive at your starting point (8600/0.6).

T62   Maggie Lakes Backpack
With Excursion N: Maggie Mountain

These three exquisite subalpine lakes, snuggled in granite cups at the foot of craggy mountains, equal High Sierra lakes in beauty and surpass many of them in accessibility. Families find this wilderness outing particularly inviting. At 9000 feet, the lakes are warm enough to make summertime swimming irresistible, yet cool enough to support the colorful Little Kern golden trout: a delight for fishermen of all ages.

Distance   19.0 miles, round trip
Steep Ascents   None
Elevation Gain   3740 feet
Skills   Easy route finding
Seasons   Spring, summer, fall (Wilderness permit required)
Maps   USGS 7.5-min. *Camp Nelson, Quinn Pk*
Trailhead   48. See car tour T46.
Description   From the parking lot trailhead (8280/0.0), 9.8 miles north of Quaking Aspen Campground, amble north along *Summit Trail 31E14.* You enter Golden Trout Wilderness at the Clicks Creek/Mountaineer Creek divide. Deep in a forest dark with red fir trees, you lose elevation gently on steep north-facing slopes; then, nearly a mile into the trip, you pass a medium campsite perched above the fledgling South Mountaineer Creek. The creek's two cascading headwater forks convene at your ford, bounding a sloping 50-foot wall of hanging gardens. Water surfaces at the wall's brink, then spreads over a profusion of ferns and wildflowers.

Ascending easily after the ford, you switchback to touch the Western Divide crest, then swing away to return via zigzags north of rocky Point 8774. Now on top of the ridge athwart the divide, saunter along the exposed crest where you have far views of Maggie and Moses mountains to the north, the Great Western Divide over the Little Kern River basin to the east and the usual brown-smudged San Joaquin Valley smog above the North Fork Middle Fork Tule River

canyon to the west.

Crisscrossing the crest all the way to Maggie Mountain, your course descends and passes Jacobsen Trail 31E21 (8360/3.7), arriving from the south. (This trail drops 3800 feet mercilessly in 5.5 miles to the Tule River fork, then eventually reaches the Forest Service's Camp Wishon Campground.) A lone, Fire Safe Area, medium campsite sits at the west edge of Jacobsen Meadow. If you are hiking here in the ebb of summer, you are likely to see yarrows, which are among the last wildflowers to survive as the ground dries. The 1- to 2-foot-tall yarrow has a somewhat flat cluster of small white flowers atop a fibrous stem with fernlike, feathery leaves. Soon your trail passes a slender brook that flows until late summer and a small campsite. Your path then passes a T junction (8127/1.3) with Mountaineer Trail 32E10 of T60. You will find another single, fairly large Fire Safe Area campsite at the south rim of Mowery Meadow, a short way down that trail to the right.

You next saunter past the tip of Mowery Meadow and climb moderately to steeply with the help of zigzags to near Alpine Meadow and a cluster of large campsites. One campsite within a former cabin's foundation and two with tables are located down a path south of the meadow; choice places to camp if you had an afternoon start on this journey. A branch of Alpine Creek begins feebly here. North of Alpine Meadow a long-gone trail reached the creek and descended to Nelson Cabin Trail. If your interest lies in viewpoints rather than obsolete trails, you push on to look for a NEVA POINT sign (8500/0.6) tacked high on a fir to the left. A faint 0.2-mile path gains 150 feet to reach Neva Point, high above Burro Creek drainage. In the westward panorama, especially vivid at sunset, the deep Tule River canyon in the middle distance contrasts (on a clear day) with the vast, smooth San Joaquin Valley in the background.

The course beyond the viewpoint turnoff zigzags up to a saddle, passing a sloping meadow; it then switchbacks down to quickly pass the T junction (8904/0.9) terminus of Griswold Trail 31E18 of T83, another trail that relentlessly drops to the river below. Your path roves beyond more meadows, one with a small campsite, then ascends to the boulder-strewn northeast shoulder of Maggie Mountain (9300/1.4). You may enjoy an ascent of this gem of a peak with its sweeping views.

Excursion N: Maggie Mountain

Maggie Mountain sits at the south end of a crescent of unnamed peaks that form the Pecks Canyon bowl. Maggie's boulder peak presents an ideal climb, difficult enough to be challenging, yet within most hikers' ability. The uninterrupted views from the top encompass mountain ranges in every direction.

Distance   2.2 miles, round trip
Steep Ascents   0.3 mile
Elevation Gain   745 feet
Skills   Easy route finding; Class 2 climbing
Map   USGS 7.5-min. *Quinn Pk*
Description   Leave the trail at the shoulder of Maggie (9300/0.0) just above a stock fence. Walk *cross-country* southwest, first climbing over a small hill, then strolling atop the ridgecrest among gnarled foxtail pines. Climb the next intervening platy hill, but stay to the north of its summit rocks. Even so, you will drop some to the saddle before ascending 450 feet in elevation over boulders interspersed with chinquapin to the top of Maggie. The highest point (10,042/1.1) of this mountain, a wedge-shaped, coarse-grained alaskitic granitoid protrusion, can be straddled with some effort. The register tablet rests lower down in a cookie tin next to the 1956 benchmark.

According to Francis P. Farquhar's *Place Names of the High Sierra*, Maggie Mountain was named for Maggie Kincaid, a San Joaquin Valley teacher, by Frank Knowles, who accompanied Clarence King to Mount Whitney in 1873. Peter Browning offers another version in his book *Place Names of the Sierra Nevada*. The Kincaids, while on a hunting trip, were visited by a government surveyor who greatly enjoyed Maggie's camp biscuits. He assigned her name to the moun-

Co-author Ruby reaches the summit of Maggie Mountain

tain she had just climbed to show his appreciation. (Later the name was added to the nearby lakes.)

*　　*　　*　　*　　*

On Summit Trail 31E14, beyond the mountain climb take-off, you pass through the hikers' passage of a stock fence and switchback down to boulder-hop a branch of Peaks Canyon creek, which flows at least until late summer. A few yards later you meet a junction (8884/0.6) near a campsite. Here in the late 1980s a trail change occurred. The Summit Trail no longer continues north into private property and the site of Pecks Cabin, but now turns abruptly left onto the former Maggie Kincaid Trail. Unless you have reservations at the Cook Ranch Bed and Breakfast, you are asked not to take the former trail. The Cook ranch house was constructed in the 1980s, but the family history goes back to the 1890s when the owner's great grandparents ran cattle in the area. For reservations call (209) 784-7279.

Briefly outlined in rocks, the trail heads west, rising gradually, then abruptly over boulder ridgelets. In this manner it continues above the outlet creek of Maggie Lakes. In time, just before reaching the edge of the lower lake, a path to the left peels off to camp-sites between the mountain slopes and a lakeside lateral moraine, thus protected from occasional winds but deprived of lake views. The Summit Trail crosses the lower lake's outlet (9020/0.9), then skirts the lake's north shore where you find numerous viewful, tree-shaded campsites—and the backside of a one-seater outhouse.

To reach the upper and largest lake, find in 0.1 mile along the trail, the rock-lined use path leading southwest from the most western campsite. On this 0.3 mile path you ford a stone-strewn inlet stream, slant up the low, spottily-forested ridge and arrive at the lake. It has a few scattered campsites. To reach the middle lake, also about 0.3 mile, start at the same campsite, but curve around the banks of the lower lake, then climb over the south moraine that separates the two lakes.

All three sparkling lakes, treasures of the Western Divide mountains, were glacier-carved from Cretaceous granitic rock. Each one's shoreline is studded with red fir, lodgepole and western white pine and intermittently ringed with heather and Labrador tea. Maggie Mountain is hidden by the slightly lower, closer, unnamed rocky peak that fills the southern view.

Beautiful Upper Maggie Lake of the Western Divide Mountains

T63   Maggie Lakes-Soda Spring Backpack
With Excursion O: Sheep Mountain

This circuit of the showiest water on the Western Divide was dubbed the "Silver Knapsack Trail" by Boy Scouts. Water along the route shimmers in glacial-carved lakes, fizzes from a bubbling soda spring and spills from pool to pool down both creeks and river. Ample campsites at points of interest and pathfinding on a secondary trail afford a mixture of comfort and challenge along the way.

Distance   35.9 miles, loop trip
Steep Ascents   0.8 mile
Elevation Gain   6545 feet
Skills   Easy-to-intermediate route finding
Seasons   Spring, summer, fall (Wilderness permit required)
Maps   USGS 7.5-min. *Camp Nelson, Quinn Pk*
Trailhead   48. See car tour T46. (This hike can be converted into a shuttle trip and shortened by 3.3 trail miles if you end at Clicks Creek Trailhead, **TH46**. There are 4.0 road miles between trailheads.)
Description   The beginning of this trip is described in T62.

Northbound Trail 31E14 Log

T62	Summit TH	8280	0.0
	Jacobsen Tr	8360	3.7
	Mountaineer Tr	8127	1.3
	Neva Point	8500	0.6
	Griswold Tr	8904	0.9
	Maggie Mtn Ex	9300	1.4
	Closed Tr	8884	0.6
	Maggie Lk outlet	9020	0.9

After a stay at Maggie Lakes, resume hiking on **Summit Trail 31E14**. Heading west, you mount a rocky passage, then meander north to rise over jumbled, hummocky chunks of granite. Next descend to Frog Lakes (9005/0.9), which house a couple of campsites. Here you cross a log-jammed, sometime stream between the two lakes. The lesser "lake" to the east, usually a saucer of dried mud, becomes a small lake only during pluvial periods.

The path next makes a brief, rocky ascent and then travels up a slope of shattered granite to ford a seasonal branch of Pecks Canyon creek. It zigzags up a glacial moraine near a deep crease sometimes carrying over-

flow water from Twin Lakes. The trail passes southeast of the lakes, where a use path branches off to reach the upper Twin. Large campsites abound at the cirque-cuddled Twin Lakes (9100/0.8): bodies of water circled with grasses and sedges at the base of rugged Sheep Mountain.

Beyond the lakes your route crosses a dry gully and gently ascends to meet the north end of a former segment of the Summit Trail (9340/0.7), now closed to the general public. Your trail ascends north, gentle at first, flanked by patches of mat lupine, pinemat manzanita and chinquapin and skirts a meadow seen in slices between lodgepole pines. It then steepens as it turns northwest up the slopes of Sheep Mountain, passes through a stock-fence gate and arrives at the Pecks Canyon Entrance (9920/0.9) to Sequoia National Park, the highest point on the trip. The park's uniform black metal sign with silver letters informs you that pets and weapons are not allowed. The wide saddle offers space for dry camping. At this point no wilderness explorer, much less peakbagger, will want to miss the inspiring views that follow an easy walk to the summit of Sheep Mountain.

Excursion O: Sheep Mountain

Astonishing views atop Sheep Mountain far surpass the meager effort needed to reach the summit.

Distance   0.6 mile, round trip
Steep Ascents   None
Elevation Gain   140 feet
Skills   Easy route finding; Class 1 climbing
Map   USGS 7.5-min. *Quinn Pk*

Description From the Summit Trail (9920/0.0) at the border between the park and the wilderness, head west *cross-country* up the wide ridge of fractured granodiorite briefly clothed with foxtail pines and spottily covered with mat lupine. You will find the register tablet under a cairn (10,060/.0.3) on the platy apex of this partially glaciated prominence.

In the foreground view to the northwest appears Dennison Ridge with Homers Nose sniffing above it from the next ridge. Center north, you can see the Hockett plateau bordered to its east by the treeless points of Vandever Mountain and Florence Peak and the prominent V of Farewell Gap; to the west, Coyote Pass and Peaks and the southern terminus of the Great Western Divide; and to the south, Twin Lakes and barely discernible Maggie Lakes.

*   *   *   *   *

After the Sheep Mountain climb, now in Sequoia National Park, ramble down the dusty trail. Keep right at the first fork and turn right at the T junction (9660/0.3) with **Summit Lake Trail**. (If you turn left at the junction, in 0.8 mile you reach Summit Lake and its many campsites.)

Contouring northeast, the trail rises and dips along slopes wooded with lodgepole pines, then angles across a wide saddle on Windy Ridge, a crest on the Western Divide. The path briefly traverses the crest. Where the trees part, distant Kern Peak comes into view above the Little Kern basin panorama. Descending zigzags introduce the meadow environs of Windy Gap, where, at a junction (9504/2.1), the route takes an abrupt change of direction to the right on **Atwell Hockett Trail**.

After heading south through a lush meadow generously sprinkled with wildflowers well into summer (no cattle grazing in Sequoia National Park), you slowly curve east on the well-built trail supported with down-slope boulders, and soon near an avalanche swath. The diagonally halved license plates tacked high on wayside trees lead snow surveyors to Quinn Cabin ahead. You pass ribbons of willows and an unmapped spring issuing forth from the south slopes of Quinn Peak. Here larkspur and monkshood thrive among a profusion of blooms. Rare strains of bleeding heart and trillium, occasionally seen along the trail in damp, shaded places, should be carefully preserved for future visitors to enjoy.

Next ford a seasonal, incipient branch of Soda Spring Creek near a campsite above the trail and arrive at nicely preserved Quinn Cabin (8320/2.0). A shovel lashed horizontally to the cabin just below the roof line demonstrates the depth of snow sometimes found by the surveyors who, after the long snowshoe trek in, have to shovel snow to uncover the cabin door. The hut is also used by the Hockett ranger on patrol; campsites can be found next to the meadow. Originally this was the summer haunt of Harry Quinn, a turn-of-the-century sheepman.

Leaving this tranquil hide-away, the trail gently descends south, then bends east near the banks of the branch of Soda Spring Creek, which winds its way through its own grove of colorful quaking aspens. A boulder-hop or a log-balancing act by you gets you across the creek dry shod. The path leaves Sequoia National Park and enters Golden Trout Wilderness. Near here the trail, now **Quinn Trail 31E13**, forks (7860/1.0): take the short left path along the creek to a soda spring (not identified on maps) and several campsites; you later return to take the right path.

This soda spring bubbles with more alacrity than any other soda spring in the Southern Sierra. Its taste is reminiscent of Alka-Seltzer, but its water can be mixed with fruit-flavored powder to create a tasty, fizzy drink. This spring gets its fizz by dissolving crystals containing carbonate as its water flows over rocks rich in minerals with that radical.

Yampah flowers grace the wet banks of a slender brook where the soda spring path more or less ends. The plant's stem supports short, bladelike leaves and numerous white blooms clustered in a flat top (umbel). Its roots and seeds are edible, but a similar looking flower with serrated leaves, water hemlock, is deadly poisonous. Equestrians carefully guide their horses away from both these plants unless they can positively tell them apart. They avoid the lovely but poisonous larkspur as well.

Return to the fork and ascend steep zigzags, cross the previously mentioned brook next to an overhanging log and gain 440 feet in elevation. The grade eases near a saddle. Here in the red fir forest, where blowdowns or broken branches litter the forest floor and trail maintenance is minimal, your path may be difficult to find. Look ahead for its contour beyond the forest litter before you leave the path to loop around the debris.

Now on a lengthy descent, proceed past a stream and meadows on steep east-facing slopes. Look for the fluttering leaves of aspen trees to the right that border the site of the Newlywed Camp. This large campsite was named for the wedding night spent there many years ago by Springville packer Frank Negus and his bride. About 0.3 mile later you pass an aged, fallen sign. It once directed visitors to Pecks Cabin on a now abandoned trail (8060/2.0) still used occasionally by the owners of the cabins near the Pecks site.

Cross a creek near the sign. Jeffrey and sugar pines, incense cedars and white firs indicate your lower elevation. Round an irregular ridge, then drop steeply on a taxing descent along another branch of Soda Spring Creek, dank with chunks of willows. Most travelers continue ahead to the dilapidated remains of Walkers Cabin (7300/1.2) even though the trail crosses the creek at an aged sign 300 feet prior to the structure. Nicknamed "Happy Camp" by Boy Scouts, the cabin built by sheepherders in 1886 is as unfit and unsafe as most late 19th century huts you find in the backcountry, but, as with the others, it has an aura of intrigue. An adequate campsite is located beside the cabin.

A use path next to the cabin commences across the creek and meadow, then merges with the Quinn Trail and heads south. Along the way the trail rises to cross a saddle, dips into a gully and offers scenes of the Great Western Divide over reddish Camelback ridge. The ridge separates the parallel flows of Soda Spring Creek and the Little Kern

River; its southern Point 7330 soon fills your eastern view. After the trail passes the point, it ends at a T junction (6440/1.9) with *Nelson Cabin Trail 32E08* onto which you continue south; you do not cross the creek. Nelson Cabin, at the site near the head of a nearby glade west of the trail, never rose above a few tiers of logs. Campsites near the junction line the creek, as do slabs that invite you to stretch out while soaking your feet.

Ahead, the roller coaster trail seems endless. You pass a stubby post signed RADIO SPOT where reception was best for shortwave radios used by backcountry rangers. Now repeater towers atop peaks offer better overall reception. Soon a fallen sign indicates a junction with abandoned Alpine Creek Trail. After walking by a sand flat, you pass a T junction with Mountaineer Creek Trail 32E10 (6290/1.6). The first segment of that trail leads near the site of Parole Cabin, demolished by fire some years ago. Harry "Parole" O'Farrell headquartered his hunter-for-hire service here in the mid-1800s. Historians say he was the first, or perhaps second, Caucasian to visit Mineral King. The site appears on old maps and some vintage signs. Today, large campsites sprawl across the creekside flat where the Parole Cabin once stood.

Now roughly paralleling Alpine Creek, you eventually descend a gravelly spit with several campsites between converging Mountaineer Creek to the right and Little Kern River to the left. Cross the creek, which here

Walker cabin built in 1886

matches the size of the river and can be swift during snowmelt. On the west bank you turn left on **Clicks Creek Trail 32E11** (6090/1.8).

Jeffrey pines shelter an assortment of campsites strung along Mountaineer Creek and Little Kern River; a good place to overnight before the 2500-foot ascent to Summit Trailhead. A soda spring seeps and barely bubbles in Mountaineer Creek near its confluence with Alpine Creek, a half mile up the fishermen's trail to the northwest. It has left interesting deposits of tufa, but the spring itself pales in comparison with the one you visited next to Soda Spring Creek. Scenic boulders, cascades and falls, especially up the creek, cradle several bathing pools and fishing holes.

Continuing the trip, the course heads south across the flood-plain gravels, then rises to roll over several slight ridges, first to meet a lateral (6220/0.5); soon after to cross Fish Creek Meadow Trail 32E12 (6180/0.3). It then curves southwest into the sylvan

Refreshing Soda Spring Creek

canyon of Clicks Creek to pass Clicks Creek Cutoff 32E16 (6340/1.0). All three of these trails reach Grey Meadow Guard Station to the east, where a summer ranger usually resides.

Shortly after the cutoff, you ford boulder-studded Clicks Creek near several campsites and zigzag up 600 feet to a gentler grade. You cross a slope abounding with wildflowers and flowering bushes that crowd a snowmelt creek and pass a use trail leading to meadow-side campsites below. On the next 500-foot gain, you crisscross a ravine displaying colorful flowers and, in late summer, various berries. The grade abates near a rocky drop of Clicks Creek, where smooth-barked aspens add textural diversity to the splendor of the creek's canyon. Cross the creek after leaving Golden Trout Wilderness and lope easily near its west side where it flows through an emerald meadow, topaz in autumn. Soon you pass corrals flanking the trail, cross the creek again, then a tributary and finally arrive at Clicks Creek Trailhead across SNF Road 21S50 (North Road) (7850/4.2).

If you plan to journey on, turn right, walk up the paved main road to **Summit Trail 31E14** (7780/0.3), which crosses the road north of fledgling Clicks Creek. As a National Recreation Trail, this path should have special charm and appeal. To the south on Slate Mountain it does, but in this segment its woodland is blemished by extensive logging and its path is often chopped by this road. Quickly after you enter the trail it ends in churned ground. You find it near the main road and on it you soon cross an access road. Now you climb 750 feet, first in dense forest near a meadowy finger of Clicks Creek.

The main road again interrupts the National Recreation Trail. You angle up the road at an offset junction (8340/1.1) and find the trail several paces ahead. On the trail you pass White Meadow and reach the highest point on this leg of your adventure. Switchbacking down the path, you follow the curve of the road, then cross it again (8410/0.8). Continue on the path next to it, eventually dipping to step over North Fork Clicks Creek. Immediately after the creek you reach a flat used mostly for parking vehicles with horse trailers (8160/0.7). Now walk north along the main road, pass a spur road, pass the SUMMIT TRAIL—1 MILE sign, then find the next piece of trail ascending to a former log-loading clearing, using part of a logging road as your path. On the final short stint you travel through a replanted clear-cut to the Summit Trailhead (8280/0.4) that you left many days ago.

T64   Lloyd Meadows Road Car & Bicycle Tour
(With Directions to Trailheads 49–54)

This Western Divide's paved, low-speed road with numerous turnouts gives drivers and bicyclists alike a chance to view a feast of flora, the precipitous Kern River gorge and the many granitic sculptures climaxed by the towering, Whitney-like pinnacles of the Southern Sierra: The Needles.

Distance   21.3 miles, one way
Steep Ascents   None
Elevation Gain   2025 feet
Skills   Easy route finding; paved road
Seasons   Spring, summer, fall
Map   Tulare County road map
Tourhead   37. The junction of Parker Pass Drive (TC Road M-99) and Lloyd Meadows Road (SNF Road 22S82) is **TH37**. This is 46.1 miles east of Ducar and 4.9 miles west of the Kern River. It departs from car tour T41.
Description   Driving north from the junction just over a half mile west of Johnsondale R-Ranch on *SNF Road 22S82* (4828/0.0/0.0), locally known as Lloyd Meadows Road, you traverse among ponderosa and Jeffrey pine, white fir, incense cedar and black oak trees thriving on terrain where moisture lingers, then among Brewer oak, mountain mahogany, buck brush, fremontia and manzanita bushes and digger pine trees growing on drier land. In autumn, the leaves of Brewer and black oaks linger on the trees, creating masses of subdued bronze color among the evergreens.

Immediately to the north your visual field includes the spire of Sentinel Peak and the fractured granitics of Elephant Knob southeast of it. Soon, after Long Meadow Creek quietly slips through a culvert under the road, you pass SNF Road 22S45 (1.3/1.3) descending east to campsites near the confluence of Long Meadow and Bone creeks.

In May of each year, this site hosts the annual Monache Gathering: a time when Native Americans celebrate spiritual traditions. Participants from a variety of tribes near and far renew their ancient culture through dance, song and purification rites such as the sweat lodge and cleansing by sagebrush smoke. Interested non-Native Americans also attend the gathering.

After crossing Bone Creek, the road passes a roadside CAMP 2 sign indicating a Fire Safe Area for camping. Then minutes beyond Nobe Young Creek, your route takes you past a fork with unpaved SNF Road 22S02 (1.1/2.4), a shortcut to the Western Divide Highway, which traverses a parallel course to yours on the upper slopes. Close ahead, your route passes narrow, paved SNF Road 22S54 (0.1/2.5) leading to the Boy Scouts' Camp Whitsett and to **TH49** of T65, a day hike up Sentinel Peak. In 0.3 mile ahead it also bisects the rutted trail rising steeply to the peak.

The 80-acre Camp Whitsett has been in operation since 1947 for Boy Scouts from ages 11 to 18. Each boy stays a week, earning merit badges or just enjoying the area. By a summer's end, more than 1000 boys will have sampled the mountain environs and private lake of this popular camp.

A brief ride subsequently takes you to a saddle on a ridge that juts from Sentinel Peak, where you will find to the right SNF Road 22S53 (1.3/3.8). Would-be Elephant Knob climbers should pull off and park in the space to the right of that road at **TH50**. The pavement next carries you generally north from the saddle and past the gate that closes the rest of the highway in winter or during rock slides. It then arrives at a large day use parking area (1.8/5. 6) to the right, **TH51**, and gated SNF Road 22S83 to the left on which day hikers walk just under a mile to the popular Alder Creek slabs of T67 featuring refreshing pools and exciting slides.

Immediately your road, SNF Road 22S82, intersects Dry Meadow Creek, and then outflanks Sand Hill Ridge as it travels in the middle plateau land between the Western Divide crest and the plunging gorge of the North Fork Kern River. At length it reaches heavily used Lower Peppermint Campground (5.3/10.9), maintained by the Camp Whitsett Boy Scouts in lieu of special user fees for their camp. All the usual amenities are offered for a small nightly fee at this shaded, comfortable camp.

In a few yards north of the camp entrance, you cross Peppermint Creek, and then shortly pass two dirt roads that fork to the right within yards of each other. The first, SNF Road 22S82F, leads 0.4 mile to Fire Safe Area Camp 6 above the falls; the next, an unnumbered road, heads to **TH52** of Ts68&69, Peppermint Falls and Upper Durrwood Camp day hikes (0.3/11.2).

To reach **TH52**, drive east on the uncoded dirt road (0.0/0.0) to the ample parking area (0.2/0.2) shaded by black oaks.

Since the campground, you see increasingly closer views of the startling Needles. A turnout (1.2/12.4) just short of crossing Needlerock Creek offers a place to pause and consider the formation of the phenomenon. There in front of you stand The Needles, a row of sheer, towering spires and narrow domes, a tribute to the power of ice wedging.

Like most rock formations you see on this trip, The Needles' granodiorite rock was crystalized nearly 90 million years ago from a huge mass of molten "recycled" rocks. Five miles deep under older rocks, where the pressure is nearly 2200 times that of the atmosphere, the rocks cooled; later pushed

up. While cooling, The Needles contracted along vertical master joints. Soil acids borne by percolating water attacked the rock along each joint, cleaving it deeply. Then as erosion stripped away the overlying debris, the rock, subjected to less and less pressure, expanded. Water that seeped down the joints froze during cold nights, creating a lateral force of 1000 pounds per square inch, and then thawed during warm days. The force crumbled rock which eroded away. Each thaw and each storm flushed more shattered rock from the sheer Needles facade, revealing the smooth spires that impassion skilled rock climbers with thoughts of daring ascents. "Skilled" is the important word here—these challenging rocks present ascents for totally competent and technically experienced climbers only.

Rocks without deep vertical joints but with flakes and cracks due to expansion, become rounded domes, like Elephant Knob. These domes peel like onions, and are also inviting to skilled climbers.

Moving ahead, you pierce a pocket of trees while crossing Needlerock Creek, and then, in 0.1 mile, pass a climbers' use path to The Needles base. Proceeding out of the creek's recess, pause at another viewpoint (2.1/14.5) to the right. A few paces on the boulders here expose the dizzying depths of the defile containing the rumbling North Fork Kern River and the massive buttes and chunky postpiles of the dissected, brownish-mauve Little Kern Basalt Flow.

Continuing northward, you first curve around Voodoo Dome, an extremity of The Needles. The roadbed here was created by blasting and bulldozing during the summer of 1969 to access the forests beyond. Ahead, a section of the Kern Flat Trail ends at a saddle. You then curve into the Freeman Grove basin, passing the entrance (3.5/18.0) to R. M. Pyles Boys Camp—not a public campground.

Founded by R. M. Pyles in 1949 and supported by contributions from individuals and companies, mostly in the oil industry, this camp has served over 18,000 boys ages 12 to 16, mostly from disadvantaged backgrounds.

Through its program of camp living, the boys build self esteem and trust for one another. Counselors keep in touch with each attendee after camp. Some boys return as workers the next year or as campers at the remote Pyles Lion Meadows Camp. Some become counselors to the next generation of campers. President Bush acknowledge Pyles Camp's success while visiting the participants in 1992.

As you proceed, a road peels off to your right to Lloyd Meadows Pack Station, a substation of Golden Trout Wilderness Packtrains based near Quaking Aspen. Next you intersect Freeman Creek and Freeman Trail 32E20 (1.0/19.0). The easternmost sequoias in the Sierra, situated not far to the southwest in the Freeman Creek Grove, are, in the opinion of National Park Service biologist Larry Norris, the most impressive grove of big trees on the Western Divide. Close-up views of the largest trees in this grove can be seen by climbing this trail from here or descending on it as in T55. In 1992, President Bush visited this grove; he hiked to the

easternmost trees, one of which now bears his name. You find it prior to a creek crossing one mile up the trail.

Norris attributes this unique grove to the funneling of Pacific storms through the gap between Slate Mountain and Jordan Peak. The masses of snow deposited here in prolonged doses soak north-facing slopes of the tall, jutting ridge crowned by The Needles, attacking the underlying rock to deepen the already rich soil. Sequoias grow well under these conditions.

Separate plant associations appear in close proximity here. This sequoia grove and underbrush need a heavy snowpack each year to survive; at nearly the same elevation, drought-tolerant digger pines and shrubs thrive a little over a mile south.

While still in the Freeman Creek watershed you pass SNF Road 20S67 (0.7/19.7) to Forks of the Kern parking area, **TH53**. Seekers of this trailhead turn right while the rest continue ahead and skip the following information.

The Needles above Lloyd Meadows Road

Traveling generally southeast, stay on the main dirt road, **SNF Road 20S67** (0.0/0.0), crossing Lloyd Meadows Creek and Fish Creek Meadow Trail. Skirt Lloyd Meadows and pass a piece of the Kern Flat Trail. You soon arrive at trailhead campsites with corrals and ample parking (2.4/2.4) **TH53**. Kern Flat Trail 33E20 of Ts70&73 descends east.

Progressing north with Hermit Rock of T56 seen protruding to the northwest and Castle Rock of T72 sitting on the ridge to the northeast, your route crosses Lloyd Meadows Creek and Fish Creek Meadow Trail in tandem and all too soon terminates (5930/1.6/21.3) at the overnight Jerky Trailhead Campground constructed in 1990, **TH54** for Ts71&72. Under the shade of black oaks and incense cedars, it offers corrals and all the comforts except tables. A good place to rest or overnight before your return trip.

T65   Sentinel Peak Day Hike

Sentinel Peak, a panorama-commanding sentry of a mid North Fork Kern River watershed, stands boldly in a rimmed basin where various vegetation offers contrast to expanses of bare rock. The adventuresome hiker will find exhilaration climbing over the crown of this peak. The technical climber will want to tackle the last 30 feet of Class 4 climbing to top the spire.

Distance   2.4 miles, round trip
Steep Ascents   0.7 mile
Elevation Gain   1390 feet
Skills   Intermediate route finding; moderate-to-strenuous hiking; Class 4&5 pitches optional
Seasons   Spring, fall
Map   USGS 7.5-min. *Sentinel Pk*
Trailhead   49. See car tour T64. From SNF Road 22S82 (Lloyd Meadows Road) turn right on paved **SNF Road 22S54** (0.0/0.0), the Forest Service road to Camp Whitsett. Drive southeast under the arched entrance sign to a SLOW DOWN sign (0.2/0.2) next to the trail just short of a road fork. Park well off the road.
Description   The Sentinel Trail was forged to the summit in the 1960s by Dave Jaqua when he was a 16-year-old Eagle Scout. Subsequent generations of scouts staying at Camp Whitsett have kept this steep, fairly direct trail passably free of brush.

The **Sentinel Trail** starts east from a black oak on the Camp Whitsett road (4720/0.0) amid thick manzanita and mountain mahogany bushes interspersed with digger pines. Quite soon the path dips into a gulch and climbs to cross paved Lloyd Meadows Road (4780/0.1).

Beyond the road you ascend steeply, almost directly north atop the south ridge, confronting a Class 2+ rock less than half way into the trip. You climb it up a slot to the right, and then scamper over slabs marked with ducks on its east side. You then return to the trail beyond.

Soon a path departs southwest to nowhere, but you continue on your trail up the steep, sandy ridge, intermittently shaded by live oaks and Jeffrey pines. Sometimes vertical lengths of white pipe mark the way. Snatches of views occur encompassing the drainages of Nobe Young and Dry Meadow creeks. The most dramatic vignettes of Sentinel Peak appear as you near it and curve around its west side to approach it from the north. Then you clamber up the rounded top crown to a heady realization that you reached a point on the formidable peak that looked impossible when you started. After a stair-step ascent up the talus atop the crown, you reach the smooth, 30-foot west wall of the summit fortress (6109/1.1). A rope placed by the Boy Scouts dangles invitingly from the top, but with its age and condition unknown, it would be risky to use.

Numerous Class 4&5 routes up the spire avail themselves to skilled climbers eager to reap the giddily sweeping summit panorama. Rewarding portions of this vista can also be found by scramblers poking around the base of the spire. Within your view rich forests delineate north-facing slopes; drought-tolerant plants indicate south-facing slopes. In autumn foliage stung by frosts into bronzy hues defines intervening drainage courses.

T66   Elephant Knob Climb

The profile of an elephant's head appears in the knob's south face. That face presents a haven of warmth during the day for technical climbers when ice glazes High Sierra ascents. This trip's climb of the backside offers an interesting challenge for non-technical climbers as well.

Distance   1.2 miles, round trip
Steep Ascents   0.2 mile
Elevation Gain   700 feet
Skills   Intermediate route finding; Class 2 climbing (Class 3–5 pitches optional)
Seasons   Spring, fall
Maps   USGS 7.5-min. *Sentinel Pk, Johnsondale*
Trailhead   50. See car tour T64.
Description   Beginning at the saddle-top junction (4737/0.0) where SNF Road 22S53 descends from paved SNF Road 22S82 (Lloyd Meadows Road), you hike southeast on a wide *firebreak/m'cyclepath* up the crest of a ridge. It soon becomes apparent in over-the-shoulder views that this ridge extends from dominant Sentinel Peak to Elephant Knob. You take the *use path* that splits to the left near the top of the first hill east of the summit rocks and descend to the following saddle. Next weave over a low hill through aisles in the brush causing you very little bushwhacking, then arrive at the third saddle.

Elephant Knob looms ahead: it is as steep and challenging as it looks. You tunnel briefly through a manzanita forest arching overhead, then your trail disappears. Unfurled ribbons marking a route occasionally flutter as you climb hands-over-feet *cross-country* up the steep, soft soil and fractured rock, spottily shaded by oak trees.

The broad rounded dome of the knob (5098/0.6) invites you to linger. Here you overlook pools and cascades set in the pine-bordered spillway of Nobe Young Creek, which arcs around the bare, steep, exfoliating Class 3–5 granite on the south face of

your viewpoint.

Sentinel Peak projects skyward

T67   Alder Slabs Day Hike

This very popular outing embodies slick-rock water slides; limpid, cerulean pools; mosaic-patterned slabs—along with the scent of pine, the shade of alders and the solace of beauty.

Distance   1.6 miles, round trip
Steep Ascents   None
Elevation Gain   200 feet
Skills   Easy route finding; easy hiking
Seasons   Spring, summer, fall
Map   USGS 7.5-min. *Sentinel Pk*
Trailhead   51. See car tour T64.
Description   The destination is paramount on this outing; the hike only incidental.

Water slides at Alder Slabs

Sturdy cut-off jeans offer the best wear for sliding along the water chutes into the cool pools. The sun quickly dries the heavy fabric while you rest on the slabs. Alders provide shade for picnickers.

From the parking lot—open between 6AM to 7PM—cross paved Lloyd Meadows Road to gated **SNF Road 22S83** (4817/0.0). In an attempt to control the land abuse and overuse that occurred here, this road remains closed to vehicle travel. To keep this popular area clean, it would help to bring extra trash bags to carry out litter left by less thoughtful people.

Walk north on the wide, dirt road, which ascends on an easy grade above the channel of Dry Meadow Creek. On this short walk you receive little shade from the drought-tolerant, middle-elevation bushes and trees that line the road. Snatches of the creek below appear along the way and massive Dome Rock ahead seems less awesome when viewed from this distance. You soon turn right on a **use path** (4970/0.7) that descends prior to the road crossing of Alder Creek. Near the confluence (4920/0.1) of Alder and Dry Meadow creeks you find the slides and pools.

The slabs here are composed mostly of granodiorite, the granite bedrock of most of the Sierra. In them appear mafic (dark) inclusions called enclaves or xenoliths. These enclaves, often composed of material more resistant to wear than the surrounding rock, usually create a rough, uneven surface. Here they appear as worn and smooth as a well-laid rock patio. Some geologists accept the hypothesis that these enclaves were unmelted mantle scooped up by granitic magma; others, that they were country rocks surrounded by upward moving magma.

The day passes quickly as you slip down the slides, splash into the pools and picnic on the slabs—a delight to all youthful spirits.

T68 Peppermint Falls Day Hike

Peppermint Creek cascades and falls 200 feet over massive slabs between a granitic dome on one side and fractured granite on the other. It then meanders along a forested flat until it falls and cascades to the North Fork Kern River. This adventure reaches the foot of the upper falls.

Distance 1.6 miles, round trip
Steep Ascents None
Elevation Gain 350 feet
Skills Easy-to-intermediate route finding; easy-to-moderate hiking
Seasons Spring, summer, fall
Map USGS 7.5-min. *Durrwood Cr*
Trailhead 52. See car tour T64.
Description An alternate approach from Camp 6 at the end of SNF Road 22S82F offers a maze of paths that descend steeply on the north side of the falls. The following description takes a gentler but longer route to the bottom of the cascades.

From the parking area 0.5 mile beyond the campground, you (and those on T69 who seek Durrwood Camp) begin hiking east on the **dirt road** (5290/0.0) to the right of the hill, then ahead on **Bean Camp M'cyclepath 32E29** (5240/0.2) where the road turns left. Descend south on the trail amid xerophytic brush to a gently sloping flat of Jeffrey pines. Shortly after you enter the pine forest, at a gully, find and take the **use trail** (4980/0.4) that branches to the right or simply leave the trail and head northwest to the creek on a cross-country route. Upon reaching Peppermint Creek (5000/0.2), pick the easiest way to climb to your best vantage point.

A few words of caution: when walking on slabs, watch carefully to avoid stepping on thin layers of decomposed granite spread over the slabs. The "D.G." is like small ball bearings and can easily roll your feet out from under you. Also, never try to cross over the creek while walking on slabs no matter how slender the flow becomes. During snowmelt the falls and cascades swell greatly, and slabs near the water become smooth and slippery and often stay that way—exceedingly dangerous.

This magnificent, tumbling water, composed of streams from the east slopes of Slate Mountain and the meadow area of Ponderosa village, is mesmerizing to watch and the slabs offer an enjoyable place to picnic.

T69 Kern River Near Durrwood Camp Day Hike

Peppermint Creek, plummeting through slick chutes, entices you to pause as you descend to the North Fork Kern. There, the wild river entrenched in a walled canyon and historic cabins visible across the ruffled water fill your day with beauty and interest. Oak-sheltered campsites secreted in back of boulder bars near the white-water rapids invite you to return for an extended stay.

Distance 4.6 miles, round trip
Steep Ascents 0.2 mile
Elevation Gain 1010 feet
Skills Easy route finding; moderate-to-strenuous hiking; not recommended for equestrians
Seasons Spring, summer, fall
Map USGS 7.5-min. *Durrwood Cr*
Trailhead 52. See car tour T64.
Description You begin your trip to the North Fork Kern River briefly east on the **dirt road** (5290/0.0) to the right of the hill, then south on **Bean Camp M'cyclepath 32E29** (5240/0.2) where the road turns left. Descend through Brewer oak and mountain mahogany on private land that remains open to hikers as long as the privilege is not abused. On the descent you are treated to beguiling glimpses of Peppermint Creek plunging more than 200 feet from a sheaf of exfoliating

granodiorite. Upon reaching a Jeffrey pine-sheltered forest, you can detour to the right on a forking path or hike cross-country for a closer view of the falls. (See T68.)

Your path levels as it crosses the pine flat, then meets a lesser path forking left, which you take (5160/0.8). The m'cyclepath you were on veers south here and fords Peppermint Creek in ¼ mile, where, if you missed the turnoff, you will realize your error.

Now on *Durrwood Camp Trail 32E44*, you continue southeast across the rest of the flat, then slant down a mild gradient while Peppermint Creek, some 250 feet down-slope, drops over polished granodiorite, pooling and cascading. Switchbacking down onto iron-rich, hence rust-stained, inter-layered sandstone, mudstone and tuff, you

Upper Durrwood Camp and cable

round a ridge. Soon you pass a use path of breakneck steepness that leads southeast down a divide to flats visible at the confluence of the creek and river.

Live and black oak offer some shade, and silk tassel appears near your path. After ¼ mile of gentle northward descent, you hike down a steep ravine and make nine tight zig-zags, each firmly buttressed with mortarless masonry. Upon reaching the Kern River floodplain several dozen yards from the river, you again travel north to reach a river-crossing cable with a flat bed attached (4280/1.3). It is not guaranteed safe and is scheduled for future removal.

The remaining cabins of Upper Durrwood Camp, a resort built by Bill Calkins during the 1920s, stand ⅓ mile upstream across the river. According to historian Bob Powers, Calkins had a path built from the Rincon Trail east of the Kern to the mouth of Durrwood Creek, on which he hauled building material for the camp. Packers later used that trail to bring hunters and fishermen to the resort. Calkins also established a bridge spanning the Kern and later had Durrwood and Bean Camp trails built to access his other lodge on South Creek. The resort thrived at first, but declined in later years. By the time the river flooded in 1966, ripping out the bridge and a cabin, the resort's current owners decided to abandon it. Miners, squatters, rafters, kayakers and others have used it since.

Here, on this oak-sheltered plain with its assortment of campsites, late blooming orangy-red California fuchsia take root. The cleft-petaled, trumpet-shaped flowers project from their centers a spray of stamens reaching beyond the petals. Fine hairs grow on the gray-green leaves and 4- to 20-inch stems. The nectar from fuchsias supply humming-birds, especially Rufous hummers, with food for their migration south.

While enjoying the crashing, wildly scenic Kern River, you may see a Rufous hummer feeding on a fuchsia. These birds are reddish brown (rufous) in color; the males of this species have a bright orange-red throat. Hummingbirds, incidentally, flap their wings 80 times per second!

T70 Forks of the Kern Day Hike

Awesome views of the precipitous North Fork Kern River gorge along with the spires and domes of The Needles await you as you hike to and from the confluence of the Little Kern and North Fork Kern rivers. Basalt postpiles, a travertine spring and numerous places to picnic, fish and bask in the beauty of the rushing rivers make this an especially pleasurable hike.

Distance 4.8 miles, round trip
Steep Ascents None
Elevation Gain 1060 feet
Skills Easy route finding; moderate hiking
Seasons Spring, summer, fall
Map USGS 7.5-min. *Hockett Pk*
Trailhead 53. See car tour T64.
Description Begin your adventure at the east end of the Forks parking lot (5760/0.0) on **Kern Flat Trail 33E20**. Stroll through a forest of fragrant pines and cedars over slopes carpeted with pungent kit-kit-dizze; slopes which suddenly lose their gentleness and plummet to the depths below. You descend easily, however, aided by a pair of switchbacks. Orangish brown-to-mauve postpiles of volcanic basalt, somewhat similar in shape but not in scope to Devils Postpile National Monument in the High Sierra, reach above the trail, a remnant of the 3.5 million-year-old Little Kern Basalt Flow. The narrow trail carved into the steep drop of the canyon wall commands almost as much of your attention as the spectacular views of The Needles and the Kern River Canyon.

The river rumbles at a dizzying depth below your path as you traverse around a ridge. Mountain mahogany, fremontia and Brewer oak keep you company while you cross into Golden Trout Wilderness. A few pinyon pines join the brush. Then a scattering of black oak, incense cedar and finally digger pine offers lacy shade. You reverse your direction from north to south, cut across a spring-fed swath of sedges and switchback to the canyon floor (4700/2.4).

Here in 1975 a campfire, fanned by gusty winds, roared out of control, spreading devastation on both sides of the river as far as Kern Flat within a few hours. If became known as the Flat Fire.

To the right the banks of the North Fork Kern River offer numerous hidden sites for a picnic. To the left flows the Little Kern River, with up-canyon banks to explore; beyond it lie the spread of a bouldery flood plain and the travertine spring. Fishermen are drawn to these waters; rafters and kayakers launch at this location for a white-knuckle journey of crashing white water. For you the Wild and Scenic North Fork Kern River is wondrous to admire but dangerous to enter; its current is much too strong to be safe except when the river ebbs very late in the season.

Rafters on a white-knuckle run of the North Fork Kern River

T71   Little Kern River Bridge Day Hike

As you hike, expansive views of the distant Western Divide dissolve into wooded, nearby scenes, then explode with color and ruggedness at the Little Kern River and its canyon, ending the day hike in a burst of beauty.

Distance   11.4 miles, round trip
Steep Ascents   None
Elevation Gain   2170 feet
Skills   Easy route finding; moderate-to-strenuous hiking
Seasons   Spring, summer, fall
Map   USGS 7.5-min. *Hockett Pk*
Trailhead   54. See car tour T64.
Description   Leave the hikers' parking lot (5920/0.0) at Jerky Overnight Campground and head northwest on a campground *connector trail*. Quickly into the journey you cross a branch of Lloyd Meadows Creek. This creek originates on the flanks of Castle Rock straddling the divide to the east, which you can see on occasion from the path. The trailside, ground-hugging web of medicinal-smelling kit-kit-dizze sporadically yields to manzanita and Kern ceanothus while black oak, ponderosa pine and incense cedar offer welcome shade for summer hikers. At the junction (6020/0.8) with *Fish Creek Meadow Trail 32E12*, marked by a MAIN TRAIL sign, you join it continuing ahead, northwest.

In the late 1970s the gentle trail ahead was constructed to replace the steep, deeply rutted path to the right of the junction. The rutted path was heavily used by motorcycles until 1978 when the establishment of Golden Trout Wilderness banned all vehicles. It now serves cattle drives.

You climb northwest on a path smooth enough for joggers and runners. Above the Lloyd Meadows Creek watershed, you catch open views of the canyon and the country to the south. In a short time after a switchback, you cross the divide and enter Golden Trout Wilderness. Soon thereafter you turn right (east) on *Lewis Camp Trail 33E01* (6925/2.1), arriving from Lewis Camp Trailhead to the west. In 0.1 mile you pass another junction with the replaced section of trail now signed CATTLE DRIVE and then pass Jerky

Meadows, the tree-hidden skimpy patch of grass to the right that seems too insignificant to carry a name. You descend along a ravine containing the meadows' outlet stream until the ravine flares and the trail levels; then you make an abrupt turn left at a junction (6730/0.7) with a closed bypass trail. At this point, where the bypass trail once separated motorcycles from hikers and equestrians, climbers seeking Castle Rock on T72 depart southeast on a cross-country route.

Heading north, then northeast, you descend in pine forest to reunite with the closed bypass trail just short of languid Jug Spring (6300/0.8). This seep issues from the base of a boulder that flanks the trail's northern edge. It supplies water for the nearby campsite and a grassy expanse containing creek dogwood, willow and wild geranium. The willows indicate the year-round flow of the water. A sign tacked on a Jeffrey pine exclaims this to be a good place to smoke! Although this sign is old, it post-dates this trail, which John Jordan forged in 1861. (See Chapter 1 for more on historic trails.)

In 0.4 mile from the spring, you again take the left fork at a split with a former motorcycle bypass trail. In a tad over 0.1

Fishing for Little Kern Golden Trout

mile while heading north, you pass another trail in the plethora of junctions on this Lewis Camp Trail. Here the path leads to Grey Meadow, as does the path in 0.4 mile at the next junction: the double-headed prongs of Grey Meadow Trail 32E15. None of these junctions should confuse you as your path remains the most pronounced. You next pass the north end of the motorcycle bypass as you descend to the Little Kern bridge (5760/1.3). Fire Safe Area campsites abound by the shores of the Little Kern River.

Here lies a scene to fill an artist's canvas. The Little Kern River, really the west fork of the North Fork Kern River, cascades and swirls in its rocky canyon—bounteous in spring with snowmelt, slack in fall. In the rock above to the north appears a brownish-mauve outlier of the Little Kern Basalt Flow. Arising from the earth's inner crust, 3.5 million years ago, via vents near present day Burnt Corral Meadows, this melted portion of crust filled ancestral Kern River watershed canyons for more than 18 miles—sometimes to depths nearing 800 feet.

To the south of the bridge rest fractured hunks of grayish granodiorite splashed with black lichen. This kind of rock, like basalt, was molten, but unlike basalt, failed to surface. Instead it cooled deep within the earth, close to 85 million years before the basalt flowed out through vents and solidified.

The suspension bridge spanning the river eerily sways underfoot. A former bridge, 100 yards downstream from the current structure, was cut and mangled in late 1955 when a tropical storm melted the snowpack, swelling the Little Kern to one hundred times its average volume.

Jeffrey pine, willow and creek dogwood along with patches of wild rose and gooseberry—all usually with a backdrop of a deep blue, crystalline sky—complete the artist's picture.

T72   Castle Rock Climb

Climbers drawn to the central Southern Sierra by the nationally known grandeur of The Needles will find that nearby Castle Rock, though it appears less dramatic in comparison, has secluded, spectacular faces, a wealth of challenging routes for climbers of all capabilities and an exciting summit panorama.

Distance   10.8 miles, round trip
Steep Ascents   0.1 mile
Elevation Gain   2200 feet
Skills   Intermediate route finding; Class 3–4 climbing (Class 5 pitches optional)
Seasons   Spring, summer, fall
Map   USGS 7.5-min. *Hockett Pk*
Trailhead   54. See car tour T64.
Description   The beginning of this trip is described in T71.

Northwestbound Trail 32E12 Log
T71 Jerky TH	5920	0.0
Fish Cr Mdw Tr 32E12	6020	0.8
Lewis Camp Tr 33E01	6925	2.1

Northeastbound Trail 33E01 Log
Fish Cr Mdw Tr 32E12	6925	0.0
Closed bypass tr #1	6730	0.7

The junction with the closed bypass trail signals you to turn right off the path toward Castle Rock, invisible from here. You begin a cross-country route southeast on a protracted gradual diagonal ascent, checking your altimeter to prevent ascending needlessly above 7100 feet, the elevation of the first saddle you reach, also out of sight from here.

Early in this first segment you leave the flared ravine and tangles of trees and cut across slopes of duff and rotten granite in conifer forests, dodging patches of chinquapin and manzanita to which the forest sometimes gives way. Less than a third along the way, you cross a tiny, undependable brook, and less than two thirds along the way, you reach the broad arc of the 7120-foot saddle between peaks 7450 and 7566 on the divide. On the last third of the trip, you cross the northeast facing slopes of Peak 7566 and regain the crest in the saddle between it and Castle Rock.

Castle Rock, now apparent in the southeast, justifies its name. Follow the short, steep length of crest that leads to a gap between a gendarme and one of the rock's stunning faces. A sheer chute plummeting southward from here along the rock's base makes this first view of that face a giddily breathtaking one. Class 5 climbers might want to start unloading equipment here. If you seek the easiest route to the summit, skirt the north face and climb the blocky east face, where ramps are linked by pitches of Class 3–4 rock.

Of the dual turrets of Castle Rock (7729/1.8) the northern one offers the more comprehensive view of the Little Kern basin, where the Southern and High Sierra meet. The higher southern turret seems the airier, perched as it is in confinement atop dazzling palisades.

Golden Trout Wilderness's Castle Rock

T73   Kern Flat Backpack

Visit spectacular gorges worn in granitic masses flanked by palisades and volcanic sculptures; traipse along exuberant rivers and quilted riverside meadows. Despite the still apparent massive devastation wrought on a segment en route by the 1975 Flat Fire, this trip remains among the most popular circuits in the Golden Trout Wilderness.

Distance   27.2 miles, loop trip
Steep Ascents   0.1 mile
Elevation Gain   3100 feet
Skills   Easy route finding
Seasons   Spring, summer, fall (Wilderness permit required)
Maps   USGS 7.5-min. *Hockett Pk, Casa Vieja Mdws* (briefly)
Trailhead   54. See car tour T64. (This hike can be converted into a shuttle trip and shortened by 4.1 trail miles if you end at **TH53**, Forks of the Kern Trailhead. There are 4.0 road miles between trailheads.)
Description   The beginning of this trip is described in T71.

Northwestbound Trail 32E12 Log

T71	Jerky Pking lot	5920	0.0
	Fish Cr Mdw Tr 32E12	6020	0.8
	Lewis Camp Tr 33E01	6925	2.1

Northeastbound Trail 33E01 Log

Fish Cr Mdw Tr 32E12	6925	0.0
Closed bypass tr #1	6730	0.7
Jug Sp	6300	0.8
Little Kern brdg	5760	1.3

On the north side of the bridge *Lewis Camp Trail 33E01* turns right and heads east to quickly dip into a tributary canyon, then ascend a moderate upgrade. At a split with a closed trail, Lewis Camp Trail is the lower path. Soon it travels on volcanic soils through a sparse Jeffrey pine forest while rounding a declivitous ridge. Above the path there is evidence of a basaltic flow; below the path appear segments of the downstream chasm through which the Little Kern River flows.

To the left the path passes Willow Meadows Trail 33E14 (5960/0.6). To the right unfold ever-improving views of Castle

Rock sitting high on the ridge; from this perspective it resembles an ancient castle on the Rhine. The trail soon swings into a gulch containing a large campsite and a transitory stream. A mile later it offers views of a cross-section slice that the Trout Meadows stream made in the basalt-capped granite; then, beyond that, of the ruffling Trout Meadows.

At the meadows, several connector trails shown on the 1987 topo map have been eliminated. You travel north along the fence containing the meadows, then turn right (6160/2.1) near the middle of the grassy expanse to cross it through an aisle created by double fencing. Beyond the aisle, hike up the slope about 150 feet where you find *Doe Meadow Trail 33E10* (6180/0.2). This trail originates 0.6 mile north above the Trout Meadows Guard Station, usually manned on summer weekends. You turn right on the trail, then make a wide arc east away from the meadows to cross above several springs. (Near the head of the last spring, the obscure Hockett Mountain Trail, now only a part of Southern Sierra memorabilia, once ascended to Hockett Meadows on Hockett Peak.) In 0.1 mile you pass a junction (6320/0.9) with one of the more obvious closed connector trails that crossed Trout Meadows.

Your southeast-heading trail crosses a field of mountain dandelions ringed by Jeffrey and ponderosa pines, slices across a seasonal stream that drains a south flank of Hockett Peak, and after a mile from the closed trail junction, nearly bumps into a trough with refreshing water piped in from Cold Spring (6460/1.2). Here at a dim junction with a long abandoned trail, your route turns abruptly left and passes a comfortable-looking campsite.

The Doe Meadow Trail then heads up a slight divide scorched in the Flat Fire of 1975. The conflagration started at the Forks of the Kern where a campfire fanned by gusty winds roared out of control and burned in a mosaic pattern. The most extensive damage occurred here but considerable destruction reached across the river as well. A forest of mixed conifers once welcomed travelers here, but now that forest is decimated and

naturally lagging behind brush in making its recovery. Blackened conifer trees still silhouette against the sky; very few conifers have returned in the 17 years since the fire. Black oak trees show heavy stump sprouting, and all around a thick mat of manzanita, Kern ceanothus and other bushes cover the vast burned area.

Switchbacks and some long side-slope traverses ease your protracted, seemingly endless descent to Kern Flat. Crossings of a stream en route give some opportunity to slake any early-season thirst. Eventually you see the river and gratefully you arrive at the Kern Flat junction (4995/3.7) with *Kern Flat Trail 33E20*, where your route turns right. (Left of this junction in 0.9 mile the trail meets a lateral to a bridge, the only safe crossing of the North Fork Kern River in Golden Trout Wilderness. Trips east of the river are described in *Exploring the Southern Sierra: East Side*.)

Now on the Kern Flat Trail, you hike south along the edge of Kern Flat's grassy meadow, then leave it while stepping across the stream you crossed on your long descent. In the narrowing canyon you parallel riverbank wattles of willow interwoven with wild rose. Riverside campsites appear at the rate of at least one every half mile until you reach Forks of the Kern. Nearly 1.6 miles past the trail junction, the canyon flares somewhat to admit Osa, then Soda creeks, which tumble in from the east. You rise slightly in passing the Osa Creek confluence, then overlook the site of a riverside shelter used by the R. M. Pyles Boys Camp until 1977, when the camp was mostly dismantled. The shelter was the first structure built after Pyles and fellow oilmen established the camp in 1949 for boys in need of guidance. The remainder of this camp and the camp to the south will one day be removed to comply with wilderness regulations.

A jaunt beyond the site takes you opposite the Soda Creek confluence. With superb views below of the river and its cascades, you soon look southward to Rattlesnake Creek spilling from an impressive gorge to join the river. In 1966 the California Highway

Commission adopted a proposal for trans-Sierra State Highway 190 to bridge the river here, eventually cross Monache Meadow on the Kern Plateau and descend through Haiwee Pass to Highway 395 at Olancha. Subsequent austere construction budgets shelved the project, and with the advent of Golden Trout Wilderness, it will not be reconsidered.

Now the path switchbacks down toward the river across from the creek, cuts briefly over dynamited granodiorite slabs, travels along soils derived from darker quartz diorite, and brushes past riverside willows passing dismantled Lower Pyles Camp. Here the canyon leads into a zone of lighter rock—granite mixed with quartz monzonite—then a mile ahead it reaches an inclusion of reddish-brown schist and quartzite.

A gauging station mostly hidden from the trail once held one end of a cable stretched across the Kern River. By pulling hand over hand, you could, in 1974, work across the river while riding a cable car, but now it exists only in Kern River annals.

Shortly after entering metamorphic rock, your canyon joins the Little Kern River canyon at Forks of the Kern, where you pass a travertine spring and then a sandy boulder-strewn floodplain. You ford the Little Kern River (4700/6.3). If the river is swift due to spring snowmelt, traipse upstream to seek a wider, shallower channel to ford—with great caution. Heavily used campsites abound here at the forks. In addition to hikers, equestrians and fishermen, this serves as a launch site for whitewater trips.

Past the Little Kern crossing, the path zig-zags west up through aprons of sedges watered by springs that issue along the Kern Canyon fault. Quite soon it traverses ⅓ mile north past a few steep downslope laterals leading to riverside campsites. The path switchbacks; chaparral replaces the scattered trees. Soon it rounds a ridge, leaves Golden Trout Wilderness and skirts seat-sized chunks of many-sided basaltic columns that rolled here from an impressive upslope postpile. Geologists will want to pause to examine the basalt flow; every one will want to ogle the wondrous cleft into which the Kern River pours southward. After switchbacking up toward the postpiles, then crossing basaltic soils just downslope from them, the trail, after a time, gains the shelter of forest and reaches the Forks of the Kern trailhead parking lot (5760/2.4).

If this is not the end of your journey, you pad west along the extended Kern Flat Trail 33E20. On it you cut through the campsites, parallel, then leave the road, dip through a grassy Freeman Creek tributary bed and con-

Cooling off at Cold Spring water trough

tinue ahead where the Kern Flat Trail forks left at an obscure, unmarked junction (5590/1.0). Now briefly on *Freeman Creek Trail 32E20*, you soon meet a signed junction north of Pyles Camp where you turn right onto *Fish Creek Meadow M'cyclepath 32E12* (5540/0.2). A sign high on a Jeffrey pine indicates public pasture at Lloyd Meadows.

Heading north near Lloyd Meadows Creek on its sandy flood plain, which seems too wide for such a paltry creek to have caused, the path passes a campsite next to the Forks trailhead road, then crosses the road (5630/0.9). Continuing ahead, it soon fords the slender creek and back to avoid a climb over boulders. Now in the welcome shade of trees, which shelter campsites scattered along the creek, the path dips through a usually dry creek branch and arrives at *Lloyd Meadows Road* (SNF Road 32S82) (5840/1.5) where a road sign says CURVES NEXT 20 MILES. Here your route leaves the trail to turn right along the paved road to Jerky Trailhead (5920/0.5).

T74   Highway 190 Car Tour:
Porterville to Western Divide Highway
(With Directions to Trailheads 55–58)

This well-used winding road visits historic towns, resort villages and spacious campgrounds as it ascends from the sunny San Joaquin plains to the wooded crest of the Western Divide mountains. Vistas unfold en route of the deeply etched canyon of the Tule River.

Distance   40.8 miles, one way
Steep Ascents   None
Elevation Gain   6515 feet
Skills   Easy route finding; paved road
Seasons   All year (snow removed)
Map   Tulare County road map
Tourhead   55. The intersection of Highway 65 and Highway 190 in Porterville is **TH55**.
Description   Before you leave Porterville, you may wish to visit the small crescent park where the city began—north on Highway 65, east on Henderson Avenue to Main Street. In the 1860s Porter Putman operated a popular station and hotel at the park's location on the Butterfield Overland Stage Route. Known as Porter's Station, the town of Porterville grew up around it. The park displays both a Historical Landmark depicting the town's beginnings and an enormous statue of a farmer that pays tribute to the surrounding furtile land, the roots of Porterville.

To begin this tour, head east on 4-lane *State Highway 190* (459/0.0/0.0). You soon pass the access road to California Conservation Corps (CCC): Sequoia District. The

CCC is a work ethic and training program. Since its start in 1976, more than 40,000 people age 18 to 23 have helped conserve and enhance the state's natural resources. It is the oldest and largest program of its kind in the country. Men and women of the corps built many miles of trails in the Southern Sierra, notably sections of the Mexico-to-Canada Pacific Crest National Scenic Trail described in this book's companion *Exploring the Southern Sierra: East Side*. The road also leads to the Porterville Developmental Center, a sprawling facility caring for those of all ages who cannot care for themselves.

Farther along, the highway narrows to two lanes. You travel past a KOA Campground to the left, and quickly arrive at a Vista Point (7.7/7.7). From here you see the spread of Success Lake snug in the vale of surrounding foothills. The reservoir, operated by the U.S. Army Corps of Engineers, contains 82,000 acre feet of water when full. The 142-foot-high, earth-filled dam spanning the Tule River was completed in 1961. The flood-control project provides both irrigation water and recreation to the public in most forms of water sports. The lake area offers picnic grounds, phone kiosks and two spacious campgrounds. The dam proved its worth when in December 1966 extremely heavy rains caused a stream of flood proportions to flow over the spillway. The water fanned out over the land below and many residents were evacuated. Damage remained minimal compared to what would have happened without the dam.

Traveling ahead, you cross the South Fork Tule River; beyond the lake you bridge the main stem Tule River. Next you drive pass the River Island Country Club, where to the left, the USFS Tule River Ranger Station (4.8/12.5) is located. (See Chapter 1 for services.)

Easy driving prevails to the town of Springville, named for a nearby soda spring. John and Rebecca Crabtree, sheep ranchers, built the first house here on the land now occupied by Roses Service Station. In 1864 John's son, William Newton, guided members of the California Geological Survey party to Mount Whitney; Crabtree Meadow and Creek near Whitney were named for him by the surveyors; the Lake and Pass were named later.

Across the highway from Roses is the historic 1912 Springville Inn. Beside it, the 1905 Patton House serves as an office for the

Farmer symbolizes Porterville's roots

Chamber of Commerce and Visitor Center. The next imposing building, Sequoia Dawn, now accommodates senior citizens, but it was constructed in 1919 to treat tuberculosis patients when rest and fresh air were the primary protocol. The large whitewashed barn at the eastern edge of town was built in 1945 on acreage used to breed and train a string of nationally known harness horses. The barn also marks the forked junction (1070/4.6/17.1) of **TH56** for Ts75&77 to Yokohl Valley, Mountain Home Demonstration State Forest and Balch Park.

Leaving Springville, your road, Highway 190, bridges the North Fork Tule River just above its confluence with the Middle Fork Tule River, which accompanies you on the right. The canyon narrows and tortuous curves begin as the road gains elevation through a country of scattered ranches and trees of oak, buckeye, and by the river, cottonwood and willow.

After entering Sequoia National Forest, the unfriendly lines of no parking signs that march along the highway represent a solution to an extreme problem of overuse. Previously, cars parked dangerously near the cliff's edge, and hordes of people descended to the pools and slides in the river below. The rowdiness, litter and water pollution that occurred necessitated restrictions. In 1992 the Tulare County Conservation Corps removed the abundant graffiti with a hydrosandblaster. Lower and Upper Coffee Camp Picnic Area (fees—no camping) and a parking turnout now provide the only legitimate access to this section of river.

The domed mountain you see to the right is locally known as Umbrella Peak; to the left is a flume. Soon the flume passes overhead, signaling an impending forked junction (7.2/24.3) with Wishon Drive, of interest for those seeking Wishon Campground and **TH57** of T76.

To reach Wishon Campground and **TH57**, drive northeast on **Wishon Drive** (TC Road M-208). Its narrow paved bed traverses high above the North Fork Middle Fork Tule River. You soon see a path

(0.7/0.7) leading steeply to river slabs and pools. Shortly beyond in a canyon crease, you pass Dunn Fire Trail 30E16 (1.1/1.8). (The 2.5-mile trail climbs abruptly through a creek-laced canyon, then over open slopes to reach Bear Creek Road. A nice winter hike.)

As Wishon Drive ascends, the surrounding slopes are covered with xerophytic shrubs, including the stunning bush poppy with its vivid yellow flowers. The road soon arrives at the Wishon Forest Service Guard Station, which has a phone kiosk, and at Wishon Campground (2.0/3.8), which has a nightly fee. The sites are scattered near the river under pines and incense cedars, and an engaging "Streamside Communities" self-guided nature trail leaves from the campground.

Drive past the campground entrance and the foundation remains of the 1900s Camp Wishon to a pullout right of the road for **TH57** (0.2/4.0) of T76.

After the road fork, Highway 190 bridges the North Fork Middle Fork Tule River and curves around Pacific Gas and Electric (PG&E) Company's 1909 power generating complex, which also houses a public phone booth. An aqueduct from a diversion dam on the North Fork Middle Fork above Wishon Campground to this complex was put into operation in 1914. After flowing through the PG&E turbines, the flume, which you passed under, carries the water to the Southern California Edison Power Plant above Springville; then the water is further transported to Springville for use there.

The road switchbacks twice after the complex and continues to twist upslope from the South Fork Middle Fork Tule River. The north slopes are sporadically dressed in chamise. The route takes you past a yawning cave left of the highway, then enters the lush canyon of Soda Creek, which is adorned with golden oaks and bigleaf maple trees. It next arrives at a cold, refreshing spring (6.5/30.8) that gushes from a pipe, drought or no—a good place to replenish your water supply. You may see people who make pilgrimages to fill a thirst of vessels from this spring.

Pierpoint Spring Resort in the village of Camp Nelson (0.4/31.2) can fill your traveling needs: store, coffee shop, motel, post office, public phone and a hillside park for your picnic. (Gas can be obtained at Ponderosa Lodge 11.4 miles ahead on the Western Divide Highway.)

While in a mixed forest where in autumn tarnished-gold leaves linger on the dark boughs of black oaks, you reach Camp Nelson's main junction (0.7/31.9). You continue on the highway. (The right fork quickly branches: Nelson Drive takes people to Belknap Campground and beyond to **TH58** of T53; Coy Flat Drive takes others 1.8 miles to Coy Flat Campground.)

More tortuous turns appear. You pass a road to the communities of Alpine Village and Sequoia Crest. The sixth largest giant sequoia, the largest outside Sequoia National Park, the Alonzo Stagg Tree, grows on private land in the Alder Creek Grove near the village of Sequoia Crest. Next you drive through Cedar Slope and curve near a roadside waterfall so well hidden in its sheltered canyon you may have only a fleeting glimpse of it. Approaching the end of this tour, you pass Camp Nelson Trail 31E30 and Summit Trail 31E14 of Ts53&54 and conclude at the junction (6970/8.9/40.8) of SNF Road 21S50 (North Road). Here Highway 190 dissolves into the Western Divide Highway of car tour T46. Popular Quaking Aspen Campground just beyond the road curve invites you to relax and enjoy the high mountain environs.

Gushing spring next to Highway 190

T75   Sierran Foothills Car & Bicycle Tour: Highway 190 to Highway 198

The three Southern Sierra foothill tours described in this book are pleasing alternatives to the busy north/south highways. The country roads are especially inviting to bicyclists. This middle section tour travels near the tree-hidden North Fork Tule River and along the seasonal Yokohl Valley Creek. This ride among low hills and valleys of geological interest follows a segment of the historic Jordan Trail.

Distance   28.7 miles, one way

Steep Ascents   None

Elevation Gain   1900 feet

Skills   Easy route finding; paved roads

Seasons   All year (Bicyclists avoid summer)

Map   Tulare County road map

Tourhead   56. The junction of Highway 190 and TC Highway J37 (Balch Park Drive) is **TH56**. This is 1.1 miles east of Springville and 14.9 miles west of Camp Nelson. It departs from car tour T74 and continues from foothill car tour T18.

Description   Heading north on *Balch Park Drive*—M-239 on road paddles—from the T junction (1070/0.0/0.0), your route leaves a mammoth white barn with its fenced track and quickly bridges hidden Mount Whitney Ditch carrying North Fork Middle Fork Tule River water from the two power plants to Springville. After traveling among a sprinkling of houses, it passes the first access road (3.4/3.4) to Mountain Home Demonstration State Forest and Balch Park: Bear Creek Road of car tour T77, departing to the right. Also to your right deciduous trees line the sometimes slack North Fork Tule River paralleling you. You take the left fork (2.7/6.1), *Yokohl Valley Road*, where Balch Park Drive curves right to intersect the trees and river on its way to the state forest and county park, a second access road to that area. Watch for this road change; the natural flow is to the right.

Your route continues ahead on Yokohl Valley Road (TC Road M-296) over pavement that was laid atop a portion of the Jordan Toll Road, which in turn followed an Indian trail. (See Chapter 1 for Jordan history.) On a gradual ascent to Blue Ridge,

the road passes random blue oaks on large private pastures near an old Yaudanchi village later called Milo. Early in the ascent it passes north of two diverting sights: a private, occasionally dry reservoir and, 0.2 mile later, far from any railroad tracks, a green caboose. Eventually your route touches steep slopes, assumes a moderate grade with many curves and offers views northeast of sheer granite comprising Dennison Peak and the west slopes of Moses Mountain. Before long the road surmounts Blue Ridge (2676/3.2/9.3), where bicyclists can relax, knowing that most of this trip elevation gain lies behind them.

From the ridgecrest the narrow road switchbacks down into the valley of Yokohl Creek. Forest frames and sifts most distant views until the third and final switchback. From there the foothills around the valley stretch toward the dark patchwork of San Joaquin Valley farmlands, backdropped by the profile of the remote coastal ranges. The road then swings rapidly around the valley's headwall to a California Department of Forestry fire-control station (2.2/11.5) perched on an overlook. The moderate descent is prolonged a bit farther; then the road closely parallels Yokohl Creek, where occasionally surfacing water nurtures a line of sycamores, cottonwoods and white oaks. A profusion of sticker weeds from now on stand ready to puncture bicycle tires.

Several miles later, you cross Chickencoop Canyon wash. A subsequent mild ascent to a gap allows your attention to wander southwest toward the defile through which Yokohl Creek veers away from your road. Slate dominated rocks in the defile are characteristic of the rocks in the roadcuts ahead. Slate is recognized by its clayey odor and shiny planes along which it breaks. Geologist Jason B. Saleeby speculated in 1977 that the slate and other Sierran rocks were deposited on an offshore continental shelf that once extended at least 300 miles north across the present Mother Lode country. He has identified, in the roadcut ahead and in surrounding ridges, the results of an undersea scrambling of washed-in rocks, slices of ocean-floor lava beds, lodes of sea-dwelling creatures' skeletons and fragments of an oceanic crust and its underlying mantle—all so transformed that only advanced geologists can sort them out.

Continuing your descent from the gap, the road arrives in a valley, a finger of Yokohl Valley, which contains few structures and fewer trees. This is grazing land with some rocky, conical hills of hornblende gabbro. In time your route passes under high-tension powerlines that extend across the Southern Sierra foothills en route from hydroelectric generators on the San Joaquin River south to Los Angeles. Built in 1911 under the auspices of millionaire Henry E. Huntington, these transmission lines represent the first long distance electrical conduits to appear in America.

Cruising along after the powerlines, you pass to the right of a roofless rock cabin, one of the many 19th century homesteads that once dotted the valley. This cabin was standing in 1874 when the Gill family bought and then cleared Yokohl and Frazier valleys to make way for grazing cattle.

Your road leads west toward the valley's narrow middle, then slices through part of Hill 685, exposing slate in the roadcut. These rocks and those of the outcrops, the soils produced by them plus the region's dry climate, low elevation and historic cattle-raising

Former homestead in Yokohl Valley

monopoly combine to create the strange starkness of Yokohl Valley.

You advance to a house and barns, the former headquarters of the Gill Ranch. When the ranch was in Gill family hands, in addition to running cattle, talc for talcum powder was mined from the nearby former sea floor and mantle fragments. The Gills soon washed their hands of the operation, however, when the talc proved too abrasive to use. Beyond, you ride into a wider part of Yokohl Valley where the stubbly granodiorite island of Rocky Hill stands straight ahead. Soon you meet *TC Road 228* (14.2/25.7) onto which you turn right.

Heading straightaway north, you pass a road to Exeter, formally a village of the Yokod (Yokohl) tribe, enter orange grove country and meet Highway 198 (Sierra Drive) (400/3.0/28.7). Here a plaque details the route of the Jordan Toll Trail. At this junction you have many choices: turn east on Highway 198 (T84) to Sequoia National Park; continue north on foothill car tour T85 to Kings Canyon Road; or return south the way you came or on alternate routes.

T76   Tule River Day Hike

Tumultuous cascades and falls of the North Fork Middle Fork Tule River, confined by bronze-toned walls, create deep swimming pools, round and long. Fern grottoes shelter brooklets with sprays of misty foliage. These inviting rewards await you on this Tule River day hike.

Distance   7.2 miles, round trip
Steep Ascents   None
Elevation Gain   950 feet
Skills   Easy route finding; easy-to-moderate hiking
Seasons   All year
Map   USGS 7.5-min. *Camp Wishon*
Trailhead   57. See car tour T74.
Description   You begin your adventure beyond the pull-out parking space (3900/0.0) by hiking up the road on which you arrived: paved, gated *TC Road M-208*. It leads to Doyle Springs Summer Home Tract. In the late 1800s, Tulare County pioneer J. J. Doyle and his nephew Wilber Doyle homesteaded property at the hot springs here. It later became a private resort, and for the owners of the cabins, it remains a popular retreat.

The road leads east along the bouldery North Fork Middle Fork Tule River and parallels a boxy concrete aqueduct across the water visible at the river's dam. The young Pacific Gas and Electric Company built the dam and aqueduct as part of a power-generating complex in the Tule River drainage early in the 1900s. The former Camp Wishon, whose foundations appear across from the trailhead, was named for A. E. Wishon, the company's general manager.

You pass a spur road that bridges the river where it skirts the aqueduct-intake dam, then arrive at *Doyle Trail 30E14* (4060/0.5) near a second gate where DOYLE SPRINGS, ESTABLISHED 1916 sign arches over the road. Now on the path heading north, you zigzag twice quite early, then trace a sinuous course up a gentle grade alternately bracketed by ground-shrouding kit-kit-dizze, exceedingly large manzanita, nook-embellishing fern and an occasional clump of poison oak. As you walk you may be bothered by swarms of tiny black flies buzzing around your face. They lay their eggs in clean, running water and are an important fish food, however annoying to hikers. After intermittently glimpsing down-slope cabins, you curl across several ravines and rise gently north. You pass Jacobsen Trail

North Fork Middle Fork Tule River falls and ponds

31E21 (4360/1.0), a lengthy, knee-punishing path between your trail and the crest of the Western Divide to your right.

Beyond the junction, your shaded path ascends on a moderate-to-steep grade high above the invisible but audible river, whose rumble wafts through the elongated canyon. Where the trail makes a lengthy traverse, if you have binoculars you can spot Jordan Lookout, a speck perched atop a peak on the divide. The trail dips through a ravine sometimes occupied by a snowmelt stream, then slants down steeply but briefly to a terrace with a couple of campsites (4640/1.3). The Doyle Trail turns to span the river here—the bridging log affords dry crossings for the sure-footed—but the path on the far side is in disrepair.

You do not cross the river, instead you leave the Doyle Trail and forge ahead, north, on *4-H Trail 30E14A*. Note as you travel through a wooded terrace, a redwood log from a northern sequoia grove that must have beached many years ago after exceedingly high water; plants have taken root in it and trees have grown around it. Campsites begin to appear below, next to the water; then, at a canyon crease just before the trail rises sharply, you scramble down to the river bank (4800/0.8). If uncertain as to where to leave the trail, continue on it until you find a slab clearing to the right. From there you will see a river falls crashing over colorful meta-

morphic rock. Go back and descend steeply among the trees to the water.

Overnighters find several campsites here in a grove of giant sequoias: Burro Creek Grove. The trees have not reached their full size, however. Some saplings bend for sunlight, some "young" trees still show immature conical shapes, while a few more mature specimens have rounded tops. The bark is not yet shredded. To sort the sequoias from the cedars, look on the ground near the trees. If you find round needles and egg-shaped cones, the tree is a sequoia. Cedars have flat needles and only flat, pointed cone-scales.

Here at the destination of this trip, the river falls into a round pond, then cascades into a walled, rectangular pool before it tumbles on—both swimming holes afford the swimmer room for several strokes (except during snowmelt when the river churns with such force that swimming is not an option). Stretch out on the colorful rocks and meld into the exquisite scene.

(If you wish to explore further, the 4H Trail continues north, rises steeply and becomes so narrow on precipitous slopes that a misstep would send you reeling. It joins a road descending to an abandoned copper mine across the river, then climbs the steep east bank where it meets the sloughing Doyle Trail. The Doyle Trail to the north improves when it joins the route of T83 at the Griswold Trail junction.)

T77   Mountain Home/Balch Park Car Tour
(With Directions to Trailheads 59–62)

The two destinations of this tour reign among the most luxuriant areas in the Southern Sierra. Mountain Home Demonstration State Forest and Balch County Park encompass groves of sky-crowned sequoias with understories of soft-leafed bushes and lacy ferns. Together they boast sparkling streams, placid ponds and a fork of the Tule River. Both offer inviting comfortable campgrounds and a network of well-maintained trails.

Distance   23.3 miles, one way
Steep Ascents   None
Elevation Gain   4000 feet
Skills   Easy route finding; mostly paved roads

Seasons   Spring, summer, fall
Map   Tulare county road map
Tourhead   56. The junction of Highway 190 and TC Highway J37 (Balch Park Drive) is **TH56**. This is 1.1 miles east of Springville

and 14.9 miles west of Camp Nelson. It departs from car tour T74.

Description Heading north from the big white barn junction (1070/0.0/0.0) on **Balch Park Drive**, the paved road enters the bucolic land of small ranches. To the right prior to a lumber yard sporting a derelict sawdust burner, you may notice a private airstrip. In 1990 a freak tornado touched down at the small airport, destroying its two hangers and the planes within them.

Your route parallels the North Fork Tule River, visible only as an inland path of sycamores, cottonwoods, alders and willows, then turns right on **Bear Creek Road** (TC Road M-220) (3.4/3.4). This road was built in 1884 along the old Jordan Trail, primarily in order to access high country timber. Heading northeast, the road immediately bridges the tree-hidden river. Then it climbs steadily to touch the entrance of SCICON— The Clemme Gill School of Science and Conservation. This school, sponsored by Tulare County schools and several conservation groups, offers outdoor experiences and the science of nature for grade school children.

Oliver Twist Tree

Bear Creek Road curves around apple orchards, dips to enter a one-lane bridge over Rancheria Creek and crosses into Sequoia National Forest (3.9/7.3). More apple orchards, thickets of blackberry bogs and a quaint bridge across Bear Creek slip by before a deep switchback turns your course southward, past the entrance (4.2/11.5) to Mountain Home Conservation Camp, a low security facility. The inmates accomplish conservation work throughout Tulare County, including trail maintenance. Then a wide space at the tip of the next switchback, known as Slick Rock (2.3/13.8), gives you a chance to view the Middle Fork Tule River canyon.

Now on a protracted stretch northeast among black oaks and ponderosa pines, you ride along the high crest between the middle and north forks of the river. About midway, you pass Dunn Fire Trail 30E16 (1.4/15.2), which drops east then south to connect with the road to Wishon Campground. In a short time you enter 4560-acre Mountain Home Demonstration State Forest (MHDSF). If you want information, take the paved road (1.9/17.1) to the headquarters.

In 1906 Thomas Hume bought the acreage that is now the forest, intending to protect the giant sequoias, which were being randomly hacked down. When he died in 1944, massive devastation followed. Hume's agent, Jack Brattin, who was responsible for the logging, said the slaughter was a "last resort" meant to shock the state into buying Hume's Mountain Home holdings for the profit of Hume's successors. (This fascinating piece of history is reported by Floyd Otter in *The Men of Mammoth Forest*.) Brattin succeeded. The acreage became Mountain Home Demonstration State Forest in 1946; it was well worth saving. Although numerous giant stumps exist throughout the area, extensive groves of approximately 5000 old-growth sequoias populate the state forest today.

Leaving the headquarters entrance, your route advances to the Methuselah Group Campground road (0.4/17.5). If you wish to see a big, probably very old tree, take this opportunity. A short walk on a path to the southeast of the spacious clearing gives access to the vaunted Methuselah sequoia. This tree is among the 50 largest sequoias known; its name suggests an ancient age as do the exposed rings, but its age will be unknown until all its rings can be counted.

Curving north, your course passes a T junction (0.7/18.2) with the Summit Road. If you are seeking Shake Camp and Hidden Falls trailheads, this unpaved road saves you 1.7 miles. A quick trip down this road takes you to two special trees. In 0.3 mile, you pass the Oliver Twist Tree, a rare kind of sequoia with spirally grooved bark. A few others with this pattern exist in the grove but seldom elsewhere, suggesting a genetic component due to the long isolation of this grove, according to the late sequoia expert Richard J. Harteveldt. A spur road to Dogwood Meadow opposite the Oliver Tree takes you in 1.1 mile, staying right at two forks, to a small turnout to the left where a brief path leads to the Genesis Tree, classified as the seventh largest tree in the world.

Remaining on the paved road, now *Balch Park Road* (TC Road M-296), you pass a pond regularly stocked with rainbow trout and arrive at Balch County Park Campground entrance (6340/0.3/18.5). The history of the park is beautifully illustrated in the museum housed in a former ranger cabin.

A. C. Balch bought the 160 acres for a $20.00 gold piece from John J. Doyle in 1923 and immediately gave the land plus 30 additional acres to the county. He gave explicit instructions on how to best preserve the area. Strangely, he did not halt the cutting of its giant sequoias, which continued until the 1950s, when the U.S. Government stopped all logging of *Sequoiadendron giganteum*.

The Visitor Center and a nature trail are also outstanding. A brochure accompanies the self-guided nature trail; it can be obtained in a box next to the museum. The Balch Tree, ranked among the top 50, stands north of the campground.

Traveling on, you reenter MHDSF, which surrounds Balch Park, and loop around Hedrick Pond where logs were stored for one of the region's succession of sawmills. The

outlets of all three ponds in the region form headwater tributaries to Bear Creek. Above the pond and road on a terrace is Hedrick Pond Campground; you may camp only in campgrounds in MHDSF. The small Sunset Point Picnic Area precedes a junction (2.4/20.9) with *Camp Lena Road* (TC Road M-247) on which you turn acutely right. (Or you may want to continue ahead where in minutes you can picnic at Old Mountain Home Picnic Area—the place of the original "Mountain Home," a resort in the 1890s. The "Summer Home" resort became Balch Park.)

Climbing a bit after the right turn, the road passes Frasier Mill Campground (0.4/21.3), MHDSF's largest. The sequoias hereabout were fed to the old Frasier Mill. Happily, several young sequoias are thriving here. Moments beyond the entrance to the campground is **TH59**, from which the northbound Bogus Meadow Trail of T78 starts to the left.

Ahead you may wish to turn into the parking lot of the Adams Memorial Grove (originally called Camp Lena) (0.5/21.8) to see the Hercules Tree. Jesse Hoskins took from 1897 to 1902 to carve a room in this tree. He reckoned without the surviving tree's sap that made the room too sticky for him to use. The carved room illustrates the anomalies people inflicted on these amazing trees: the tunnel tree in Yosemite was another example.

Passing the site of the Enterprise Mill, you again meet the unpaved *Summit Road* (0.8/22.6) and turn abruptly left onto it to a triangle junction (0.1/22.7) with the River Road. People wishing **TH60** of T79 or Moses Gulch and Hidden Falls campgrounds follow the bracketed directions.

The *River Road* (0.0/0.0) descends past logging roads to a junction (2.2/2.2) with the Moses Gulch Road. To reach Hidden Falls Campground (0.3/2.5) and **TH60** at either of the camp's parking lots, stay on the River Road. To reach Moses Gulch Campground turn right and descend on *Moses Gulch Road* to the camp's loop road (1.0/3.2).

The Summit Road continues north past a

driveway that peels off to the right to Balch Park Pack Station (0.1/22.8). The road balloons at **TH61** for T80 (0.2/23.0) to allow corrals and parking for cars and horse trailers. A loop hike here to the Adam Tree is a good way to end your tour. Ahead is Shake Camp trailhead, **TH62** (6460/0.3/23.3), again with ample parking and corrals, along with Shake Camp Campground.

(If you wish to make a loop trip home, return past Frasier Mill Campground to the Camp Lena Road/Balch Park Road junc-tion. Then continue westward on Balch Park Road, which eventually curves south, over-laps 3.4 miles of your ingress route and ends at the big white barn and Highway 190. En route you can detour on TC Road M-276 to the Blue Ridge Lookout, perched on a spindly tower, where you will see stunning panoramic views. Along the route after the detour, you will see a monument erected in 1990 com-memorating the skirmish at Battle Mountain in 1856 between the Tulare County Native Americans and the settlers.)

T78   Bogus Meadow Day Hike

You can experience the profound and infectious serenity of the sequoias in the area of this lotus-filled bogus meadow, and, viewing nearby authentic pot holes, you can conjure up images of the Native Americans who lived in these halcyon woods.

Distance   2.6 miles, round trip
Steep Ascents   None
Elevation Gain   500 feet
Skills   Easy route finding; easy-to-moderate hiking
Seasons   Spring, summer, fall
Map   USGS 7.5-min. Camp Wishon
Trailhead   59. See car tour T77.
Description   Your northbound trek begins beside paved Camp Lena Road (6180/0.0) in MHDSF several dozen yards east of the entrance to Frazier Mill Campground. The ***Bogus Meadow Trail*** initially borders a trickling brook with banks of bracken fern, then switchbacks up onto a nearby selec-tively logged ridge and slants up its crest. Mature sequoias spared in late 19th and early 20th century logging appear near the end of the switchbacks. A closed path (6660/0.8) to the right that becomes a road, heralds a dip in your trail above which the funnel-shaped clearing of unsigned Bogus Meadow (6680/0.1) appears. Columbine, meadow lotus and various wild plants jam this clearing—and what is a meadow with no room for grass? Bogus!

The trail next bends southwest and splits. The path ahead leads to a logged section of forest, but you take the left path where you immediately arrive at bedrock showcasing Indian mortars (6680/0.4). The deep bowls (mortars) in the bedrock were created by hand-held rocks grinding against the bedrock. Native Americans reduced their acorns and nuts to a powdery substance in this manner. Usually such sites are not advertized, but MHDSF willingly shares them with you. This place invites you to picnic and spin images of the activity that took place here in another era.

T79   Hidden Falls and Cascades Day Hike

North Fork Middle Fork Tule River careens between towering pale and bronzy rock and whirls down shadowy clefts. Sparkling creeks churn over beds of granite and rush to unite with the river. Giant sequoias stand tranquil amidst this scene. All these features enrich your travel along this challenging trip.

Distance   8.8 miles, loop trip
Steep Ascents   0.1 mile

Elevation Gain   1500 feet
Skills   Easy route finding; moderate hiking

Seasons Spring, summer, fall

Maps USGS 7.5-min. *Moses Mtn* (Trail does not appear on provisional edition), *Camp Wishon*

Trailhead 60. See car tour T77.

Description This trip begins and ends at Hidden Falls Campground, a walk-in facility in MHDSF. Situated on a riverside terrace, it offers stunning views of the hidden falls that spill into a narrow, chiseled gorge. (It could also begin and end at Moses Gulch Campground.)

From either parking area at Hidden Falls, walk alongside River Road, cross the river on a sometimes submerged concrete slab and find the *River Trail* (5990/0.0) immediately east of the slab. Hike up the path to a water faucet where the trail splits. You take the right fork. (The left leads to campsites.) Shaded by an awning of sequoia and fir boughs, you make your way north on a mild grade, dipping occasionally into shallow ravines. Sturdy sequoias along the way touch the heavens from riverside bluffs; one giant cuddles a trunk-sized boulder at its base.

Quite soon you reach a connector path (6380/0.7) that branches northeast and weaves 0.2 mile up a steep slope to join the Eastside Trail. If you find this unmarked path, it can save you 0.6 mile.

On the River Trail you continue up-river to a fork. Take the upper: both unite quickly with *Long Meadow Trail* (6620/0.4), on which you turn right. You quickly meet a T junction with the *Eastside Trail*. Turn right again. A direction of signs and a sequoia with a burned-through base mark the location. Now on undulating trail, you pass a grassy spring, round a nook with a transitory brook at the edge of sequoia habitat and pass the unmarked connector path (6620/0.3) ascending from the River Trail.

The ensuing trail through medicinal-smelling kit-kit-dizze, the dominant ground cover along this trip, continues to roll southeast, crossing the corrugated slopes of the river's deep canyon. Where your path crosses a ravine, a crag appears to the east in a climber-luring vignette. Then the path enters Sequoia National Forest and crosses a

The Hercules Tree in which a room was carved

stream that spins frothily over metamorphic rock in an avalanche chute. Soon views through portals in the forest reveal across the river canyon, the jumble of bronzy cliffs that make up a flank of Moses Mountain. Eventually the course rounds a large south-trending ridge and shortly afterward passes the McAnlis Trail (6900/1.1).

After rising on a mild grade you intersect a pair of chutes, the second of which contains thickets of willows and a seasonal branch of Galena Creek. Then you cross on an open slope mantled with snow brush and manzanita and round another ridge upon which a campsite sits. Next descend nearly 140 yards to a slim Galena branch thick with ferns, thimbleberries and wildflowers. Following that you skid another 100 yards down the steep, gravelly path to an avalanche-scoured granite chute. Here silvery Galena Creek (6840/0.7) slides and pools.

This refreshing, picture-perfect series of cascades invites you to tarry. A campsite can be found downstream. To continue, cross the chute but take special care: the slabs may be slippery. (If the creek abounds with water, return to the McAnlis Trail and descend on the path which becomes road, then turn right on the River Road and hike northwest to Hidden Falls Campground.)

Beyond the crossing, the path abruptly ascends upslope across bark debris, then it turns parallel to the slope and eventually crosses a saddle. Now in Silver Creek drainage, the trail descends, sometimes steeply, sometimes via switchbacks and cross-slope traverses, then slips into the Silver Creek recess where it fords the slender creek below a minifalls. A campsite rests to the right of the creek.

After scrambling out of this ravine you drop into the next, which harbors a branch of Silver Creek. Ford this stream, which is bordered with dense vegetation and proceed on a long moderate traverse across forested slopes to a T junction (6480/1.8) with **Griswold Trail 31E18**, on which you turn right.

Galena Creek with picture perfect cascades

Heading west now, you soon zigzag down. You might entertain yourself by counting the zigzags on the way—there are plenty! But be grateful! The trail once headed straight down. At the base you turn right on **Doyle Trail 30E14** (5360/1.3). (If you enjoy poking around old mines, turn left on the deteriorating path 0.5 mile to an abandoned copper mine next to the river.)

Reentering the world of sequoias, you walk north past prospectors' quests for riches that pock the slopes, and in a short time, descend to bridge Silver Creek on logs. A "fixer-upper" retirement hut squats in the curve of the trail. You next traverse above the river to a boulder-hopping ford of Golena Creek, stroll along a terrace, and, where the trail splits, take the right fork. Cross the Tule River and continue along the west bank for 0.1 mile. You then switchback up to the end of the trail at **Moses Gulch Road** (5520/1.3) where you turn right. Secluded campsites of Moses Gulch Campground line a loop road 0.1 mile to the south and along your road as you head north. The end of the road's cul-de-sac (5580/0.2) marks the beginning of the **River Trail**.

The path north follows the river, then switchbacks higher on the canyon slope. It soon takes you atop a length of fallen sequoia into which steps have been carved. The trail then winds into a bouldery floodplain and eventually mixes with paths to campsites in the sylvan setting of Hidden Falls Campground. Other paths lead to the brink of the gorge carved by the river and to sites overlooking the poetic beauty of Hidden Falls. You soon spot the camp's parking lot (5990/1.0) and complete this scenic loop trip.

T80   Shake Camp Loop Day Hike

The stately Adam Tree, featured on this loop, is a handsomely shaped sequoia. It stands near its companion the Eve Tree, which was axed to death. Also featured is a curious hole called an "Indian Bathtub" ground deep and wide in a huge boulder.

Distance   1.8 miles, loop trip
Steep Ascents   None
Elevation Gain   450 feet
Skills   Easy route finding; easy-to-moderate hiking
Seasons   Spring, summer, fall
Maps   USGS 7.5-min. *Camp Wishon, Moses Mtn* (briefly)
Trailhead   61. See car tour T77.
Description   Leaving the Summit Road in MHDSF, the **Loop Trail** (6440/0.0) proceeds west on a logging road. A group of lacy dogwoods grace the road's entrance; shaggy-barked sequoias stand ahead. The Loop Trail turns right off the road and takes you alongside a ravine, then leaves the ravine in which a curious block of concrete sits askew. Switchbacks aid the ensuing ascent; then the path parallels a road to your left, then dips back into the ravine.

Soon you see the Adam Tree (6730/0.7), which, like most old sequoias, shows burn scars at its base. Old giants like this survive numerous wild fires. These fires clear the understory of brush and allow the sequoia seeds to take root. The Adam Tree is second largest to the Genesis in MHDSF; the 22nd in giant sequoia hierarchy. Not far ahead, to the left, the Eve Tree stands tall and dead with its gaping wound. Before saws were used on sequoias, the trees were girdled with axes to remove the bark. This also removed the life sustaining cambium. Why the tree was abandoned by loggers is unknown.

Symbolically, the Eve Tree recalls the flagrant destruction vested upon the environment worldwide. In this case the age-old giants were felled wantonly to make humble products like shingles and fences. The Adam Tree, escaping the axe and saw, represents hope for enlightened policies: intelligent management and ample preservation of the world's bounty.

You next cross a ravine and its slender

Eve Tree was axed to death

brook. Here occur denizens of moist places usually found near sequoia groves—the California hazelnut, a relative of the commercial filbert. The hazelnut found ripening here in late summer and fall can be ground by those who would emulate Native Americans, to make a high protein bread. The bush stands 5 to 12 feet tall, has smooth bark and soft, finely haired, roundish leaves with a point. Its nut grows encased in an inch-long, hairy tube.

You walk past another similarly garbed ravine with a seasonal brook, then cross a retired road before you approach a trailer-sized granite boulder signed INDIAN BATH-TUBS (6800/0.3). Here on top of the boulder the Yaudanchi Indians worked in relative safety while viewing the nearby land. The mortar holes are much too large for acorn grinding, and many theories abound as to their purpose. Several of these "Bathtubs" have been found on Southern Sierra west slopes north of the Tule River. If you wish to climb to the top of the boulder where the deeply rounded mortars are located, a rickety ladder may still be leaning against the rock.

Ahead, an exposed, often hot section of dusty trail yields views of the Maggie ridge to the east and passes a room-sized cistern holding water for Shake Camp Campground below. A closed section of the old trail stretches next to it. Substantial logging is evident here and along this entire loop trail. Your path curves sharply south and descends among incense cedar and fir to exit (6440/0.8) near the entrance where you began.

T81   Moses Gulch Day Hike

Plummeting waters, towering sequoias, a steep canyon and a luxurious understory of plants all allure you to take this one small trip.

Distance   6.6 miles, loop trip
Steep Ascents   None
Elevation Gain   1440 feet
Skills   Easy-to-intermediate route finding; easy-to-moderate hiking
Seasons   Spring, summer, fall
Maps   USGS 7.5-min. *Camp Wishon, Moses Mtn*
Trailhead   62. See car tour T77.
Description   This delightful jaunt begins at the Shake Camp Campground trailhead, but it can also begin at Moses Gulch or Hidden Falls campgrounds: the trip passes both.

Leaving the Summit Road at the trailhead (6460/0.0), the junction of two trails, the *Moses Gulch Trail* to the right takes you south past the corrals. The trail begins its contour around a southeast-trending ridge first as a path, then as a logging road and once again, at the ridgecrest, resumes as a path, now heading north. The route cuts across steep slopes and occasionally offers remarkable views of the North Fork Middle Fork Tule River canyon.

The path rounds Moses Gulch, in which crowds of thimbleberry and California hazelnut bushes vie for ground among the boulders. Young sequoia trees grace the banks of its seasonal brook. Now leading southeast, the trail descends among cinnamon-barked sequoias intermingled with other conifers and black oaks and switchbacks to the first of several dirt-road crossings (6070/1.3). TRAIL signs mark the off-set sections of trail.

Turn left on the River Road for 0.1 mile, then right to resume on trail. Heading south you switchback to return to the canyon, then southeast to trace woodsy Moses Gulch. You pass sequoias with burned-out centers and a fallen giant nourishing young cedars. Soon you cross Moses Gulch Road (5760/0.3) and angle left to find your trail. The trail descends, sometimes abruptly, to again reach **Moses Gulch Road** (5520/0.4), on which you again turn left. The main section of Moses Gulch Campground spreads 0.1 mile south, but some walk-in sites appear along the road as you head north. The River Trail, the next leg of your romp, begins at the end of the road's cul-de-sac (5580/0.2). This trail has been in place for some time, but it was omitted on the provisional topo map. Heading north on the **River Trail**, you trace the base of the river canyon's slopes, then zigzag momentarily up them. Afterwards you climb onto a slanted, fallen sequoia into which steps were carved, and walk down it toward its roots. Once there, jump off the tree and over a brook, which flows into a pool fringed with sword ferns.

The path winds from riverside terrace to boulder floodplain to canyonside and eventually intertwines with a network of paths serving the Japanese gardenlike Hidden Falls Campground. Just east of the terraced, widely-spaced campsites here, the river plummets into a chasm, and several spur paths split off from your trail to take you to the chasm's brink. Allow time to enjoy this hidden falls. Your trail leads up an embankment to a parking lot. There your route heads right on the River Road past another parking place and across the North Fork Middle Fork Tule River on a sometimes submerged concrete slab (5990/1.0).

Beyond the slab you resume hiking the River Trail northward up the road bank and

"Indian Bathtubs" ground in boulder

then, 40 yards from the road, branch right, away from a lateral that heads to more walk-in campsites scattered amid sequoias next to the river. Rambling awhile up a mild grade across the canyon's steep east-bank slopes, you advance in thick stands of white fir, sugar pine, incense cedar and sequoia. Your trail continues to parallel the lyrical river. Then it splits: the upper path is preferable. Both forks meet at a junction (6620/1.1) with **Long Meadow Trail 31E15**, onto which you turn left. (The trail is signed at the junction with the Eastside Trail several paces up.)

On the last leg of your journey, head down, northwest, past a sequoia-shaded picnic site perched next to one of the river's many cascades; a good place for you to lunch. Ford the rock-strewn river at Redwood Crossing—springtime torrents sometimes make this difficult. At such times you might check out the fallen sequoia that bridges high above the creek. It may be wise to straddle the log, scooching along on the seat of your pants.

The trail quickly crosses a terrace west of the river, then bends south and starts a gradual ascent across steep, east-facing slopes. Sequoias drop out of the close-at-hand forest; soon the path momentarily leaves the forest to cross an avalanche chute. Here on the flank of Moses Mountain, a mishmash of metamorphic and granitic rocks, red penstemons decorate your ford of a snowmelt stream. Here, too, unlimited views of the immense west face of the Western Divide appear. The route leaves the state forest, enters the national forest, then returns to state forest again. It shortly tops a slight ridge, then drops on a mild grade to the Shake Camp trailhead (6460/2.3), completing your loop hike.

Kit-kit-dizze: west side's dominant ground cover

T82   Moses Mountain Climb

"Immersed in color" describes this trip. This challenging peak in Golden Trout Wilderness displays great jumbled cliffs with myriad shades of reds and browns. Reddish-barked giant sequoias flourish near its flank. Add the deep blue and green tones of the nearby river and you have a palette of subtle and lively colors that few other mountains in the huge wilderness can match.

Distance   10.0 miles, round trip
Steep Ascents   0.7 mile
Elevation Gain   3000 feet
Skills   Intermediate route-finding; Class 3 climbing (Class 4 & 5 pitches optional)
Seasons   Spring, summer, fall (Wilderness permit required)
Maps   USGS 7.5-min. *Camp Wishon* (briefly), *Moses Mtn*
Trailhead   62. See car tour T77.
Description   From the trailhead and corrals (6460/0.0) immediately south of Shake Camp Campground in MHDSF, *Long Meadow Trail 31E15* leads north over a crest of stumps. It then leaves the logged area to traverse steep slopes shaded with cedar, fir and pine high above the invisible, inaudible North Fork Middle Fork Tule River. Graceful-limbed California hazelnut, thorny-stemmed snow brush and stiff-branched chinquapin comprise the understory growth. The dusty, undulating trail becomes banked

with kit-kit-dizze; openings in the forest provide eastern views of Maggie Lakes' peaks perched high on the Western Divide. On this first leg of the journey the trail drifts in and out of the squared-off parcels of MHDSF.

After a brief contour around a canyon, you ford the river on boulders at Redwood Crossing (6520/2.2). As an alternative during snowmelt, some hardy people perform a fine balancing act on a sloping fallen log high above the water. Soon after the crossing you pass a picnic site near a colony of colorful sequoias. Ascending moderately, you quickly pass an end of the River Trail. A few steps later, you meet an end of the Eastside Trail (6613/0.1). A large sequoia burned through sections of its base marks this junction.

Now leaving MHDSF and entering Golden Trout Wilderness, your trail turns left at the junction, weaves up-canyon, affords westward glimpses of Moses Mountain and crosses a seasonal creek. The route cuts across a small meadow, then Long Meadow, both with a generous spray of Bigelow sneezeweed, and arrives at two good-sized campsites. An additional small site lies across the river. Sequestered among sequoias next to the euphonious river, this is an ideal place to spend the night.

When you continue the mild upgrade up-canyon, ducks east of the campsite indicate one approach to a North Maggie Mountain climb. You pass another meadow and a couple large campsites, then turn to boulder-hop the river (7140/1.2). Here consider the alternative routes by which multi-colored Moses can be climbed. Basically you stay on the trail until it curves north, then leave it anywhere along the curve, or from the following meadow with a snow-survey pole, or from the avalanche area beyond the meadow. All routes entail some bushwhacking and some Class 3 climbing. (People on T83 remain on the trail.)

Ascend west on a *cross-country* route to timberline. Turn south about 300 feet below the crest to traverse over rock ribs and gullies, enjoying en route spectacular views afar and clumps of yellow alpine columbine nearby, until you appose the peak. Then turn to climb it (9331/1.5). Off to the west the great sheer face of Dennison Peak stands in profile, while to the east, a parade of peaks rises on the Western Divide. Climbers inspired by the sight of so much rarely climbed rock will find more of the same close at hand on the flanks of Moses Mountain.

The mountain's name, "Moses," may refer to an old fisherman nicknamed for his age: Frank Knowles, a local denizen, was said to have named the mountain for him during the 1870s. It seems more likely that Moses Peabody, a government surveyor working in the area in the early 1900s, who named Maggie Mountain, named this mountain for himself.

T83   Summit Lake-Maggie Lakes Backpack

This loop trip circles a northwest corner of Golden Trout Wilderness. Here await ageless sequoias clustered in the deep canyon of a cascading river and craggy peaks towering over secluded lakes. Here awaits the essence of Southern Sierra beauty and wonder.

Distance   23.2 miles, loop trip
Steep Ascents   0.5 miles
Elevation Gain   5440 feet
Skills   Easy route finding
Seasons   Spring, summer, fall (Wilderness permit required)
Maps   USGS 7.5-min. *Camp Wishon, Moses Mtn, Quinn Pk, Camp Nelson* (briefly—but trail not mapped on this provisional edition)
Trailhead   62. See car tour T77.
Description   The beginning of this trip is described in T82.

Northbound Trail 31E15 Log

T82	Shake Camp TH	6460	0.0
	Redwood Xing	6520	2.2
	Eastside Tr	6613	0.1
	river xing	7140	1.2

After leaving the Moses Mountain approach, you stride ahead on *Long Meadow Trail 31E15* in a fir forest. Continuing up-canyon for a stretch, inland from, but parallel to, the North Fork Middle Fork Tule River, you soon curve east where, at a T junction (7550/1.3), Touhy Gap Trail 30E13 leads north into Sequoia National Park. You, however, approach the river (7640/0.3) and boulder-hop it above its confluence with a rock-strewn, seasonal branch fed by the overflow from Summit Lake.

Soil seems to have washed away from the west-facing canyonside ahead; it looks as though a great deal of water rushed down its slopes. In 1924 a dam was built across the outlet of Summit Lake to supply extra water when needed for the power project on the Tule River. The dam was later cut through when it was determined to be in Sequoia

National Park. Perhaps the resultant flood caused at least some of the apparent gouging.

Long Meadow Trail 31E15 now begins its 1700-foot ascent to the Western Divide crest. It passes a ledge-perched campsite, then, while venturing near the wilderness border, gains elevation by a clutch of zigzags and switchbacks. In the upper third of the ascent, the route turns southeast to climb in cobbles not far from the overflow creek. In this lushly wildflowered, shrubby exposure, craggy Moses Mountain appears in a southwest view while rocky Windy Ridge, topped by Sheep Mountain, stretches in the nearby east.

After crossing the often dry outlet, the trail enters Sequoia National Park (no pets or weapons allowed), fords the outlet (9320/2.5) again and reaches serene Summit Lake. Campsites among the lodgepole pines surround the lake. Brook trout, rumored to hide among the sedges, ply the water. Labrador tea and heather furnish lakeside cover for marmots and golden-mantled squirrels.

The path, now **Summit Lake Trail**, hugs the west shore of Summit Lake beyond the outlet stream, then climbs out of the bowl where it soon passes a left lateral trail (9415/0.4) to South Fork Meadow. A short easy-to-moderate climb ensues, generally east amid firs and pines, then meadows, before the next junction (9660/0.6). Here the route turns right on a *lateral trail* to climb to the park's Pecks Canyon Entrance at a broad saddle on the Western Divide (9920/0.3). There is a medium campsite here. An easy walk-up to the view-filled summit of Sheep Mountain to the southwest is a must for all adventurers passing this way. (See T63: Ex-0.)

Once again in the Golden Trout Wilderness of Sequoia National Forest, now on **Summit Trail 31E14**, you descend past a stock-fence gate on the slopes of Sheep Mountain, rounding south mostly under a canopy of fir and pine boughs. The moderate grade eases and soon a COOK RANCH BED AND BREAKFAST—20 MINUTES sign confronts you at a closed section of trail (9340/0.9). If you have reservations at the ranch, continue straight ahead on the private

trail, formerly a section of the Summit Trail. (For reservations call (209) 784-7279.) If not, turn right to continue on the Summit Trail, this section formerly known as Maggie Kincaid Trail. Head southwest down the path on a mild grade, cross a gully and you arrive at grass-lined Twin Lakes (9100/0.7) glistening at the glaciated foot of Sheep Mountain. Large campsites ring the peaceful lakes.

The Summit Trail crosses the outlet crease, descends on a moraine along the creek's deepening gully, then fords a seasonal fork of Pecks Canyon's creek. The path next negotiates a granite slope close to the lilting creek, effects an easy rocky ascent, then drops to cross the log-jammed, usually-dry stream between the two Frog Lakes (9005/0.8). Only one Frog Lake appears on maps, as the eastern "lake" usually remains a dry, cracked-mud hollow. A migration of mallards enjoy the wetter shallows of the western lake. Two campsites flank the lake northeast and southeast.

Chunks of granite mantle a rise not far south of Frog Lake, and the course meanders over this rise. Then it drops through a bouldery passage and arrives at the lowest of the Maggie Lakes, snug in a glacier-scooped bowl and backed by an eye-catching fin often mistaken for Maggie Mountain.

The three Maggie Lakes, the centerpiece of this loop trip, offer ample campsites, good fishing and swimming. A lateral (9020/0.8) briefly lined with rocks, departs southwest 0.3 miles to the largest and uppermost lake. It starts next to a campsite on the northwest edge of the lowest lake, crosses the stony inlet stream and slants diagonally up the ridge to the upper lake. The middle lake is tucked behind the moraine at the south of the lowest lake. The pine-and-fir-shaded shores of all three abound with heather and Labrador tea.

The Summit Trail leaves the lateral trail junction and leads east along the shore, past campsites and the open-ended outhouse. After it fords the lake's outlet, Pecks Canyon's creek, it passes a traceable but unmaintained segment of a trail to private land. It then climbs over boulder ridgelets on its way to meet the south end of the closed section of the Summit Trail mentioned previously. With a campsite nearby, the route turns right at the junction (8884/1.0) to ford a branch of the creek in Pecks Canyon and proceeds south switchbacking up the shoulder of Maggie Mountain, through a stock-fence passage to the ridgetop (9300/0.6). Here climbers of Maggie Mountain, an interesting, attainable peak, leave the trail for a cross-country trek up the ridge. (See T62: Ex-N.)

Next drop from the ridge of Maggie, skirting past meadows and a small campsite. You arrive at a T junction (8904/1.4) with *Griswold Trail 31E18*, on which you turn right. It would be difficult to find someone who lists this next section of knee-bruising, unrelenting though shaded trail, which drops 3800 feet in 4.0 miles, among their favorite paths. Plan to rest frequently along the descent.

This is a section of the Dennison Trail that was among the first to span the Sierra Nevada. Originally a game trail, it was improved by Native Americans and then by pioneering Caucasians. Its current name commemorates Art Griswold, who engineered its realignment in 1930, adding some 50 zigzags to ease the grade and better serve his Shake Camp pack station.

The trail heads west, first climbs over a low ridge near the divide where there is a campsite, then drops on 11 zigzags down a southwest-facing ridge in and out of Golden Trout Wilderness to near another large campsite ensconced in a swale. The subsequent 12 zigzags on south-facing slopes to a wedged flat offer vistas of the Western Divide's steep convoluted western facade. A mile traverse to a broad saddle breaks up the zigs and zags, entering MHDSF midway. The zigzaggery resumes and takes you past a T junction (6480/3.5) with the Eastside Trail. Your trail then descends along the crest of a shaded west-trending ridge, enters Sequoia National Forest and finally ends at a T junction (5360/1.3) with *Doyle Trail 30E14*, on which your route goes to the right.

Now heading northwest well above the North Fork Middle Fork Tule River, you pass prospectors' digs and a framed mine shaft

Peaceful Summit Lake in Sequoia National Park

and once again enter the domain of magnificent giant sequoias. Soon you cross a minibridge of logs spanning Silver Creek and curve behind a weathered metal-roofed, wood cabin near a few campsites. After ascending to traverse steep slopes, you drop to boulder-hop Galena Creek, then continue through woods on a riverside terrace where you reenter MHDSF. Here you take the right fork at a riverside trail split, then cross the river and continue briefly along the west bank before climbing to intersect Moses Gulch Road (5520/1.3). Doyle Trail 30E14 ends here. Moses Gulch Campground lies to the south; a few campsites lie to the north.

Your course, now the *Moses Gulch Trail*, continues at an off-set junction to the right. It ascends moderately to the north of a stream's canyon called Moses Gulch, through selectively logged trees among sequoias. A lush growth of ferns, hazelnuts and thimbleberries decorate the slopes while black oaks, white firs and incense cedars intermingle with the giant trees. The trail then crosses Moses Gulch Road (5760/0.4) and resumes to the left at a road curve, again next to the gulch. All of the off-set trail junctions at roads have TRAIL signs. The grade steepens along the canyon, then the trail temporarily turns north, switchbacks up a slope and again crosses a dirt road (6070/0.3)—this one the River Road.

Find the path to the left at a road curve and on it again ascend steeply. Soon you contour across Moses Gulch, which you have been following since Moses Campground, and round a ridge on which a logging road usurps the trail for 0.1 mile. Then again on trail to the left of the logging road, pass corrals and arrive at Shake Camp Trailhead (6460/1.3), your starting point for this experience among Southern Sierran charm and beauty.

Giant sequoias of Mountain Home Demonstration State Forest

Section 4

Sequoia and Kings Canyon National Parks
Jennie Lakes Wilderness
& Surrounding Area

Serene lake number five of the Mosquito Lakes chain

T84   Highway 198 Car Tour:
Visalia to Sequoia National Park
(With Directions to Trailheads 63–77)

The wonder of the giant sequoia trees, which are the largest living things on earth; your awareness of the rugged distant Great Western Divide mountains; and the proximity of domes, rivers, lakes, wildlife and wildflowers combine to make a visit to this revered park an unforgettable experience.

Distance   57.1 miles, one way

Steep Ascents   None

Elevation Gain   6500 feet

Skills   Easy route finding; paved road; large vehicles use Highway 180

Seasons   All year; snow removed—usually to Grant Grove

Map   Tulare County road map

Tourhead   63. The junction of highways 65 & J27 at Highway 198 east of Visalia is **TH63**. This is 15.5 miles east of Highway 99.

Description   Before beginning this tour you may wish to walk through the Nature Conservancy's Kaweah Oaks Preserve, one of the last stands of handsome native valley oaks, *Quercus lobata* (white oak). Drive 1.7 miles west on Highway 198. Turn right on Road 182, drive 0.5 mile to the open field on the left with the preserve sign. Climb over the stile and walk a short distance up the dirt road to the information kiosk, picnic tables and trailheads.

To reach Sequoia National Park from the junction (325/0.0/0.0), drive east on *State Highway 198* (Sierra Drive). At the point where the road curves northeast, you pass a T junction (400/3.0/3.0) with Yokohl Valley Road, the end of the second foothill car tour (T75) arriving from the south.

You quickly enter Lemon Cove, which was the site of a Gaweah Indian village; the derivation "Kaweah" honors that tribe. The town has inviting fruit stands and a bed and breakfast inn. The first house in the townsite has been refurbished as a women's clubhouse and community center. You next pass a junction (498/6.1/9.1) with Highway 216, which is **TH64**, the beginning of the third Sierra foothill tour (T85).

You start your mountain ascent passing

right of Limekiln Hill and the dams of Lake Kaweah: spillway elevation 694 feet. This linear lake operated by the Army Corps of Engineers, was completed in 1962 with a capacity of 150,000 acre feet of water. It has a nicely planned campground near the east end, Horse Creek Campground (fee), day areas and boat ramps that give access to water recreation of all types.

Soon after crossing Horse Creek, the lake shrinks to river size, and the river absorbs its south fork branch. You pass South Fork Road (10.1/19.2), but those heading for **TH65** and the South Fork Campground turn right.

Drive south on paved *South Fork Road* (TC Road 348) (0.0/0.0), passing California Department of Forestry and Three Rivers Rural Fire Station before pausing at Blossom Road (0.7/0.7). (It, followed by Old Three Rivers Drive, offers a minor shortcut west to the highway.) You bridge the South Fork Kaweah River twice before rising high in its canyon. You lose the pavement before crossing the river again, then negotiate a few switchbacks, enter Sequoia National Park (no entry fee) and arrive at South Fork Campground (12.0/12.7).

A camp host who issues wilderness permits and collects camp fees has replaced the summer ranger. You will find **TH65** for Ts86&87, Hockett plateau backpack and river day hike, at the east end of the campground beyond the sites.

Still on Highway 198, you next pass North Fork Drive (0.4/19.6) at **TH66** for T88, a car tour to Kaweah Colony sites. The town of Three Rivers follows, offering amenities and accommodations. The pleasant town seems

1930s sign welcomes visitors

to stretch along the Kaweah River from the South Fork almost to the East Fork. The hamlet of Hammond sits at the beginning of the twisty, lengthy Mineral King Road (1170/3.9/23.5), **TH67** of car tour T89.

Your state highway bridges the river below the confluence with the east fork, then ends upon entering Sequoia National Park at a pay station (2.0/25.5). The road ahead becomes *Generals Highway*, thus named because on the plateau it travels between the world's first and third largest trees: General Sherman and General Grant.

Now within the park, you drive past the wooden 1930s sign intricately carved by a member of the Civilian Conservation Corps (CCC). A picture of this frequently photographed sign serves as an introduction for visitors' pictorial memories of the beauty of the park. You soon arrive at Ash Mountain Headquarters and Visitor Center (1.0/26.5). (See chapter 3 for services.) Special park rules: no firearms; no pets on trails; camp only in campgrounds; camp 4 miles or beyond from the trailhead while in wilderness.

Before leaving the Ash Mountain area, pause to compare the coast redwood with the

giant sequoia growing in the picnic grounds across the street. Coast redwoods are the world's tallest trees while giant sequoias are the largest by volume; botanists say they are distantly related. Redwoods grow from stump sprouting or seed and when mature have a narrow conical crown. Sequoias grow only from seed and develop a rounded crown when mature. Particularly notice the difference between the leaves (needles) of the two trees. To help preserve the coast redwoods, Congress formed a national park just as it did many years earlier to preserve the giant sequoias.

Sequoia National Park was formed simultaneously with General Grant National Park in 1890. The successful thrust for park status was championed both by Col. George Stewart, editor of the *Visalia Delta,* and by naturalist John Muir. Sequoia National Park was enlarged in 1926 to include the back country to the summit of Mount Whitney and again in 1978 to include Mineral King. The administration of the park has adhered to the policy adopted by Col. John Roberts White, superintendent from 1920 to 1938, 1941 to 1947, who, against great pressure, held commercialism to a minimum.

Continuing on this tour, your car can slip under Tunnel Rock if it is less than 7 feet 9 inches high. An interpretive sign at the rock states that the original road, built in 1926, was the one that curves around to the right, but in 1934, with a flair for the dramatic, it was enlarged by building a section under the granite boulder.

You next pass Potwisha Campground (2.8/29.3), **TH68** of T100 (the Marble Falls hike departs from its north end), then arrive at Hospital Rock Picnic Area (2.3/31.6). Leave your car and explore the informative exhibits of local Indian history, the pictographs and the bedrock mortars here. Before white settlers arrived, these sites were occupied by the Patwisha tribe of Monache Indians, which were bands of Shoshone Indians. The pictographs, however, exist from an earlier tribe. Those seeking **THs69&70** and Buckeye Flat Campground, follow the bracketed instructions.

Take the road branching off to the right from the picnic area. Head east on the narrow paved road (0.0/0.0) to a left fork (0.5/0.5) signed MIDDLE FORK TRAIL. Those seeking that trail, T102, take the dirt road to the parking area at **TH70** (1.3/1.8). Those heading for T101, Paradise Creek hike, remain on the paved road to Buckeye Flat Campground, **TH69** (0.2/0.7). The trail begins at campsite 25.

Your route, the Generals Highway, turns north gaining 3600 feet of elevation on 12 miles of tortuous road. It climbs among successions of wildflowers through plant zones ranging from brush to broad-leafed evergreens to coniferous forests. The road passes misty springs and several viewpoints with roadside exhibits. The surrounding rock changes from speckled granite to reddish metasedimentary, and the ascent affords increasingly cooler temperatures.

In time you pass the T junction (8.2/39.8) with Crystal Cave Road. Be sure to take this opportunity to visit Crystal Cave, which is at the end of the 6.4 mile road. The cave displays spectacular marble stalactites, stalagmites and flowing draperies. Annually more than 60,000 visitors take the 50 minute guided tour through the 48° cavern. Purchase your tickets as soon as possible at Ash Mountain or Lodgepole visitor centers as tour sizes are limited—open summers only. Spelunkers need to obtain permission to explore the other more than 100 caves in the park, all of which are closed to the general public.

Continuing on your highway, crossing the park's plateau from south to north, you may have noticed that rusty-barked giant sequoias have already appeared in the surrounding conifer forest, some furnishing textured backdrops for ethereal dogwood trees. The Four Guardsmen, 1000+ year old sequoias that march across the road's path, make the official announcement that you have entered Giant Forest, the most beautiful of all sequoia groves. It was named in 1875 by John Muir, the country's most noted and influential naturalist.

Col. White, the highly regarded superintendent of earlier years, and his successors had long sought a major change for Giant Forest. They wished to remove the possible adverse impact that visitors to its village had on the sequoia grove. This desire is about to be realized. If you arrive at Giant Forest Village (2.2/42.0) after the year 2000, you will find only a few buildings remaining. Wuksachi Village, 5.9 miles ahead, away from sequoias, will replace the activities here. However, the road to Moro Rock and Crescent Meadow will still leave from Giant Forest for those seeking **THs71&72**.

To reach **THs71&72**, turn right on paved *Moro/Crescent Road* (0.0/0.0). Very quickly, take a signed, short detour left to drive atop a fallen sequoia, the Auto Log, just as cars of all vintages have done since 1917 when the tree fell. Look north of the Auto Log about 0.1 mile to locate the unnamed 12th largest sequoia. Beyond the Auto Log turn off, you reach a forked junction (1.2/1.2). Take the right fork to the edge of the plateau where the road flares, providing parking (0.5/1.7) for the famous Moro Rock, the climb of T103 at **TH71**.

To reach Crescent Meadow of T104, take the left fork at the junction, ride through the Tunnel Log, wind among sequoias to the end of the road (1.4/2.6) at **TH72**, Crescent Meadow. This serves also as the trailhead for the spectacular transSierran High Sierra Trail built between 1927–1932. The route is

Tunnel Rock on Generals Highway

Popular 48° Crystal Cave

described in detail in *Sierra South* by Winnett et al.

Continuing on the Generals Highway, you quickly reach Round Meadow (0.2/42.2) of **TH73**. Three easy day hikes described in this book and numerous other hikes begin in this vicinity: T105 north to Sunset Rock, a place to be as the day wanes; T106 on the Trail for All People, a wheelchair accessible, self-guided nature trail looping Round Meadow, is ideal if you have time for only a less than a mile hike. To the right of the highway, T106 continues on the Hazelwood Trail where interpretive signs touch on the human influences that shaped the park.

Driving ahead, eagerly viewing the many giant sequoias, you reach the master of them all: The General Sherman Tree (1.9/44.1), **TH74**. Allow time to let the impact of this tree take effect: it is the world's largest living

organism. Immerse yourself in the behemoths: take the 2.0 mile Congress self-guided nature trail of T107 that begins here. This stop marks the northern boundary of Giant Forest's 8000 mature sequoias.

Now through a passageway of tall conifers, you drive past the Wolverton exit (0.7/44.8). But turn right here if you are interested in wintertime cross-country skiing or snow shoeing (lessons/rentals/marked trails); or summertime pack station, picnic area and **TH75** of Ts108&109, the exquisite Pear Lake/Moose Lake/Alta Peak loop.

To reach **TH75**, turn right on ***Wolverton Road*** (0.0/0.0). Pass the spur road (0.3/0.3) to the Horse Corral Pack Station and turn left on the loop road to the parking area at **TH75** (1.1/1.4). The winter facilities here at Wolverton, Sequoia National Park's cross-country ski center, concentrate solely on this type of skiing; the lifts for alpine skiing were removed in 1991.

Beyond the Wolverton exit, you experience a gentle descent to the vast Lodgepole Campground (1.5/46.3). The park's complex here includes a Visitor Center, market, deli, gas station, permit and ticket office, and other amenities such as the shuttle service to popular features that was initiated in 1993. The trip through this glacial-carved valley to magnificent Tokopah Falls (T110) begins at the bridge in the campground, **TH76**.

Moving out of the canyon campground of lodgepole pines, you immediately cross Marble Fork Kaweah River, then Clover Creek over a bridge of beautifully crafted, arched stonework. Soon to the right a road (1.6/47.9) leads to Wuksachi Village where new buildings will replace the ones at Giant Forest. Red Fir Maintenance Station, part of the new project built in the 1990s, and the heliport straddle Generals Highway. A bit farther ahead, Halstead Meadow shelters a secluded picnic site. Traveling on, you see the dome of Little Baldy, then gain elevation that climaxes at Little Baldy Saddle (5.0/52.9) **TH77** of T111, Little Baldy hike. If you can walk 1.7 mile uphill on a path, this old lookout site will reward you with panoramic views.

Crossing the watershed divide between Kaweah River's Marble and North forks, you descend to the premier campground of Dorst (1.6/54.5). Captain Joseph Dorst, United States Army, first acting superintendent of the park, would be immensely proud of the facility bearing his name. It offers widely separated RV accommodating campsites, walk-in campsites, group sites, an ideal area for the handicapped and an amphitheater. Throughout the beautiful campground are magnificent stonework retaining walls. The old campground was completely rebuilt and reopened in 1992.

A pocket of statuesque Lost Grove sequoias (6660/2.6/57.1) draws your attention shortly before the highway crosses out of Sequoia National Park to enter Sequoia National Forest. This makes a good turn-around point. (If instead you wish to journey ahead through the national forest and upper Kings Canyon National Park, refer to car tour T112: points of interest are described from north to south, the reverse of your direction.)

T85   Sierran Foothills Car & Bicycle Tour: Highway 198 to Highway 180

This foothill tour, like the two others described in this book, takes the traveler into quiet country where time seems to stand still. The terrain is brushed in pastels. In spring a profusion of flowering redbud bushes along the route further evokes a Renoir quality to this adventure. This is a pleasant, leisurely way to avoid busy highway travel. It is particularly appealing to bicyclists.

Distance   30.5 miles, one way
Steep Ascents   None
Elevation Gain   4835 feet
Skills   Easy route finding; paved roads
Seasons   All year
Map   Tulare County road map
Tourhead   64. The junction of Highway 198 and Highway 216 is **TH64**. This is 24.6 miles east of Highway 99 and 10.5 miles west of Three Rivers. It departs from car tour T84 and continues from car tour T75.
Description   From the T junction (498/ 0.0/0.0), turn left onto **State Highway 216** and proceed along fenced pasture land to bridge the Kaweah River. Immediately after crossing the river you turn right onto paved **TC Highway J21** (0.6/0.6), marked 243 on roadside paddles and named DRY CREEK ROAD. For ¾ mile you ride northeast along the river's riparian woodland of sycamores, cottonwoods and willows, then curve north where Dry Creek replaces the river, and the riprap of Lake Kaweah's dam makes a cameo appearance to the east.

Hills spottily dotted with oaks incline to the right and left, but your road seems fairly level as it gently gains elevation. In springtime, the countryside's velvet grass abounds with a montage of wildflowers. A few structures appear within fenced grounds. You almost expect to meet a carriage carrying a woman in a long flowing dress, parasol in hand, and a nattily dressed man managing the horses.

Maybe not carriages, but in this sparsely populated country, you may see golden eagles. They perch on high boughs of trees. Eagles build stick nests in large trees, or sometimes on cliffs, and they return to them year after year, each time adding more sticks. The mature golden eagle of dark brown plumage soars gracefully with wide spread wings that span up to 7.5 feet. The immature bird in flight shows a white patch under each wing and a white tail tipped by a brown band. Young and old feed on rabbits, rodents and sometimes carrion that they see while soaring, then dive to grasp with their outstretched talons.

Boulders make an appearance, and a creek trickles under a 1938 cement bridge crossing. The road narrows, the ascent steepens, and soon you see Dry Creek far below; then you and it travel at the same

A pair of Golden eagles

elevation. The redbud bushes begin to appear. In spring this deciduous bush covers itself with pinkish-red or purplish clouds of delicate flowers. When the blooms wane, round, bronzy-green leaves, heart shaped at the base, spread alternately on its long stems. The bush ranges from 8- to 20-feet high.

Well into the journey, after ascending a hairpin curve, you suddenly pass a covered tennis court and a large structure. This begins a slightly more populated section of your country tour. A couple miles later you pass a T junction (16.9/17.5) with Stagecoach Drive, TC Road M-453. (Immediately east on this road you would reach M-Bar Guest Ranch, and in 1.5 miles, the privately owned Sierra Lake Campground and Restaurant.) Your road soon ends at a junction (1.0/18.5) with State Highway 245.

(If you wish a loop tour along similar country roads, turn left here. On the loop you stay on Highway 245 until a left turn on Highway 216 takes you to your starting point. The return section of the loop is 27.3 miles.)

On this tour you continue north to Highway 180 from the junction, now on *Highway 245*. After some narrow, tight curves, you arrive at the quiet community of Badger

(0.9/19.4) tucked in an oak forest. Here and farther north a maze of paved country roads offers extensive opportunities to explore numerous hamlets and wooded country-sides. Badger boasts a few houses, an inn and banks of the wildflower baby blue eyes. As you exit the village the community of buildings to the right once belonged to Synanon, a well-known rehabilitation settlement for alcoholics. It has changed hands many times since Synanon. To the left, the California Department of Forestry's Badger Forest Fire Station blends with its tree-covered background.

Shortly after crossing into Fresno County your route descends slightly, climbs up a gentle grade beside a runoff fork of Badger Creek, then turns back and forth on switchbacks through a triple-deck canopy consisting of ankle-high kit-kit-dizze, waist-high manzanita and fremontia and overhead crowns of buckeye, oak and pine. The road next passes the end of Dunlap Road (4.8/24.2).

Still ascending, a fruit stand beckons as you reach a saddle and briefly contour across the divide between a watershed of Kings River and the headwater bowl of Badger Creek, a feeder of the distant Kaweah River. You quickly pass the Pinehurst Division of Highways Station, the community of Pinehurst, which has a lodge and market, then Sequoia National Forest's work center. At the junction with Todd Eymann Road (1.5/25.7), you swing south, then north, through little communities, round Logger Point offering patches of dogwood among the trees and snatches of San Joaquin Valley far off. You cross Mill Creek. Now you turn west to meet State Highway 180 (5430/4.8/30.5), which leads east to Kings Canyon National Park (T112) and west to Fresno.

T86   Hockett Lakes-Summit Lake Backpack

Garfield Grove of sky-reaching giant sequoias; brooks in fern-lined crannies; lakes in tree-hemmed hollows; vistas, meadows, wildflowers, mountains: this collection of attractions combine to make this journey on the Hockett plateau a memorable occasion.

Distance   27.7 miles, semiloop trip
Steep Ascents   2.8 miles
Elevation Gain   6100 feet
Skills   Easy route finding
Seasons   Spring, summer, fall (Wilderness permit required)
Maps   USGS 7.5-min. *Dennison Pk, Moses Mtn*
Trailhead   65. See car tour T84.
Description   Often people prefer to reach the Hockett plateau by other trails, then leave through Garfield Grove despite the long car shuttles required for such routes. The daunting elevation gain and the possible high temperatures at the South Fork entry explain this preference. However, a mid-afternoon start and a short first day hike to Snowslide Campsite help mitigate these disadvantages.

At the junction to the south of the trailhead parking area (3620/0.0), the *Garfield Hockett Trail* begins its ascent under shade of redbud, California laurel and golden oak. Quite soon a closed path abuts the trail. Your trail curves southeast to ascend cross-slope, closely bordered by a thick cover of bushes and trees.

In the early stage of this ascent around the north slopes of Dennison Ridge, your sinuous course visits numerous nooks overarched with trees of dogwood, bigleaf maple, nutmeg and alder. The accompanying ground cover of thimbleberry bushes and ferns connotes a cool, moist soil. Occasionally in these moist places you may see pink bleeding heart flowers. These moist pockets alternate with trees and brush of drier slopes where white Chinese houses bloom and rosey-clustered twining brodiaea spiral around wayside shrubs.

When trees and shrubs part, you can see Homers Nose on the northern ridge: the high peak head with the bulbous dome nose. The muffled music of falling water echoes as you approach Putnam Canyon. After snowmelt you cannot count on water at trail height: its source, Big Spring, issues forth down-canyon. Snowslide Canyon follows, identifiable by the boulder-strewn path across it. (See T87 for the story of its landslide.)

Just east of the avalanche canyon, you enter Garfield Grove with its giant sequoias. The grove was named in the memory of James A. Garfield, 20th President of the United States, assassinated while in office. This grove is continuous with the Dillonwood Grove across Dennison Ridge, and as such ranks among the largest giant sequoia groves known. For nearly 3.0 miles you walk among the scattered titans.

Shortly, next to a giant, you pass a use path (5840/3.4) dropping sharply to a series of ideal campsites known as Snowslide Campsite, the first overnight area en route. Here the graceful, soft green leaves of Pacific dogwood and California hazelnut complement the rusty-red shred of sequoia trunks. Just beyond, a brook spills refreshing water over mossy boulders; although not shown on maps, it seems to be a fairly reliable source of water. You will find other campsites from here to the lakes.

Beyond the campsite lateral, the trail leads up a stiff grade for nearly ⅔ mile, then crosses a ridge. There it resumes a mild grade, then again ascends steeply. In time the path crosses a series of Garfield Creek branches. Each branch, abundant with flora, spills in scalloped cascades nestled in cool recesses; each has its own appeal that invites you to linger.

The path soon rounds a granitic ridge bristly with manzanita, bitter cherry and snow brush. It next passes the dim Summit Lake Trail (7250/2.0) to the right, sometimes marked with ducks. (This unmaintained route to the Tuohy Creek Trail, beautifully crafted by the CCCs in the 1930s, crosses Dennison Ridge in 1.5 miles; there it passes more giant sequoias, including the 11th largest, the King Arthur Tree. This tree reigns from its throne near the crest, 100 yards below the trail. The trail no longer appears on newly published maps.)

At length, having left the headwall of Garfield Creek, exchanging sequoias for red firs, you pass old directional signs. These mark an abandoned section to the left, of the historic transSierra Hockett Trail. From here to South Fork Meadows your route overlays that old trail. Next you drop to cross the

South Fork Kaweah River and pass the Touhy Creek Trail (8270/2.7) on which you will return to this point.

With the elevation gain of 4700 feet behind you, you still climb a ladder of zig-zags to reach the Hockett Lakes. Once on the level beyond the zigzags, and before the lakes' sometimes dry outlet (8560/0.7), turn left and walk north *cross-country* to the southernmost lake (8580/0.1). These quiet 5- to 8-foot-deep pools amid a lodgepole pine forest offer excellent swimming. If you wish to overnight here, you will find a pair of campsites at the first lake. In the damp soil surrounding the water, the Sierra star tulip, a tripetaled white lily related to the mariposa lily, blooms profusely. This eye-catching flower hugs the ground, but sends its long narrow leaves well above. Native Americans enjoyed its sweet bulb.

Upon leaving Hocket Lakes, you return to the trail and turn left (8560/0.1). Now on a clockwise loop around the southwest tip of the tranquil Hockett plateau, you hike east until you meet the first of many junctions (8610/0.2). Take the right fork here and at the next T junction (8530/0.7): both direct you to

South Fork Meadows. Now on the *Atwell Hockett Trail*, continue ahead, southwest. Along this path you are sure to notice halved license plates nailed high on a few trees; they guide snow surveyors to Quinn Cabin. Next pass the Touhy Cutoff (8525/0.3) that arrives to your right. The spread of deep green, flower-flecked South Fork Meadows offers a pleasing interlude. Shortly beyond, you pass a use trail peeling off to the right in the trees to a packers' campsite with a bear proof food storage box. At the next fork (8603/0.9) you again turn right and cross Hunter Creek on a low log. You advance on rock steps past exfoliating granite to the fifth junction since Hockett Lakes. Here you turn right on the *Cyclone Meadow Trail* (8840/0.6).

Your route takes you over a log crossing of the South Fork Kaweah River, then climbs steeply for 200 feet. It next ascends gradually near Kaweah River, then near the river's headwaters at Cyclone Meadow. Shortly after the meadow the route passes your return trail (9390/1.7); remember this point—the sign indicates SUMMIT LAKE AND SUMMIT MEADOW.

Inviting Hockett Lake rimmed with pines

Continue ahead south, past yet another junction (9415/0.3), this one on the Kaweah/ Tule rivers' divide. Descend to tree-lined Summit Lake (9320/0.2): a glittering, isolated lake perched just north of Windy Ridge and the park's border. Abundant campsites tempt you to unfold your tent. Brook trout as well as swimmers enjoy this placid lake of around 25 feet in depth. (More routes to Summit Lake are described in two other loop trips in this book, Ts63&83.)

When you must leave, return to the junction directing you to Summit Meadow (9390/0.5) and turn left. Heading northwest, then west, you descend gradually to pass a meadow heavily freckled with white marsh marigolds and yellow buttercups. Later pass a shallow pond resting to the left slightly away from the path.

After ascending the slopes of Peak 9596, you again lose elevation, then climb over a low hill where dry camping is possible. Next, turn sharply right onto the **Tuohy Creek Trail** (9140/2.9) and head north. Descend a short way until you see one of the park's aging signs. This marks the south end of the unmaintained section of trail through Garfield Grove; you passed the north end on your long ascent in. It also directs you west to Summit Meadow.

Descending nine switchbacks of diminishing length in a red fir forest, you hear Tuohy Creek long before you cross it. You pass the west end of the Tuohy Cutoff Trail (8480/

1.3), then you cross the creek again. John Tuohy was one of the group who encouraged Congressman Vandever to introduce the Sequoia National Park bill in 1890. Tuohy, who himself herded sheep for 20 years in the Kaweah River watershed, observed the damage they caused to the land. He, along with others in the group (John Muir called sheep "Hoofed locusts"), insisted that sheep, shepherders and loggers as well be excluded from the park. It was Tuohy who recommended the land chosen for the park, and he placed Garfield Grove and Hockett plateau within its original borders.

A ground carpet of lush plants precludes camping from here until you meet the river. When you cross Tuohy Creek to a flat at the confluence of the creek and river, there are several large packer-type campsites. Then you recross the creek, cross the river, turn left on the **Garfield Hockett Trail** (8270/1.0) where you again cross the river. (If you are not looking for a campsite and are not eager to make four water crossings, you can find your way cross-country alongside the creek: follow the creek past its confluence with the river until you meet the Garfield Hockett Trail in about 0.2 mile. This route is incorrectly shown as trail on your 7.5 minute topo map.)

Now on your incoming trail, you retrace your steps west, down the 4700 feet of elevation you labored so hard to gain, to your starting point (3620/8.1).

T87   South Fork Kaweah River Day Hike

On this trip you explore two of Sequoia National Park's most appealing features: tumbling water and big trees. The South Fork Kaweah River in early season showcases powerful pounding cascades that dominate all other sights and sounds. Several big sequoia trees appear en route, and just across the river—in elevation, the lowest in the world naturally growing sequoia thrives.

Distance   10.2 miles, round trip
Steep Ascents   0.2 mile
Elevation Gain   2360 feet
Skills   Easy route finding; moderate-to-strenuous hiking
Seasons   Fall, winter, spring
Maps   USGS 7.5-min. *Dennison Pk,*

Moses Mtn
Trailhead   65. See car tour T84.
Description   *The Ladybug Trail* (3620/ 0.0) begins at the eastern end of the South Fork Campground, leading east to a bridge crossing of the South Fork Kaweah River. It then passes through a bouldery flood plain

before rising onto a terrace. Some of the wild country's wildest flora and fauna have been seen here: poison oak, mountain lions and rattlesnakes. In minutes the route runs past an obscure trail to highly vandalized Clough Cave. Entrance by permission only. An endangered species of bat finds this cave to his liking.

Another obscure trail, a challenging climb to Homers Nose, slants up the ridge prior to usually dry Pigeon Creek. A beaten use trail forks off to the river. The Ladybug Trail ascends moderately to steeply, offering views of the racing river far below and the cascading ribbon of Putnam Canyon's creek ahead. The path occasionally crosses ledges chipped from a mostly metamorphic reddish-brown rock called flysch. This type of rock consists of sand and laminated clay shales high in calcium carbonate. However, Sierran bedrock granodiorite accounts for most of the rock en route.

You soon drop into Squaw Creek canyon and, in the shade of incense cedars and alders, cross the slender stream on a slender log. After returning to South Fork canyon, you pass above popular Ladybug Camp, a group of campsites near the river named for the beetle that winters here en masse. A thunderous 30-foot falls drops downstream from the first campsite. At the curve of a

Refreshing dips

switchback (4540/1.8), make a detour down the use trail, which leads across slabs to the confluence of Garfield Creek and the river, particularly impressive during snowmelt. Pools here offer refreshing dips when the water slacks late in summer.

A careful observer will notice reinforcing bars protruding from the rock just above the confluence—all that remains of a bridge that collapsed as a result of a heavy 1969 snowpack. The former Ladybug Trail, originally a section of the historic Hockett Trail, crossed the river here to climb the ridge between the river and the creek. That section of the trail was abandoned and the bridge was not rebuilt.

A conical-crowned sequoia stands several dozen yards downstream of the confluence. Drawing on his comprehensive knowledge of sequoias, the late Richard J. Hartesveldt concluded that nowhere else has the sequoia naturally extended its range to such a low elevation—4360 feet. Hartesveldt reported that the sequoia's seed was swept here from the Garfield Grove in December of 1876. Historian Floyd Otter wrote of intense rain and snowmelt that turned the land to mush late one night. A mass of sopping soil and rock abruptly gave way along Dennison Ridge and plummeted down what is now Snowslide Canyon, plucking sequoias from the Garfield Grove, pouring through Garfield Creek's defile and finally damming the South Fork Kaweah River with debris from a swath 12 feet deep, ½ mile wide and 1½ miles long. The river downstream was dry for a day while the dam backed up runoff torrents. Then the dam's breaching that night sent a destructively huge surge of water down upon farming communities of the San Joaquin Valley.

Return to the switchback and the Ladybug Trail, which switchbacks again to send you along grassy slopes. You can see rounded-topped sequoias of the Garfield Grove across the river and the dome called Homers Nose to the north. Leaving the open grass for a forest of black oak and incense cedar, you drop to a log crossing of Cedar Creek (5100/1.3). Stately sequoias of the South Fork Grove rise above flats that are now off limits for camping in order to protect the trees. This peaceful place invites a pause for quiet contemplation.

An ascending traverse east on the ridge takes you past a junction (5280/0.1) with the Cahoon Trail, marked by a metal sign with perforated letters. The Ladybug Trail drops steeply to cross a seep and rises just as steeply before it nears river cataracts at Whiskey Log Camp (5200/0.8). Some mighty flood deposited sequoia logs here. Several scattered campsites in this idyllic setting kindle thoughts of a return with backpack.

In a quest for more sequoias of the South Fork Grove and more remote communion with the river, you climb the trail up the slender ridge between the creek and the river, pass an area of numerous blowdowns, observe sequoias across the river and reach a campsite. Here you begin to see immature sequoias on your side of the river. Beyond a second campsite a large cinnamon-colored trunk of a mature tree appears. Beyond it, you hike to a river bluff where you view picture-perfect cascades. Although the trail continues, the eastward progress of this trip ends here (5600/1.1).

T88   Kaweah Colony Sites Car & Bicycle Tour

This journey, especially interesting to history buffs, takes you along the scenic North Fork Kaweah River where you visit two historic sites of the utopean Kaweah Colony. You drive along a road that was originally forged with pick and shovel by the colonists.

Distance   7.1 miles, one way
Steep Ascents   None
Elevation Gain   585 feet
Skills   Easy route finding; paved road
Seasons   All year (Bicyclists avoid summer)
Map   Tulare County road map
Tourhead   66. The junction of Highway 198 and North Fork Drive in Three Rivers is **TH66**. It departs from car tour T84.
Description   In 1885 a group of about 160 visionaries led by Burnette Haskell identified an enterprise which would enable them to put into practice their utopian ideal: a community where everyone had an equal say in policies, and where each contributed to the labor, which was valued. Their income was to come from the timber of Giant Forest. The enterprise depended on getting government approval of their legal claims to the forest and on building a road on which they could haul the timber.

In 1886 the group began to construct their road with pick and shovel. As the road slowly progressed the colonists established a forward tent camp up river called Advance. By 1890 they had carved their road, all by hand, up the steep slopes to the forest—

around 18 miles and 4500 feet elevation gain. They then set up their mill and began cutting timber. But they had not succeeded in obtaining legal title to the land, and in late 1890 Giant Forest became part of the newly established Sequoia National Park. As a result, the most beautiful grove in the world of massive giant sequoias has been preserved unlogged.

The colonists protested their loss but to no avail. They then sought compensation for their road, which was used to access the park until 1927. They also tried to reestablish their

1897 Kaweah Post Office

dream in Mineral King where they cut and milled timber at Atwell Mill. Both efforts failed and the disheartened people slowly disbanded. Their interesting story is told in a fine booklet, *Kaweah Remembered* by William Tweed, sold in the park. It presents pictures of the colonists and an in depth account of their endeavor.

To begin this tour turn left from the junction of Highway 198 (875/0.0/0.0), travel north on **North Fork Drive** (TC Road 357). You immediately bridge, then follow, the North Fork Kaweah River, winding among scattered houses and ranches to reach the Kaweah Post Office (2.7/2.7). The building blends with an old valley oak whose ample branches seem to enfold it. The tiny aged post office was built in 1897 on the site of the colony's first settlement, but after its demise, and still serves the community of Kaweah.

Traveling on, you again cross the river, then follow its curves as the canyon closes in. Just after the road makes a U turn in a tight ravine, you rattle over a cattleguard and make a turn to the left on a road (1460/4.4/7.1), which descends to the parking area of Advance, the site of the colony's tent camp. A large sign marks the area. The fenced-in foundations with standing chimneys, no doubt historic, survive from a time later than the tent camp.

(After you tramp around the wooded, historic site—the end of this tour—you may wish to investigate further. The colony's road climbs and narrows beyond Advance, loses its pavement and clings to steep slopes. In 2.9 miles, at a fork with a road descending to the river, your road ascends into a small private section and is gated. The road beyond the private section climbs steeply in Sequoia National Park to Crystal Cave Road. It no longer supports vehicle travel, but as the Colony Mill Trail, makes a great spring or fall hike. Check with the park for the current access policy, then obtain 7.5-minute topographic maps Shadequarter Mtn and Giant Forest.)

T89   Mineral King Car Tour
(With Directions to THs78–80)

Once you have visited Mineral King, the memory of its grandeur will beckon you to return. In its forested valley, resting at 7500 feet, you are dwarfed by the great jagged, multicolored peaks. As the snow melts from these windswept alpine summits, you are surrounded with the music of tumbling creeks. You may even see curious and wild animals who call this valley home. To reap the rewards of this pristine wilderness, you must first experience the tortuous but historic Mineral King Road, which with its many curves offers its own element of beauty and excitement.

Distance   24.6 miles, one way
Steep Ascents   None
Elevation Gain   6655 feet
Skills   Easy route finding; mostly paved road; not recommended for trailers or RVs.
Seasons   Spring, summer, fall
Map   Tulare County road map
Tourhead   67. The junction of Highway 198 and Mineral King Road (TC Road M-375) northeast of Three Rivers is **TH67**. This trip departs from car tour T84.
Description   Equestrians pulling horse

trailers could choose other entries into the Mineral King area; the closest, via Hockett Meadows, is **TH65**, the South Fork entry. Check available turning and parking space there before driving through the campground.

A park entry sign on the Mineral King Road suggests you allow 90 minutes to reach the valley, and it indicates the availability of campsites within the campgrounds. Overnight stays outside the campgrounds or within a radius of four miles on the trails from the trailheads is forbidden. This regulation has greatly improved the cleanliness and sanitary conditions near the trailheads.

Mineral King was governed by Sequoia National Forest as a game refuge from 1926 until 1978. During that time property was leased for summer cabins. In 1965 Walt Disney Productions, with Forest Service approval, proposed an alpine ski village on the floor of Mineral King valley. Their plans consisted of a five-story hotel, numerous restaurants and stores, skating rinks, stations for tramways and ski lifts radiating in all directions, swimming pools, tennis courts, a golf course and an improved access road. After a lengthy battle spearheaded by the Sierra Club in opposition to the project, approval was removed. In 1978 Congress voted to transfer Mineral King to Sequoia National Park, thus securing its wilderness character.

Occupation of Mineral King by Native Americans closely followed the receding glaciers, which covered the area from 1.5 million to 10 thousand years ago. No record of Caucasian visitation appears until 1858 when cattleman Hale D. Tharp explored the valley, and 1864 when Harry O'Farrell, alias Harry Parole, commemorating his release from prison, rode in seeking game for his employer John B. Hockett. (Hockett and his crew were carving a toll road across the

Sierra south of Mineral King.) Then after James Crabtree discovered silver in 1872, the valley bristled with miners for ten years. At that time it was optimistically named "Mineral King." Although silver was extracted from some prospects, it had a high lead content that was too expensive to remove. Loggers arrived following the road's completion, but logging did not prove profitable either and few people remained. Recreationists began to trickle in. In 1903 the trickle swelled to a flood of over 200 Sierra Club members who used the valley as a trailhead for their four-week hike to Mount Whitney. (Apparently 139 hardy men and women reached the summit!) Today Mineral King is a popular destination for those seeking wild beauty and an outstanding wilderness experience.

The road on which you travel above the East Fork Kaweah River was built in response to Crabtree's discovery of a large silver vein, the White Chief Mine. In 1878 enterprising John Crawley formed the company that built "The Mineral King Wagon and Toll Road" to transport ore and the swarms of prospectors. For the first two miles you drive on a piece of that twisty, somewhat steep road to a saddle south of Red Hill. There the old toll road, now a private road to Old Bear Ranch, plummets to the

1923 gracefully arched bridge over East Fork Kaweah River

floor of the gorge and climbs wildly up River Hill before it returns to the river and reaches Oak Grove. Fortunately for today's travelers, a five mile section of road built in the 1920s bypasses that nightmare plunge and climb. Car passengers today can see snatches of the old road winding along the canyon's far side beyond River Hill. The rest of your ride from Oak Grove to Mineral King is on the original road bed.

From the junction (1170/0.0/0.0) in Hammond, a foothill village that developed around the hydroelectric plant in 1898, turn right to travel eastward on the *Mineral King Road*, soon passing the old road turn off. Paralleling above you snakes the power plant's aqueduct, mostly invisible until it, you and the river merge at Oak Grove (6.5/6.5). There the trestled flume, the curving road and the 1923 gracefully arched bridge meet to form a picture of man's late 19th, early 20th century achievements.

Now traveling on the north side of the Kaweah, again on the original road, you pass a ranch house. This is all that remains of the once busy community of Oak Grove, where a Civilian Conservation Corps (CCC) camp was located. Between 1933 and 1942 the CCC built many roads, trails and facilities in both Sequoia and Kings Canyon national parks. You next pass over the conduits of two creeks: Grunigen, named for early homesteaders, and Squirrel whose name has little to do with its inviting potholes that entice hot passersby. Soon after, you cross into Sequoia National Park and gain 800 feet to the 1930s Lookout Point Ranger Station, a park entrance pay station (3.7/10.2).

The road, reported to have a total of 698 curves, continues to round in and out of every furrow on the steep slopes high above the river. Occasionally it supplies fugitive vistas of Sawtooth Peak, a bare mountain with an off-center point, the emblematic peak of Mineral King. Passing from chaparrel to mixed forest, the route suddenly curves below sentinel giant sequoias at Redwood Creek—no doubt eliciting exclamations of admiration. A sign here recounts the fascinating events of early travelers.

Still ascending at a maximum speed of 15- to 20-miles per hour, you pass a road gate,

The winter wonderland of Mineral King

closed after Thanksgiving or the first heavy snowfall. Nearly two miles later, you pass the trail to Paradise Peak, then note Atwell Mill Campground (8.9/19.1), the largest of the two fine campgrounds in Mineral King. Drive ahead past the camp to its east end for parking at **TH78** of Ts90–93. As with so many place names in the Southern Sierra, Atwell Mill Grove, Trail, Creek and Campground commemorate a use that was not beneficial to the land. At Atwell's mill, which stood here in the late 1800s, many mighty sequoias were reduced to trivial products, such as fence posts and roof shingles.

Traveling on you arrive at Cabin Cove. This land belongs to the park, and when the leases expire the village will probably be removed. This holds true for the villages of Faculty Flats and Mineral King as well. Silver City (1.6/20.7), in contrast, was established on private land owned by Jim Mehrten. From the late 1800s to the present, this village has served the people of Mineral King valley. Since 1934 this tradition has continued through the Jones family, owners of the restaurant complex. They offer food, rental cabins, hot showers and lead-free gasoline pumped from a vintage gas tank. (Phone (209) 561-3223).

In one mile past Silver City you reach the avalanche slash of Highbridge Creek. The creek and the angle of north slopes in the bowl of Mineral King are conducive to avalanches and many have occurred.

The next group of land-lease cabins, called Faculty Flats, built by Los Angeles area school personnel in the 1930s, cluster at the foot of the valley. Beyond, you pass attractive Cold Springs Campground (2.6/23.3), then the Mineral King Ranger Station (0.1/23.4) (wilderness permits) and the picnic area. Parking for the Tar Gap Trail of T94 at **TH79** (0.2/23.6) spreads upslope to the left beyond the station. Shortly after, you will see parking (0.6/24.2) for Sawtooth/Monarch/Timber Gap trails.

In the 1870s a mining town occupied the latter parking area. A tram to transport ore scaled the slopes to Empire Mine above to the north. As you gaze upon those metamorphosed rocks you may understand why the early miners were so excited: miners in other locations found extensive ore veins in contact zones between reddish metamorphics and grayish granite like this. But this mine produced little and its tram and the town were destroyed by avalanches.

The road continues to a fork (0.3/24.5): you find the Mineral King Pack Station and the trail to Franklin Pass and Farewell Gap at the end of the road ahead, 0.3 mile, but no public parking; the right fork leads you over the bridge to Mineral King cabins and parking (7830/0.1/24.6) at Eagle Crest Trailhead, **TH80** for Ts96–99 and return of T93.

When you stop here to stroll along the river or admire the views, you are likely to see a Yellow-bellied Marmot. The mostly brown, stout, Yellow-bellied Marmot lives above or near tree line in meadows with rock outcrops or talus. When not eating he suns on lookout rocks cluttered with his droppings. This lovable rodent eats grasses and forbs in abundance to acquire a fat layer for the long winter hibernation in his burrow. He also enjoys munching on unguarded camping equipment and most anything in your backpack. The Yellow-bellied Marmots of Mineral King are unlike all other marmots known, in that in spring and early summer they dine on car wiring and hoses!

T90   Paradise Peak Day Hike

This trek to a former lookout site ascends steeply in a forest of some of the world's loftiest sequoias, both in height and in elevation. Paradise Peak, rising on a divide between the East Fork and Middle Fork of the Kaweah River, provides sweeping views of Sequoia National Park and beyond.

Distance   9.2 miles, round trip
Steep Ascents   0.3 mile
Elevation Gain   2847 feet
Skills   Easy route finding; moderate-to-strenuous hiking
Seasons   Spring, summer, fall
Map   USGS 7.5-min. *Silver City*
Trailhead   78. See car tour T89.
Description   From the trailhead parking east of Atwell Mill Campground, walk west past the campground down the Mineral King Road 0.3 mile to a curve where you will find your trail. Ascend north under cover of white fir, incense cedar and sugar pine on the *Atwell Redwood Trail* (signed PARADISE RIDGE TRAIL) (6515/0.0). Many zigzags and switchbacks aid your stiff climb. Through occasional west windows where manzanita replaces trees, you catch far reaching views of the East Fork canyon, and, across the nearer canyon, of the rounded crowns of Atwell Grove sequoias. Soon you hike among the grove's giants: their reddish boles are bathed in waves of soft, flowing fronds of bracken fern. Three of the largest sequoia trees live in this impressive grove: the 21st, 25th and 32nd.

Your trail switchbacks steeply upward. At the west end of one switchback, a post marks an obscure use trail to Cabin Cove. As the leases expire at the Cove and the cabins vacate, the use trails their occupants trod since the 1930s disappear. Your trail advances to, but switches away from, Atwell Creek, the only reliable water on this side of the divide. Then, with wafts of minty pennyroyal greeting you, it arrives at an open area mottled with snow brush and soon tops the forested ridge of red fir at a saddle set on the divide (8460/3.0). Hikers on T91 continue ahead here.

You, however, turn left onto *Paradise Peak Trail*. You ascend easily up the ridge, quickly passing a camping possibility overlooking the East Fork canyon. The trail, peppered with ducks and occasionally reinforced with rocks, assures easy pathfinding despite numerous blowdowns. After rounding the north side of Hill 8863, look down the southeast slopes for sequoias to find the

uppermost tree. This tree, at 8800 feet, is the highest naturally growing sequoia known in the world.

The trail ascends a ridge, leaves it to curve south, then turns abruptly west to climb up through a rock garden with an exuberant melange of mountain pride, purple penstemon, Indian paintbrush and lupine to reach the summit outcrop (9326/1.6). Rock steps lead to a crack on the summit rock where a Class 2 climb affords an ascent to the top. The lookout was dynamited when abandoned during the mid-1950s, and only scattered bits of wreckage remain. A park radio relay tower now sits at one end of the summit rock.

To the north you can pick out nearby Castle Rocks. Then, across the Middle Fork canyon, you can see the Generals Highway snaking up the slopes, Moro Rock, Alta Peak, Big and Little Baldy Ridge and curved, forested Shell Mountain. To the south beyond the canyon of the East Fork lies the Hockett plateau. All of these places except Castle Rocks are visited on trips in this book.

Paradise Peak sans lookout

T91   Paradise Ridge–
Middle Fork Kaweah Canyon Backpack

This trip is tailor-made for backpackers who seek a measure of solitude en route and who tolerate ascending but relish descending. It climbs steeply up over a ridge and down on a lightly trodden trail, then traverses gently along Sequoia National Park's deepest canyon. Linking two large sequoia groves, the route crosses several channels seething with whitewater and ends beneath the park's emblematic dome, Moro Rock.

Distance   21.7 miles, shuttle trip
Steep Ascents   0.3 mile
Elevation Gain   3465 feet
Skills   Easy route finding
Seasons   Spring, fall (Wilderness Permit required)
Maps   USGS 7.5 min. *Silver City, Lodgepole, Giant Forest* (briefly)
Trailheads   78&70. This trip begins at **TH78**. See car tour T89. It ends at **TH70**. See car tour T84. There are 29.0 miles between trailheads.
Description   Enjoy this trip after peak snowmelt when Cliff and Granite creeks become less dangerous to cross. The beginning of this trip is described in T90.

Northbound Atwell Redwood Trail Log
T90 Atwell Redwood Tr   6515 0.0
   saddle   8460 3.0

Leave the divide on *Atwell Redwood Trail* to switchback north amid red firs while descending into the Castle Creek watershed. Shortly the switches abate and you skirt a sometimes boggy patch garnished with an array of wildflowers. The numerous successively blooming, colorful flowers, supplemented with ferns and thimbleberry bushes, appear in plush nooks and sloping meadows throughout the descent to Cliff Creek, sometimes so lavish they crowd over the trail.

In one mile from the saddle you step across a Castle Creek tributary, the first reliable water north of the crest. Immediately, you pass a destination sign for the dim, long abandoned Castle Creek Trail—you will pass its north end later in the trip.

Ascending mildly now, you may notice on dry patches of ground, yellow-throated gilia. You can recognize this bloom by its five shocking pink petals and purple dots at the

flower's yellow center. Also known as mustang clover, these bright flowers, with whorls of narrow leaves, are white in color at lower elevations.

Hovering some distance to the left appear the turrets of Castle Rocks. A small campsite, the first since the ridge, sits next to a slender creek crowded with creek dogwood. You soon cross another creek downslope of flower-decked Little Sand Meadow (8120/2.9), which indeed shows little, in fact, no sand. Open spaces flanking the trail just beyond the meadow serve well for camping, the last until Cliff Creek.

Your path, heading north, steepens as it parallels the Castle Creek/Cliff Creek divide, then zigzags down a ravine. Where the ravine swerves northwest, the trail abruptly turns right, east, crossing the divide at a saddle overgrown with snow brush—pick your way among the scratchy low-growing bushes.

Descending steeply now, the zigzagging path seems to tumble down the oak- and cedar-shaded slopes covered with medicinal smelling kit-kit-dizze. The descent abruptly ends at billowing Cliff Creek (5520/2.6). First the path bisects a dreamy campsite snuggled at the feet of giant sequoias; the reward at the end of a rainbow-flowered descent.

Several weeks after the snowmelt runoff peaks, you can wade across the creek a few yards below the path. A large blowdown bridges it 0.3 mile upstream, but the climb there and back on steep slabs with a backpack may be more dangerous than a careful wade.

Beyond the creek the path switchbacks up steep slopes among the Redwood Meadow Grove of hardy sequoias, levels, and meets

Timber Gap Trail (6040/0.7). An ideal, short shuttle trip would be to return to Mineral King along this scenic trail over Timber Gap, around 9.5 miles. At this junction are a pair of cabins used by rangers and trail crews, and a Redwood Meadow public pasture, sunny with yellow coneflowers.

North of the junction lies a single large Redwood Meadow campsite among sequoias, replete with faucet water and outhouse! After the campsite your route meets the first of three trails (6020/0.2) to Bearpaw Meadow and ultimately Giant Forest. You take the left fork, now **Middle Fork Kaweah Trail**. It drops via zigzags to pass a ledge campsite above Granite Creek. Cross the creek: another difficult ford during snowmelt. Astute observation reveals foundations of a former bridge above the trail crossing.

A large camping area spreads across a terrace next to the creek's north bank. Your trail mounts the low ridge dividing the creek from the Middle Fork Kaweah River. Midway on the ridge you pass the second path (5495/1.0) to Bearpaw Meadow. As your trail approaches the river, a small campsite sits above and off the trail on the south bank. The route crosses a steel-girdered bridge (5460/0.1) that displays puzzling twisted steel hand rails. The river churns beneath, spinning frothy whitewater against the sides of its bouldery chasm.

Beyond the bridge the trail ascends through a woodland on a westward course, which it maintains high above the river to the trailhead. After rounding a ridge, the third and most direct trail (5820/0.9) to Bearpaw Meadow and the High Sierra Trail branches east off a switchback.

Your Middle Fork Trail falls into a pattern of rounding corrugated ridges and canyons. Some creases hold seasonal streams—you soon pass one with horsetails near a small campsite. The trail also loses elevation overall despite some steep climbs. Along the way openings appear amid the forested ridges to eastern views upward of the sharply pointed Great Western Divide peaks, and downward to the canyon of Cliff Creek you crossed earlier; and western vistas of the valley of the Middle Fork Kaweah River and the unmistakable dome of Morro Rock.

Two switchbacks help your descent to a retreat with wild currant and strawberry plants. Later the trail rounds the ridges far below Sugarbowl Dome and descends moderately to steeply into the deep canyon of Buck Creek, passing an immense west-facing slab. The branches of Buck Creek drain Alta Peak, invisible to the north, coalescing into one mighty stream, more a river than a creek. A 1959 bridge (4950/2.1) affords passage

Early season waters of rushing Buck Creek

that most of the year would otherwise be an impossible wade. A large campsite straddles the trail east of the creek; a small one sits to the west; and at low water one rests on the sandy floodplain.

Trees in Buck Canyon include a few bigleaf maple and California nutmeg. The deciduous 6- to 10-inch maple leaf, sometimes mistaken for a sycamore leaf, sports five pointed lobes deeply separated and edged with smaller points, atop a 10-inch stalk. The tree's sap is sweet like eastern maple. The nutmeg, on the other hand, displays sharp-pointed, evergreen needles in two flat rows flanking the center stem. The shiny dark green needles show two narrow whitish lines on their underside. The fruit resembles the well-known spice but has no commercial value. Both these trees prefer moist canyons.

An arduous ascent brings you past unsigned, unmaintained Seven-Mile Hill Trail. A gradual descent carries you through sometimes hot and sunny brush of mountain mahogany, buck brush and manzanita. White with purple five-spot, orange California poppies, yellow violets and blue brodiaea add colorful interest to the path's borders. In quick time your route reaches a springtime wade across Mehrten Creek, and then passes a use path descending to a campsite. In 0.4 mile your trail passes the obvious but unsigned, unmaintained Castle Creek Trail (4720/2.8), which travels down the slope to campsites. (That trail can be traced to the river but not beyond even though we met its southern end earlier.)

Continue on the Middle Fork Trail, heading west through predominant incense cedar, black and golden oak groves. In a couple of miles you glimpse in a fleeting moment the falls of Panther Creek. You then switchback past a terraced campsite and cross Panther Creek (3840/2.4). Treat the lower pool as off-limits for refreshing yourself, as the falls drops immediately beyond the pool's rim.

The trail climbs sharply out of Panther Creek's canyon, then weaves through thickets of chamise and other drought resistant plants. Sporadic views of Castle Rocks high across the Middle Fork valley and the Great Western Divide far to the east offer distractions on the sometimes hot trek to the Moro Creek crossing (3140/2.8). A pool north of the crossing offers marvelous refreshment. In spring, bush poppies clothe the slopes in butter-yellow polka dots; in all seasons poison oak lurks trailside. Soon the cars come into view, toy-sized at first, and you quickly end your journey at **TH70** (3340/0.2), 1.5 miles from Buckeye Flat Campground.

T92   East Fork Falls Day Hike

This short trip offers an ideal introduction to Mineral King adventures for hikers of all ages. A relic at the sawmill site, sequoias saved from destruction, Indian "bathtubs" of unknown purpose, and a river gorge sprayed with spindrift from a churning falls acquaint visitors with the marvelous diversity in the valley of Mineral King.

Distance   2.6 miles, round trip
Steep Ascents   None
Elevation Gain   575 feet
Skills   Easy route finding; easy-to-moderate hiking
Seasons   Spring, summer, fall
Map   USGS 7.5-min. *Silver City*
Trailhead   78. See car tour T89.
Description   From the trailhead parking lot east of Atwell Mill Campground, follow the campground road west bearing left through two consecutive forks to arrive at the beginning of the **Atwell Hockett Trail** (6500/0.0) between campsites 16&17. In the campground, young sequoias reach for sunlight among the stumps of parent trees under the deep shade of white firs, incense cedars, sugar and ponderosa pines. On the wide trail

you hike among dainty white gayophytum blooms. Soon to the right, the long meadow grass parts around an Erie Gity Iron Works flywheel, revealing the site of the Atwell sawmill (6420/0.2).

Toppling and milling of giant sequoias and other conifers followed the completion of the Mineral King Road in 1878. The mill, built here at A. J. Atwell's behest, reduced the giants to shingles and posts—their brittle wood otherwise unusable. Two years later, realizing no profit, the mill shut down.

In 1890 most of the land adjoining, but not including, Atwell's passed into U.S. Army protection as Sequoia National Park. The Kaweah colonists, attempting to regain their utopian dream after the loss of Giant Forest (See T88), reopened the mill. Apparently unaware that the mill was outside the park, Captain J. H. Dorst, the first park superintendent, was so incensed when logging resumed there that he and his troops illegally seized the mill and shut it down again. By 1898 the mill was reactivated, furnishing posts for the 5.7 mile roadside flume that shunts East Fork Kaweah water from Oak Grove to generate power in Hammond.

Despite the clamor of conservationists for government purchase and protection of the remaining sequoias, the threat of logging was not banished until 1920, when philanthropist D. E. Skinner bought the property and transferred it to National Park Service jurisdiction. The grove, with its 600+ sequoias, despite efforts to name it for Skinner, honors the man who long ago tried to despoil it!

Beyond the mill site, look for a path (6400/0.1) to the right next to a tree stump. This obscure short lateral leads to bedrock boulders with 5-foot round, 3-foot deep Indian "bathtubs." Smaller potholes, scattered throughout the Southern Sierra were created by Indians grinding nuts, but although there remains much speculation, no one seems to really know what purpose these larger tubs served.

Back on the trail, you descend through a mushy trickle as you near, then cross Deadwood Creek, which spills and splashes among mossy boulders. As you approach the river, its distant muted hiss grows to a roar. You pass to your left a faint, closed path to Cabin Cove. Beyond a stone ledge developed by a sledgehammer-wielding construction crew, you drop to a burly log bridge (5925/1.0) spanning the East Fork Kaweah River gorge, the end of your trip. The nameless, bounding falls accompanied bankside by giant sequoias sends billows of droplets to dampen the bridge and the exuberant nearby flora. A precarious path squeezes between the river, bluffs and trees at the far end of the bridge to a bouldery picnic site upstream.

(If you continue on the main trail, you will see the scars of a natural fire that burned freely among the sequoia trees in 1991. Since it has been determined that fire promotes sequoia germination, the park allows some fires to run their course: this was one of them. Many seedlings developed, but most appear to be white fir.)

T93   Hockett Meadows–Little Kern River Backpack
With Excursions P–S: Cahoon Rock/Evelyn Lake, Blossom Lakes, Bullfrog Lakes, Vandever Peak

This adventure takes you to the land of the Hockett plateau, where wildflowers thrive in nature's gardens, deer herds congregate in tall grass meadows and lakes repose in glaciated bowls. The route then loops around to the rushing Little Kern River, whose headwater freshets plunge down flaming rock walls. The numerous side trips offered expand and extend your adventures.

Distance   30.7 miles, shuttle trip
Steep Ascents   None

Elevation Gain   6420 feet
Skills   Easy route finding

Seasons   Spring, summer, fall (Wilderness permit required)

Maps   USGS 7.5-min. *Silver City, Moses Mtn, Quinn Pk, Mineral King*

Trailheads   78&80. This trip begins at **TH78**. See car tour T89. It ends at **TH80**. There are 6.0 miles between trailheads.

Description   The beginning of this trip is described in T92.

Southeastbound Atwell Hockett Trail Log

T92	Atwell Mill CG	6500	0.0
	mill site	6420	0.2
	Indian site	6400	0.1
	bridge	5925	1.0

Beyond the East Fork bridge, you begin an extensive but mild climb to Hockett Meadows, continuing on the **Atwell Hockett Trail**. Abruptly turning southwest, you rise above the East Fork Kaweah River, passing through a 1991 natural burn in the East Fork Grove. Park biologists are monitoring this part of the grove closely for sequoia seedling growth. Only a dozen or so of the 353 sequoias comprising the grove can be seen along the trail, but they, like all these giant trees, leave a lasting impression.

After a mile, your course fords a trickling fork and shortly thereafter leads across boulder-studded Deer Creek, crowded with leopard lilies, monkey flowers and bracken ferns. This ford lies on the slick brink of a gra-

nite bluff where the creek spills in a lacy fall. The path then switchbacks and curves above the Deer Creek drainage. One mile from the Deer Creek crossing, the trail leaves the East Fork Grove at an outpost of distinguished sequoias.

Eventually you cross steep-sided granite, heavily dynamited to create a path. Here you have open views of the East Fork canyon, from which you can hear sounds of cars geared down to tackle the sinuous Mineral King Road, seen weaving along the canyon slopes. You next ford a plant-smothered creek that falls over slabs below the trail, and hike a steady upgrade around a ridge into the Horse Creek watershed. Immediately to the south the highest point claims the name of Cahoon Rock—really a mountain—and the highest point west of that forms the head of Homers Nose.

After stepping across more brooks in flower-decked coves on furrowed southwest-facing slopes, you boulder-hop Clover Creek (8040/5.8). The first real campsite en route, room for four tents, sits above the path just prior to the ford. A sloping meadow profuse with wildflowers intervenes between Clover Creek and your next ford, Corner Creek. Then in quick time the Tar Gap Trail merges with your path (8575/1.2).

You pass the obscure, unsigned Horse

Evelyn Lake rests in a rock-bound cirque

Creek Trail, which angles into the woods a few dozen feet from the junction and in no time you reach capacious campsites under red firs next to the crossing of Horse Creek. This makes an excellent place to camp; a handy cable relieves you the effort of finding the right branch on which to safely hang your food from marauding bears.

Several logs aid in a dry crossing of Horse Creek (8545/0.2) during high water; and, later on the trail, log bridges cross over bogs aflight with shooting star wildflowers. Your ascending course then deflects west to round a ridge that separates the Horse Creek and Whitman Creek watersheds, and drops to a T junction with the Evelyn Lake Trail (8505/1.5).

Before you spreads the impressive expanse of verdant Hockett Meadows. At its south end just ahead, you see a log cabin where a park ranger resides from June to September. When not on patrol, he raises a U.S. flag indicating his presence. Feel free to seek his advice. A part of the meadow by the cabin is fenced off for administrative use. The vast spread of grass beyond the fenced area attracts large gatherings of deer, most often seen at dusk. To the west of Hockett Meadows flanking the Evelyn Lake Trail, you find a cluster of campsites, two cables and an outhouse.

The first of several side trips begins at the junction of the Evelyn Lake Trail.

Excursion P: Cahoon Rock/Evelyn Lake

Plan a full day or an overnight to take advantage of the views from easily attained Cahoon Rock and the swimming and fishing at Evelyn, a deep water lake hugged by boulders.

Distance   8.0 miles, round trip
Steep Ascents   0.2 mile
Elevation Gain   1375 feet
Skills   Easy route finding; moderate-to-strenuous hiking; Class 1 climbing.
Maps   USGS 7.5-min. *Silver City, Moses Mtn* (briefly)

Description   Initially on the *Evelyn Lake Trail* (8505/0.0), you parallel Whitman Creek, passing the camping zone and then cutting across a boggy meadow outlet on log bridges. Next, a handy blowdown makes for an easy ford of Whitman Creek, named for Capt. William Whitman, acting park superintendent in 1912.

About 50 feet later you pass the long abandoned, barely visible Eden Grove Trail that forks right; it does not appear on current maps. You continue ahead across a glade and its inlet stream. After ascending round-ended switchbacks, you reach the Cahoon Trail junction (8820/1.5). Take the left fork to Cahoon Rock.

On the *Cahoon Trail* you gently climb to the right of a Whitman Creek branch, then to the right of a grassy meadow. You next slog through the tip of the meadow. Beyond, you ascend on switchbacks in woods of red fir and western white pine, climb a canyon left of its creek and its lush greenery and in time level off and curve left to ascend the peak from the south. On the broad top where evidence of camping exists, you reach a cluster of rocks. Climb these to the summit (9278/1.0), where you may sign the register.

This mountain was named for George W. Cahoon, and the lake for his wife Evelyn. They homesteaded acreage southwest of here in 1885. The lookout that long stood here was moved north to Yosemite National Park in 1977, and the lookout's foundations were dynamited. The views to the east include multicolored Vandever Mountain peeking through a granite gap of snaggletoothed peaks. To the west, Homers Nose, a mountain whose dome resembles the bulbous proboscus of pioneer Kaweah resident, Joseph Homer. Hardy climbers who prevail the bushwhack ascent from the South Fork to the nose report its Class 5 climbs "are not to be sneezed at."

Return to the Evelyn Lake junction (8820/1.0). Now on the right fork, the *Evelyn Lake Trail*, you ascend north via zigzags to near the top on Hill 9061, where you can enjoy far-reaching views. After a traverse you reach the top of Hill 9020, from which you glimpse the sparkling water of Evelyn Lake caught in its rock-bound cirque. Here you descend, sharply zigzagging under forest cover, to the lake (8700/1.5). This idyllic lake invites an extended stay. A hitching post and a couple of campsites appear near the trail, well above the water's edge. More remote sites can be found past the lake's outlet at the wooded southwest end—a hefty scramble over rocks.

*   *   *   *   *

Continuing on the Atwell Hockett Trail beyond the Evelyn Lake junction, the trail passes west of the ranger station and Hockett Meadows, bridges Whitman Creek and ascends easily into a fringe of lodgepole pines that obstructs views of the meadow below. During snowmelt this vast meadow is transformed into a glossy lake. In quick order your path reaches the first of three consecutive junctions (8580/1.1): on all you stay left. (At this first junction a trail cuts across Sand Meadow to Hockett Lakes; the next junction meets the Garfield Hockett Trail (8530/0.9) to Garfield Grove; the last is a cutoff to the Tuohy Trail (8525/0.3).) After cutting across a lobe of peaceful South Fork Meadows, bisected by the South Fork Kaweah River, and passing a lateral to a packers' campsite that includes a food storage box, your route forks left onto the **Wet Meadows Trail**

(8603/0.9), leaving the Atwell Hockett Trail just before it fords Hunter Creek.

Here you climb gently east among wild-flowers that bloom well into summer. In early season the whole plateau resembles a park, with plush meadows of tall grass; slopes of ferns, lupines and soft thimbleberry plants; numerous trees whose spreading crowns offer shade; and flowers that bloom every-where like tossed confetti. Most of the better known flowers nod in the soft breezes here, but look for the delicate little elephant heads. Their tiny pink blooms alternate on the stems and each has a "head, trunk and two elephant ears." The plant prefers moist soil.

You boulder-hop over Hunter Creek, the outlet of lower Blossom Lake, then begin the exit of your romp on the Hockett plateau. Now you embark on a steady ascent. Your trail curves about to gain elevation among lodgepole and red fir trees, then at length levels out and meets a cutoff trail (9562/2.3) to the Wet Meadows Entrance. If the Blossom Lakes are your next destination, continue straight ahead, again ascending, until you meet the Blossom Lakes Trail (9860/0.4). It exits your trail on the water-shed divide between the Kaweah and Kern rivers and the boundary between Sequoia Park and Sequoia Forest.

A tranquil middle Blossom Lake

Excursion Q: Blossom Lakes

In its hidden setting, days away from all trailheads, scenic lower Blossom Lake, with its chain of lovely upper lakes, invites you to sample splendor and solitude.

Distance   2.0 miles, round trip
Steep Ascents   None
Elevation Gain   160 feet
Skills   Easy route finding; easy hiking
Map   USGS 7.5-min. *Quinn Pk*
Description   Turn left, heading north on the *Blossom Lakes Trail* (9860/0.0), which rises on a gentle-to-moderate ascent. Along the undulating climb of the divide, you find a few foxtail pines joining the forest cover and chinquapin among the boulders. Then you drop to the lake (9860/1.0). A couple of large lodgepole-shaded campsites lie along the east side. The glacial-scooped lake, with its excellent fishing for brook trout, sits below slopes of chiseled granite. Fingers of sedges with pinkish-purple shooting stars stretch into the lake, which is garlanded with Labrador tea and red heather.

To reach the upper group of lakes, climb up the slabs next to the lakes' outlet. Begin on the east side (right); then, when you can ford easily, cross the outlet and resume climbing on its west side. Look for ducks and two large cairns: they lead to a fracture in the headwall that presents the best way to climb up to the next lake. This lake, the first in the middle lake chain, equals the lower in appeal. The second, a good-sized, oblong body of water captured within walls of granite, looks deep and ideal for swimming, while several of the shallow-surfaced tarns along the mid-level outlet invite wading.

The bouldery terrain of the middle lakes area appears inhospitable to camping, but sites could probably be found. Much time would be needed to explore all the satellite lakes including the upper cirque lake, which rests at 10,500 feet, 300 feet higher than the middle lakes.

*   *   *   *   *

From the Blossom Lakes junction, the trail heads south along the divide, where it leaves Sequoia National Park at the Wet Meadows Entrance (9824/0.7) and enters the Forest Service's Golden Trout Wilderness. Here the Wet Meadows Trail acquires a number, *31E11*, and begins a long descent east to the Little Kern River. After three switchbacks the course arrives at a roofless log cabin built by the Pitt Brothers and large campsites near a splashing stream.

As the descent continues, you cross the inlet stream to Wet Meadows, observe paths branching left to campsites and see bits of the meadow to the north framed by red firs and backdropped by the rugged, nameless peaks of the Western Divide mountains. After another set of switchbacks you arrive at Deadman Camp spread next to a glade housing a rain gauge and snow pillow. The pillow constantly measures the snowpack's water content and radios measurements to the water resource agencies.

A little further travel leads you to a broad, forested flat with several campsites and a trail junction (8965/2.0). (Quinn Trail 31E13 heads south to the Quinn Snow Survey Cabin. Unmaintained Little Kern Trail 31E12 branches east to travel through the superb country along the Little Kern River to Rifle Creek.)

You continue on Wet Meadows Trail 31E11, descending past more campsites. Hop atop boulders over Wet Meadows' outlet creek below a cascade moistening creek dogwoods and willows. As you curve north into drier climes, the canyon of the Little Kern River opens to your view, and you can identify the distant, distinctive Needles south of the canyon. After miles of descent you now begin a 2500-foot ascent along the Little Kern River that culminates at Farewell Gap, 4.3 miles ahead. The river is heard but unseen until it explodes before you in a thundering falls over russet metamorphic rocks. Shortly after, you bridge the Little Kern (8440/1.6) on a broad red fir log.

Immediately on the east side, you pass signs indicating a junction with a trail heading south. (Much of this path, which meets the Little Kern Trail, was washed away in the high waters of 1966. It was abandoned.)

Several campsites appear at the junction. Advancing up river on open slopes, you pass a signless post by a path (8800/0.5). This post marks a cutoff to the Farewell Gap Trail above. Just beyond, you step over a small creek. Then in several minutes the lower tiered logs that remain at Broder Cabin appear between the trees on a bluff across the river. A sign nailed on one of two large red firs marks the steep path that crosses the river to the cabin site and ideal campsites.

Your trail switchbacks once and ends at an acute angle junction (9085/0.5) with *Farewell Gap Trail 31E10*. Your course turns left and heads north on this trail, up-canyon. (T99 to Silver Lake continues south on this trail.) Quickly the path crosses a creek redolent of swamp onions, then continues to ascend on a bias across southwest facing slopes luxuriant with plants watered by snowmelt creeklets. The path presently gains elevation through two sets of widely spaced switchbacks.

You may forget to watch your footing as your gaze lifts to the steep canyon walls composed of Pre-Cretaceous metamorphic rock that rise about you—see cover picture. These muted gold, red, rust, magenta and brown slopes, dotted with greens of foxtail pines and red firs, soar around 2000 feet. Lofty cirque-tucked snowpacks lasting well into summer give birth to silvery streams that plummet down these precipitous slopes. The bowl resounds with the symphony of falling water.

Soon the trail passes several fine campsites perched among foxtail pines flanking the river, then passes above Bullion Flat where a large exposed campsite spreads on the valley floor. Just beyond and prior to Bullfrog Lakes' outlet stream, your trail passes a fork (9920/1.7) with the steep Bullfrog Lakes Trail. This appealing side trip makes an enjoyable day hike. If you take it, hang your backpacks off the ground, as unattended they will surely be chewed by marmots.

Excursion R: Bullfrog Lakes

These lakes lie in a fractured-rock crescent, glistening intense blue against the austere, treeless beauty that surrounds them.

Distance   1.6 miles, round trip
Steep Ascents   0.3 mile
Elevation Gain   820 feet
Skills   Easy route finding; moderate-to-strenuous hiking
Map   USGS 7.5-min. *Mineral King*
Description   *Bullfrog Lakes Trail 31E05* (9920/0.0) splits to the right of Farewell Gap Trail 31E10 and ascends east above the valley floor. At its third switchback it meets a

Slivers of streams form the Little Kern River's headwaters

short cutoff heading north to the main trail; your route turns right. From here on, the trail ascends steeply, zigzagging on open slopes of hornfels sparingly dotted with pines. These rocks—once thin-bedded sandstone and siltstone—have metamorphosed to the point of breaking irregularly, unlike slate. Then the trail crosses an extension of Mineral King's slates and phyllites as it curves away from the outlet creek that tumbles over and slickens this vivid vermillion rock. A set of ensuing zigzags leads to a bench on which small campsites perch under foxtail pines.

You then progress to the lower of the two Bullfrog Lakes (10,740/0.8). Some Labrador tea and red heather soften the lake lines and at least three-medium campsites can be found among the boulders. A hefty 250-foot scramble takes you to the upper cirque lake.

Scanning the bowl you notice a definite division between grayish granitic and reddish metamorphic rocks, and you see rocky, pyramid-shaped Florence Peak standing solid to the north.

*   *   *   *   *

On a traverse, still heading north, after Bullfrog Lakes junction, you cross one creek that drains overflow from the lakes and a second that tumbles from a tiny tarn near the crest. You hike along sodden slopes spattered with the ephemeral colors of numerous wildflowers. Across the canyon a peak points to Vandever Mountain. You pass the unmarked northern end of the cutoff trail (10,080/0.2) to Bullfrog Lakes, then shortly after, climb a set of ten switchbacks that delivers you to Farewell Gap (10,680/1.2). Here you leave Golden Trout Wilderness and the headwaters of the Little Kern River to reenter Sequoia National Park. Here, also, you have a chance to climb Vandever Mountain.

Excursion S: Vandever Mountain

At times this mountain looks foreboding, at times inviting, but here is your opportunity to scale one of the most widely visible and identifiable peaks of the Mineral King basin.

Distance   1.2 miles, round trip
Steep Ascents   0.6 mile
Elevation Gain   1460 feet
Skills   Easy route finding; Class 1–2 climbing
Map   USGS 7.5-min. *Mineral King*
Description   From the trail (10,680/0.0) at Farewell Gap, you head left, *cross-country* directly west, to dip to the lowest point on the pass where you stash your backpack. Proceed straight up the grade on loose metamorphic rock chunks. The degree of slant changes little as you eventually climb to and over the often lingering horizontal snowbank near the top. Then you reach the ample summit (11,947/0.6) and the Sierra Club's register box among the rocks.

Vandever Mountain pays homage to Congressman William Vandever. In an 1890 legislative session, with one year left to serve and only three to live, Vandever introduced the bills that established Yosemite, Sequoia and General Grant (now enlarged as Kings Canyon) national parks.

The views are startling nearby and far. You can pick out nearby lakes, find just about any of your favorite peaks and identify several river drainages. Note in particular the precipitous west face of Vandever—a classic rock climbers' ascent. Adventuresome skiers have been known to descend the slope on which you arrived.

*   *   *   *   *

Dry camping here at the gap is possible but undesirable due to the usual fierce winds. Now the long, long descent to the trip's end looms ahead. You descend untold numbers of switchbacks, zigzags and U turns into highly scenic Farewell Canyon. On the ninth switchback from the gap, photographers will find the ideal setting to capture Mineral King framed by a sturdy foxtail pine in the foreground. On the slopes along the way, some backpackers will notice powder blue forget-me-nots. The tiny five-petaled flower with a yellow ring at its throat blooms in loose clusters atop a stem with alternate oblong leaves. At length a welcome spring sends water across the trail to join the juvenile East Fork Kaweah River. Stop here for a breather and waterbottle refill.

Eventually you pass the only camping area on this stretch: a broad, tree-covered shelf way below the trail to the left with access to the river. Closely thereafter you pass the Franklin Pass junction (9358/2.7),

and many curves later you wade across Franklin Creek. In time your trail straightens out for the last leg: you pass the corrals and reach the bridge where you turn left to your journey's end at Eagle Crest Trailhead (7830/3.7).

T94   Ansel Lake Backpack
With Excursion T: Eagle Crest

Banked in part by flower-flecked sod, in part by shattered slabs and rocks, remote, hidden Ansel Lake occupies a thin-rimmed bowl of towering boulder-heaped walls: a product of the ancient Horse Creek glacier.

Distance   23.8 miles, round trip

Steep Ascents   0.4 mile

Elevation Gain   3450 feet

Skills   Intermediate route-finding

Seasons   Spring, summer, fall (Wilderness permit required)

Maps   USGS 7.5-min. *Mineral King, Silver City*

Trailhead   79. See car tour T89.

Description   Park 0.2 mile east of the ranger station. To locate the trail, enter Cold Springs Campground, hike west up the road found next to the bulletin board and pay station. You will see the trail to the left past the campsites. (The parking lot to the right affords parking for the walk-in campsites, not for the trailhead.)

The ***Tar Gap Trail*** (7490/0.0) rises quickly under white fir shade on an ascent that is moderate to steep despite several switchbacks designed to ease the grade. Where it crosses slopes moistened by seeps, it passes among populations of ferns and thimbleberry bushes; on drier soil it passes among infrequently seen plants of dainty, white-petaled sargent's campion. This flower's clefted petals open from a sac at their base, and its thin leaves grow opposite on an equally thin stem.

You soon pass an abandoned Mosquito Lakes trail (8044/0.5), which ascends left. Although no longer maintained, this trail remains the preferred route over its replacement by many who seek the Mosquito Lakes. You immediately hop across Mosquito

Creek, and after climbing over a minor ridge, ford Mineral Creek, another dashing stream.

Beyond the creek's recess, you begin a long scalloped pattern, traversing around ridges and retreating into creases; the latter often shelter impetuous creeks crowded with seasonal efflorescence—one such is Fowler Creek, the next stream you ford. Namesake State Senator Thomas Fowler, a flamboyant Irish-emigrant entrepreneur, took control of Mineral King mining in 1878 after the original investors had pulled out, declaring its silver too costly to extract. Under Fowler's direction, mines on Empire Mountain near Timber Gap were enlarged and connected via tramway with a mill near the valley floor. He learned the hard way that the first investors were right, and retired from mining bankrupt, discouraged and ill.

Ahead the undulating but overall ascending path passes through a boulder chute. On the ridge above, the displacement of rock caused by weathering and by the scraping effect that glaciers had on the Sierra, is clearly visible. The next open boulder field presents the best views in this trip of the East Fork canyon, forested Paradise Peak (T90), the serpentine road to Mineral King and the ever encroaching brown smog of San Joaquin Valley.

You next ford the several branches of Deer Creek. About 0.2 mile after the initial branch, you find a large campsite (8240/3.7) spread below the trail in the forest, the first site beyond the trailhead's four-mile zone of no camping. Another large campsite rests within the next mile below the trail near a meadow and its stream. Soon you outflank a ridge, the end of the rim above that contains Tar Gap—far removed from this Tar Gap Trail. You pass a cabin-sized boulder standing trailside as you enter into the Horse Creek watershed.

The varied trail along this watershed presents in intervals sloping granite dynamited to create the path, sun-baked terrain covered with manzanita and snow brush, moist slopes filigreed by seasonal flowers and cool forests of red fir replacing lodgepole pine trees. In time the route crosses the braided effervescence of Clover Creek, then of Corner Creek; it then descends to the forked junction (8580/3.8) with the Atwell Hockett Trail that paralleled below your path for many miles. From the junction you pace off 100 feet ahead on the *Atwell Hockett Trail*, then look in the forest to the left for the unsigned, unmaintained *Horse Creek Trail*, which you take. (Before turning off the main trail, you may elect to overnight at Horse Creek, 0.2 mile ahead, where a food storage cable serves the several large campsites.)

There may be a duck at the junction of the Horse Creek Trail; there is an old blaze on a fir about 20 feet in. Although inconspicuous here the path quickly becomes more defined.

It weaves east, initially strewn with blowdowns, through the gradually inclined, glaciated valley of Horse Creek. Lodgepole pines offer shade; many varieties of Southern Sierra wildflowers bloom profusely. The path veers toward, but not in sight of, Horse Creek, then follows it, remaining inland. The trail passes camping opportunities along the broad flats and a packers' campsite with a built-up fireplace 300 feet to the right prior to the path's entry into a young pine forest.

You will notice numerous ducks and some triangular tree blazes that mark the path, but waist high plants in occasional boggy areas obscure markers and path alike. Usually you can find the trail by angling toward the creek. Your ascent increases and you begin to notice recessional moraines. These cross-valley dikes of rounded boulders and finely ground rocks were left in a long prehistoric cold spell when intense storms stalled the melting of the Horse Creek glacier. A glacier acts as a conveyor belt for rocks that it picks up or plucks from its head and flanks and dumps at its foot: spread evenly when the glacier shrinks fast, but usually left in elongated heaps when it slowly recedes as is the case here.

After crossing several rills in plant-intense bogs, you turn south to a boulder-hop ford of Horse Creek (9140/1.6), marked at the far

Remote Ansel Lake (center oval) from Vandever Mountain

end by a blaze inland from the creek. Some campsites lie to the right. In the valley beyond, you ascend on alternating steps and ramps whose pattern is determined by the spacing of cracks in the granite beneath. Glaciers quarried rocks from along the cracks readily, but skimmed over the least cracked bedrock, leaving a series of sloping slabs. You gradually arch south where you traverse a forested terrace with camping possibilities; then, after nearing the base of bouldered south-ridge chutes, you curve east to ford Horse Creek (9640/0.7) a second time.

The path, now lined with abundant ducks, zigzags up increasingly steep slopes. At length it reaches a timberline bench (10,340/1.1) embellished to the right by a pair of hidden tarns and a few secluded camping areas. At this point along the trail, an interesting side trip to Eagle Crest begins for experienced hikers who enjoy cross-country hiking with map and compass.

Excursion T: Eagle Crest

During the late 1960s and early 1970s, Walt Disney Productions envisioned a sandwich bar capping Eagle Crest. Their plan, long defunct, for a ski resort in Mineral King linked the crest to other tourist facilities in the basin by means of an aerial tramway across Eagle Lake. Now, instead, you can lunch there in solitude.

Distance 2.6 miles, round trip
Steep Ascents None
Elevation Gain 520 feet
Skills Intermediate route finding
Map USGS 7.5-min. *Mineral King*
Description Leave the trail (10,340/0.0) on the bench containing the tarns, which is prior to the exposed granite slabs below Ansel Lake. Contour **cross-country** northwest while climbing over hunks of granite at the foot of a west-trending ridge, then weave your way north down to an island-dotted tarn with campsites (10.240/0.5). Head north from the tarn to the broad area between several high points. From here, rising steadily, you climb out of vegetation over

boulders to reach the giddying crest (10,660/0.8) overlooking cirques in which Eagle and upper Mosquito lakes nestle. (See Ts96&97 to these lakes.)

* * * * *

Pushing east to Ansel Lake you find an intervening 120 vertical feet of polished slabs, which you climb left of the outlet. You easily reach the lake (10,500/0.5) where campsites spread at the north and east sides. Ansel Lake was named for Ansel Franklin Hall, a ranger in Sequoia National Park, 1916–17. This remote treasure, the end product of what must have been a huge chunk of ice, rests among boulders and flowered banks. The reddish, twisted foxtail pines soften the harsh stone walls.

Looking at the walls around Ansel, you realize that their rims barely reached above the glaciers that helped grind away the canyons. To experience the results of this action, climb 450 vertical feet of boulders northeast to a rim notch and peer straight down 1000 feet into the valley of White Chief. Breathtaking! If you are a stalwart, non-acrophobic hiker and wish a loop trip, climb over the first notch northeast, to the right of the crest-residing foxtail pines, and lower yourself from the jagged arête on a frightening vertical ladder of widely spaced rock rungs; backpacks should be lowered by rope. This connects with the end of T98. Most people take a look over the thin rim, glance at the brownish, carved face of Vandever Mountain (T93: Ex-S), and happily return to the rugged serenity of Ansel Lake.

A less challenging way to access White Chief valley, suggested by rangers at Mineral King station, would be to take Excursion T to the island-dotted tarn. From there turn east to climb over the saddle south of White Chief Peak. (For peakbaggers, climber John Palmieri ranks the enticing ascent of White Chief Peak a Class 3 climb from the saddle.)

T95   Mineral King Nature Trail Day Hike

This fascinating, easy hike will expand your appreciation and knowledge of the plants, trees and geology in the surrounding terrain. The plaques along the trail are exceptionally interesting and informative. Also, the extension of this trail connects Cold Spring Campground with the Eagle Crest Trailhead.

Distance   2.4 miles, round trip
Steep Ascents   None
Elevation Gain   400 feet
Skills   Easy route finding; easy hiking
Seasons   Spring, summer, fall
Map   USGS 7.5-min. *Mineral King* (Trail does not appear on provisional edition)
Trailhead   79. See car tour T89.
Description   Did you know that corn lilies are also called skunk cabbage? That there are 24 species of willow and 25 species of currant and gooseberry in the Southern Sierra? Have you noticed that western juniper trees often appear singly far removed from other junipers? It seems that juniper seeds need to be partially digested by birds in order to sprout, and birds carry seeds far away from parent trees. More information awaits.

This easy hike begins between campsites 6&7 (7460/0.0) at the most easterly point of Cold Springs Campground. The *Nature Trail* rises gently south of the East Fork Kaweah River. It passes among a kaleidoscope of colorful wildflowers, gray-green sagebrush and evergreen and deciduous trees. The short trail loops back (7600/0.3)

from the last plaque describing the difference between Jeffrey and ponderosa pines, red and white firs.

You take the **connector trail** that branches off the top of the loop to continue ahead. You veer next to the river, soon switchback, pass over wooden planks bridging seeps and descend to near the river again. Here you see Sawtooth Peak on the Great Western Divide looming above the Black Wolf Falls of Monarch Creek in the east; and, while glancing at that uniquely bold peak, you pass left of a mushy meadow containing Iron Spring hidden among the thick vegetation.

You next cut across drier slopes with avalanche-bent quaking aspens and arrive at the end of a residential road. Staying on this road to the right of Mineral King village, you thread your way through the small community of aged cabins, pass a RESIDENTS ONLY, NO PARKING sign and arrive at the end of the paved Mineral King Road and trailhead parking for trails heading up Farewell Canyon (7830/0.9).

T96   Mosquito Lakes Day Hike

This fascinating chain of lakes, like most High Sierran lakes, was left after fingers of glaciers deepened the canyon in the various stages of the Pleistocene epoch—the ice age. The six lakes progress upward from lushly forested to barren rockbound.

Distance   10.8 miles, round trip
Steep Ascents   0.2 mile
Elevation Gain   2190 feet
Skills   Easy-to-intermediate route finding; moderate-to-strenuous hiking
Seasons   Spring, summer, fall (Wilderness permit required for backpackers only)
Map   USGS 7.5-min. *Mineral King*
Trailhead   80. See car tour T89.

Description   Begin your hike at the end of the Mineral King Road across the East Fork Kaweah River at the trailhead known as Eagle Crest (7830/0.0). Climb the west slopes of Farewell Canyon on *Eagle Crest Trail*. You immediately pass the 1930 Honeymoon Cabin tucked under the boughs of mature juniper trees. Restored in 1988 by the Mineral King Preservation Society, it stands as an example of how the society would like to preserve all the cabins in the community. Passing sagebrush, snow brush and currant bushes, you soon mount a wooden bridge to cross the braided waters of Spring Creek bounding below Tufa Falls; then in a short time you boulder-hop Eagle Creek. With captivating views of Crystal Creek cascading down the steep east slopes of Farewell Canyon, you quickly meet a T junction (8340/1.0) where the crest trail ends and those heading for White Chief valley (T98), part company. You turn onto the *Eagle Lake Trail* which ascends steeply west to the right at the junction.

Avalanche-bent quaking aspen trees

The trail climbs under a diaphanous awning of red fir needles next to an occasional understory cover of chinquapin. The accompanying roar of rushing water echoes in the canyon. Far below, the pack station appears in miniature. A pair of switchbacks precede a sloping meadow generously endowed with wildflowers. The path turns back and forth in the meadow until it passes the upslope point where some of Eagle Creek's water emerges. The trail curves southwest to climb along the creek's dry canyon, and then arrives at Eagle Sinkhole where boisterous Eagle Creek drops into the ground, a phenomenon common in limestone. For a short time the trail climbs above the hole alongside the robust creek, and then levels in forest where it meets a T junction (9016/1.0). Here people bound for Eagle Lake on T97 depart.

From the junction, your route forks right on *Mosquito Lakes Trail*, heading northwest. It soon leaves the forest to zigzag up slopes flowered with yellow groundsel. This common plant grows from 1- to 5-feet tall in wet meadows, as here, or along creek banks. Its flowers, which have small yellow discs and indifferent yellow petals, gather in a flat-top cluster atop a stem with serrated, arrow-shaped leaves. Blue lupine appear. Before returning to a forest of red fir and western white pine, northeast views of Mineral King's symbolic peak, Sawtooth Peak, occur, and again you see Crystal Creek's long descent to the river.

The trail makes a set of switchbacks, and then rounds Miners Ridge above a saddle next to the point tagged "Miners Nose." After six switchbacks and an easy descent, the trail reaches Mosquito Lake #1 and a junction (9060/1.6) with the former trail. (The unmaintained trail descends to join the Tar Gap Trail, and then reaches Cold Spring Campground; a much shorter, albeit steeper route than your trail.)

Cross the outlet of the lowest Mosquito Lake, which is lined with grass and willow and forested with lodgepole pine. A privy remains but the lake is closed to camping, allowing the hardened sites to recover. Abundant brook trout ply the waters here and at the other lakes. This tranquil lake may be the destination for most day hikers; those with some pathfinding skills may wish to continue to the upper lakes.

Tree blazes mark some of the trail and ducks indicate the rest of the way on the unmaintained path to the upper lakes. Ascend south above the west side of the lake. You will find some steep climbs. Cross over a brush-hidden outlet stream and pass east of invisible side lake #2. While following ducks, zigzag up among boulders left of the outlet to reach lake #3 (9590/0.7). This lake, excellent for swimming and fishing is surrounded on three sides by rock-strewn walls. It offers ideal lodgepole pine-shaded camping.

Continuing on, the ducked trail climbs the ridge west of lake #3, passes a descending path to the head of the lake, crosses the usually dry but brushy outlet from shallow lake #4, then heads over slabs bypassing to the left of small lake #4. It next crosses over the stream from lake #5 and arrives at its west bank (9920/0.7). Fewer trees shade campsites on this dramatic lake, nearly enclosed by bouldery walls. The route reaches the uppermost lake by continuing west of lake #5 heading south up the final ascent to the west side of cirque lake #6 (10,020/0.4). Only brush survives at this

barren, beautiful lake.

The large amount of rock debris here and at other Mineral King lakes indicates the granite was fractured and easily broken away by weathering and by quarrying of ice. The slab benches between the lakes were more resistant and they emerged with glacial polish and directional scratches.

The platform of Eagle Crest sits high on the southeast ridge behind the point on Miners Ridge. (See T94: Ex-T.) Eagle Lake nestles behind the east ridge.

T97   Eagle Lake Day Hike

A montage of bold walls, jumbled rocks and open forests surround the crystalline waters of sky blue Eagle Lake, a favorite destination for fly fishermen and photographers.

Distance   6.8 miles, round trip
Steep Ascents   0.1 mile
Elevation Gain   2210 feet
Skills   Easy route finding; moderate-to-strenuous hiking
Seasons   Spring, summer, fall
Map   USGS 7.5-min. *Mineral King*
Trailhead   80. See car tour T89.
Description   The beginning of this trip is described in T96.

Southbound Eagle Crest Trail Log
T96 Trailhead   7830 0.0
    White Chief/Eagle Lk trs
    jct   8340 1.0
Southwestbound Eagle Lake Trail Log
    Eagle Crest Tr   8340 0.0
    Mosquito Lks Tr jct   9016 1.0

Leaving the Mosquito Lakes Trail junction, *Eagle Lake Trail* continues ahead, soon switchbacks and zigzags, then suddenly presents you with an extended climb among boulders: a jungle of talus left by rock fall and glaciers that carved the lake and cut Miners Ridge. The open path and elevation gain reward you with northeast views of Sawtooth Peak poking above Mineral Peak and the silver ribbon of Crystal Creek.

In time you return to forested slopes and eventually arrive at Eagle Lake (10,040/1.4), an ample body of water in an amphitheater of muted red-brown meta-

morphic and creamy granite walls. The unobtrusive dam you see was built here in the early 1900s, similar to those at Franklin, Crystal and Monarch lakes; it retains water for use in late summer to spin the turbines of the Southern California Edison plant at Hammond. Shortly you pass a path branching right to a privy. Beyond the jetting rocky point, you pass flats on the lodgepole-shaded slope offering numerous campsites. You are asked not to camp between the path and the lake. Above the lake you see lofty Eagle Crest occupying the south mountain rim (T94:Ex-T).

(Experienced mountaineers sometimes combine this trip with a hike to Mosquito Lakes: a loop trip best accomplished in two days. The route with the least vertical drops on either side of the intervening rim begins on the slopes about 50 feet south of the dam, the location of the outhouse in 1993.

Climb cross-country, west, on a Class 2 scramble up Miners Ridge between Eagle and the Mosquito lakes. Climb past timberline, although a few trees march farther up the slope to your right. A few scattered ducks now mark the way. Ascend steeply near the bushes that cling among the boulders as you advance to the rim. Climb over the serrated arête.

Below you lies the second to highest

Mosquito Lake. Although the route drops steeply on the west side of the rim here, it is not as abrupt at this point as further to your left. You can see where others have zig-zagged slightly to the right down the uppermost steep slope. When you reach the extensive boulder field, the steepness abates somewhat. As you near the lake begin to angle left, eventually rounding the top of the lake to its west side where you pick up the fishermen's path next to the water near camp-sites. This path leads to the unmaintained, ducked trail connecting the rest of the Mosquito Lakes. (See T96.))

T98   White Chief Valley Day Hike

Perhaps a Michelangelo could have sculpted a David from the gleaming white marble found in this valley. Instead, this marble was poked and pocked in search of silver. Word of the silver claim set off a Mineral King prospecting frenzy in 1873. The marble presents only one facet in a melange of valley color and interesting historical discoveries.

Distance   7.6 miles, round trip
Steep Ascents   0.2 mile
Elevation Gain   2225 feet
Skills   Easy-to-intermediate route finding; moderate-to-strenuous hiking
Seasons   Spring, summer, fall
Map   USGS 7.5-min. *Mineral King*
Trailhead   80. See car tour T89.
Description   The beginning of this trip is described in T96.

Southbound Eagle Crest Trail Log

T96 Trailhead	7830	0.0
White Chief/Eagle Lk trs		
jct	8340	1.0

Straight ahead, south, the *White Chief*

Trail steepens noticeably after you leave the trail junction. Metamorphics click under-foot, and the ubiquitous Junco plays hide-and-seek in the trees and bushes. This 5- to 6-inch, berry and seed eating bird, recognized by his black hood and gray tail with white outer feathers, is among the most visible birds in the Southern Sierra.

You soon edge near the canyon of White Chief's slender flowing creek, which disappears upstream and reappears again farther up, typical of streams in areas with porous limestone and marble. After rounding a minor ridge and before crossing the creek, you may notice off to the right a few

Co-author Ruby at sublime Eagle Lake

logs, the remains of James A. Crabtree's cabin. Crabtree claimed he was guided to the area by Indian apparitions in 1873 when he found what appeared to be a promising silver deposit later known as the White Chief Mine.

At the cabin site you cross the creek, usually dry here, and skirt a meadow repository for trees that became victims of avalanches. Rising above the now flowing creek, you arrive at a cluster of red fir, lodgepole and foxtail trees shading the only good campsites (9340/1.5) in the valley. You share the site with a herd of tame deer—antlered bucks, does with spotted fawns—all seem to move without fear among campers.

Beyond the campsites, late blooming explorer gentians thrive on the slopes. These deep blue blooms add new life and color to fields of fading flowers. Their 1½ inch funnel-shaped flowers with five pointed petals open skyward, and their opposite ovate leaves join at the stems. High on the rock-bound wall to

the right a trickle descends from White Chief Lake hidden in its high cirque to the north of White Chief Peak.

The trail continues south, crosses the canyon's creek and climbs past privately owned White Chief Mine, bored in snow white marble. Pure white marble is composed essentially of the mineral calcite. Its parent rock, limestone or dolomite, more often carries impurities that result in colored marble, even black marble. Insoluble minerals, including silver, can accumulate in the weathering of soluble rock such as limestone or its end product marble. A miner may think he has a rich deposit based on surface assays, only to find the ore insufficient when a shaft is sunk. This probably happened here, as apparently Crabtree's original assay was favorable. Caves and mines found in the White Chief area, although apparent and accessible, are off limits unless permission to explore is granted by the park, or in the case of White

White Chief Lake and valley; distant Sawtooth Peak

Chief, by the owner.

The path, now indicated by ducks, rises on ledges and dips to cross the upper limits of the creek, curves around and reaches the high meadow (10,040/1.3). If the winter snowpack was normal, a shallow tarn nourishes wildflowers and a variety of ground animals. The meadow snuggles at the base of 1000-foot, glacial-cut rock walls with precipitous rims. Beyond the rim to the south lies Ansel Lake (T94). To the east rises the face of Vandever Mountain (T93:Ex-S).

T99   Silver Lake-Franklin Lakes Backpack
With Excursion U: Florence Peak

Silver Lake—remote, isolated, aloof—shines like a silver dollar at the foot of craggy slopes. The Franklin Lakes—accessible, popular, inviting—complement their wine-red backdrop with waters of intense cobalt blue. This adventuresome journey crosses three lofty passes and several headwater bowls on the mountains of the Great Western Divide.

Distance   24.8 miles, semiloop trip
Steep Ascents   0.7 mile
Elevation Gain   6700
Skills   Easy route finding; not recommended for equestrians
Seasons   Spring, summer, fall (Wilderness permit required)
Maps   USGS 7.5-min. *Mineral King, Quinn Pk*
Trailhead   80. See car tour T89.
Description   Horses unused to mountain terrain have fallen from several places along the rugged route of this trip; pack animals seem to travel successfully.

From the Eagle Crest parking area west of the East Fork Kaweah River, you amble across the bridge, and then turn up on the pack station road to pass the stables—no trailhead parking allowed here. Beyond the stables you find unfenced poles skewered across the width of the road marking the beginning of the **Farewell Gap Trail** (7860/0.0).

To the right across the canyon as you head south, Tufa Falls dashes out at mid-slope; its name is derived from the calcite rock deposited by the spring. The water above the falls flows underground; below, called Spring Creek, it tumbles down the canyon slope to be one in a symphony of headwater creeks that become the euphonious East Fork Kaweah River. Soon you ford the ample spread of Crystal Creek. Its flow, like Franklin Creek's, is controlled by Southern California Edison, whose dams contain the snowmelt waters of Crystal and Franklin lakes. You leave the road to continue on trail (7961/0.8), which leads through bands of black cottonwood trees while noticeably rising above the canyon floor. (The closed section of the road you left heads into Aspen Flat where a soda spring flanks the river—a lovely day hike.)

Westward views discover cataracts splashing down lichen-blackened phyllite cliffs in white relief. Ahead, groves of foxtail pines embellish deeply-green, steeply-rising Farewell Canyon. Underfoot, streaky reddish-brown slate chips and fractured sandstone that clink add to the coloristic ensemble.

Presently you boulder-hop Franklin Creek at the lip of one of its many plunge pools. The ensuing 12 switchbacks, whose several curves abut the canyon of Franklin Creek, receive shade from occasional red fir trees; otherwise, the route is exposed. The park asks you to remember that shortcutting switchbacks breaks down the trail, is unsightly and is costly to repair. You soon assume a lengthy ascending traverse, then negotiate 7 more switchbacks, often passing the former trail that traveled straight up the ridge, and arrive at the forked junction (9358/2.5) with Franklin Pass Trail. You will return to this point on Franklin Pass Trail from the loop of your trip.

Branching right at the junction, still heading south, the path arrives in 0.2 mile at a cluster of foxtail pines. Sharply below, a ledge supports several large, shady campsites and offers a short but steep scramble down the ledge to water.

Your straight away path continues high above the nascent river, and then curves into an alcove flowing with spring water and splashed with rock fringe. This matted plant has ovate leaves that grow opposite on a creeping stem and supports numerous inch-wide, deep-pink flowers with four heart-shaped petals. The plant clings to rocky crevices. It becomes especially decorative when growing in colonies on multicolored metamorphic rocks, as is displayed across the canyon.

Now you brace for an ascent of 21 switchbacks followed by a traverse of rocky slopes that takes you to Farewell Gap (10,680/2.7). You may see a sky pilot on these slopes: a cluster of deep-blue flowers on a single stem. This unforgettable, foot-high flower grows only in high places—as its name suggests. Here Vandever Mountain (T93:Ex-S) slants up to the right and an unnamed peak slants up to the left, together forming the V gap that ranks among the Sierra's most distinctive, conspicuous passes. The views are enticing, but the winds often blow fiercely, making it undesirable to linger or camp here.

At the gap you enter Sequoia National Forest's Golden Trout Wilderness and the colorful sculptured-bowl headwaters of the Little Kern River. This magnificent scene, captured by camera, graces the cover of this book. Now on Farewell Gap Trail *31E10*, after a clinking descent south on 10 switchbacks, you pass an obscure branch of Bullfrog Lakes Trail 31E05 forking left across metamorphic chunks. As you descend, the aroma of mint, onion and sage from penny royal, swamp onion and sagebrush floats up from the flower and shrub masses that cover the slopes. Along the way you step across several snowmelt rills, and then ford a stream from a tiny cirque lake high above. You then quickly ford Bullfrog Lakes' outlet. Several steps beyond, you pass

Bullfrog Lakes Trail 31E05 of T93:Ex-R (9920/1.4), which forks back and ascends steeply to the lower Bullfrog Lake.

You soon pass above an exposed valley floor campsite, and then stroll by a right lateral to foxtail pine-shaded campsites across the river. After cornering through two pairs of widely spaced switchbacks and stepping across a slender creek, you meet Wet Meadows Trail 31E11 (9085/1.7) switchbacking downslope. Unless you want to camp at Broders, you continue ahead.

Now the route parallels the lower trail. The path edges on platy slate that occasionally sloughs off the steep slope, leaving a very narrow trail requiring good balance. Below, Broders Cabin site and its fine campsites spread west of the river. If you plan to camp on the ridge ahead, obtain your water at the next creek crossing, about 0.2 mile before a zigzagging connector trail from the path below joins yours (9056/0.6).

You quickly reach red fir trees where campsites appear at the curve around the ridge. Just beyond that point a closed section of the Lion Meadows Trail forks downslope. You traverse easily east where you glimpse views of impressive bluffs upslope and vistas of the Little Kern canyon downslope. In the curve of a canyon a few dozen yards before Shotgun Creek, you turn up-canyon onto *Shotgun Pass Trail 32E01* (9000/1.0).

This trail twists upslope sharply as it winds north among boulders and cuts through a low layer rife with plants. Where the trail nears the creek, a small campsite is situated. Then the gravelly path traverses the base of east-facing slopes, outflanking two willow meadows with a small campsite between them. At length Shotgun Pass appears through the gunsight V formed by two blond snags, then the route advances nearly 500 yards to skirt a spring fringed with ephemeral floral sparklers. Beyond, the trail briefly climbs up ledges of a granite outcrop, fords a rivulet, weaves awhile up a steep, wooded slope and finally crosses into the bowl containing Silver Lake (10,520/1.4) and several scattered campsites.

Peaks of more than 12,000 feet flank the

nearly round lake, and Shotgun Pass sits challengingly at the head of the bowl. Gnarled old foxtail pines gather by the lake and inch up the slopes: their reddish bark mellows the harsh granite starkness. A coarse sand beach welcomes swimmers and loungers; golden trout await the fishermen.

The crow-sized gray, black and white Clarks Nutcracker harshly breaks the silence when he "Kraaas" at you. He begs for food or steals it when you are not looking. But this bird, found at tree line on high mountain ranges, usually uses his long, sharply pointed bill to probe for his favorite food, pine seeds.

After crossing the outlet, the route heads through a camping area to the foot of the east slope where the path again becomes defined. It then leads diagonally north up a moderate grade, passing a left lateral to large camp-sites near the inlet and on the upper bench. The trail angles steeply up decomposed granite slopes past timberline, then curves and turns among a network of boulders and ledges until it finally reaches Shotgun Pass (11,440/1.0).

At the pass the trail crosses into Sequoia National Park over the Great Western Divide

that reaches north and south in a sinuous line of barren, jagged peaks. South, beyond Silver Lake, hazy waves of ridges dip into the Little Kern basin; north, rise the peaks of the High Sierra, including Mount Whitney to the northeast on the Sierra crest.

Leaving the pass, the ducked path, not in the park's system of well-defined trails, declines north-northwest across bouldery slabs, then turns northeast to run down the first slight ridge beyond the pass. After a spell of moderate descent, the route bears north and gradually diverges from the ridge to cross a timberline bench. Here it skirts foxtail-sheltered flats suitable for camping and then nearby, weaves downslope beside a brook. Zigzags complete this quick descent and triangular blazes now help mark the way. Then a short stretch of path resembling a dry watercourse leads to a broad meadow cross-hatched with meandering channels. Pyramid-shaped Florence Peak towers dramatically above the meadow. The path resumes across the expanse of grass at a north-northeast bearing and continues in that direction through a bench forested with lodgepole pines. Campsites begin to appear as the trail

Attractive Silver Lake with the trail to the left

descends to Rattlesnake Creek. A burn at one site marks a campfire that flared out of control. The path crosses Rattlesnake Creek above a meadow, then vanishes; but the black and silver junction sign appears just ahead (10,278/1.8).

Turning west on the *Franklin Pass Trail*, you gain elevation on a moderate ascent, then pass campsites spread between the trail and creek after a few helpful switchbacks. You soon reach a willowy meadow that floors a sheer-walled cirque. You may wonder how you can climb those awesome walls. You accomplish the feat by ascending the north wall on 35 heavily dynamited switchbacks. Not surprisingly, footing can be precarious. Spectacular views of Rattlesnake drainage abound, especially of Florence Peak, whose slopes skid 1800 feet to the basin.

The trail splits below an east viewpoint overlooking Forester Lake. Both paths lead west and rejoin beneath Peak 11,973. Then the route turns southwest to Franklin Pass (11,740/2.1). Here confident peakbaggers may choose to climb Florence Peak; the rest pause to ogle familiar peaks including Langley, Whitney and Kaweah; and, with compass and topo in hand, identify many more.

Excursion U: Florence Peak

Gouged on four sides by glaciers, Florence Peak appears a nearly perfect pyramid. Perhaps Khufu, the pharoah of Egypt who ordered the building of the great

Pyramid-shaped Florence Peak

pyramid in 2600 BC, first visited Florence Peak and copied her design.

Distance   1.2 miles, round trip
Steep Ascents   0.3 mile
Elevation Gain   750 feet
Skills   Easy route finding; Class 2 climbing
Map   USGS 7.5-min. *Mineral King*
Description   Franklin Pass offers the best route up the boulders of steep Florence Peak. Leave the trail where it switchbacks away from the pass (11,720/0.0), then on a *cross-country* route descend southwest to cross the pass. Continue southwest following Florence's sharp-edged ridge, climb around the pinnacles and stay left of but close to the ridge to avoid the steeper northeast-facing slope that plummets to the valley of Rattlesnake Creek. Next clamber up Florence's thin neck where the north and east ridges nearly converge, presenting interesting drops on either side. Finally, scramble west up her slanted head to the summit (12,432/0.6) and the Sierra Club's register.

Florence's pyramid shape straddles the border between Sequoia Park and Sequoia Forest on the Great Western Divide and soars highest of all peaks in the Southern Sierra south of Mineral King. Views from her summit include peaks and ridges at great distances in all directions. Near views to the north highlight Franklin Lakes, to the south Bullfrog Lakes and in between to the east the lakes of Rattlesnake Creek drainage.

*   *   *   *   *

The final stage of the loop begins with the switchback at the pass, the first of 15, followed by a prolonged traverse northwest just downslope from the crest. This traverse on barren scree treats you to a stunning setting across the canyon: the marbled wine-red hornfels of Tulare Peak and Peak 12,146 abutting the creamy granite of Florence Peak. These three peaks form the sheer headwall that contains the intensely blue Franklin Lakes and the glistening Mine Dump Rock Glacier. The rock-mantled glacier is said to be the southernmost active body of ice in the United States.

On the descent flower-festooned midway

springs add variety. After the last of the switchbacks you may wish to pause on the foxtail-covered bench between the lakes, where lie a few isolated campsites.

The trail now descends north of the lower, larger and most popular lake, abundant with brook trout. It soon passes a path to an outhouse and several entrees to large, terraced campsites between the lake and the path. The two food storage, bear-proof lockers located here are for the use of all nearby campers. The dam at the outlet was built of native rock masonry in 1904–05. Beyond the dam the path switchbacks down near campsites next to the outlet; a food storage box is also located here. Much later, after a zigzag down slopes salted with marble, the trail passes an obscure silver mine and nearby spring to ford Franklin Creek. Then the path works its way around the lower slopes of Tulare Peak, passing below century old mining prospects

Billowing Marble Falls

including the Lady Franklin Mine, and makes its way to the junction (9358/4.5) with the *Farewell Gap Trail*, ending the loop part of your trip. Here you retrace your steps down to the trailhead (7830/3.3).

T100   Marble Falls Day Hike

The Marble Fork Kaweah River thunders in falls and cascades over dazzling white marble at this trip's destination. There you sit on a grassy ledge to observe one of the river's powerful falls or on slabs close enough to feel the cascades' spindrift.

Distance   6.8 miles, round trip
Steep Ascents   None
Elevation Gain   1500 feet
Skills   Easy route finding; easy-to-moderate hiking
Seasons   Fall, winter, spring
Map   USGS 7.5-min. *Giant Forest*
Trailhead   68. See car tour T84.
Description   Your outing begins north of the loop road through Potwisha Campground, off Highway 198, on a gravelly *road* (2150/0.0), chained off to cars. Shortly after your walk begins, you pass a side road leading to a river gauging station and a locked cable car affording a river crossing for Southern California Edison personnel. Your route crosses Edison's concrete-lined aqueduct on a diagonally planked bridge, proceeds next to the aqueduct, then, opposite a control gate, turns right on *Marble Falls Trail* (2190/0.2).

On the trail you climb up three switchbacks before heading generally north, the direction of this trip. Slopes here blaze with the daisylike flower, common madia. This easily identifiable 1- to 2-foot high, yellow flower has a maroon center and a maroon base spot on each of its many three-lobed petals. Its stems and linear leaves are sticky and hairy.

Hiking along the mostly sunny trail, you steadily gain elevation as you curve in and around canyon creases and ridges. Bushes of chamise, yerba santa, fremontia and occasional spikes of yucca accompany you—also patches of poison oak. You may also encounter a rattlesnake warming himself on the trail in the morning, or cooling himself in brush at midday. You may notice twining brodiaea spiraling up a bush here and there. It can grow 7- to 8-feet long from a small corm. Numerous pinkish-lavender flowers appear in dense heads at the end of its stems. Indians used the corms for food, and they must have used the twining stems in many ways.

You curve into nooks, sometimes ornamented with creek dogwood and redbud bushes, that furnish welcome shade from boughs of laurel, oak, buckeye and sycamore trees. A few shady places have trickling streams that keep bracken fern moist. Colorful outcrops of metasedimentary rock present along the trail. Curving around one such platy ridge you are treated to views of the Kaweah's churning white-water far below, its rumble wafting up Deep Canyon. The last nook before you reach your destination houses a brook cascading down glistening white marble balconies festooned with ferns. A side path reaches a bench carved from steep slopes.

You switchback directly out of the nook above the bench, then gently descend. Take the use path to your left to a small grassy ledge from which you can view the powerful falls. Beyond the use path, Marble Falls Trail ends (3640/3.2) at boulders and slabs close to cascades where the river spills over sections of sparkling marble in giant plumes with arching rainbows.

The falls here belong to a series: one down-canyon, the rest up-canyon and out of sight as the river curves. The farthest above received the name "Marble Falls."

T101   Paradise Creek Day Hike

Wildflower enthusiasts enter paradise on an early season hike along this creek-hugging trail. Although low in elevation, this short walk along a dancing creek in the bower of oaks, buckeyes, laurels and alders remains temperate.

Distance   4.8 miles, round trip
Steep Ascents   None
Elevation Gain   1020 feet
Skills   Easy route finding; easy-to-moderate hiking
Seasons   Fall, winter, spring
Maps   USGS 7.5-min. *Giant Forest, Lodgepole* (briefly)
Trailhead   69. See car tour T84.
Description   At campsite #25 of Buckeye Flat Campground, start your stroll on *Paradise Creek Trail* (2820/0.0) shaded by golden oak trees near spring flowering redbud bushes and buckeye trees. Rise on a bluff overlooking a spillway and dam, then cross the turbulent Middle Fork Kaweah River (2840/0.2) on a sturdy wooden bridge with a noticeable middle sag.

The rock reinforced trail ascends amid boulders with spreads of common madia and Indian pink. On this garden stroll the trail also passes poison oak, untouchable in any season; and it is unblessed with tiny ticks—mostly active in late winter and spring. Check yourself and your clothing often.

Soon you amble above a gorge where the creek shoots into rock-bound pools, switchback up a minor ridge and curve around a lush nook with bracken ferns and a mossy-banked rivulet. Here to the north you see the slim side of Moro Rock anchoring the south edge of Giant Forest.

While walking next to the creek, look for the deep purple wildflower called Chinese houses, one of the most delightful of California's wildflowers. The 1- to 2-foot-high plant with opposite lanceolate leaves boasts of several whirls of blooms along its central stem. Each flower in a whirl has two light colored, upward bending petals with maroon dots and three purple petals that curve down: the effect creates a pagodalike appearance, thus its common name. But you may envision rings of dancers with full flowing purple skirts.

Cross alder-hugged Paradise Creek, which in spring requires a wade. Switchback up on the west bank, then 0.1 mile later wade across again. At this crossing you find nosegays of another special wildflower, bleeding heart. These 1- to 2-foot-high plants have bluish-green leaves and heart-shaped pink flowers that hang in clusters: their tips flair at the base where the stamens and pistil appear. Because it is unlawful to pick wild-flowers on public land, these delicate plants will remain to adorn the banks of Paradise Creek year after year.

You next switchback above the creek.

Now the trail narrows and the flora encroach upon it. Continue to the slender 15-foot waterfall where the path crosses a branch of the creek (3840/2.2)—the destination of this trip.

T102   Middle Fork Kaweah Canyon Backpack

Castle Rocks, a group of fins and spires, and Moro Rock, a prominent dome, contain the Middle Fork Kaweah canyon, which is nearly as deep as the Grand Canyon. They and the Great Western Divide dominate views along this up-canyon journey. Numerous streams, pools and shady recesses offer refreshing pauses along the way. This is an ideal overnight for a beginning backpacker. An abbreviated version presents a fine day hike.

Distance   11.0 miles, round trip
Steep Ascents   None
Elevation Gain   2400 feet
Skills   Easy route finding
Seasons   Fall, winter spring (Wilderness permit required)
Map   USGS 7.5-min. *Lodgepole*

Trailhead   70. See car tour T84.
Description   Begin hiking on the *Middle Fork Kaweah Trail* at the end of the access road (3340/0.0) east of Buckeye Flat Campground, 3385 feet below famous Moro Rock, invisible from here. You cross slopes bright with sunny yellow springtime flowers of bush

Alder-hugged Paradise Creek

Sunny-yellow bush poppies

poppies, a 4- to 20-foot bush with blooms of cupped, four petals surrounding many stamens. Its blue-green, lanceolate leaves face sideways, making them less exposed to the drying sun. These bushes germinate only after a fire; in this case, perhaps the 1969 controlled burn. You immediately descend to cross Moro Creek (3140/0.2) in a hidden recess just below the creek's raucous falls and placid pool.

Beyond the creek's shade of alders and laurels, you enter an aisle among high chamise bushes. These bushes stump sprouted thickly in the wake of the burn. Patches of poison oak pop up along the trail. If the identity of this plant evades you, give wide berth to any thornless bush or vine that produces leaves in groups of three.

Soon you boulder-hop a lively, unnamed creek and curve into two more shady nooks with seasonal flows and flourishing creek dogwood; the last nook offers a medium sized campsite. All along you gain elevation; sometimes the pitch is moderate to steep. The river, 200 to 400 feet below, usually remains out of sight, but its roar resounds in the broad canyon. Sporadic views of Castle Rocks (best approached from Paradise Peak of T90) and the Great Western Divide compensate for the trail's exposure. In a short time you descend abruptly into the canyon of Panther Creek (3840/2.7).

Beginning backpackers, as well as day hikers, may find this enchanting creek with its oak-shaded campsite perched on a ledge, an ideal place to stop. The creek's two pools lure hot, tired hikers into their refreshing domain. But be cautious—only dip into the pool above the trail crossing. Hundred-foot Panther Falls drops immediately beyond the rim of the lower pool, and it is life-threatening to get that close, especially during snowmelt's strong current.

Eager to continue, you venture on along the trail, climb a pair of switchbacks, and then traverse the slopes among a mixed woodland of incense cedar and black and golden oak; Indian pink flowers add spots of color. Pass another rill with a possible campsite, and then look for an unmarked but obvious trail descending the steep slopes. This is the unmaintained **Castle Creek Trail** (4720/ 2.4). Descend on it to a large campsite next to a small creek or proceed farther to a camping area next to Mehrten Creek (4560/0.2). A good campsite across the creek became strewn with twigs and branches when a blowdown crashed next to it.

This is a fine place to practice bear-bagging your food; Bruin's rounds sometime include a stop here. The Castle Creek Trail descends 0.9 mile, sometimes steeply, to the river where another campsite sits on a sandy stretch during low water.

A Castle Rocks spire

T103   Moro Rock Day Hike

Jutting abruptly from the Giant Forest plateau in Sequoia National Park, 4000 feet above the canyon floor, the enormous oblong dome of Moro Rock attracts numerous visitors. Its fascination stems from the massiveness of the monolith, the accessibility of it, the vast tableau surrounding it and the violence shaping it: freezes, exfoliations, earthquakes.

Distance   0.6 mile, round trip
Steep Ascents   None
Elevation Gain   265 feet
Skills   Easy route finding; moderate hiking
Seasons   Spring, summer, fall
Map   USGS 7.5-min. *Giant Forest*
Trailhead   71. See car tour T84.
Description   At the trailhead, before beginning the ascent of Moro Rock, pause to read the display about its geologic and human history. The first steps up the rock, built in 1917, were wooden with single railings. The stairway climbed straight up the crest. In 1931, the wooden steps were replaced with the stone you see and were considered so exceptional that they were entered into the National Register of Historic Places in 1978.

Signs at the trailhead and at the top warn of the severe lightning hazard when thunderstorms envelop Moro Rock. Some people intentionally ascended the rock during such a storm and were fatally struck by lightning. Take the warnings seriously.

At the beginning of **Moro Rock Trail** (6460/0.0), consisting of 400 steps and several interpretive stations, you ascend the aggregate concrete stairs placed on dynamited ledges. Even with the rock as a wall on one side and the sturdy hand rail on the other, you can feel giddy as you view the great depths. Courageous rock climbers shun the steps and ignore the giddiness to scale the precipitous sides of this immense granodiorite dome. Occasionally a few of their popular climbing routes are closed to allow peregrine falcons to nest undisturbed.

Surprisingly, here and there black oak, white fir and sugar pine have taken root, and vivid dark pink mountain pride penstemon thrive in cracks in the stone. These flowers add a splash of color and astonish onlookers, as they appear to grow right out of the rock.

Mountain pride penstemon grow between 6 to 12 inches from their matted bases. Their tubular flowers open with two lobes bent up and three lobes protruding and bent down. Their ovate leaves grow opposite on a stem that supports several blooms.

Finally, or in minutes, depending on your physical condition, you arrive at the long, narrow summit enclosed by railings (6725/0.3). The convoluted Great Western Divide on the distant eastern skyline stands as a product of a contest between forces building mountains and forces eroding them; the same contest has produced Castle Rocks, southeast across the Middle Fork valley and the dome on which you stand.

Roped-up rock climbers

Cloud-covered Middle Fork Kaweah River canyon from Moro Rock

T104   Crescent Meadow-Sequoia Trail Day Hike

Meadows exploding with wildflowers, terrain sanctified by august sequoias, paths distant from bustling crowds: this trip is an ideal introduction to Sequoia National Park's remarkable frontcountry.

Distance   5.4 miles, loop trip
Steep Ascents   None
Elevation Gain   750 feet
Skills   Easy route finding; easy-to-moderate hiking
Seasons   Spring, summer, fall
Maps   USGS 7.5-min. *Lodgepole, Giant Forest*
Trailhead   72. See car tour T84.
Description   This loop hike links several paths from a maze of trails that meander among the sequoias and meadows in Giant Forest. Although well-signed at the many intersections, you have to have a sense of where the features of interest to you are located and how you wish to return. If you want map details, you can purchase a map of Giant Forest trails at the Visitor Center.

This trip begins on the ***High Sierra Trail***

(6700/0.0) east of the Crescent Meadow parking area. Follow the paved path down the toe of Crescent Meadow where a treasure trove of wildflowers burst forth as summer approaches. You cross Crescent Creek on wooden bridges, then turn left at the fork (6740/0.1), leaving the famous High Sierra Trail.

Now heading north, ***Tharps Log Trail*** nears the meadow, crosses the creek, then turns right to leave the meadow at a junction with a trail to Chimney Tree. Still on Tharps Log Trail, your route ascends gently, advances west of Log Meadow, a lobe of the crescent, then reaches Tharps Log. Hale D. Tharp grazed cattle in these meadows and lived in the hollow log each summer from 1861 to 1890. Native Americans introduced Tharp to Giant Forest, but he received the honor of being its founder.

Beyond the log house, you continue ahead past another path (6835/0.8) to the left to Chimney Tree. Gently ascend on duff now to pass a research area and measuring device. Cross Crescent Creek again, then its branch at the head of Log Meadow, hike through a junction, and climb nearly 200 feet in elevation to yet another junction (7040/0.5), the fifth so far—the last two leading down to the High Sierra Trail. Stay left.

Now on the *Trail of the Sequoias* and free of crowds, you wander northward among the sequoias. The painted symbols on metal triangles nailed high on trees indicate skitouring routes—these routes marked in this manner are found throughout the park's forests. This land is equally lovely hiking in summer or cross-country skiing in winter.

In the summer you are likely to hear the Solitary Vireo singing his brief ascending—pause—descending paired notes. This 5- to 6-inch olive green perching bird with yellowish flanks and white wing bars, often serenades Southern Sierra hikers in wooded areas.

Alongside the path you see many young sequoias that have taken root and several mammoths that have fallen. You soon walk between two sections of a broken, fallen tree. After fording a snowmelt creek and rills, you descend easily to cross the mushy headwaters of Crescent Creek in a broad canyon. Next, in a burn area, you achieve a mild gain to a low saddle, then gradually drop to meet the Chief Sequoyah Tree. Some believe these giant sequoia trees, *Sequoiadendron giganteum,* were named for the Cherokee Indian who invented a system of writing for his people—a giant among men.

At this point among awesome giant trees, you find an offset five-way intersection (7060/2.1) of paths. Your route, the *Circle Meadow Trail,* heads south to the fourth largest sequoia, the stunning President Tree, and the stately Senate group of sequoias. Here it passes among the Senators—threading the aisle between the Democrats and Republicans—so to speak, on the way to Circle Meadow. Above Circle Meadow the path switchbacks around a fallen giant and soon dips to meadowside. At the next junction (6980/1.0) stay left onto the *Crescent Meadow Trail* and left through the next two junctions, right through the third, then skirt the west side of Crescent Meadow and return to the parking area (6700/0.9) where you began.

T105   Sunset Rock Day Hike

This nearly level path leads you atop a massive dome in Sequoia National Park from which you can see waves of interlocking distant ridges; occasionally some forming profiles against brilliant reds and oranges. This trip is unforgettable during flaming sunsets.

Distance   1.6 miles, round trip
Steep Ascents   None
Elevation Gain   Negligible
Skills   Easy route finding; easy hiking
Seasons   Spring, summer, fall
Map   USGS 7.5-min. *Giant Forest*
Trailhead   73. See car tour T84.
Description   You will find the *Sunset Rock Trail* in Giant Forest to the west of Round Meadow; it begins at the Generals Highway (6415/0.0). Immediately descend to ford Little Deer Creek across a wooden bridge—you find these bridges throughout the park's frontcountry; a luxury for those used to boulder-hopping or wading across creeks in the backcountry. A connector trail to Round Meadow succeeds the ford. You ascend easily above the creek, shaded first by white firs and sugar pines, then by ponderosa pines, incense cedars and black oaks as well.

Off the trail to the right, park biologists have an experimental plot of land enclosed by an electrically charged fence. The tests in progress include monitoring the effects of ozone on trees. The plot includes two giant sequoias and a nursery of planted seedlings.

You soon traverse inland from the steep slopes of the Marble Fork Kaweah River, pass an obscure path traveling to the right that finds its way to the Marble Fork bridge, then in a few steps walk onto the large exfoliating, pocked granodiorite dome of Sunset Rock (6412/0.8). The rock's position allows you to catch interleaved western ridges in bold relief at sunset. For reference, Crystal Cave tunnels into the backside of the ridge west-northwest, and Little Baldy's bare head (T111) protrudes to the north.

Massive, flat-topped Sunset Rock

T106   Self-Guided Nature Trails Day Hike

The Trail for All People in Sequoia National Park winds among sequoias that circle brilliant Round Meadow; the Hazelwood Trail weaves among giants whose trunks are veiled with dogwood. These two accessible and easily walked loops offer information and beauty that will enrich your visit to the parks.

Distance   1.6 miles, loop trips
Steep Ascents   None
Elevation Gain   Negligible
Skills   Easy route finding; easy hiking
Seasons   Spring, summer, fall
Map   USGS 7.5-min. *Giant Forest*
Trailhead   73. See car tour T84.
Description   Round Meadow lies several steps to the left of Generals Highway in the south portion of Giant Forest. Its wide, paved, nearly level path with interpretive signs was designed for both foot travelers and people in wheelchairs.

Begin clockwise on the *Trail for All People* (6385/0.0). You learn from information presented en route the relationship of forests to meadows and the names of some of the abundant meadow flowers. You learn to recognize young sequoia trees and to appreciate the benefit of forest fire. Your attention is drawn to the birds of the forest and the firs and pines that may be forgotten in the overwhelming presence of the mammoth trees.

On the return around the loop, you pass a 1.5 mile trail (6380/0.4) to the General Sherman Tree; then you cross a tributary to Little Deer Creek. You learn that the rock that lies under the forest and the sequoias that

lie across the forest floor are also a part of the "symphony" described on the last interpretive sign linking forest, meadow and stream. Then this loop ends where it began (6385/0.3).

Now continue onto the *Hazelwood Trail* (6380/0.2) across the highway. Here a stand of mature sequoias, an unmarked, unnamed 17th largest tree among them, ornaments a gentle vale circled by a trail with uneven paving. A fallen giant forms a frame above your entry into this magnificent stand.

Dogwood flowers seem to float

On the trail as you gaze at the sturdy behemoths, you also see dogwoods that lend their graceful beauty: creamy white blossoms in early summer and flamboyantly colored leaves in fall. The white flowers that seem suspended on the branches are really petal-like brats: the centers of the brats, composed of numerous blooms of greenish-yellow petals, are the flowers. The elliptical leaves with slightly wavy edges grow opposite on the reddish twigs.

Interpretive signs on this loop focus on earlier people who had divergent thoughts on Giant Forest's use: Hale Tharp grazed his animals here; John Muir wished to preserve the big trees; the Kaweah Colony hoped to log the forest. You learn about people who had an impact on the management of the forest: George Stewart campaigned for park status; Walter Fry shaped the park's future; Col. John White enforced sound environmental policies; and Richard Hartesvedt shared his expertise of sequoia trees. The poetic observations also given set the tone for the rest of your park visit. John Muir wrote that the big trees are nature's forest master-pieces, and that one naturally walks softly and with reverence among them (6380/0.7).

The General Sherman Tree

T107   General Sherman Tree Loop Day Hike

Everyone who visits Sequoia National Park visits the General Sherman Tree: it stands as the largest living organism on earth! To learn more about the sequoias and to enjoy other behemoths, hike the nearby self-guided Congress Trail.

Distance   2.0 miles, loop trip
Steep Ascents   None
Elevation Gain   250 feet
Skills   Easy route finding; easy hiking
Seasons   Spring, summer, fall
Maps   USGS 7.5-min. *Giant Forest, Lodgepole*
Trailhead   74. See car tour T84.
Description   A pamphlet with information and illustrations corresponding to the numbers on the trail can be purchased at the Visitor Center if not at the trailhead. With your pamphlet you learn how these wondrous trees grow, why they become so old and how

they finally die. You learn how to identify sequoias of all ages. Information includes identification of associated plants and animals as well.

The General Sherman Tree's excellent growing conditions helped produce its immense size: it weighs nearly 1400 tons and stands 274.9 feet high. In 1975 its age was estimated by increment borings to be between 2300 and 2700 years old—down from previous estimates of 3500 years. Sequoias rank among the fastest growing trees worldwide, and the old general still adds to his girth each year.

The self-guided **Congress Trail** heads east, then turns south from the General Sherman Tree (6880/0.0). Its asphalt path passes numbers along the trail. You immediately cross several branches of Sherman Creek, one crossing so cozy to a mini-falls that you feel the spray during early season. Continue on the Congress Trail past the junction (6840/0.6) with a shortcut that returns you to the parking lot—many named trees are yet to come.

At the embattled-appearing Chief Sequoyah Tree you meet the Trail of the Sequoias and briefly overlap the route of T104. Here you may admire the well-shaped, fourth largest, President Tree and the staid Senate group. Looping back on a lower trail, you arrive at the House group—both groups like their namesakes stand around in clusters seemingly inactive. But these distinguished trees, genetically endowed to outlive many civilizations, are a constant benefit to the environment; just by existing, they enrich mankind.

Farther ahead, be sure to include the off-loop walk south on the Alta Trail (6915/0.8) to the Lincoln Tree, the fifth largest. The Lincoln Tree is best described by Wendell Flint in *To Find the Biggest Tree:* "The Lincoln resembles the president it was named after, rugged and adorned with lumps and bumps." Flint's tree measurements assist the park's ranking of sequoias. Past the Lincoln Tree, off the trail to Circle Meadow, stands the second largest of all trees, the beautifully scallop-trunked Washington Tree. A few hundred yards southeast along the trail soars the tenth largest tree, the Franklin.

Back on the loop trip, you head north, doubling back just below your ingress trail to the parking lot (6840/0.6).

Suspended over a chasm 2000 feet deep

T108   The Watchtower Day Hike

The Watchtower in Sequoia National Park, a vertical-walled point on Tokopah Valley's south rim, projects like a peninsula 1800 feet above a sea of granite, the valley floor. Nothing along the easily traveled rim trail prepares you for the experience of viewing this sudden, awesome drop and expanse.

Distance   6.6 miles, round trip
Steep Ascents   None
Elevation Gain   1645 feet
Skills   Easy route finding; easy-to-moderate hiking
Seasons   Spring, summer, fall
Map   USGS 7.5-min. *Lodgepole*
Trailhead   75. See car tour T84.
Description   Water, toilets and a food storage box are located near the trailhead at Wolverton. Please leave no food in your car and cover articles that appear to contain food.

From the north side of the parking lot (7275/0.0), climb up the seven stairs to the bulletin board and hike north on the ***Lakes Trail*** to an intersection (7340/0.2) on a broad ridge. (The left trail accesses the horse corrals and also heads on a long descending traverse to Lodgepole Campground.) You turn abruptly right where you pass a closed trail to Long Meadow, then ascend easily up the ridge dividing the watershed of Marble Fork Kaweah River and Wolverton Creek. You follow the creek for 1.8 miles.

Although the fir-clad ridge you are on drops steeply north to the campground and river, detouring to the edge reveals only the dense lodgepole forest below. Sets of switchbacks help you gain elevation, and the tin hornlike "ank-ank-ank" of the Red-breasted Nuthatch marshals you along your way. This small blue-gray bird with a rust-colored tummy and a black and white horizontal striped cap feasts on seeds tucked under the scales of cones; its loud call resounds throughout the conifer forests of the park.

You near a meadow vividly dressed in deep green, decorated with a multitude of wildflowers; then in time you cross a spring-fed stream that alerts you to the ensuing junction (8060/1.6). Here people on T109 arrive past Panther Gap from the loop part of their trip. You turn abruptly left, heading north, again crossing the same stream and then arrive at a trail split (8300/0.3). Nordic skiers and early season hikers struggle up the right fork via The Hump; you take the easier Watchtower fork. Now you slant gently north, then northeast to pass through another sloping meadow, this with its creek on the far side. After what seems to be a lengthy traverse, you switchback to the crest of the Watchtower (8920/1.2)—not named on topos.

Those sure of foot and fearless of heights leave the trail to make their way along the crest to the 8973-foot projection called the "Watchtower." Far below miniature appearing people move along the winding trail to Tokopah Falls (T110). To the east, the sinuous headwaters of the Marble Fork spill in glittering threads from lakes and snow-packs seen as far as the granite Tableland and the divide between Kings Canyon and Sequoia national parks.

Here on the rim, skilled rock climbers who have checked with the Park Service, stretch their ropes east of the crest across the gaping chasm from the trail to the tower. They then belay across the sheer drop—they even look down while crossing the abyss!!

For a lengthier day hike, continue on to Heather, Aster, Emerald or Pear lakes (described in T109).

Top of sheer-sided Watchtower

T109   Moose Lake Backpack
With Excursion V: Alta Peak

The lakes you pass on this trip—Heather, Aster, Emerald and Pear—rate among the most visited lakes in all of Sequoia National Park: their accessibility, stunning beauty and responsive fish account for that. In contrast, Moose Lake resides miles from maintained trails, and its magnificent stark shores require great effort to reach. It has the best fishing of all.

Distance   18.3 miles, semiloop trip
Steep Ascents   0.6 mile
Elevation Gain   4100 feet
Skills   Intermediate route finding
Seasons   Spring, summer, fall (Wilderness permit required)
Map   USGS 7.5-min. *Lodgepole*
Trailhead   75. See car tour T84.
Description   The beginning of this trip is described in T108.

Eastbound Lakes Trail Log

T108	Wolverton prkg	7275	0.0
	ridge jct	7340	0.2
	loop jct	8060	1.6
	The Hump fk	8300	0.3
	Watchtower	8920	1.2

The sudden, sheer cliff drops do not end with the Watchtower; the 1930s-dynamited *Lakes Trail*, on which you continue, hugs the steep granite walls, then passes the east end of The Hump fork (9300/0.7). Just beyond, the trail curves around seclusive Heather Lake (9240/0.1), discontinuously wreathed in red heather. This lake, like Aster, Emerald and Moose, was carved from Cretaceous granodiorite by glacial action during the Pleistocene epoch, the ice age that began close to three million years ago. Note the glacial polish on the slabs approaching the lake. A barely private privy sits north of the trail, but no camping is allowed either here or at Aster Lake.

You next switchback over a ridge; it and the ridge to the east border Aster and Emerald lakes (9220/1.1). Aster sits in bouldered but serene surroundings below the trail, while Emerald embraces a dramatic essence in an amphitheater of humbling crestline rocks rising 1800 feet skyward. Emerald Lake, one of the most studied subalpine lakes in the country, has had its bottom scraped and poked to collect algae, aquatic plants, fish and sediment to test the effects of acid rain.

You may camp at Emerald and Pear lakes only in numbered sites: 10 sites at Emerald; 12 at Pear. These strictly enforced rules have helped the lakes retain their unspoiled attractiveness. You will find sparkling clean, odor-free, solar-powered toilets here and at Pear Lake. At both lakes food storage boxes provide safe keeping for your food from bears day and night, but dauntless marmots chew everything—suspend your backpack on a rope if you plan to leave it unattended.

To reach Pear Lake, you again arch around a ridge; this ridge extends directly below Alta Peak. You pass a lateral to the Pear Lake Ranger Station/wintertime ski hut that forks off the trail half way between the lakes. You soon descend to Pear Lake (9560/1.0), a granite-walled body of sparkling water, the largest of the four lakes.

Up to now the physical effort has been reasonable and the exquisite surroundings have been rewarding—many may choose not to go on. Those who elect to continue to Moose Lake need to have a sense of direction, the ability to match a topo map to the terrain and the strength and balance to climb over unwieldy boulders with an often unwieldier backpack.

One recommended route to Moose Lake with definitive landmarks is as follows: From the campsites on the north end of Pear Lake, note the saddle north-northeast on the ridge and angle up to it, *cross-country*, first staying below the slabs, then climbing up their fractures. Instruments atop the saddle collect an assemblage of data for park scientists. Some of the projects here and throughout the park include studies of soil and snow chemistry, snow hydrology, plant physiology and over-all effects of air pollution.

Below the saddle to the northeast, a meadow and trees, then an ascending linear grove of shrubs indicate the outlet stream of a lake hidden above the talus bench to the east. To reach that lake involves the most difficult climb on this trip. It requires a 400-foot elevation gain, half-mile Class 2 scramble up the large, jumbled boulders right of the outlet to the lake. In a drought year, you may find this lake and the next lakes just muddy hollows.

(Some hikers climb on a 290° bearing from the south side of this first lake up to a definite ridge notch, east-southeast and descend via a chute to Moose Lake.) You, now on the north shore of lake #1, angle 90° to the left and climb northeast up the greenery of the next outlet to lake #2. Your next land-mark, a group of lakes above the slabs east-southeast require a 90° angle to the right, then ascend from the south side of lake #2. Climb the slabs on relatively easy zigzags to lakes #3. Cross between the two largest lakes, then climb to the ridgecrest left of the highest block.

Below you by 400 feet lies the vast, brilliant blue waters of Moose Lake in a garden of boulders backdropped by the dis-tant serrated peaks of the Great Western Divide. No tree has taken root for miles around. As you turn in all directions, it is an other-world experience of ghostly pointed peaks and barren rocks, all shaped in part by the huge ice sheet that once covered it. Back to Planet Earth, drop to a small tarn north of Moose, then to the shoreline (10,560/2.5). Make your way along the west edge to the south end of the lake where sheltered camp-sites decorated with bouquets of cascading phlox cluster in the saddle above (10,620/ 0.8).

Concentric rings dancing upon the lake's surface indicate the presence of hungry brook trout and the best fishing on this trip, causing even a tired fisherman to reach for his rod. Other hikers relax and marvel at this wonderland of rock, water and sky.

To continue your loop trip, find the unmaintained **path** leaving south from the campsites. Follow it through a meadow to the edge of rock slides. Swirling slope patterns across Buck Canyon catch your eye, but your full attention is needed: the trail disappears among boulder fields. Your goal now is south to the upper edge of the forest on the bare ridge to your right that you have been following. Here you have three choices: The old trail descended to near a pond southwest

Exquisite granite-walled Pear Lake

of the little lake in the canyon known as Little Moose Lake, then climbed the ridge to the tree line; some hikers climb to the ridgecrest and then descend to tree line; or, the route suggested here, find the way ahead that suits you best over the steep boulder field to the beginning of the trees on the ridge where you again find the path (10,120/1.0).

The path zigzags and switchbacks to descend under forest cover southwest from the ridgecrest to a meadow called "Last Chance." The undulating path continues through slopes occasionally draped with bracken fern or with lupine. In quick time it arrives at extensive Alta Meadow. Here it becomes maintained *Alta Trail* and wanders among waist- to shoulder-high flowering plants with Alta Peak and Tharps Rock hovering above. The route climbs a sandy path, then levels beyond the meadow, passing ample campsites on a spacious red fir-shaded ridge (9400/2.1). A creek just beyond adds to the attractiveness of the camping area.

You round open, steep slopes with sweeping views of Farewell Gap and Vandever Mountain, Paradise Peak and Castle Rocks beyond the Middle Fork valley. (Each of these features, except Castle Rocks, is visited in this book.) You then pass medium-sized campsites next to a spring-fed creek and minutes later arrive at Alta Peak

Trail (9300/0.9). Alta Peak sits at the hub of your loop trip and provides a comprehensive picture of the country you have traveled and the Sierra beyond.

Excursion V: Alta Peak

When an engineered trail leads up a peak you can expect a fire lookout or the remains of one, but this trail was built just to access a lofty peak with exciting views of the Great Western Divide.

Distance   3.8 miles, round trip
Steep Ascents   0.6 mile
Elevation Gain   1910 feet
Skills   Easy route finding; Class 2 climbing; Class 5 pitches optional
Description   Ascend north on the *Alta Peak Trail* (9300/0.0) under boughs of red fir, then quickly turn east to ford a creek just below its spring, next to a small campsite. Continue on an extended traverse along the foot of outstanding Tharps Rock to cross the nascent creek from which you may have drawn water if you camped on the ridge next to Alta Meadow, visible below.

The path makes a reverse turn around a mature red fir and advances above Tharps Rock. En route slender ¼-inch jewel flowers are just noticeable. Their heart-shaped leaves

Spectacular views of the Great Western Divide from Alta Trail

hug the stem on which bloom budlike yellow flowers with spreading thready tips. This plant prefers dry, rocky soils.

As the main trail turns right, away from Tharps Rock, a use trail (10,580/1.5) leads to that outcrop where climbers enjoy Class 5 climbing. A novice can ascend a short way up its ridge. This colorful, lower in elevation rock soars more prominently than the summit outcrop of Alta Peak.

The last leg of Alta Peak Trail twists east-northeast on decomposed granite among boulders, rises above outliers of foxtail pines, heads toward a north ridge, then arrives at a gravelly platform on which sits the summit block. The north point of this flat treats you to amazing views of Emerald, Aster and Pear lakes below. Big Moose Lake to the northeast hides behind higher towers on this cupped, glacial-carved rim.

A crease to the right on the summit rock leads you to the register atop this steeply curved half dome of Alta Peak (11,204/0.4). The east face drops abruptly. All around rise the remarkable peaks of the High Sierra, including Triple Divide Peak to the east on the Great Western Divide, separating the Kings, Kern and Kaweah watersheds.

*　　*　　*　　*　　*

Beyond the Alta Peak Trail, the path continues to descend west where, in about 0.3 mile, a spring bursts from beneath the trail: dry upslope, a lively brook downslope—reminiscent of River Spring on the Kern Plateau (T88, described in the east side companion to this book). A half mile later, the trail passes above tiers of campsites on a shaded slope alongside Mehrten Creek above Mehrten Meadow. Shortly thereafter, it passes a lateral that descends 2.2 miles to the High Sierra Trail (8960/1.1).

After completing a curve around a minor ridge, you traverse the steep south-facing slopes of the captivating headwater bowl of Panther Creek. Then step across one of the creek's spring-fed branches and cross the ridge divide. A short descending switchback delivers you to Panther Gap (8320/1.0).

At the gap a sharp turn right sends you switchbacking north to descend among fern-clothed slopes embroidered with wildflowers and threaded with spring-fed brooks. This enchanting scene brings your loop to an end for you soon arrive at a T junction with the *Lakes Trail* (8060/0.9), your incoming route. Here you turn left to walk again above Wolverton Creek to return to your starting point (7275/1.8).

T110　Tokopah Falls Day Hike

Churning headwaters from High Sierra lakes crash down Tokopah Falls in Sequoia National Park, loudly echoing off soaring canyon walls. This sublime scene—the upper Marble Fork Kaweah River and glaciated Tokopah Valley—draws many visitors.

Distance　3.4 miles, round trip
Steep Ascents　None
Elevation Gain　610 feet
Skills　Easy route finding; easy-to-moderate hiking
Seasons　Spring, summer, fall
Map　USGS 7.5-min. *Lodgepole*
Trailhead　76. See car tour T84.
Description　The *Tokopah Valley Trail* (6750/0.0) begins at the north side of Lodgepole Campground's bridge across the Marble Fork Kaweah River. The shaded trail travels east along the river's edge. Straight,

slender lodgepole pines that usually prefer to grow at higher elevations in the Southern Sierra inhabit this cool, well-drained valley, especially the campground. This widespread tree is easily recognized by its two-needle bundles and its ¾- to 2-inch, egg-shaped cones. Because the trees often live in pure stands, when stressed, a whole forest can fall prey to its natural enemy, the needleminer moth. The name lodgepole refers to the Indian's use of the trunks for teepee poles.

The path becomes squeezed between outcrops and the river, then ascends easily among boulders. Quite soon glades appear and trees part, offering fleeting glimpses of Watchtower's sheer face (T108) that forms the valley's south wall. Then rugged cliffs of the north wall come into view.

After you cross a variety of streams, among them Horse Creek, and observe a number of lethargic, pudgy, brown marmots

sunning on boulders, the dramatic gorge bisected by frothy water suddenly opens before you. For a closer look make your way along the path among talus blocks to the foot of clamorous Tokopah Falls (7360/1.7). Here you can sit on rocks deposited by the ancient river of ice that chiseled the jointed granodiorite and helped shape the gorge.

T111   Little Baldy Day Hike

A well-banked trail leads to the domed summit of Little Baldy in Sequoia National Park, the former site of a fire lookout tower with panoramic views.

Distance   3.4 miles, round trip
Steep Ascents   None
Elevation Gain   715 feet
Skills   Easy route finding; easy-to-moderate hiking
Seasons   Spring, summer, fall
Map   USGS 7.5-min. *Giant Forest*
Trailhead   77. See car tour T84.
Description   At Little Baldy Saddle (7340/ 0.0) on the Generals Highway northwest of Lodgepole Campground and Wuksachi Village, a set of steps ushers you onto the *Little Baldy Trail*, then a set of switchbacks helps you gain elevation. Beyond that the trail angles up northwest-facing slopes in a forest of pines and firs with an understory of chinquapin and snow brush.

If you climb this dome in the morning or late afternoon, you may hear the Western Wood Pewee, a fly-catcher, voice his trailing, harsh, one-slurred note "pee-eer" loud and often. This 6-inch, olive-gray bird has two whitish wingbars. You will probably hear it before you see it. Numerous in the Southern Sierra, this bird ranges throughout the west from Alaska to Mexico.

After the traverse, three sharp switchbacks turn you south to hike over lesser domes on the ridge to Little Baldy. You soon attain the summit by climbing up the east side. From the broad dome (8044/1.7) you turn away from the San Joaquin Valley and its smog to the west, to view forested Shell Mountain (T118:Ex-W) and other high peaks of the Jennie Lake Wilderness that stand out 6.0 air miles to the north. The upper reaches

of Marble Fork Kaweah River (T109), seen against the Great Western Divide peaks, fill the eastern view. The series of Kaweah River canyons and intervening ridges are easily recognized to the south. Massive Sunset Rock (T105) seems miniature.

Marble Fork's Tokopah Falls

T112   Highway 180 Car Tour:
Fresno to Kings Canyon National Park

Rolling country, handsome Grant Grove and picturesque Jennie Lakes Wilderness highlight this tour, which begins on Highway 180, a National Scenic Byway, east of Fresno.

Distance   38.9/30.9 miles, one way
Steep Ascents   None
Elevation Gain   6850 feet
Skills   Easy route finding; paved roads
Seasons   All year; snow removed—usually to Giant Forest
Map   Tulare County road map
Tourhead   81. The junction of Highway 63 and Highway 180 is **TH81**. It is 30.0 miles east of Fresno.
Description   From the junction (1440/0.0/0.0) drive east on *State Highway 180* past a sign advising you of conditions ahead. While ascending among lightly populated, oak-rich foothills, you pass Ruth Hill Road, the first in a web of paved country roads crisscrossing the foothills south of your highway—ideal for exploring and bicycle riding. The paved road to the left that you pass as you drive beyond Squaw Valley hamlet travels to the Kings River. (En route it skirts Dalton Mountain, an 1891 hide-out of robber Grat Dalton, then passes the site of the first dude ranch in California, now the Wonder Valley Ranch Resort.)

Your route, Highway 180, follows Mill Creek, then intersects the hamlet of Clingans Junction where old Highway 180 branches right from your road to continue along the creek. On the outskirts of the hamlet, the highway arrives at Hume Lake Ranger District station of Sequoia National Forest (7.3/7.3). (See Chapter 3 for services offered.) This book describes several trips on this district's land, squeezed between Sequoia National Park and Kings Canyon National Park: Ts117&118 in Jennie Lakes Wilderness and Ts116, 119&121.

In the mountains next, but still driving in high gear, you rise on steep slopes where road turnouts offer dramatic valley views. En route, the plant communities advance from oak and brush to a mixed forest of buckeye,

black oak, incense cedar and pine. You soon enter Sequoia National Forest, swing through a hairpin curve, then pass an intersection. (On the road north from the intersection you can find your way to Delilah Lookout, open to visitors, or to campgrounds on the Kings River.)

Still on Highway 180, rounding McKenzie Ridge, you pass Highway 245 (5430/13.2/20.5) (foothill car tour T85) slanting in from the east. Less than a mile later, at Happy Gap, named by the early mill suppliers happy to be at the top of the grade, a road to the right travels north to the cabins around private Sequoia Lake, a converted cow pasture. (The Sanger Lumber Company created this artificial lake in the late 1800s to facilitate their logging operations—now it is the locale of a YMCA camp.)

The appearance of sequoias signals the Big Stump Entrance Station of Kings Canyon National Park (2.9/23.4). Here a park ranger collects entrance fees and dispenses campground information. Free passage is given to people heading for national forest land. Minutes later a large parking area (0.7/24.1) gives access to picnic tables, drinking faucet, restrooms and the Big Stump Nature Trail.

The giant sequoia stumps found in Big Stump Basin and in other logged sequoia areas offer scientists an opportunity to study rings of trees that lived 2000 years or more. In reference to climate, the studies revealed that in the last 1000 years, the climate overall was much drier than the present century. What we consider drought may really be the norm.

For a nominal fee you can obtain a pamphlet here for the self-guided nature trail around Big Stump Basin, a mile loop of little elevation gain. The pamphlet is written in the first person voice of a mythical old timer who, as a young boy, felled giant sequoias in the

Big Stump Basin. The literature provides insight into conflicting philosophies that surrounded these trees: some people focused on how to use them; others sought to preserve and protect them.

In 1890 these differences were resolved when Congress elected to protect the trees and established General Grant National Park. In 1940, Congress enlarged the park to include Redwood Mountain and the great wilderness to the north and east. It changed the name to Kings Canyon National Park. Once again, in 1965, the park was further enlarged: this time to include the easternmost canyon of the Kings River and parts of the Tehipite Valley. Sequoia and Kings Canyon National Parks are administered as a single unit from Ash Mountain headquarters.

Beyond the parking area, a wide curve heads you east to The Wye (6220/1.0/25.1), a triangle junction with Generals Highway. Those seeking Sequoia National Park or **THs82–87** turn right; everyone else continues left on Highway 180 and skips the following description.

— — — — —

After taking a right turn on *Generals Highway* (0.0/0.0), you drive southeastward along the Kings-Kaweah Divide into Sequoia National Forest. Quickly, you reach the roadside Redwood Mountain Overlook. A stop here allows you to view Redwood Mountain and to read the informative interpretive sign. From this overlook you gaze upon the world's largest giant sequoia grove—five square miles of sequoias! Just under a mile later you arrive at Quail Flat (3.5/3.5). Those taking the hike through the groves of Redwood Mountain, T113 at **TH82**, turn right on the rough, unpaved road. (The road to the left heads north to Hume Lake.)

Traveling on, threading the boundary between forest land left and park land right, be sure to stop at the pullout to the left. A Kings Canyon Overlook exhibit identifies the High Sierra peaks soaring over vast canyons of the Kings River. Look between the trees for precarious Buck Rock Fire Lookout (T116) balanced on a needle rock to the

northeast.

Now you drive past two trailheads each providing areas of intimate and exciting knowledge for you of this special land. In 0.1 mile from the viewpoint, Buena Vista Peak Trail (1.1/4.6) to the right, T114 at **TH83**, offers a 2.0 mile hike with 405 feet elevation gain to a scenic point. Minutes later to the right, Big Baldy Ridge of T115 at **TH84** (2.0/6.6) suggests a view-packed hike of 5.8 miles round trip. Seconds later, to the left, SNF Road 14S11 (0.1/6.7), Big Meadows Road, peels off to **THs85&86** and Big Meadows Campground. Also, this 9.0 mile, paved road to Horse Corral Meadow makes an excellent bicycle tour.

Those seeking Buck Rock Lookout (T116) and Jennie Lakes Wilderness (Ts117&118) turn onto *SNF Road 14S11* (0.0/0.0), the road to Big Meadows. Drive east past marked cross-country ski routes to SNF Road 13S04 (2.8/2.8). Those heading for the lookout turn left here and drive north on *SNF Road 13S04*, a bumpy, unpaved road. Continue past the small Buck Rock Campground to park at the SNF Road 13S04B fork (2.1/4.9), **TH85**.

For Jennie Lakes Wilderness, continue past the lookout road on SNF Road 14S11 to the Big Meadows parking area across from the ranger station (0.9/3.7), **TH86**. A phone kiosk and rest room stand at the trailhead. The campground is 0.3 miles farther.

On Generals Highway about a mile beyond the Big Meadows turnoff, you pass the road to privately run Montecito-Sequoia Inc. family camp and winter resort: for information about the resort, phone 1-800-843-8677. Shortly thereafter, hikers and climbers seeking the exciting ascents of Chimney Rock T119 of **TH87**, turn right on SNF Road 14S29 (2.2/8.9). Check your mileage and watch for it; it may be unsigned.

You next arrive at the Forest Service's Stony Creek complex (3.1/12.0), another place of interest on this journey southeast. It provides campgrounds, picnic area, shower, laundromat, general store and is also a point of entry into Jennie Lakes Wilderness. Beyond, you cross into Sequoia National Park, then enter the Lost Grove (6660/1.8/13.8) with its stately sequoias. To continue further on this highway, T84 describes the Generals Highway from south to north.

—   —   —   —   —

From The Wye heading north on Highway 180, you soon pass to the right the main road to the cabins of Wilsonia, a private inholding surrounded by national park. To the left you pass the entrance (1.3/26.4) to Sunset Campground and amphitheater for evening programs; then you enter Grant Grove Village whose market, gas station, cafe, post office, lodge and fine Visitor Center stand ready to serve your needs.

Continuing on, a right turn at the next intersection (0.4/26.8) takes you to Crystal Springs Campground and an opportunity to view the wonders of this park by car on a 2.5-mile, tortuous road, unsuitable for large vehicles, to scenic Panoramic Point. A left turn takes you past Azalea Campground and Columbine Picnic Area to **TH88**, the beautiful General Grant Tree and the superb 0.4 mile, nearly level, self-guided nature trail of T120. A stable here offers guided equestrian rides.

Ahead on Highway 180 you reenter Sequoia National Forest and arrive at a turnout for McGee Vista Point. Stop at the vista point to scan the slopes for traces of the 1955 fire that burned 17,500 acres. Following the conflagration, an incredible number of seedlings were planted. You next reach Cherry Gap where in just over two miles on the road to the left, you access the Chicago Stump. The stump was called the General Noble Tree when it was cut down in 1892. Its bark was removed and sent to the Chicago World's Fair where the shell was reconstructed for display. The tree was apparently comparable in size to the Boole Tree. The stump of the oldest known giant sequoia, 3200 years old when cut, is also in the vicinity of the Chicago Stump.

The Highway descends, and you need to watch carefully to the left for your turnoff onto unpaved Converse Basin Road (SNF Road 13S55) (6380/4.1/30.9) to the Boole Tree, T121 at **TH89**. Although signed, the road can easily be missed. Highway 180 travels on beyond the scope of this book to the awesome canyon of the mighty Kings River. For greater in-depth road and park information, look for the park's excellent booklet *Exploring Mountain Highways* by William C. Tweed.

T113   Redwood Canyon Day Hike

This challenging trip into the world's largest giant sequoia grove offers you the opportunity to walk among these awesome trees far from Kings Canyon National Park crowds. Although a shorter loop is available, the long distance and significant elevation gain contribute to this unforgettable experience.

Distance   9.9 miles, loop trip
Steep Ascents   None
Elevation Gain   1880 feet
Skills   Easy route finding; moderate-to-strenuous hiking
Seasons   Spring, summer, fall
Map   USGS 7.5-min. *General Grant Grove*
Trailhead   82. See car tour T112. From Quail Flat (0.0/0.0) on the Generals Highway, turn south on the rough dirt road. It hangs on steep slopes as it descends, then

forks (1.8/1.8). Take the left fork to Redwood Saddle (0.1/1.9), **TH82**.
Description   From Redwood Saddle (6180/0.0) the **Sugarbowl Trail** climbs south into the five square mile grove of giant sequoias that includes 2100 trees larger than 10 feet in diameter, 15,000 larger than one foot and thousand upon thousands of smaller trees. Today the Redwood Mountain Grove reigns as the largest sequoia grove in the world, but it was once second in size to the Converse Basin Grove (T121) until that basin

was completely cut down between 1897 and 1907.

You quickly enter a long term research study area. The focus of these studies is how to protect giant sequoias as well as the giants of several species that stand about you in solemn repose. While ascending the ridge-crest, you pass areas of burn. These scars remain from intentional fires designed to open the canopy, clear the soil and heat the sequoia cones to cause them to release their seeds.

You leave the crest to hike along the west side, then switchback to the east side where you see broad vistas of Big Baldy's sheer granite facade (T115), a contrast to the intimate view of the surrounding trees. You next descend to a saddle, then ascend along the east shoulder of the mildly rising ridge, eventually passing below the summit. (Peak-baggers turn right to climb cross-country less than 0.1 mile to the 7001-foot summit. While doing so you cross a retired section of the Sugarbowl Trail.)

Continuing on, you enter the Sugarbowl

group of giants, tempting you to tarry. Here a destination sign indicates miles yet to walk. You continue on, turn acutely north, then east, then negotiate long-legged switchbacks down a moderate grade across corrugated east-facing slopes. Early on you sight shining Buck Rock Lookout (T116) northeast.

Below the switchbacks you come upon an area where a prescribed 1977 burn flared out of control. Now a shaggy cover of hundreds of sequoia saplings grow in the burned area. In 1983 these trees were a foot or two high; ten years later many reached six feet or more. Because each needs sunlight, many in the crowded area will eventually die, but some will live to be like the old giants you see around you.

At the canyon floor, the Sugarbowl Trail ends and you turn right on the **Redwood Canyon Trail** (5520/4.5) to amble briefly south along Redwood Creek. (Redwood Canyon Trail continues down-canyon, and with permission you can camp along it even though this is considered park "frontcoun-try." It also travels up-canyon near the valley

Mule deer at foot of giant sequoia

floor, then returns to Redwood Saddle, a route which shortcuts your trip by 3.5 miles.)

You quickly meet a junction (5520/0.1) with the **Hart Tree Trail**, which you take. It immediately crosses Redwood Creek—on an upstream log during snowmelt. In 0.5 mile you arrive at the Fallen Goliath. Giant Sequoias seldom die of old age. They die most often by toppling over, perhaps weakened by an extensive fire burn, undercut by excessive water or downed by strong wind, which maybe is analogous to the biblical David's sling shot and stone. Goliath's girth measures a hefty 21 feet in diameter.

The course climbs the west slopes of Redwood Canyon, gradually, sometimes steeply, passes several seasonal creeks, and, still among sequoia trees that have sheltered it nearly continuously, it arrives at a lateral (6120/2.0) to the Hart Tree—the second sequoia up from the trail.

Only recently has this tree fallen in rank from the top four among giants. Of the trees measured in 1931, this was the tallest and fourth largest in volume, and it received much publicity. Perhaps its notoriety even helped to include this grove in the park's expansion. In 1993, according to mathematician Wendell D. Flint's measurements, it was the 23rd largest by volume. At 260 feet tall, it fell

junior to another tree in this grove, one of the two tallest known in the world, both at 310 feet. It is even uncertain whether this or the 278-foot tree below it is the true Hart Tree. Nevertheless, these are two admirable trees and among the largest by volume in the world.

On an ensuing switchback you descend to either boulder-hop East Fork or cautiously cross on a fallen sequoia. Resuming the gradual ascent, you reach, then stride 60 feet through, a log tunnel. Beyond, an occasional tree-framed portrait of the rugged face of Buena Vista Peak (T114) appears as you approach the foot of Hart Meadow. You then cross Buena Vista Creek.

Descending now, the route curves past a granite slab and down a long, twisty zigzag into northern Redwood Canyon. It passes shake-sided "Pierce Cabin," built when desultory logging took place before Redwood Canyon received the protection of park status in 1940. After fording several branches of Redwood Creek, the path joins Redwood Canyon Trail (6100/3.0), then switchbacks up to return to Redwood Saddle (6180/0.3).

Having emerged from your walk among giant sequoias, you might imagine what it was like in the late Tertiary period when a forest this size would have been a small swath of the giant sequoia forest that covered much of western North America.

T114   Buena Vista Peak Day Hike

This family excursion in Kings Canyon National Park offers neophyte hikers the excitement of peakbagging with the thrill of edging near a summit's precipice or the pleasure of relaxed viewing from the ample space atop.

Distance   2.0 miles, round trip
Steep Ascents   None
Elevation Gain   405 feet
Skills   Easy route finding; easy-to-moderate hiking
Seasons   Spring, summer, fall
Map   USGS 7.5-min. *General Grant Grove*
Trailhead   83. See car tour T112.
Description   From the parking area (7200/0.0) off Generals Highway on the **Buena Vista Peak Trail**, you switchback once then

ascend moderately in the shade of white fir, ponderosa pine and incense cedar; occasional groupings of manzanita occupy open spaces. You soon curve among cabin-sized boulders—some seem precariously balanced. You will see a few bitter cherry bushes here— they occur also along the roadside of Generals Highway, sometimes in thickets. Identify the bush by the leaves: oblong and roundish at the tips, bunched on young, shiny red twigs; and by the flowers: loosely clustered, five-petaled, white with many

stamens. The blooms cast an almondlike fragrance. In late summer animals enjoy the bitter red berries.

Hiking generally south, aided by granite steps, you cross exfoliating slabs where rocks line the path, then traverse below the bulging peak. With the help of a switchback, then another set of stone steps, you ascend the ridge northwest, slanting up to climb to the summit (7605/1.0).

A stunted Jeffrey pine struggles to grow on the granodiorite rock, and huge boulders define the top. To the east you can see Buck Rock Lookout (T116) sitting on its stone pillar; to the south stretches Big Baldy Ridge (T115); and far beyond from north to south the jagged peaks of the High Sierra appear in profile; to the west you can make out the rounded tops of giant sequoias along Redwood Mountain's crest (T113).

Chimney Rock's "campanile' and "martello tower"

T115   Big Baldy Ridge Day Hike

An exciting trek for all hikers, this traverse along Big Baldy Ridge in Kings Canyon National Park offers a fascinating array of botanical, geological and ornithological attractions as well as photogenic scenery. Beyond the last peak where most will stop, a finger ridge extension lures you to the limits.

Distance   5.8 miles, round trip
Steep Ascents   None
Elevation Gain   900 feet
Skills   Easy route finding; easy-to-moderate hiking; Class 5 pitches optional
Seasons   Spring, summer, fall
Map   USGS 7.5-min. *General Grant Grove*
Trailhead   84. See car tour T112.
Description   From a parking area (7580/ 0.0) near the Big Meadows Road, where the Generals Highway curves across a slight saddle, the **Big Baldy Trail** climbs among chinquapin and snow brush to quickly enter the park. The ascent varies from easy to moderate with a touch of steepness. The path leaves the cross-country ski markers and

curves west of Hill 7879. Here the slopes show a wedge of hornfels, schist and purer volcanic rock.

Traveling along the crest, you glimpse nosegays of phlox in the red fir forest. You may hear a resonant "boom—boom—boom." If particularly fortunate, you may see the instigator of those owllike sounds: a Blue Grouse standing on a rock expanding and contracting air sacs on each side of his neck. They resemble a bunch of yellow corn kernels when inflated. He could be advertising his territorial claim or calling for a mate. This bluish-gray 1½-foot bird with bright orangish-red eye combs, feeds on pine needles during winter. In summer he seeks lower ground for insects, seeds and berries.

Stories about birds who mate for life, show affection and share family duties do not refer to the Grouse. After a pompous display, he impregnates the female and leaves—but you do have to admire the "booms" that resound throughout the mountains.

You soon round a jutting ridge and from there see the sheer, fluted facade of Big Baldy, presenting Class 5 climbs. Next contour back on the crest again where you transfer from metasedimentary to granitic terrain, then zigzag up a rise to a breathtaking traverse on a brink of exfoliating granite to Big Baldy's benchmark summit (8209/2.2). Here you view the varied horizons of the High Sierra,

the San Joaquin Valley and maybe the Coast Range.

The next peak south beckons, and the path traces 300 feet of rock ridgecrest, zigzagging into timberland. After 0.3 mile it rises by twists and turns on talus slopes to attain Overlook 8169 (8169/0.7). To the southeast you can see the ridge, the domes, "campanile" and "martello tower" on Chimney Rock (T119) that attract climbers. To the south you can see the knife-edged, rock-bound crest that intrigues scramblers, and many find their way 0.2 mile to the jumble of rocks on the slender point of the ridge.

T116   Buck Rock Lookout Day Hike

Balanced atop a bare chiseled pinnacle, breathtaking Buck Rock Lookout is one of the most exhilerating viewpoints in the Southern Sierra.

Distance   0.6 miles, round trip
Steep Ascents   0.1 mile
Elevation Gain   140 feet
Skills   Easy route finding; easy hiking; Class 5 pitches optional
Seasons   Spring, summer, fall
Map   USGS 7.5-min. *Muir Grove*
Trailhead   85. See car tour T112.
Description   You begin your trip to Buck Rock on **SNF Closed Road 13S04B** (8360/0.0) at its fork north from SNF Road 13S04. Stroll north along the spur road several feet, then bypass its locked gate. Continue below a radio relay facility through a red fir forest interspersed with chinquapin clumps. You see Buck Rock looming directly north. A parked car where your road ends at a swale (8360/0.2), indicates the lookout is manned and open during visiting hours. The attendant will be glad to answer questions.

While climbers scan the seamy rock for challenging Class 5 routes, most people elect to climb it via the trail. On **Buck Rock Trail 29E09**, you start north from the swale, zigzag and then climb several gulf-bridging flights of giddying stairs. Midway up, a gate bars further progress during winter and also ensures the lookout employee's privacy after visiting hours. Even if the gate is locked when

you arrive, the climb to it is exciting and the view rewarding.

Shortly thereafter, you top the rock and take in the immense sweep of landscape visible from the lookout's vantage point (8500/0.1).

Breathtaking Buck Rock Lookout

T117   Weaver Lake Day Hike

The rough, ice-carved face of imposing Shell Mountain rises abruptly from the south shore of Weaver Lake's smooth surface. Occasionally brook trout puncture the lake's calm, sending rings to lap against the jumbled boulders and forested shore.

Distance   7.2 miles, round trip
Steep Ascents   None
Elevation Gain   1110 feet
Skills   Easy route finding; easy-to-moderate hiking
Seasons   Spring, summer, fall
Map   USGS 7.5-min. *Muir Grove*
Trailhead   86. See car tour T112.
Description   From the Big Meadows Road (7600/0.0), *Jennie Lake Trail 29E05* heads southeast, touches a velvet finger of Big Meadows, then cuts within the edge of Big Meadows Campground and across the meadows' soggy outlet stream. The path gently rises at the foot of one of the many exfoliating domes on this rolling tableland, then it turns to follow a frolicking branch of Big Meadows Creek 0.1 mile before crossing it. The path ascends atop, then curves away from another expansive dome—note this point for your return trip lest you veer off course.

Tiny blue-eyed Mary and yellow dwarf monkey flowers announce the end of winter along the path, which is sparsely shaded by Jeffrey pines. The trail curves around a ridge offering open views of the lofty mountains of Kings Canyon National Park, then descends to pass an unmapped path forking north to Big Meadows Campground. A destination sign and register box at Fox Meadow mark this fork. Shortly, at a junction (8160/2.1) where Jennie Lake Trail turns right, you take *Weaver Lake Trail 30E09* straight ahead.

Immediately, heading east, you boulder-hop a purling creek followed shortly by an entrance into Jennie Lakes Wilderness. You then ford a fan of seasonal creeks and the outlet stream of Weaver Lake, all uniting downstream to form Weaver Creek and flow into Big Meadows stream. Presently you arrive at a rock-lined, unsigned junction (8620/1.2)—you will see diverging tree blazes. Here you turn right onto Weaver Lake's *access trail*.

Climb south on the gently ascending path, breach a curtain of red fir trees and approach handsome Weaver Lake (8707/0.3), back-dropped by the craggy, colorful face of towering Shell Mountain. Several campsites spread in clearings among the boulders of the Labrador tea-lined north shore. Shell Mountain peakbaggers (T118:Ex-W), if at all visible, appear as specks atop the mountain's 9594-foot apex.

Enchanting Weaver Lake tucked at foot of Shell Mountain

T118   Jennie Lakes Wilderness Backpack
With Excursion W: Shell Mountain

In 1984, a 10,500 acre expanse of picturesque lakes, streams, meadows, forests and mountains became Jennie Lakes Wilderness. This loop trip just north and west of Sequoia and Kings Canyon national parks, exposes you to many of the wonders of this wilderness.

Distance   20.2 miles, semiloop trip
Steep Ascents   0.2 mile
Elevation Gain   3430 feet
Skills   Easy route finding
Seasons   Spring, summer, fall
Map   USGS 7.5-min. *Muir Grove*
Trailhead   86. See car tour T112.
Description   The beginning of this trip is described in T117.

Southeastbound 29E05 Trail Log

T117 Prkg area	7600	0.0
Weaver Lk Tr	8160	2.1

Leaving the junction with Weaver Lake Trail, the path on which you will return to this point, you turn abruptly right to hike on *Jennie Lake Trail 29E05*. From here to Poop Out Pass you climb around the flanks of Shell Mountain, ascending almost continuously on a moderate grade. In a dark forest of red fir, lodgepole and western white pine, you pass into Jennie Lakes Wilderness, hop across the spring-fed outlet stream of Poison Meadow, then saunter past the meadow, which lies laterally on the east side of the trail. Beyond a pocket glade, you leave the trees to enjoy views southwest of Big Baldy Ridge (T115), Chimney Rock (T119) and the quilted plains of San Joaquin Valley.

Turning east around a Shell Mountain ridge, the rocky path descends among pinemat manzanita to cross a seasonal headwaters branch of Stony Creek. It then climbs past a T junction (9040/2.7) with a 5.0-mile, ridge-straddling trail to Stony Campground, another trailhead access to this wilderness. Your trail next arrives at well-named Poop Out Pass (9140/0.3). This broad pass offers camping room or places to stash packs for those who wish to enjoy the supreme 180° views from atop Shell Mountain.

Excursion W: Shell Mountain

Gaze down the abrupt precipice from the top of Shell Mountain to Weaver Lake, then beyond to the wider, exhilarating views.

Distance   2.4 miles, round trip
Steep Ascents   0.2 mile
Elevation Gain   455 feet
Skills   Easy-to-intermediate route finding; Class 1 climbing
Description   The forested backside of Shell Mountain to the northwest is barely visible from Poop Out Pass (9140/0.0), whereas the slabby slopes of Peak 9567 to the south beckon. To find the route, face northwest, take a compass bearing, and make your way *cross-country* through a tangle of lodgepole pines and red firs for 0.3 mile on the spacious pass. Then climb steeply up to the ridgecrest—take note of where you arrived for your return trip.

Now you turn right to curve around the top of a canyon that cleaves Shell Mountain between you and the mountain's summit. The summit, the highest pancake of granite rocks, sits at the south end of the curve. An easy ascent of the peak (9594/1.2) reveals a box with a passel of notes and signatures, adding an interesting dimension to the climb.

From the summit, look directly down to Weaver Lake, then northwest to Big Meadows; raise your sights to Buck Rock Lookout atop an obelisk rock (T116). Look due north to the deep canyons of South Fork and Middle Fork Kings rivers flanking the Monarch Divide peaks. You see other peaks arrayed against the horizon as well.

*   *   *   *   *

Several trails go down the canyon beyond Poop Out—all steep. The best choice, probably the newest trail, descends along the ridge and switchbacks. Beyond the switchback it crosses a snowmelt creek where the fragmented paths meet. Now the path traverses east, largely on exfoliating granodiorite slopes. Views of the ragged Sierra appear. Then curving southeast, it rises easily through forest to an unmarked junction (9012/2.0) with a short path to Jennie Lake, prior to the lake's outlet.

In 1897 the head ranger for the Kings River District, S.L.N. Ellis named this lake for his wife. Cradled next to the fractured facade of a Kings Kaweah Divide peak, Jennie Ellis Lake rests in all its splendor. Campsites gather on the red fir-shaded north shore; Mountain Chickadees and Solitary Vireos seranade early risers; brook and rainbow trout swim in the placid water.

Upon leaving, a climb of five switchbacks takes you east from Jennie Lake's north shore, then the trail curves right reaching a saddle. The ensuing path touches the park border and stays near or on the crest, offering en route a few views southeast of deeply-gouged Mount Silliman. The path soon reaches JO Pass (9410/1.7). Ellis named this pass for the letters "J O" cut on a tree, probably by a sheepherder. (The trail from the pass to the south takes hikers in about 8.0 miles to Lodgepole Campground.)

You turn sharply left on *JO Pass Trail 30E11*, and head north past a brook and campsites over peeling rock and boulder steps. You descend easily in a stately forest to a boulder-hop ford of a Boulder Creek tributary. Generous campsites sit nearby. In the upstream meadow close to the receding snowline if you are hiking early season, you will see a garden of marsh marigolds in bloom. A 4- to 12-inch leafless stem supports this bowl-shaped flower of six to nine pure white petallike sepals around a sometimes large yellow center cushion of many stamens. Its round leaves grow on a long stem. When in bud, this lovely flower looks pale blue.

A gain of elevation on switchbacks and an easy walk take you to a junction (8980/3.1) with *Weaver Lake Trail 30E09*, onto which you turn left. (If you took a right turn you would travel via Rowell Meadow to Horse Corral Meadow on Big Meadows Road, 7.0 miles east of your trailhead.)

Heading west, you drop sometimes steeply, then turn south to slant down west-facing slopes in Boulder Creek's scenic headwater bowl. At the south curve of the bowl you ford four branches of Boulder Creek, often requiring a wade across, but in summer boulder-hopping will suffice. Boulder Creek gathers numerous streams to eventually become a major tributary to the South Fork Kings River.

After the creek crossings you regain your lost elevation by the time you reach a pair of saddles. Beyond the second and broader saddle, you descend for 0.6 mile to the forked junction (8620/4.4) with Weaver Lake's access trail. If you plan to visit Weaver Lake, watch for the rocks that line the unsigned junction to your left. Should you see a #3 tacked on a tree, you have missed it. On the lake's *access trail*, you weave among red fir trees to the north shore with its several campsites (8707/0.3).

Weaver is smaller than Jennie Lake but similarly striking. Both lakes cuddle against towering glacial-scooped rocks: here the face of Shell Mountain. At both, rock shadows dance on the rippling water and white-flowered Labrador tea edge their forested shores; both lakes invite an extended stay.

Upon returning to the *Weaver Lake Trail 30E09* (8620/0.3), you turn left and head west, pass out of Jennie Lakes Wilderness, cross a bouncing brook and meet your incoming route at a T junction (8160/1.2) next to the brook. Follow your footsteps on *Jennie Lake Trail 29E05* to your starting point (7600/2.1).

T119 Chimney Rock Climb

Peakbaggers will delight in this climb. Their only route involves a scramble up talus on Chimney Rock's steep northeast slope. Rock climbers will delight in the sheer walls that fall away sharply on all but the talus side. Easy accessibility, inspiring views and the exhilarating challenge make the ascent exciting for both types of climbers.

Distance 0.8 miles, round trip
Steep Ascents 0.4 mile
Elevation Gain 615 feet
Skills Intermediate route finding; Class 2 climbing (Class 3–5 pitches optional)
Seasons Spring, summer, fall
Map USGS 7.5-min. *Muir Grove*
Trailhead 87. See car tour T112. From Generals Highway (0.0/0.0) turn south on paved **SNF Road 14S29**, unsigned at the highway. Check your mileage. Your road crosses Woodard Creek and arrives at a signed junction (0.5/0.5); bear right and traverse south on steep slopes past spur roads. Leave the road (2.8/3.3) on a short spur to a cul-de-sac, **TH87**, just before a sharp turn north followed by a marked descent.
Description A deeply rutted **use path** (7100/0.0) is located about 25 feet south of the pavement above the cul-de-sac saddle. It climbs west amid a logged red fir forest, then slants up behind a row of adjoining cylindrical concrete tanks, each with its own peaked roof. The path zigzags steeply, then

leads to the crest of a visible shoulder on the southeast ridge emanating from Chimney Rock. However, your route leaves the path (7530/0.3) about 150 feet below the crest where you see the jumble of rocks to the right on the slope of Chimney Rock.

Now you scramble **cross-country** hands-over-feet up the boulders, avoiding chinquapin and Brewer oak, to the peak of Chimney Rock (7711/0.1). From this lofty fortress Big Baldy Ridge (T115) stretches immediately west-northwest, while an array of High Sierra turrets and jags form the distant eastern horizon. The "campanile" and "martello tower" stand in the southern foreground, separated from you by a gulf.

The obvious path leading southwest from where you turned off the path is the best route for rock climbers. It crosses the ridgecrest in 150 feet, then weaves down a brief, steep stretch in a manzanita-packed col and exits west via a short granite ledge. The ledge adjoins a timbered swale between a tall campanilelike spire and a martello-tower-topped hidden precipice where you begin your climb.

T120 General Grant Tree Day Hike

Wheelchair access and nearly level pavement make the General Grant Tree in Kings Canyon National Park accessible to all. It was proclaimed the Nation's Christmas Tree by President Calvin Coolidge, and each December a tour leaves Sanger, California to gather for a Christmas celebration at its snowy feet. President Eisenhower declared this tree a Living National Shrine in memory of Americans who died in war. Although the General Grant Tree measures less in volume than the General Sherman Tree, its symmetry and full crown place it ahead of the Sherman in beauty.

Distance 0.4 mile, loop trip
Steep Ascents None
Elevation Gain Negligible
Skills Easy route finding; easy hiking
Seasons All year

Map USGS 7.5-min. *General Grant Grove*
Trailhead 88. See car tour 112. Turn left on **Grant Tree Road** (0.0/0.0) near Grant Grove Village. Drive past a campground and

a picnic area to Grant Tree parking lot (1.2/1.2), **TH88**.

Description   To fully enjoy General Grant Grove, purchase a brochure for the self-guided trail at the Visitor Center. However, signs identify tree names, and informational plaques rest at special points of interest. The sequoia groves in these parks were explored during the Civil War, which explains why the largest trees are named for that war's heros. In the early 1900s it became fashionable to name the trees after states. Trees no longer receive names.

Begin on the right fork of *Grant Tree Trail* at the north end of the parking area (6320/0.0); the guided tour, accessible to all including wheelchairs, loops counterclockwise.

You soon arrive at a point where the entire General Grant Tree can be photographed, and everyone toting a camera takes aim. Other tree species identified for you among the revered sequoias include white fir, incense cedar, sugar and ponderosa pine and Pacific dogwood.

In a short time you arrive at the General Grant Tree, the third largest living thing on earth. It has been growing for an estimated 2000 years and reaches the height of a 27-story building: 267.4 feet. Its base would lap across a three-lane highway. Try to allow time to absorb its enormity and beauty. While on the loop, take note of the Robert E. Lee Tree; it ranks 13th by volume. Also note the California Tree; its top was set afire by lightning in 1967. It took a tree climber dragging a fire hose to put out the fire. Very few sequoias have been climbed.

At the top of the loop you find the Gamlin Cabin. Constructed in 1872, this artifact of man was built by the Gamlin brothers, lumbermen who claimed 160 of these acres. It was moved a few times, used periodically and has been partially reconstructed. Shortly beyond you see the Centennial Stump. In 1875 a cross section of this giant sequoia was sent to America's Centennial Exhibition in Philadelphia. No one believed its great size; it was laughed at and called the "California Hoax." Current measurements reveal that it would not have been listed among the greatest giants.

The Fallen Monarch, hollowed by fire before it fell, once housed people and animals and now serves as a tunnel tree, a further demonstration of the mammoth size of these trees. Circle back to the parking area (6320/0.4).

An ideal follow-up to the self-guided tour is the 1.5-mile stroll on the North Grove Loop Trail found at the west end of the bus and RV parking area. Here you can view majestic giants of the Grant Grove away from the Grant Tree crowds.

T121   Boole Tree Day Hike

The singular Boole Tree grows in a forest of stumps at Converse Basin. Before logging, this forest was the largest giant sequoia grove in the world. Nearly 75% of the wood from felled trees was wasted; the rest ended up ingloriously as fence material or roof shingles. This last trip in the book illustrates the need for constant vigilance of our national treasures.

Distance   2.9 miles, loop trip
Steep Ascents   None
Elevation Gain   600 feet
Skills   Easy route finding; easy-to-moderate hiking
Seasons   Spring, summer, fall
Map   USGS 7.5-min. *Hume*
Trailhead   89. See car tour T112. Unpaved *Converse Basin Road* (SNF Road 13S55)

(0.0/0.0) leads north from the end of this book's coverage of Highway 180, 1.3 miles north of Cherry Gap. In 0.3 mile, roads begin to branch to the right and left; you descend on the middle road. To the left, a half mile from the highway, soars a 133-foot snag believed to be the dead tree on which John Muir counted 4000 annual growth rings. If the count were confirmed, it would be the oldest known giant sequoia. Its age can not be verified due to extensive burns and decay, but by increment borings and estimations its age at death is thought to be between 3000 and 3500 years. The oldest giant sequoia known, near the Chicago Stump west of Cherry Gap, was 3200 years old when cut.

Continue into Converse Basin. Shrubs and trees have hidden the stumps that once stood so harshly, except at Stump Meadow (1.8/1.8), where the ground water is too great for regrowth. The road then becomes rougher and ends in a cul-de-sac (0.8/2.6) at **TH89**. **Description** From the cul-de-sac take *Boole Tree Trail 28E02* (6260/0.0) to the right. Ascend eastward easily then moderately in heavy foliage along the drainage of a little creek. Cross the creek twice, the second time at the head of a slender meadow, then switchback to a saddle. Here you meet a *lateral* (6740/1.0), on which you descend to the Boole Tree (6680/0.2) and its interpretive plaque.

The Boole Tree sits in the northeast corner of what was the 2600-acre Converse Basin Sequoia Grove. Nearly every tree in the basin was cut between 1897 and 1907, mostly by the Sanger Lumber Company, which realized no profit. The logs were milled in the basin, then sent 54 miles by flume to Sanger, where they were refined. That was the longest flume in the world—it since burned in part and the rest was dismantled.

The one specimen tree that was left bears the name of the general manager of the lumber company who oversaw the grove's destruction, Frank A. Boole—honored like a conqueror! The impressive tree, once thought to be the largest in the world, now ranks eighth, but remains the largest in a national forest. It stands 269 feet tall with the greatest ground perimeter of all sequoias—113 feet. For decades it stood alone overlooking Kings River canyon. Now trees have grown around it, many of which are second growth sequoias. It will take two thousand years for them to grow to the magnificence of the ones that were lost.

Return to the saddle, where you continue to the right on the *Boole Tree Trail* (6740/0.2). Rising above the saddle you see the top of Boole Tree in the canyon to the right, then the distant jagged Sierra peaks. You soon descend west along a ridge, passing a wooden building with antennae and solar panels, then walk through plantations of planted pines. After a cattlegate, you arrive at a viewpoint of Kings River canyon (6640/0.6). Here, you pause before losing elevation on short switchbacks to travel south, where you complete the loop (6260/0.9).

After visiting numerous cathedral groves of giant sequoias from the Trail of 100 Giants in the Western Divide mountains, 60 air miles south, to Grants Grove in Kings Canyon National Park—all impressive, all saved from the saw—it seems appropriate that the last trip in this book visits this individual sequoia. Seeing the Boole Tree's splendid presence stand where a grove of thousands near its size once stood generates a spirit of thankfulness to those who gave their time and money to preserve the remaining groves enjoyed by so many, and to those today who continue the effort.

This concludes an exhausting 877.4 miles of trails and cross-country routes with an unbelievable 186,126 feet of elevation gain, and an extensive 787.5 miles of car tours in the beautiful, spacious Southern Sierra.

Part 3
Appendix

Tripfinder Table

Trip Number	Car	Bicycle	A-T Bike*	Day Hike	Climb	Backpack	Equestrian*	Side Trip	Winter	Spring	Summer	Fall	Distance (Miles)	Steep Assents (Miles)	Elevation Gain (Feet)	Route Finding	Climbing (Class)	Difficulty (Day Hikes)	One Way	Shuttle	Round Trip	Loop	Semiloop
			Activity							Season					Data						Type		
Section 1 Highway 56 to Highway 178																							
1								•	•	•	•	•		0	0								
2	•	•							•	•	•	•	35.0	0	4095	E			•				
3	•	•							•	•	•	•	28.0	0	2735	E			•				
4			•	•					•	•		•	4.6	0	830	E		E-M			•		
5						•	•		•	•		•	20.2	0.2	3700	E					•		
6	•	•							•	•	•	•	25.0	0	4245	E			•				
Ex-A	•	•					•		•	•	•	•	6.6	0	360	E					•		
7				•					•	•	•	•	1.2	0.1	585	E-I	2				•		
8				•					•	•	•	•	1.0	0.5	855	E	2				•		
9				•					•	•	•	•	0.8	0.1	400	E	2				•		
10	•		•	•			•		•	•		•	10.4	0	1965	E		M			•		
11	•	•							•	•	•	•	39.7	0	6170	E			•				
Ex-B	•	•					•		•	•	•	•	8.0	0	930	E					•		
12		•		•			•		•	•	•	•	5.2	0.1	1210	I	1				•		
13	•								•	•	•	•	33.2	0	1780	E			•				
14	•	•							•	•	•	•	13.4	0	395	E			•				
15			•	•					•	•		•	5.4	0	970	E		E-M			•		
16			•			•	•			•		•	18.6	0.9	4430	E-I						•	
Section 2 Highway 178 to Parker Pass Drive (J22)																							
17								•	•	•	•	•		0	0	E							
18	•	•							•	•	•	•	68.2	0	3700	E			•				
19								•	•	•	•	•		0	0	E							
20			•	•					•	•		•	6.6	0	700	E		E-M			•		
21	•	•							•	•	•	•	35.4	0	1350	E							•
EX-C	•	•							•	•	•	•	4.0	0	320	E					•		
EX-D	•								•	•	•	•	1.6	0	100	E					•		
EX-E	•								•	•	•	•	0.4	0	120	E					•		
22			•	•			•		•	•		•	2.8	0	405			E			•		
23			•						•	•		•	6.0	0	200	E		E			•		
24			•			•	•		•	•		•	13.9	0.4	2540	E				•			

Trip Number	Car	Bicycle	A-T Bike*	Day Hike	Climb	Backpack	Equestrian*	Side Trip	Winter	Spring	Summer	Fall	Distance (Miles)	Steep Assents (Miles)	Elevation Gain (Feet)	Route Finding	Climbing (Class)	Difficulty (Day Hikes)	One Way	Shuttle	Round Trip	Loop	Semiloop
	Activity								Season				Data						Type				
25			●	●			●		●			●	5.2	0.2	920	E		E-M			●		
26			●	●			●		●			●	6.8	0	1250	E		E-M			●		
27	●								●	●	●	●	45.7	0	5515	E			●				
28				●					●	●	●	●	6.0	0.1	900	E		E-M			●		
29						●			●	●			3.8	0.5	1975	I	1				●		
30			●	●						●	●	●	3.2	0	730	E		E-M				●	
31	●		●	●		●				●	●	●	6.4	0	600	E		E				●	
32	●									●	●	●	27.6	0	2225	E			●				
33	●		●							●	●	●	14.0	0	1650	E			●				
EX-F	●		●							●	●	●	4.0	0	735	E					●		
34	●									●	●	●	36.3	0	3915	E						●	
34			●							●	●	●	29.3	0	3915	E						●	
35					●					●	●	●	3.2	0.5	1204	I	2				●		
36					●					●	●	●	8.2	1.2	3300	I	2				●		
37				●						●	●	●	3.2	0	1105	E		M			●		
38			●	●			●			●	●	●	2.4	0.5	1080	E		M-S			●		
39				●						●	●	●	2.4	0	350	E		E-M			●		
40						●				●	●	●	1.8	0.1	510	I	2				●		
41	●	●								●	●	●	51.0	0	5900	E			●				
42		●				●	●			●	●	●	14.6	0.3	3500	I						●	
43				●						●		●	4.6	0.1	1060	E-I		M			●		
44				●						●	●	●	0.6	0.1	375	E	1				●		
Section 3 Parker Pass Drive (J22) to Sequoia National Park																							
45				●						●	●	●	0.8	0.2	520	E	2				●		
46	●	●								●	●	●	25.1	0	4060	E			●				
47				●						●	●	●	0.6	0	100	E		E				●	
48			●	●			●			●	●	●	1.2	0	545	E		E-M			●		
49			●			●	●			●	●	●	11.0	0.3	2230	E				●			
50				●						●	●	●	0.4	0	100	E		E			●		
51				●						●	●	●	4.0	0.1	1165	E		M			●		
52			●	●			●			●	●	●	9.4	0.2	2045	E		M-S			●		
EX-G				●						●	●	●	0.8	0.1	305	E	2				●		

Trip Number	Car	Bicycle	A-T Bike*	Day Hike	Climb	Backpack	Equestrian*	Side Trip	Winter	Spring	Summer	Fall	Distance (Miles)	Steep Assents (Miles)	Elevation Gain (Feet)	Route Finding	Climbing (Class)	Difficulty (Day Hikes)	One Way	Shuttle	Round Trip	Loop	Semiloop
													Activity										
53			●	●			●			●	●	●	4.3	0	0	E		E		●			
54			●	●			●			●	●	●	5.2	0	1035	E		E-M		●			
55			●	●			●			●	●	●	6.4	0.2	1370	E		M			●		
56				●						●	●	●	1.8	0.4	765	I	4				●		
57						●	●			●	●	●	30.4	0	5675	E					●		
Ex-H			●				●			●	●	●	4.0	0	225	E		E-M			●		
58						●	●			●	●	●	45.2	1.6	10,200	E-I						●	
Ex-I				●						●	●	●	1.0	0.4	755	I	2				●		
Ex-J				●						●	●	●	2.2	0.1	510	I	2				●		
Ex-K				●						●	●	●	1.4	0.3	550	E	1-2				●		
59						●	●			●	●	●	50.4	0.5	9110	E							●
Ex-L				●						●	●	●	1.6	0.2	605	I	1				●		
60						●	●			●	●	●	20.0	0	4350	E-I						●	
61		●	●				●			●	●	●	1.6	0	515	E		E-M			●		
Ex-M				●						●	●	●	2.0	0.2	500	I	1				●		
62						●	●			●	●	●	19.0	0	3740	E					●		
Ex-N				●						●	●	●	2.2	0.3	745	E	2				●		
63						●	●			●	●	●	35.9	0.8	6545	E-I						●	
Ex-O				●			●			●	●	●	0.6	0	140	E	1				●		
64	●	●								●	●	●	21.3	0	2025	E			●				
65				●						●		●	2.4	0.7	1390	I		M-S			●		
66				●						●		●	1.2	0.2	700	I	2				●		
67				●						●	●	●	1.6	0	200	E		E			●		
68				●						●	●	●	1.6	0	350	E-I		E-M			●		
69				●						●	●	●	4.6	0.2	1010	E		M-S			●		
70				●			●			●	●	●	4.8	0	1060	E		M			●		
71				●			●			●	●	●	11.4	0	2170	E		M-S			●		
72						●				●	●	●	10.8	0.1	2200	I	3-4				●		
73						●	●			●	●	●	27.2	0.1	3100	E						●	
74	●								●	●	●	●	40.8	0	6515	E			●				
75	●	●							●	●	●	●	28.7	0	1900	E			●				
76			●	●			●		●	●	●	●	7.2	0	950	E		E-M			●		

Trip Number	Car	Bicycle	A-T Bike*	Day Hike	Climb	Backpack	Equestrian*	Side Trip	Winter	Spring	Summer	Fall	Distance (Miles)	Steep Assents (Miles)	Elevation Gain (Feet)	Route Finding	Climbing (Class)	Difficulty (Day Hikes)	One Way	Shuttle	Round Trip	Loop	Semiloop
77	●									●	●	●	23.3	0	4000	E			●				
78				●						●	●	●	2.6	0	500	E		E-M			●		
79				●						●	●	●	8.8	0.1	1500	E		M				●	
80				●						●	●	●	1.8	0	450	E		E-M				●	
81				●						●	●	●	6.6	0	1440	E-I		E-M				●	
82						●				●	●	●	10.0	0.7	3000	I	3				●		
83						●	●			●	●	●	23.2	0.5	5440	E						●	
Section 4 Sequoia and Kings Canyon National Parks & Surrounding Area																							
84	●								●	●	●	●	57.1	0	6500	E			●				
85	●	●							●	●	●	●	30.5	0	4835	E			●				
86						●	●			●	●	●	27.7	2.8	6100	E							●
87				●				●	●	●		●	10.2	0.2	2360	E		M-S			●		
88	●	●							●	●	●	●	7.1	0	585	E			●				
89	●									●	●	●	24.6	0	6655	E			●				
90				●				●		●	●	●	9.2	0.3	2847	E		M-S			●		
91						●	●			●		●	21.7	0.3	3465	E				●			
92				●						●	●	●	2.6	0	575	E		E-M			●		
93						●	●			●	●	●	30.7	0	6420	E				●			
Ex-P				●				●		●	●	●	8.0	0.2	1375	E	1	M-S			●		
Ex-Q				●				●		●	●	●	2.0	0	160	E		E			●		
Ex-R				●						●	●	●	1.6	0.3	820	E		M-S			●		
Ex-S					●					●	●	●	1.2	0.6	1460	E	1-2				●		
94						●				●	●	●	23.8	0.4	3450	I					●		
Ex-T				●						●	●	●	2.6	0	520	I					●		
95				●				●		●	●	●	2.4	0	400	E		E			●		
96				●				●		●	●	●	10.8	0.2	2190	E-I		M-S			●		
97				●				●		●	●	●	6.8	0.1	2210	E		M-S			●		
98				●				●		●	●	●	7.6	0.2	2225	E-I		M-S			●		
99						●				●	●	●	24.8	0.7	6700	E							●
Ex-U					●					●	●	●	1.2	0.3	750	E	2				●		
100				●					●	●		●	6.8	0	1500	E		E-M			●		
101				●					●	●		●	4.8	0	1020	E		E-M			●		

Trip Number	Activity								Season				Data						Type				
	Car	Bicycle	A-T Bike*	Day Hike	Climb	Backpack	Equestrian*	Side Trip	Winter	Spring	Summer	Fall	Distance (Miles)	Steep Assents (Miles)	Elevation Gain (Feet)	Route Finding	Climbing (Class)	Difficulty (Day Hikes)	One Way	Shuttle	Round Trip	Loop	Semiloop
102						●	●		●	●		●	11.0	0	2400	E					●		
103				●						●	●	●	0.6	0	265	E		M			●		
104				●						●	●	●	5.4	0	750	E		E-M				●	
105				●						●	●	●	1.6	0	0	E		E			●		
106				●						●	●	●	1.6	0	0	E		E				●	
107				●						●	●	●	2.0	0	250	E		E				●	
108				●				●		●	●	●	6.6	0	1645	E		E-M			●		
109						●				●	●	●	18.3	0.6	4100	I							●
Ex-V				●						●	●	●	3.8	0.6	1910	E	2				●		
110				●						●	●	●	3.4	0	610	E		E-M			●		
111				●						●	●	●	3.4	0	715	E		E-M			●		
112	●								●	●	●	●	38.9	0	6850	E			●				
113				●				●		●	●	●	9.9	0	1880	E		M-S				●	
114				●						●	●	●	2.0	0	405	E		E-M			●		
115				●						●	●	●	5.8	0	900	E		E-M			●		
116				●						●	●	●	0.6	0.1	140	E		E			●		
117				●				●		●	●	●	7.2	0	1110	E		E-M			●		
118						●	●			●	●	●	20.2	0.2	3430	E							●
Ex-W				●				●		●	●	●	2.4	0.2	455	E-I	1				●		
119				●						●	●	●	0.8	0.4	615	I	2				●		
120		●								●	●	●	0.4	0	0	E		E				●	
121			●	●				●		●	●	●	2.9	0	600	E		E-M				●	

* Tours, trips and excursions that can double for all-terrain bicycle and/or equestrian use.
Ex– Optional excursion of prior trip.
E– Easy; I– Intermediate; A– Advanced; M– Moderate; S– Strenuous

Glossary

Arête Narrow, rugged, usually glacial-carved, mountain ridge

Bearbagging Method of counterbalancing two food bags hung from tree branch with bags 12 feet from ground and 10 feet from tree trunk

Belay Secure person or object by rope

Bench Comparatively level platform or terrace, sometimes raised, breaking degree of slope

Blaze Mark carved on, or object nailed to, tree to mark trail

BLM Bureau of Land Management, U.S. Department of Interior

Blowdown Tree toppled by wind

Bushwhack Move through country covered with scrub

Cable Wire strung between two trees on which food bags can be hung out of bear's reach

Cairn (pronounced kern) Many rocks stacked to mark summit, junction or point of interest

Cirque U-shaped basin resulting from ice action at head of glaciated canyon

Clear-cut Area cut and cleared of everything by loggers, leaving only bare soil

Cow path Trail resulting from repeated use by cattle

Cross-country Across land without a trail

Cul-de-sac End of road with turn-around area

CDF&G California Department of Fish and Game

Dry camp Campsite with no nearby water

Duck Low stack of several (usually three) rocks to mark trail

Food storage lockers Heavy metal bear-proof boxes placed at campsites and popular camping areas in Sequoia and Kings Canyon national parks

Glade Open space in forest

Glen Narrow secluded valley

M'cyclepath Motorcycle trail open to all users

Moraine Rocks, etc., carried by glacier and deposited at its lower end (terminal moraine) or its sides (lateral moraines)

MHDSF Mountain Home Demonstration State Forest

Multi-use Term used by agencies to designate areas open to many uses: logging, grazing, mining and recreation

OHV Off highway vehicle

Packers' campsite Ample campsite developed by packers, usually have crude table, stools, grill and often littered

Pass Passage between two mountains

Peakbagger Term applied to person who climbs to tops of peaks

Plate tectonics Theory stating earth's crust divided into irregular mobile sections called plates

Prospect Place where mineral deposit was sought

Riparian Flora, usually trees, lining watercourse

Saddle Horizontal section on ridge between two higher points

Scree Sheet of coarse, loose, decomposed granular rock on mountain side

Selective logging Only selected trees cut in grove

Sierra crest High ridges and peaks forming eastern edge of Sierra

Skiing Alpine: down hill; nordic: cross-country

Slash Tree debris left by loggers

Snag Upright, dead tree

SNF Sequoia National Forest, U.S. Department of Agriculture

Stock driveway Path used to drive cattle to and from cattle allotments

Swale Low area of land, sometimes marshy

Switchback Sharp-angled curve reversing direction of trail or road on steep slope

Tailings Rock debris left at mine site

Talus Collection of boulders that fell on or at base of slope

Tarn Small lake, usually one that fills cirque

Topographic map (Topo) Detailed map indicating elevations by contour lines

Traverse Move across land such as a slope, usually at slight angle

Trending   Term used in this book as ridges decreasing in elevation toward a direction or canyons narrowing in width toward a direction

Use trail   Nonconstructed trail developed by repeated use

Vale   Valley

Xerophyte   Plant adapted to very dry climate

Zigzag   Short wide curve in trail usually in series on slope

Bibliography
Biology

Behler, John L., and King, F. Wayne, 1979. *The Audubon Society Field Guide to North American Reptiles and Amphibians*. New York: Alfred A. Knopf, 743pp.

Cutter, Ralph, 1984. *Sierra Trout Guide*. Portland: Frank Amato Publications, 108pp.

Drummond, Roger, 1990. *Ticks and What You Can Do About Them*. Berkeley: Wilderness Press, 65pp.

Fisk, Leonard O., 1969. *Golden Trout of the High Sierra*. Sacramento: California Department of Fish and Game, 15pp.

Flint, Wendell D., 1987. *To Find the Biggest Tree*. Three Rivers: Sequoia Natural History Association, Inc., 116pp.

Hartesveldt, R. J., et al., 1981. *Giant Sequoias*. Three Rivers: Sequoia Natural History Association, Inc., 77pp.

Klauber, Laurence M., 1972. *Rattlesnakes, Their Habits, Life Histories and Influence on Mankind*, Second Edition. Berkeley: University of California Press, 1536pp.

Little, Elbert L., 1980. The *Audubon Society Field Guide to North American Trees Western Region*. New York: Alfred A. Knopf, 639pp.

Munz, Philip A., 1963. *California Mountain Wildflowers*. Berkeley: University of California Press, 115pp.

Niehaus, Theodore F., 1974. *Sierra Wildflowers Mt. Lassen to Kern Canyon*. Berkeley: University of California Press, 223pp.

Ryser, Fred A. Jr., 1985. *Birds of the Great Basin A Natural History*. Reno: University of Nevada, 604pp.

Spellenberg, Richard, 1979. *The Audubon Society Field Guide to North American Wildflowers Western Region*. New York: Alfred A. Knopf, 862pp.

Stocking, Stephen K., and Rockwell, Jack A., 1989. *Wildflowers of Sequoia and Kings Canyon National Parks*, Revised Edition. Three Rivers: Sequoia Natural History Association, Inc., 48pp.

Storer, Tracy I., and Usinger, Robert L., 1963. *Sierra Nevada Natural History*. Berkeley: University of California Press, 374pp.

Sudworth, George B., 1967. *Forest Trees of the Pacific Slope*. New York: Dover. (1908 reprint with new Foreword and Table of Changes in Nomenclature), 455pp.

Thomas, John Hunter, and Parnell, Dennis R., 1974. *Native Shrubs of the Sierra Nevada California Natural History Guides:34*. Berkeley: University of California Press, 127pp.

Twisselmann, Ernest C., 1967. *A Flora of Kern County, California* (Reprinted from *The Wasmann Journal of Biology, Vol. 25, Nos. 1&2*). San Francisco: The University of San Francisco, 395pp.

Udvardy, Miklos D. F., 1977. *The Audubon*

Society Field Guide to North American Birds Western Region. New York: Alfred A. Knopf, 852pp.

Verner, Jared, and Boss, Allan S. (Technical Coordinators), 1980. California Wildlife and Their Habitats: Western Sierra Nevada, General Technical Report PSW-37. Berkeley: Pacific Southwest Forest and Range Experiment Station, Forest Service, U.S. Department of Agriculture, 439pp.

Geology

Darke, R. M., 1991. BLM Fieldtrip Road Log: Bakersfield Colleqe to White Wolf Grade. Bakersfield: Bureau of Land Management publication, 7pp.

duBray, Edward A., and Dellinger, David A., 1981. Geologic Map of the Golden Trout Wilderness, Southern Sierra Nevada, California. Miscellaneous Field Studies Map MF-1231-A Restin: U.S. Geological Survey

Foster, Robert J., 1971. Physical Geology. Columbus: Charles E. Merrill Publishing Co., 550pp.

Hill, Mary, 1975. Geology of the Sierra Nevada. Berkeley: University of California Press, 232pp.

Jenkins, Olaf P., 1964. Geological Map of California Bakersfield Sheet. Washington DC: Army Map Service, Corps of Engineers, U.S. Army.

Jenkins, Olaf P., 1965. Geological Map of California Fresno Sheet. Washington DC: Army Map Service, Corps of Engineers, U.S. Army.

Matthes, F. E., 1965. Glacial Reconnaissance of Sequoia National Park, California. U.S. Geological Survey Professional Paper 504-A, 58pp.

Moore, James G., and Sesson, Thomas W., 1985. Geologic Map of the Kern Peak Quadrangle, Tulare Country, California: U.S. Geological Survey Map GQ-1584.

Moore, James G., and Sisson, Thomas W., 1987. Geologic Map of the Triple Divide Peak Quadrangle, Tulare County, California. U.S. Geological Survey Map GQ-1636.

Robinson, Russ, 1991. Eastside San Joaquin Valley Fieldtrip. Bakersfield: Bureau of Land Management publication, 12pp.

Ross, Donald C., 1987. Generalized geologic map of the basement rocks of the southern Sierra Nevada, California Open-File Report 87–276 (preliminary report). Menlo Park: U.S. Geological Survey, Department of the Interior, 28pp.

Schaffer, Jeffrey P., 1994. "Yosemite Valley and the Sierra Nevada: relative ineffectiveness of glaciers in an ancient granitic landscape." Berkeley: Department of Geography, University of California, 22pp.

Stokes, William Lee, 1960. Essentials of Earth History An Introduction to Historical Geology, Third Edition. Englewood Cliffs: Prentice Hall, Inc., 532pp.

Tarbuck, Edward J. and Lutgens, Frederick K., 1987. The Earth: An Introduction to Physical Geology, Second Edition. Columbus: Merrill Publishing Company, 591pp.

Troxel, Bennie W., and Morton, Paul K., 1962. Mines and Mineral Resources of Kern County, California County Report 1. San Francisco: California Division of Mines and Geology, 370pp.

Wilkerson, Gregg, et al., 1989. Kern Fault Zone, Clear Creek Mining District-Loraine Mining District Geology Field Trip. Bakersfield: Bureau of Land Management publication, 37pp.

Wilkerson, Gregg, et al., 1990. Kern Canyon Geology-Archaeology Field Trip Overview. Bakersfield: Bureau of Land Management publications, 19pp.

History

Boyd, William Harland, 1972. *A California Middle Border The Kern River Country, 1772–1880*. Richardson: The Havilah Press, 226pp.

Boyd, William Harland, Ludeke, John, and Rump, Marjorie (Editors), 1982. *Inside Historic Kern*. Kern County Historical Society, Inc. Bakersfield, Fresno: Pioneer Publishing Co., 274pp.

Brown, Henry McLauren, 1988. *Mineral King Country Visalia to Mount Whitney*. Fresno: Pioneer Publishing Co., 94pp.

Brown, Henry McLauren, 1991. *Kern Canyon Country*. Porterville: Edwards Senior Press, 40pp.

Browning, Peter, 1986. *Place Names of the Sierra Nevada From Abbot to Zomwalt*. Berkeley: Wilderness Press, 253pp.

Burmeister, Eugene, 1977. *The Golden Empire Kern County, California*. Beverly Hills: Autograph Press, 168pp.

Felzer, Ron, 1992. *Mineral King Southern Sequoia Park and part of Golden Trout Wilderness* High Sierra Hiking Guide, Third Edition. Berkeley: Wilderness Press, 97pp.

Field Enterprises Educational Corporation, 1958. *The World Book Encyclopedia*. Chicago: Merchandise Mart Plaza.

Gauer, Milly, 1990. *Springville Centennial*. 32pp.

Handbook 145, 1993. *Sequoia and Kings Canyon*. Washington DC: Division of Publications National Parks Service. U.S. Government Printing Office, 127pp.

Harper, John L., 1982. *Mineral King Public Concern With Government Policy*. Arcata: Pacifica Publishing Company, 223pp..

Jenkins, J. C. and Robinson, John W., 1979. *Kern Peak-Olancha High Sierra Hiking Guide #13*, Second Edition. Berkeley: Wilderness Press, 90pp. (Out of print)

Nelson, Joseph S., 1991. *Ardis Manly Walker*. Kernville: Kern Valley Historical Society, 51pp.

Otter, Floyd L., 1963. *The Men of Mammoth Forest*. Ann Arbor: Edwards Brothers, Inc. 169pp.

Powers, Bob, 1974. *North Fork Country*. Tucson: Westernlore Press, 159pp.

Powers, Bob, 1979. *Kern River Country*. Glendale: Arthur H. Clark Co., 101pp.

Roberts, George, and Roberts, Jan, 1986. *Discover Historic California*. Whittier: New Fortress publications, 330pp.

Selters, Andrew, 1987. *Triple Divide Peak King River Canyon, Northern Sequoia* High Sierra Hiking Guide, Second Edition. Berkeley: Wilderness Press, 102pp.

Sequoia National Forest Interdisciplinary Team, 1982. *Peppermint Recreation Area Information Booklet*. California: Sequoia National Forest, 12pp.

Signor, John R., 1983. *Southern Pacific-Santa Fe Tehachapi*. San Marino: Golden West Books, 272pp.

Tweed, William C., 1980. *Sequoia-Kings Canyon The Story Behind the Scenery*. Las Vegas: K. C. Publications, Inc. 64pp.

Tweed, William C., 1984. *Exploring Mountain Highways A Road Guide to Sequoia and Kings Canyon National Parks*. Three Rivers: Sequoia Natural History Association, Inc., 48pp.

Tweed, William C., 1986. *Kaweah Remembered The Story of the Kaweah Colony and The Founding of Sequoia National Park*. Three Rivers: Sequoia National History Association, Inc., 16pp.

Walker, Ardis M., 1974. *Francisco Garces Pioneer Padre of the Tulares*. Visalia: Visalia, California, 74pp.

Index